Staging Philanthropy

Social History, Popular Culture, and Politics in Germany
Geoff Eley, Series Editor

(continued on last page)

Staging Philanthropy

Patriotic Women and the National
Imagination in Dynastic Germany,
1813–1916

Jean H. Quataert

Ann Arbor
THE UNIVERSITY OF MICHIGAN PRESS

361.7082
Q2s

Copyright © by the University of Michigan 2001
All rights reserved
Published in the United States of America by
The University of Michigan Press
Manufactured in the United States of America
⊗ Printed on acid-free paper

2004   2003   2002   2001   4   3   2   1

A CIP catalog record for this book is available from the British Library.

Library of Congress Cataloging-in-Publication Data

Quataert, Jean H. (Jean Helen), 1945–
    Staging philanthropy : patriotic women and the national
imagination in dynastic Germany, 1813–1916 / Jean H. Quataert.
        p.   cm. — (Social history, popular culture, and politics in
Germany)
    ISBN 0-472-11171-X
    1. Women in charitable work—Germany—History.   2. Women
philanthropists—Germany—History.   3. Patriotism—Germany—History.
4. Germany—Politics and government.   I. Title.   II. Series.
HV541 .Q38   2001
361.7'082'0943—dc21   00-010714

In Memory of
Nancy Hannah (1933–1997)
and to
Sharon Levit,
for opening new vistas on the past and future

Contents

Illustrations

Tables

Preface

This book grows out of my own engagement with issues of war and national consensus, which was rekindled during the Gulf War in the early 1990s. With the onset of hostilities, I observed the silencing of debate in the proliferation of "yellow ribbons" and, in Vestal, my small town in upstate New York, experienced at firsthand efforts at consensus building through parades and ceremonies. And yet these activities coexisted uneasily with deep ambivalences, stirred by historical memory, about the human costs of war. Serendipitously, at that moment my friends at the German Historical Institute—Stig Förster and Roger Chickering—asked if I would join an ongoing comparative research project on "total war," starting with the mid-nineteenth-century American Civil War and German Wars of Unification. It seemed a way to combine personal and professional passions. I could turn my feminist commitments to the interrelationship between nationalism, war, and state building and rework these "traditional" themes in history through the lens of women's lives and gender analysis. I wanted to understand how identification with such abstract notions as "state," "nation," and "national community" is made and contested in daily life.

Over the years, I have profited from the support of friends and colleagues. I am pleased to be able to thank them here. Richard Trexler has been an inspiration, not only for his own work on civic rituals, but also for our ongoing exchange of ideas concerning community solidarity, women, and sacrifice, even if we part company over agency. He encouraged my interest in ritual behavior as integral to power and politics. Howard Brown offered a very spirited reading of the introduction and conclusion. Stig Förster, James Retallack, George Stein, and Deborah Cohen read chunks of the manuscript and offered very useful comments for revision. I also want to thank John Röhl for helpful bibliographical suggestions at key moments of revision. Molly O'Donnell helped broaden my perspective on the colonial context, as did Kenneth Orosz. Specific chapters were also read by Kevin Slick, Jennifer Evans, and other graduate students in history, particularly Dianne Criswell, Morgana Kellythorne, Rebecca Willis, Matthew Lungerhausen, and Ronald Applegate.

I presented parts of the argument at various German Historical Institute conferences, which were invaluable for broadening and deepening my understanding of the changing relationship between civilian and soldier, home front and battlefield in the nineteenth century. I took my case as well to Rutgers, Harvard, and Emory universities. I received indispensable cooperation from the staffs at the Generallandesarchiv, Karlsruhe, the Landeshauptarchiv, Koblenz, as well as the Stadtarchiv, the Geheimes Staatsarchiv Preussischer Kulturbesitz, and the Staatsbibliothek in Berlin, and also from the staff of the Hoover Library and its archives. I want to acknowledge as well their long-distance help in sending me materials after I returned from my research trips. In addition, the Interlibrary Loan Service staff members at Binghamton University tracked down countless volumes of printed materials and newspapers, and their efforts are truly appreciated.

The artistic eye of Michael Tanzer (1941–2000) helped me analyze form, design, and color in the Red Cross posters included in this work. I am grateful for the impact he had on this book and I will deeply miss his always challenging perspectives on the world. I also want to thank Kenneth Orosz for helping me with the tables, Costa Sakellariou for the maps, and Nadir Özbek for the index. The series editor, Geoff Eley, whose insights into German nationalism have shaped my own approach, read the manuscript with great attention; he encouraged a more equitable balance between "'anthropology" and "sociology" as methods. I appreciate these suggestions and hope I have done them justice.

As always, my husband, Donald Quataert, lived through all the phases and stages of the completion of this book. He remains, variously, perceptive, helpful, calming, and patient.

JHQ
Vestal, New York
December 2000

Abbreviations

DRK	*Das Deutsche Rote Kreuz. Entstehung, Entwicklung und Leistungen der Vereinsorganisation seit Abschluss der Genfer Convention i.J. 1864.* Vol. 1, *Centralkomitee der Deutschen Vereine vom Roten Kreuz. Landesvereine vom Roten Kreuz.* Vol. 2, *Frauen-Hilfs-und Pflege-Vereine unter dem Roten Kreuz.* Vol. 3, *Kranken-und Mutterhäuser vom Roten Kreuz.* Ed. Dr. Kimmle. Berlin, 1910.
GK	Generallandesarchiv, Karlsruhe
GSPK	Geheimes Staatsarchiv Preussischer Kulturbesitz, Dahlem, Königliches Geheimes Civil-Cabinet, I, HA, Rep. 89
HIA	Poster Collection, Hoover Institution Archives, Stanford, California
LK	Landeshauptarchiv, Koblenz
KZ	*Neue Preussische Kreuz-Zeitung*
Mitteilungen	Mitteilungen des Badischen Landesvereins vom Roten Kreuz (Baden state Red Cross communiqués)
VZ	*Vossische Zeitung. Königlich privilegirte Berlinische Zeitung von Staats-und gelehrten Sachen.*

Introduction: Dynastic Legitimacy and Women's Philanthropy in German State and Nation Building

> Social solidarity . . . through the union of . . . humanitarian sentiment and the most noble public spirit.
>
> —Gräfe, 1844

At an elaborate public ceremony in October 1896, the magistrates of Koblenz unveiled a monument to the memory of Empress Augusta, who had died six years earlier. By official intent, the marble structure was placed in the new public gardens along the Rhine River, named, appropriately, Empress Augusta Park in recognition, as one mayor put it, of "her prominence in all areas of public life and particularly her benevolent care *(Fürsorge)* for her favorite residence city, Koblenz."[1] Before taking over the Prussian throne, between 1850 and 1858 Prince William and Princess Augusta had resided in Koblenz. The monument depicts a regal figure of authority, flanked below by relief panels capturing moments of women's philanthropic ministerings to the war wounded, sick, and needy (fig. 1). Its spatial relationships reproduced social hierarchies even as its messages evoked norms of community solidarity. The royal patron, distant yet immediate, oversees the work of the women, who serve as intermediaries between dynastic concern and individual misery and need. The monument

---

1. GK, Abt. 69 (Geheimes Kabinett der Grossherzogin Luise), no. 188, 1, Die Denkmalfragen für die Höchstseligen Majestäten, betr., 1890–91, mayor of Koblenz, January 9, 1891, to Duchess Luise of Baden. Also, no. 188, 9, Gluckwünsche zum Denkmals-Enthüllung in Coblenz am 18 Oktober 1896. This is a typical collection in the Civil Cabinet archives, capturing the participation of individuals and members of associations *(Vereine)* in important dynastic family events, which always were public and political.

Fig. 1.   The Empress Augusta Monument in Koblenz

still stands today in Koblenz, a living testimony to a once vital world of dynastic rule, patronage, and display that has all but receded from memory.

The granitelike solidity of the monument, however, froze in time what was in fact a highly publicized and dynamic set of exchanges in the ceremonies of authority and power. At the center of these performances of rule were carefully orchestrated visits by the royal female guests to the philanthropic and welfare institutions of the particular locale hosting the dramatic gathering. Indeed, elaborate ceremonies in and around the hospitals, sanatoria, asylums, and orphanages drew public attention to the institutions and their staff as well as to the work of the women and men in voluntary philanthropic service such as, in the Koblenz case, the members of the local Prussian Patriotic Women's Association (Vaterländische Frauen-Verein), under royal patronage. The correspondence in the Civil Cabinets, the offices that linked court and state, highlights the importance of these publicized ritual interactions for the royal patrons, the female elites, and the municipal officials in local communities. And the shared recollections of many German memorialists across the political spectrum, too, are a testimony to their ubiquity and familiarity.[2] As performances of loyalty, these carefully choreographed ceremonies worked simultaneously to reinforce it.

Ten months after the unveiling of the monument to Empress Augusta, in August 1897 a similar ritual voyage to Koblenz's philanthropic institutes occurred during the celebrated unveiling of the new monument to William I on the Deutsches Eck, the built promontory at the confluence of the Mosel and Rhine Rivers.[3] Philanthropy, indeed, was a stage on which to enact wider state identities around issues of community obligations and responsibilities.

The philanthropic practices of patronage, gift giving, and personal visitations were well-known elements in the dynastic repertoire. They

---

2. Only a sample of the literature can be offered here. Gertrud Bäumer, *Lebensweg durch eine Zeitwende* (Tübingen, 1933), 73; August Bebel, *Aus meinem Leben* (Stuttgart, 1914), 1–7, 18–19, including opposition to a visit by the crown prince; Friedrich Meinecke, *Erlebtes, 1862–1901* (Leipzig, 1941), 28–29, 33–34, 79–80, and 162 for a variety of references to public processions and festivities. Meinecke's subsequent memoir contains much reflection on the Baden court after his move to Freiburg, including positive memories of the duchess Luise. See his *Strassburg, Freiburg, Berlin, 1901–1919. Erinnerungen* (Stuttgart, 1949), 67–68, 107–8, 131.

3. For details on the August 1897 event that reveal just how important the memory of Empress Augusta was in the ceremony for Emperor William I, GK, Abt. 69, no. 225, Den Besuch in Coblenz am 31 August 1897, betr.; and also, *KZ,* no. 404, August 30, 1897, and no. 406, August 31, 1897. The *Kreuz-Zeitung* was the leading Conservative newspaper published in Berlin.

were, however, one part of a duality, a symbolic, institutional, and gender pairing, that reflected the complexities of traditional rule *(Herrschaft)* as both coercion and persuasion, force and favor. Their highly stylized and repetitive performances were set in a context that linked war making and community welfare as the mutually constitutive expressions of dynastic political legitimacy—the one implying the other.

These seemingly distinct poles of statecraft were intertwined in practice. Thus, for example, during a large military maneuver in Hanover in 1874, William I gave the city five hundred thaler earmarked for those ill with trichinosis; against the backdrop of similar exercises fifteen years later, Empress Auguste Victoria visited the local hospitals, including those for military personnel. German military historians have argued that the growing tension between the new kaiser, William II, and his military advisors by the late nineteenth century made these long-established maneuvers "displays of pomp," not opportunities to advance military tactics or test principles. These historians have missed the coupling of the messages that was so vital to state-building on the ground.[4]

The philanthropic imperative was at the heart of one pole of dynastic ritual communication, doing its larger work even in the absence of explicit mention of its complementary image. Despite their importance for state rule, however, philanthropic rituals and practices have received little attention from historians of national identity and state formation in nineteenth-century "Germany." German scholars such as Christoph Sachsse and Florian Tennstedt analyze philanthropy in terms of social discipline and its place in structuring a capitalist labor market; others, as Ewald Frie, place it in a complex of welfare forms in modern Germany responding to, as well as shaping, the pressures of bureaucratization and rationalization.[5] In the German literature, philanthropy rarely is viewed as a site for the production of definitions of community membership and state identities.[6]

---

4. For a short history of the army maneuvers see *KZ,* no. 209, May 6, 1914, and for the powerful mix of military and philanthropic gestures, no. 299, October 1, 1874, and no. 434, September 17, 1889. For the tensions between William II and his military advisors, Wilhelm Deist, "Kaiser Wilhelm II in the Context of His Military and Naval Entourage," in *Kaiser Wilhelm II: New Interpretations,* ed. John C. G. Röhl and Nicolaus Sombart (Cambridge, 1982), 180.

5. Christoph Sachsse and Florian Tennstedt, *Geschichte der Armenfürsorge in Deutschland vom Spätmittelalter bis zum 1. Weltkrieg,* vol. 1 (Stuttgart, 1980), and *Fürsorge und Wohlfahrtspflege, 1871 bis 1929,* vol. 2 (Stuttgart, 1988). Ewald Frie, *Wohlfahrtsstaat und Provinz. Fürsorgepolitik des Provinzialverbandes Westfalen und des Landes Sachsen, 1880–1930* (Paderborn, 1993), 2–7.

6. Recent collections outside the German context, however, raise new questions about philanthropy, elite formation, and political struggle. Among the more provocative new studies is Jonathan Barry and Colin Jones, eds., *Medicine and Charity before the Welfare State*

Although overlooked in the scholarship, the dynastic ceremonies of rule and the rituals of patronage, which extended deep into civil society, were essential elements in the politics of German state-building in the "long" nineteenth century. They were opportunities to constitute sets of relationships that spoke equally of hierarchy and community. Through an emerging network of institutions and organizations, dynastic philanthropic practices established common bonds that increasingly linked patriotic groups in distinct localities together over a growing swath of territory. The causal dynamics, however, were complex and went in two directions. The ritual process was not imposed solely "from above" but mediated "in between" in the specific institutional and associational milieu of each locality. Over time, the bases of dynastic legitimacies were reconfigured by these patterns of interaction between the apparatus of dynastic court authority and the changing sociohistorical context of civil society. The living force of dynastic state symbols was their ongoing enactment in the local routines of community relations.

These complex patterns of interaction are at the root of a transformation that makes dynastic identities critical for the "long" nineteenth century. Their new forms elevated the symbol of the *Landesmutter* (Mother of the People) to prominence in the constellation of state identities. This remaking of royal authority was part of the same processes of change at once restructuring the Germanic states and mobilizing their citizenry for war in light of the French Revolution and the Napoleonic occupation. It was a conservative response to the newfangled notions of popular obligations and rights that were recasting the basis of state legitimacies as well as the preconditions of modern warfare. Dynastic groups in Germany made community welfare and its defense part of newly gendered social obligations and in ways that worked to safeguard conservative interests.

As an increasingly pervasive symbol of community well-being, responsibility, and care, the dynastic *Landesmutter* also oversaw a civilian mobilization for the purposes of war. The new female symbol, in effect, served to link the emerging world of the male "citizen-soldier," which rested on the newly proclaimed state obligation of universal military service, with a voluntary ethic of care, which stressed collective community

---

(London, 1991), particularly the chapter by Sandra Cavallo, "The Motivations of Benefactors: An Overview of Approaches to the Study of Charity," 46–62. For a comparative study that analyzes voluntarism as an indication of the vibrancy of civil society distinct, however, from the autocratic state, Adele Lindenmeyr, *Poverty Is Not a Vice: Charity, Society, and the State in Imperial Russia* (Princeton, N.J., 1996). By the end of the century, Lindenmeyr writes, communities in the diverse multiethnic empire used philanthropy to "create or solidify" their identities (226).

responsibility for the wounded soldiers, the veterans, and their families. Indeed, dynastic practices intertwined the soldier and the civilian volunteer in an elaborate system of honors and rewards, feasts and festivals that bound them to the state. After 1864, this ethic became institutionalized in the German Red Cross, which tested an increasingly complicated set of gender roles and relations.[7] While it drew primarily on aristocratic women volunteers to run and staff the widening network of charitable associations and institutions, it used men in key administrative posts and, in time, employed its own professionally trained medical personnel. The dynastic world of voluntary philanthropy was instrumental in the continued evolution of a patriotic civil elite.

These civic "duties" sanctioned by dynastic patronage provided the foundation for an acquisition of new state identities. In a recent work in the context of German reunification, Jürgen Habermas points to the significance of self-conscious public activities and roles that sustain a wider sense of community membership. In his analysis, one form of national identity was acquired through "self-conscious striving" and an "identification with a role which demanded a high degree of personal commitment, even to the point of self-sacrifice."[8] He draws attention to the importance of universal conscription—in essence the foundation of formal male citizenship in the nineteenth century—and to patterns of organization for civil rights. Designed to reanalyze issues of citizenship in the post-1989 era, his approach nonetheless offers a way to think about women's participation in state-building and nationalism prior to their formal political membership in the state, which in Germany occurred only in 1918, after the demise of the monarchy. The emerging world of formal electoral and party politics in the nineteenth century all but excluded women.

Women in voluntary philanthropic service under dynastic state patronage, however, acquired a civic identity through the public roles and activities that were named "patriotic" by the dynasty. Prototypical, as we will see, was the Patriotic Women's Institute in the Duchy of Weimar, officially constituted in 1817 out of the earlier war work of civilians in the struggles against Napoleon; in time, it served as model for similar philanthropic undertakings in the Germanic Confederation. These charitable

---

7. John F. Hutchinson, *Champions of Charity: War and the Rise of the Red Cross* (Boulder, Colo., 1996). Written primarily from the perspective of the male-headed International Committee in Geneva, the study hints at, but fails to sustain, an analysis of the significance of gender and dynastic rule in the formation of the national components of the International Red Cross.

8. Jürgen Habermas, "Citizenship and National Identity: Some Reflections on the Future of Europe," in *The Nationalism Reader*, ed. Omar Dahbour and Micheline R. Ishay (Atlantic Highlands, N.J., 1995), 334–35.

interventions in the community were understood as "patriotic" by the growing number of patrons, the scores of female volunteers, and, increasingly, the wider public itself. They drew privileged women in local communities into their ministering orbit—most consistently, the wives of aristocrats, those of the urban patriciate, and, especially, of government officials at the local, state, and, later, imperial levels—constituting, in effect, a service elite of civil volunteers. Given the mutual interdependency of dynastic state authority and the institutions of civil society, however, this process was not simply one that incorporated increasing numbers of women into the state, as if the so-called state were a given. Rather, the daily routines of charitable activities and the ritual forms that enveloped this philanthropic culture worked to constitute an understanding of the state itself.[9]

Notions of the state, indeed, were being shaped by the activities of these women on the ground. Through their work, the state could be seen, for example, as "caring." And, over time, with the growing medicalization of society and the insertion of modern medical science into the planning for war, the state, too, could derive a new legitimacy as "curing." These interactions, then, made the dynamics of gender an integral part of the process of state-building in Germany. And, by insinuating a war culture into daily life and helping make the necessity of war part of state and national identity, they worked as well to provide some of the preconditions for the evolution toward modern "total" war in the twentieth century.[10] The dynastic-loyal Red Cross was giving institutional form to the relief and medical sides of a "home front" in the making and keeping alive the memory of war work in peacetime.

A perspective that ties the institutions of voluntary philanthropy at the local level to the dynastic court and its symbolic and ritual practices offers a new way to assess the extremely complicated processes of identity-

---

9. My perspective differs from such historians as Ute Daniel, who see these philanthropic activities as signifying women's incorporation into the state. See Ute Daniel, "Die Vaterländischen Frauenvereine in Westfalen," in *Westfälische Forschungen* (Zeitschrift des Provinzialinstituts für der Landschaftsverbandes Westfalen in Lippe), ed. Karl Teppe, vol. 39 (Münster, 1989), 158–79.

10. Total war is a complicated subject. The Prussian model of a conscript army under professional direction was Germany's path to modern war, involving the disciplined management of military force and the continued importance of central state direction over military and civilian mobilization. I found particularly useful for comparative discussion Stig Förster and Jörg Nagler's introduction, Wilhelm Deist, "Remarks on the Preconditions to Waging War in Prussia-Germany, 1866–71," and Roger Chickering, "The American Civil War and the German Wars of Unification: Some Parting Shots," in *On the Road to Total War: The American Civil War and the German Wars of Unification, 1861–1871,* ed. Stig Förster and Jörg Nagler (Cambridge, 1997), 1–25, 311–25, 683–91.

formation, for members of the wider community as well as of the [nation]-state, itself. How is an entity as abstract as the state invested with meaning? What elements deepen a sense of community beyond the legal definitions of membership in a sovereign and mapped territorial polity? To expand the problematics at the heart of Benedict Anderson's "imagined" national community, why are people so willing to die in its name or sacrifice for its glory? What explains the fact, indeed, that these deep-seated identities and loyalties are mobilizable even in the face of profound and apparently insurmountable social inequalities and injustices?[11]

While these are broad and complicated questions of a general nature, my study combines several distinct scholarly approaches to seek their answers in the context of nineteenth-century German history, a period that saw the formation and demise of the first German nation-state out of the evolving territorial dynastic and city-states after 1815. It uses basic archival research to reconstruct a neglected history of the philanthropic state women's associations *(Frauen-Vereine)* that, after 1864, gave institutional form to the "German" Red Cross under dynastic, aristocratic, and military tutelage. It expands this institutional and sociological history, however, by also examining their symbolic practices in order to analyze how institutions and their custodians are represented and received in the wider community. This study assumes that ideas have their own complex material forms and seeks their expressions at the level of institutions, rituals, and behavior. Thus, this book is not a history of ideas in isolation nor, for example, of distinct authors of texts on patriotism, nationalism, or humanitarianism. Rather, my study looks to the enactment of ideas, particularly in the practices and rituals around gift giving and sacrifice, the central motifs that worked to construct an understanding of "patriotism" in the philanthropic institutions and associations under dynastic patronage.[12] It seeks a sociological profile of the backgrounds, interests, and motives of leaders and members while highlighting the ritual forms of their behavior in public.

The patriotic women's associations have been overlooked in German history. No previous study has drawn a composite picture of their patterns of institutional growth and influence over the "long" nineteenth century.

---

11. Benedict Anderson, *Imagined Communities: Reflections on the Origin and Spread of Nationalism,* rev. ed. (London, 1991), 1–4, 141–44; and also David Cannadine and Simon Price, eds., *Rituals of Royalty: Power and Ceremonial in Traditional Societies* (Cambridge, 1987), 19.

12. Useful for an assessment of distinct approaches to the materiality of ideas, Peter Schöttler, "Mentalities, Ideologies, Discourses: On the 'Third Level' as a Theme in Social-Historical Research," in *The History of Everyday Life: Reconstructing Historical Experiences and Ways of Life,* ed. Alf Lüdtke, trans. William Templer (Princeton, N.J., 1995), 72–115.

These associations, however, came to embrace the largest numbers of female volunteers in German society: by the end of the *Kaiserreich,* the Prussian Patriotic Women's Association (Vaterländische Frauen-Verein) alone had a membership of eight hundred thousand women. In their philanthropic and ritual work, furthermore, they were joined by other patriotic groups such as the Prussian Women's and Young Ladies' Association (Preussische Frauen und Jungfrauen-Verein) in Berlin; its historic life, from 1814 to 1916, nearly perfectly duplicates the chronology of this book. These patriotic groups, drawing on aristocratic leadership, however, stood apart from the bourgeois women's movement, object of considerable interest by German historians. Feminist scholarly research has centered on the struggles to change women's lives; it has been less interested in a philanthropic voluntarism that, seemingly, reproduced the conservative gender and political order. Similarly, contemporary memoirs of life at the German courts present a seriously skewed image; if not fully overlooked, women at court are seen as frivolous, the source of much political and religious intrigue; their multiple connections to civil society and their place in decision making in matters of state are glossed over fully.[13]

There are, however, a number of case studies of patriotic women's activities in distinct eras of the nineteenth century. For Württemberg in *Vormärz* and the revolutionary years, 1848–49, the collection edited by Carola Lipp devotes considerable attention to patriotic women's work; tellingly, the analysis is placed within the context of an emerging bourgeois

---

13. An informative study of women's social activism is Elisabeth Meyer-Renschhausen, *Weibliche Kultur und sociale Arbeit. Eine Geschichte der Frauenbewegung am Beispiel Bremens, 1810–1927* (Cologne, 1989). Meyer-Renschhausen, however, duplicates the feminist bias against aristocratic women; she fails to understand their role in the reform efforts of *Vormärz* and, after the emergence of the women's movement, all but discontinues examination of local women's patriotic work. An example of the biases in the memoirs of the German courts is Robert Zedlitz-Trütschler, *Zwölf Jahre am deutschen Kaiserhof* (Berlin, 1924), 34, 45–46, 67, 160, 211, where women are depicted, variously, as "bigoted" and "small-minded." Also, Catherine Radziwill, *Memoirs of Forty Years* (New York, 1915) and her *Secrets of a Dethroned Royalty* (New York, 1920).

While this book is not about the German dynastic court, there are four female rulers who figured prominently in the evolution, development, and symbolics of patriotic philanthropy. Queen Luise of Prussia, 1776–1810, became the archetypical *Landesmutter* after her death and symbol of "German" patriotic and nationalist struggles. Princess, Queen, and, later, Empress Augusta of Prussia/Germany, 1811–90, was married to William I, the unification kaiser and son of Queen Luise. Augusta oversaw the formation of the Prussian Patriotic Women's Association and later was patron of the German Red Cross. Her daughter, Luise of Baden, 1838–1923, the granddaughter of Queen Luise, founded the Baden Women's Association in 1859 and was active overseeing women's associational life in the state until her death in 1923. In 1890, after Augusta's death, Auguste Victoria (married to William II), Empress of Germany, became the patron of the Red Cross until the end of the monarchy in 1918.

reform movement.[14] For the *Kaiserreich*, there are the studies of Roger Chickering and Ute Daniel as well as the observations of Hans-Ulrich Wehler.[15] Chickering demonstrates how patriotic rhetoric legitimized women's public presence, but he fails to assess the broad political implications of the philanthropic acts themselves. Furthermore, by limiting his analysis to the post-1871 era, he misses a half century of previous organization that shaped the structure of the German Red Cross. Thus, he neglects the women's essential role in medical war preparation. Daniel provides a thorough case study of the Patriotic Women's Association in Westfalia, which she carries through to the Weimar Republic and the early Nazi era, but does not link it to issues of state-building or nationalist struggle. Wehler, in turn, devotes a number of pages to the patriotic women's organizations in his broad interpretation of German social history. He erroneously explains their significance solely by a teleology that leads to National Socialism, a logic that is not sustained by the historical record.[16] To be sure, the work of these patriotic women does not fit an emancipatory trajectory, but it nonetheless had a significant impact on state-building and struggles over identity-formation in the century.

In analyzing this important yet neglected history, my study takes seriously the question of political style. It borrows heavily from the insights of cultural anthropologists interested in how meaning is created in the theater of politics. Dynastic state and national identities were cultural forms, best understood as genres of cultural performances that imparted meaning through the power of their emotional and cognitive elements. These ritual and symbolic forms, furthermore, were not "mask[s] of force" nor simple instruments of manipulation but themselves types of power that constituted relationships, ties of loyalty, and bonds of solidarity. This approach stresses the power inherent in the ceremonies of power, which is essential to the reproduction of authority and the creation and perpetuation of

---

14. See particularly, Sabine Rumpel-Nienstedt, "'Thäterinnen der Liebe.' Frauen in Wohltätigkeitsvereinen," in *Schimpfende Weiber und patriotische Jungfrauen: Frauen im Vormärz und in der Revolution 1848–49*, ed. Carola Lipp (Moos, 1986), 206–31.

15. Roger Chickering, "'Casting Their Gaze More Broadly'? Women's Patriotic Activism in Imperial Germany," *Past and Present* 118 (February 1988): 156–85; Daniel, "Vaterländischen Frauenvereine in Westfalen"; and Hans-Ulrich Wehler, *Deutsche Gesellschaftsgeschichte*, vol. 3, *Von der "Deutschen Doppelrevolution" bis zum Beginn des Ersten Weltkrieges, 1849–1914* (Munich, 1995), 1095–96.

16. Wehler draws too simple a line from patriotic women in imperial Germany to Nazi electoral successes in late Weimar; some former members of the Prussian Patriotic Women's Association crossed the powerful ideological and class divides in the Weimar Republic and ran as Progressives, particularly in more liberal southwest German cities and regions of Baden and the Rhineland. See, for example, Barbara Koops, "Frauen in der Koblenzer Kommunalpolitik, 1918–1933," *Koblenzer Beiträge zur Geschichte und Kultur* 4 (1994): 82.

political legitimacies.[17] At the same time, it recognizes the contestations around identity-formation. The emergence of a wider sense of community remained always incomplete and disputed.

This promising interpretive perspective ties into an earlier literature in German history. For example, Thomas Nipperdey acknowledged in 1968 that German political historians to date had paid insufficient attention to the power of symbolic forms. He developed a typology that shows how distinct understandings of "the nation" were embodied in the different national monument styles designed and implemented in the nineteenth century. He places the 1897 unveiling ceremony at the Deutsches Eck in the "patriotic cults of William II," although tellingly he omits mention of the October events to honor Empress Augusta. Later, George Mosse, in an equally pathfinding study of the symbolism inherent in the struggle over identity, stressed the new "political style" of nineteenth-century nationalism. Nationalists communicate their values, Mosse argues, through a seductive secular liturgy, which draws on powerful myths and symbols as well as gestures and dress. He downplays the written programmatic appeal of nationalist movements in emphasizing their performative, emotional side. Reflecting an earlier project, however, both authors place their study in a line of development that culminates in National Socialism.[18] The sym-

---

17. The quote comes from the introduction to Cannadine and Price, *Rituals of Royalty,* 19. The anthropological literature is integrated into the main empirical body of this study, so only its outline will be noted here. I have drawn on three interrelated types of studies. One is on symbols and their meaning. Useful here are Victor Turner, *The Ritual Process: Structure and Anti-Structure* (Ithaca, N.Y., 1969); and Raymond Firth, *Symbols: Public and Private* (Ithaca, N.Y., 1973). The second type of study looks to the nature of political rituals and their power. See, specifically, David I. Kertzer, *Ritual, Politics, and Power* (New Haven, 1988); Zdzisław Mach, *Symbols, Conflict, and Identity: Essays in Political Anthropology* (Albany, N.Y., 1993); and John J. MacAloon, ed., *Rite, Drama, Festival, Spectacle: Rehearsals toward a Theory of Cultural Performance* (Philadelphia, 1984). Here, performance, in the sense of doing, is distinguished from representation. The third type of study deals directly with the rituals of royalty and the pageantry of the political "center." In addition to the collection edited by Cannadine, see Clifford Geertz, "Centers, Kings, and Charisma: Reflections on the Symbolics of Power," in *Local Knowledge: Further Essays in Interpretive Anthropology* (New York, 1983), 121–46, and also his *Negara: The Theatre State in Nineteenth-Century Bali* (Princeton, N.J., 1980).

18. Thomas Nipperdey, "Nationalidee und Nationaldenkmal in Deutschland im 19. Jahrhundert," *Historische Zeitschrift* 206 (1968): 529–85, in particular 543. Also, George L. Mosse, *The Nationalization of the Masses: Political Symbolism and Mass Movements in Germany from the Napoleonic Wars through the Third Reich* (Ithaca, N.Y., 1975). The teleology is less pronounced in Nipperdey; his typology leads to a *Volksgemeinschaft* without dynastic leaders, foreshadowing the Nazi racial community. His subsequent investigations of nineteenth-century Germany do not go beyond this earlier perspective, and women still are omitted from the analysis. See Thomas Nipperdey, *Deutsche Geschichte, 1800–1866*, vol. 1, *Bürgerwelt und starker Staat* (Munich, 1983), 278–82, 300–313, and *Deutsche Geschichte, 1866–1918*, vol. 2, *Machtstaat vor der Demokratie* (Munich, 1992), 250–65 and 595–609.

bolic and ritual paths in Germany seem to lead, tragically, to the manipulative pageantry of aestheticized fascist politics and, thus, in some way, to
the horrors of the Third Reich. This implicit linkage of rituals and fascism
meant that many subsequent German historians were unwilling to deal
with the symbolic forms of politics and their place of power in the dynastic
state system of central Europe. Besides, ritual forms of communication
were seen as incompatible with an emerging "modern" rational, bureaucratic state system.[19]

The British historian Eric Hobsbawm has no such qualms. He draws
attention to the German Empire in the last third of the nineteenth century
as one of Europe's newest nation-states. In a widely cited work, Hobsbawm argues that new nations "invent traditions" as they struggle to construct a viable national identity in the face of bewildering industrial, social,
and political changes. In the need to create common bonds among region-
ally and ethnically diverse groups of peoples, those at the "center" promote an invented set of traditions, ceremonies, and ritual time. This identity, rooted in a shared connection to the past, becomes the criterion for
membership in the political community. Similar processes of constructing
state identities "from above" were at work as well in the new nations of
Asia, Africa, and the Middle East after decolonization. Indeed, a line of
analysis is opening that connects aspects of German nation-state building
with those in former colonized areas of the world, offering a fertile ground
for reconceptualizing the complicated patterns of nationalisms through
comparative methods.[20]

However persuasive the notion of "invention" might seem, the com-

---

19. Werner K. Blessing, "The Cult of Monarchy, Political Loyalty, and the Workers'
Movement in Imperial Germany," *Journal of Contemporary History* 13, no. 2 (April 1978):
357–75. "Modernization" here is seen to undercut monarchical identity. Also, Isabel V. Hull,
"Prussian Dynastic Ritual and the End of Monarchy," in *German Nationalism and the European Response, 1890–1945,* ed. Carole Fink, Isabel V. Hull, and MacGregor Knox (Norman,
Okla., 1985), 13–41. Hull takes ritual politics seriously but posits a basic tension between its
dynastic and nationalist forms.

20. Eric Hobsbawm, "Mass Producing Traditions: Europe, 1871–1914," in *The Invention of Tradition,* ed. Eric Hobsbawm and Terrance Ranger (Cambridge, 1983), 265–307. For
possible connections between German state-building and the "last wave" of state formation
after 1945, Clifford Geertz, "After the Revolution: The Fate of Nationalism in the New
States," in *The Interpretation of Cultures: Selected Essays* (New York, 1973), 234–54; and, for
similar observations, Helmut Walser Smith, *German Nationalism and Religious Conflict: Culture, Ideology, Politics, 1870–1914* (Princeton, N.J., 1995), 238–39. These approaches anchor
part of German nation-building on a continuum with other countries rather than setting it on
a unique path toward fascism. For a careful effort to distinguish the emergence of middle-
class radical nationalism in the 1890s from "extremist nationalism" of the Nazi movement in
the 1920s, Wolfgang J. Mommsen, *Imperial Germany, 1867–1918: Politics, Culture, and Society in an Authoritarian State,* trans. Richard Deveson (London, 1995), 100.

memorative ceremonies in late-nineteenth-century Germany were hardly invented in the sense of an imposition of new forms, styles, or symbols on passive local communities. The dynastic ceremonies of rule and the spaces of institutional patronage emerging in local communities affirm not Hobsbawm's assertions of invention but Benedict Anderson's telling insights into "official nationalism": powerful voices in and around dynastic courts confronted, channeled, and ultimately appropriated the nationalist impulses in ways that relegitimized dynastic rule.[21] Indeed, Anderson forces an examination of the restructuring of dynastic authority over the course of the nineteenth century. Significantly, dynastic rule was connected to the emergence, placement, and evolution of a patriotic public sphere, a new institutional and associational space through which dynastic interests increasingly bent the malleable and charged notions of "fatherland," "patriotism," and "nation" to their purposes. Anderson also draws attention to the coexistence of many conflicting definitions of nationalisms in civil society.

Several distinct "publics" emerged early in the nineteenth century to engage public opinion in the struggle over German "national" identity: bourgeois, patriotic, and plebian (or, perhaps more to the point, later in the century, socialist) publics. Their intensive interaction shaped the debates and actions in the political arena, infusing the very notions of state and nationhood, including their symbolic representations and performances, with decisively different emotional contents. Only one, however, has received detailed theoretical treatment and explication by its advocates as well as its vocal—mostly feminist—critics.[22] Prompted by the influential work of Jürgen Habermas, the bourgeois public, for a time, became an object of avid research among social scientists interested in the maintenance and erosion of legitimate rule and the liberal patterns of state formation in Europe. As an alternative legitimacy to the processes of political integration of the territorial states, duchies, and principalities in the

---

21. Anderson, *Imagined Communities,* 83–111.

22. Jürgen Habermas, *The Structural Transformation of the Public Sphere: An Inquiry into a Category of Bourgeois Society,* trans. Thomas Burger (Cambridge, Mass., 1992), 175–76, 225, for a succinct formulation. For a critical analysis of its male bias, Joan Landes, *Women and the Public Sphere in the Age of the French Revolution* (Ithaca, N.Y., 1988). For a reappropriation of the notion of public sphere for feminist analysis, Belinda Davis, "Reconsidering Habermas, Gender, and the Public Sphere: The Case of Wilhelmine Germany," in *Society, Culture, and the State in Germany, 1870–1930,* ed, Geoff Eley (Ann Arbor, Mich., 1996), 397–426, and for a recent study that, through comparison, complicates the assumed correlation between associational life and democratic values and reasoned habits, Frank Trentmann, ed., *Paradoxes of Civil Society: New Perspectives on Modern German and British History* (New York, 2000), 24–29, his critiques of Habermas, particularly.

Germanic Confederation after 1815, it often is conflated with the German bourgeois nationalist movement.

By contrast, the competing "patriotic" configuration has not been identified as clearly. Standing between the bourgeois public and transcendent notions of the state was a patriotic public sphere. Anchored in the associations of civil society, this public served as an intermediary between the individual and the state. Claiming the mantle of disinterested social welfare in both civilian and military life, it expressed an identity based on civic activism. It was an effort to dominate public opinion by those seeking new ways to conserve the social order. At the same time, its activities worked to configure state legitimacies. In dynastic systems, it was a gendered formation that rested on aristocratic women's agency. It would be interesting to see if alternative but comparable patterns emerge in republics. I hope to make a case for the validity and usefulness of the concept for historical research.

To be sure, some authors recently have moved the debate beyond the original bourgeois context. For example, Christopher Clark looks at the politics of pietist revival on aristocratic patrimonial estates in early-nineteenth-century Prussia. He writes persuasively, "Much attention has been given to the role of voluntary associations in the formation of bourgeois political society, but a tendency to link them exclusively with the phenomenon of 'bourgeoisification' has led to the almost complete neglect of those strands of early nineteenth-century organizational culture that were emphatically non-bourgeois."[23] He is referring directly to the organization of conventicles and caritative associations, which emerged for a time to oppose the reforming impulses of the Prussian bureaucracy.

A distinctly patriotic public simultaneously was carving out its own legal space in associational life. Its place, however, was directly in the center of public affairs, not solely within the protective confines of the patrimonial estates; its prototype originated not in Prussia but in the Duchy of Weimar, and it drew into leadership positions titled aristocrats and estate owners from diverse geographical areas as well as nobles and professionals in government and municipal service. The importance of this public space is captured well later in the century by the Conservative *Kreuz-Zeitung*. Commenting in 1893 on placing a monument to Augusta near the Opera House in Berlin, the author notes that "the works of this noble queen stand right at the center of service for the public weal *(öffentliche*

23. Christopher M. Clark, "The Politics of Revival: Pietists, Aristocrats, and the State Church in Early Nineteenth-Century Prussia," in *Between Reform, Reaction, and Resistance: Studies in the History of German Conservatism from 1789 to 1945,* ed. Larry Eugene Jones and James N. Retallack (Providence, R.I., 1993), 59–60.

Wohlfahrt), and so her monument belongs also in the spotlight of public life *(öffentliches Leben)*, in the center of the capital."[24]

As a quasi-private philanthropic formation, this public was deeply enmeshed in the struggles over legitimacy—and at times, too, some of its constituent elements stood as an alternative to the bureaucratic state. It was, nonetheless, loyal and royal (although its ties to the dynasty were clarified only after 1848) and consistently Christian, appropriating a "religion of the deed"—an injunction on the pious to charitable acts—for state purposes. In effect, it intermingled religious and political imagery in the sacralization of patriotic acts. It extended its reach deep into civil society, relying on the work of the autonomous, voluntary *Verein*. After 1871, a wider German national identity was mediated by this framework sponsored by the dynastic courts.[25]

Many German historians prefer the term *monarchy*, which, arguably, fits the view of state-building as a modern, rational bureaucratic process. The choice permits historians to contrast dynastic absolutism of an earlier era with the monarchical states in the nineteenth century.[26] Despite the preference, however, the label "dynastic" Germany lends a coherency to a historical century that dates from 1813 to 1916. It captures a number of key aspects of social and political life that otherwise are dismissed as meaningless vestiges: the pervasive use of the old dynastic "subject" identity *(Untertan)*, which coexisted with notions of citizenship; the sacralization of dynastic family time in the politics of associational life; and the shaping of collective memories of war around dynastic and aristocratic lineages. Born out of the legal and bureaucratic reforms of the Napoleonic era and tested in war, this dynastic formation, however, could not survive the social strains of "total" war that it unleashed. In 1916, before the for-

---

24. *KZ,* no. 79, February 16, 1893.

25. My study departs from the concept of a "German national public" coined earlier by Roger Chickering in *We Men Who Feel Most German: A Cultural Study of the Pan-German League, 1866–1914* (Boston, 1984), 167–207. Chickering still anchors his analysis in the bourgeois public, which is both "critical" and "acclamatory" (177).

26. For an illustration of the contrast, Nipperdey, *Deutsche Geschichte, 1800–1866,* 78–79, with reference to the south German states. There is, however, no standard usage among historians of the nineteenth century. For example, a recent study employs the dynastic framework to assess modern technological change in Prussia. See Eric Dorn Brose, *The Politics of Technological Change in Prussia: Out of the Shadow of Antiquity, 1809–1848* (Princeton, N.J., 1993). At other times, an antidynastic position becomes the criterion of modern nationalist politics. For example, Smith, *German Nationalism,* 128. In addition, there is a whole body of literature that looks at German history from the perspective of the dynastic courts and the persons of the monarch. Among the more prominent studies, John C. G. Röhl, *Kaiser, Hof und Staat. Wilhelm II. und die deutsche Politik* (Munich, 1987); and the collection edited by Röhl, *Der Ort Kaiser Wilhelms II. in der deutschen Geschichte* (Munich, 1991).

mal overthrow of the monarchy two years later, its legitimacy had been eroded irrevocably.

The perspective of "dynastic" Germany, with its linkages to an evolving patriotic public sphere, revisits several controversial lines of interpretation in nineteenth-century German history. In the first place, it moves the discussion of nationalism and national identity away from its moorings in the telos of modernization. It transcends the liberal conceptual categories that typically have framed the linear analysis of "modern" change. By exploring the connections between politics and philanthropy, it returns to the contemporary vocabulary of the age, which encased the philanthropic mission in the language of patriotism.[27] And it simultaneously exposes the limits of the normative claims to distinct spheres of public and private life, court and civil society, to the autonomy of the liberal association and even to the commonsense distinctions between wartime and peacetime.

Through the lens of gender, my arguments therefore help rethink some of the ties between nationalism, modernity, and elite-formation. State-building is a more complicated process than a progressive line of secular, rational, and bureaucratic development. It reveals, rather, the "paradoxes" of modernity, to borrow the phrase from Young-Sun Hong, a slow, contradictory, and asynchronic emergence that reproduced and reinvigorated older patterns of deference as well as reciprocities of obligations and needs upholding social privilege.[28]

---

27. There are other studies exploring these linkages. For German history, see Nancy R. Reagin, *A German Women's Movement: Class and Gender in Hanover, 1880–1933* (Chapel Hill, N.C., 1995), 8. Reagin offers a distinctly new analysis of women's organized activities on the local level, combining social work and party orientation, feminist and nationalist politics. Her view of nationalism, however, is rooted solely in formal "nationalist" associations. For a comparative study of North America, Paula Baker, "The Domestication of Politics: Women and American Political Society, 1780–1920," *American Historical Review* 89, no. 3 (June 1984): 620–47. Baker broadens the understanding of American government and politics by the focus on women's voluntarism in the nineteenth century.

28. Young-Sun Hong, "World War I and the German Welfare State: Gender, Religion, and the Paradoxes of Modernity," in Eley, *Society, Culture, and State,* 345–69. Hong has rethought the process of modernity, and thus her analysis differs from those of the "critical" school who acknowledge tensions between modern and premodern formations. For example, Wehler, *Deutsche Gesellschaftsgeschichte,* 3:461, 468, and 1250–95, on the Janus face of imperial Germany. In Wehler's analysis, the tensions a priori are a function of the analytic construct imposed on the empirical material, that is, the gap between a dynamic modern economic base and a traditional political system, rather than inhering in the processes of modernization themselves. For the idea of "defensive modernization" as a bridge between traditional antimodernism and modernity, Ursula Baumann, *Protestantismus und Frauenemanzipation in Deutschland 1850 bis 1920* (Frankfurt am Main, 1992), 274–76.

The dynastic institutions and associations shaping municipal welfare and civilian defense consisted of a complex mix of traditional and modern elements. Well into the twentieth century, they perpetuated older forms of beneficence of rule *(herrschaftliche Fürsorge)*—immediate personal relief, gift giving, soup kitchens, the distribution of coal during the winter months, among others—matched by new social and preventive interventions targeting such groups as infants, children, and youth. Their increasingly coordinated program of civilian defense was modern, underwriting and utilizing new scientific medical research and inventions. At the same time, it was couched in the traditional language of humanitarian and Christian duties to defend the state from its external enemies. It rested on a vocabulary of female voluntarism and sacrifice while, simultaneously, training a growing staff of competent nurses and aides. Paradoxically, it was shaped partly by the equally complex forces of feminist "modernities," which, however, it worked to channel and contain. Indeed, the simultaneity of old and new is acknowledged in the literature on the ritual forms of politics and struggle by such German historians as Alf Lüdtke, Bernd Jürgen Warneken, and Dieter Düding.[29] The German path to modernity was crooked and tortuous, some of its parts accepting the inevitability—indeed, the desirability—of war. But other parts helped fashion a conservative Christian national identity, which served as the basis of community rebuilding in West Germany after the horrors of fascism and the devastations of the Second World War.[30]

Nationalism, too, emerges in a different light in the dynastic century. To frame it solely through bourgeois class analysis is to narrow the perspective, a tendency exacerbated by the pronounced male bias in the literature. This standard approach also expresses the seductive pull of "modernization theory." The linkage is explicit in many of the "master narratives" of the nineteenth century by such prominent German histori-

---

29. Alf Lüdtke, "Trauerritual und politische Manifestation: Zu den Begräbnisumzügen der deutschen Sozialdemokratie im frühen Kaiserreich," in *Massenmedium Strasse. Zur Kulturgeschichte der Demonstration,* ed. Bernd Jürgen Warneken (Frankfurt am Main, 1991), 120–48; and Dieter Düding, Peter Friedemann, and Paul.Münch, eds., *Öffentliche Festkultur. Politische Feste in Deutschland von der Aufklärung bis zum Ersten Weltkrieg* (Hamburg, 1988). It also is characteristic of the new approach to charity that disproves the assertion that "modern" state welfare regulations inevitably replace private charitable interventions. See, for example, Barry and Jones, *Medicine and Charity,* 2–3.

30. This observation is supported by Baumann, *Protestantismus und Frauenemanzipation,* 166; and Paul Weindling, *Health, Race, and German Politics between National Unification and Nazism, 1870–1945* (Cambridge, 1989), 184. I accept the challenge put by Mommsen, *Imperial Germany,* 101, paraphrasing Nipperdey, to think of multiple time frames that extend to, as well as transcend, the Nazi era, 1933–45.

ans as Nipperdey and Wehler.[31] The same forces of modernity propelling bourgeois class formation—industrialization, urbanization, growing literacy, and professionalization—are seen to underpin the emerging nationalist movements in the period before unification. After 1871 and the compromises with the Bismarckian state, nationalism becomes integrative, overcoming the divisions within the bourgeoisie caused by modernization itself and functioning, equally, as a strategic instrument of rule, a successful manipulative technique designed to stave off democratic political reform. Given the mounting class and social tensions, however, it is radicalized after 1890. Here, in Wehler's assessment, it tragically takes a "pathological" turn that ends in fascism.[32]

In contrast, my study finds other interpretations more cogent and convincing. It accepts the basic premise of Geoff Eley that nationalism was a divisive force in German politics and focuses on the dynastic variant—official nationalism—and its secularizing religious appeal. Here, I am indebted to Helmut Smith's study of the confessional tensions and conflicts in the struggle over German national identity; Smith's work, too, transcends the classic contours of bourgeois class analysis. With Celia Applegate, I look to multiple spatial identities and see the rich texture of local worlds mediating abstract identities, but I insert the rhetoric of consensus—of national belonging—much more in the fabric of struggle.[33] In addition, my study complicates the relationship between patriotism and nationalism, demonstrating how patriotic acts, indeed, worked to constitute national identities.

Given my emphasis on official nationalism, this study shares with the self-identified "critical" school of German history an interest in the role of

---

31. The term is from Jonathan Sperber's review essay "Master Narratives of Nineteenth-Century German History," *Central European History* 24, no. 1 (1991): 69–91. I am drawing on the following larger studies for this paragraph: Hans-Ulrich Wehler, *The German Empire, 1871–1918,* trans. Kim Traynor (Leamington SPA/Dover, 1985), as well as *Deutsche Gesellschaftsgeschichte,* vol. 2, *Von der Reformära bis zur industriellen und politischen "Deutschen Doppelrevolution" 1815–1845/49* (Munich, 1987), 394–404, and *Deutsche Gesellschaftsgeschichte,* 3:190–91, 230–51, 483–85, 923–61, 1067–81. Also, Nipperdey, *Deutsche Geschichte, 1800–1866* as well as *Deutsche Geschichte, 1866–1918,* vol. 1, *Arbeitswelt und Bürgergeist* (Munich, 1988) and vol. 2, *Machtstaat vor der Demokratie.* My interest here is on their narratives of nationalism, which exhibit a surprising convergence, despite the distinct approaches, methods, and interpretations that each author brings to the subject. Also, Hagen Schulze, *The Course of German Nationalism: From Frederick the Great to Bismarck, 1763–1867,* trans. Sarah Hanbury-Henison (Cambridge, 1991).

32. Hans-Ulrich Wehler, "Wie 'bürgerlich' war das Deutsche Kaiserreich?" in *Bürger und Bürgerlichkeit im 19. Jahrhundert,* ed. Jürgen Kocka (Göttingen, 1987), 273.

33. Geoff Eley, *Reshaping the German Right: Radical Nationalism and Political Change after Bismarck* (Ann Arbor, Mich., 1990); Smith, *German Nationalism;* and Celia Applegate, *A Nation of Provincials: The German Idea of Heimat* (Berkeley and Los Angeles, 1990).

elites in the politics of legitimacy. But it casts the interpretation no longer in debates over "feudalization," "aristocratization," or "imitation," as an inquiry into the power of static premodern social vestiges.[34] Nor does it see elite behavior solely as manipulative. Supported by the dynastic court apparatus that it defended, the evolving gendered service elite of volunteers expressed its own distinct identity comprised of aristocratic, religious, and bourgeois elements—a veritable *Sonderkultur,* in the formulation of Hermann Bausinger—that long outlived the dynasty.[35]

Chapter 1 assesses the historical context for the reformulation of dynastic authority in more gendered family idiom and the material forms that embodied and reproduced notions of the *Landesmutter* as symbol of humanitarian service and care after 1815. In the aftermath of 1848, "patriotic" philanthropy increasingly was channeled toward dynastic-military interests. Chapter 2 describes the growing effort by dynastic groups to draw women's voluntary associations into the state components of the emerging German Red Cross. The outcome, however, reflected negotiation and compromise between privileged women, their royal patrons, and the bureaucratic states.

The next four chapters place patriotic philanthropy at the center of struggles over the gender patterns of civic duties, the nature of obligations, and the extent of rights constituting the new national community after 1871. These efforts were part of "official nationalist" institutional and cultural strategies to perpetuate dynastic rule. Organizationally, the four chapters follow the "ideological" distinctions at the heart of dynastic rhetoric between municipal relief services in peacetime and the institutional planning for medical services in wartime. The division was more blurred in reality, however. Women's public peacetime charitable work, for example, was justified partly by its training ground for wartime.

Chapter 3 looks to the place of patriotic women's associations in the evolution of municipal poor relief services in Germany, which remained an important element giving shape to the emerging authoritarian welfare state. Chapter 4 turns to distinct genres of cultural performances around relief service, which worked to communicate the conservative social and gender values at the heart of the official nationalist imagination. Chapter

---

34. These debates are crystallized in the collection by Kocka, *Bürger und Bürgerlichkeit,* 10, 48–53, 258–59, 281–87, including a commentary by David Blackbourn. For the self-definition of the school as "critical," Wehler, *Deutsche Gesellschaftsgeschichte,* 3:466–67; also, 712–26, for his reassessment of aspects of the controversy. For a welcome call to transcend this same debate, George Steinmetz, *Regulating the Social: The Welfare State and Local Politics in Imperial Germany* (Princeton, N.J., 1993), 217–20.

35. Hermann Bausinger, "Bürgerlichkeit und Kultur," in Kocka, *Bürger und Bürgerlichkeit,* 132.

5, then, traces the complex institutional development of civilian war preparedness emerging under military control after 1878, whereas chapter 6 deals with its cultural forms and genres, which kept alive the memory of individual and community sacrifice in wartime. These ritual forms played an important role in the militarization of imperial German society.

Chapter 7 uncovers tensions and contradictions in this patriotic community itself that surfaced glaringly in 1913, a centenary year celebrating "German" liberation from Napoleon officially designed to proclaim community cohesion. It revealed, however, multiple fault-lines, including deep divisions within the nationalist community over gender. Nonetheless, when war broke out, the women and men in medical war service remained loyal to the dynasty, even as state legitimacy eroded around them. The conclusion assesses the cumulative impact of patriotic subjectivities for social organization and nationalist struggles in the century and confronts the gender paradoxes in their complex material life.

Throughout the "long" nineteenth century, an evolving patriotic public, anchored in the legal norms of associational life, fostered a visible space for elite women to help shape the contours of community welfare and participate in its defense. It was less a simple creation from above than a product of mutual interaction between dynastic interests and their local associations through which images of the state, indeed, were revisioned. The institutional practices and ritual forms that linked royal patrons and volunteers in Christian service demonstrate how such abstract notions as patriotism, nationhood, and militarism acquired their distinctive conservative definitions and became a powerful part of daily life. As a performance out in the public limelight, patriotic philanthropy molded an official nationalism that defended conservative legitimacies against continuous protests on the right and the left. Its legacy, however, was as complex as its past: the patriotic public helped to fashion a conservative Christian national identity, which long outlived the dynasty.

CHAPTER 1

The *Landesmutter* and Philanthropic Practices in the New German Dynastic States, 1813–1848

In 1835, a Protestant pastor in the Rhineland issued a public appeal to humanitarians *(Menschenfreunde)* everywhere. Remarkable in content and style, it spoke of new relationships that were being forged between institution building and state identity as well as individual behavior and social capital. Addressing a potential group of educated patrons, the manifesto simultaneously drew on and redeployed a host of symbols around community care, obligations, and responsibilities. If anthropological methods help decode the symbolic frameworks through which people experience reality, in complementary fashion historians' sensitivity to change helps uncover the emergence and transformation of new symbols in society.

Societies, of course, cannot create any symbolic system.[1] The pastor's appeal reflected a set of historic events that, during the wars against Napoleon, had drawn elements from Old Europe together in new combinations: ties of charity and secular authority tested in Renaissance Italy, confessional changes that inserted poor relief right into the heart of statebuilding, and new values of religious calling that underpinned feminine identity. They elevated a distinct symbol of dynastic authority to new prominence—the mother of the people *(Landesmutter)*—and supported its institutionalization in philanthropic practices in civil society. In its

---

1. Kertzer, *Ritual, Politics, and Power,* 4, who argues that symbols do not arise spontaneously, nor is their redefinition a matter of chance; rather they reflect the immediate distribution of power.

material forms, indeed, this symbolic framework would play a powerful role in the ongoing transformation of German society and politics.

Acknowledging that a large number of institutions were working to reduce misery and want in the decade of the 1830s, Pastor Friedrich Scheibler nonetheless announced his own plan to raise money to endow a female philanthropic association. Such an institute would meet multiple needs, and his list added up to a clear statement about the purposes of Christian love: "to feed the hungry, clothe the naked, aid the sick, take in abandoned widows and orphans, support destitute girls reduced to begging, and ease the burdens of honest yet feeble old people no longer able to work." In the insecure economic climate of the decade, success required, or so he argued, stability and durability, which could be guaranteed best by charitable gifts *(milde Gabe)* turned into a permanent fund. Emboldened by the Christian spirit, Scheibler was calling on his brothers and sisters of both confessions in the religiously mixed environs of the Rhineland to support his noble venture. And he laced the manifesto with assurances that by these acts of charity the benefactors would receive God's abiding pleasure and reap due rewards in heaven. He also promised future patrons that the poor, indeed, would pray for them.[2]

The pastor's solicitation, in part, grew out of a religious revival of piety that had swept through German territories in response to the revolutionary wars and the Napoleonic occupation. Religious authority, institutions, and property had been profoundly shaken by the secular reforms and territorial adjustments of the revolutionary decades. While admittedly complex and confessionally diverse, this movement reinvigorated religious commitments and, after 1815, reawakened a sense of mission and social activism, which expressed itself in charitable works.[3] Pastor Scheibler was aware of the proliferation of religiously inspired philanthropic institutes elsewhere, and he addressed an audience outside his locality. For him, the "kindness" of the public spoke to the presence of a wider sacred community bound together in its concern for the female poor and destitute. Furthermore, he drew on a vocabulary that increasingly was circulating in urban settings. In German civil society, the word *humanitarian* was being

---

2. LK, Abt. 403, no. 7363, Frauenvereine im Oberpräsidialbezirk, Bl. 5–12, Montjoie, May 1, 1835.

3. For a useful description of the importance of this religious revival for women's Christian activism and subsequent embrace of bourgeois feminism, Catherine M. Prelinger, *Charity, Challenge, and Change: Religious Dimensions of the Mid-Nineteenth-Century Women's Movement in Germany* (New York, 1987). For more general discussion of the religious revival, James J. Sheehan, *German History, 1770–1866* (Oxford, 1989), 555–65; Nipperdey, *Deutsche Geschichte, 1800–1866,* 74–75; and, most recently, David Blackbourn, *The Long Nineteenth Century: A History of Germany, 1780–1918* (New York, 1998), 134–37.

invested with honor, and he sang the praise of those who accepted the "duty of love" at the root of the charitable impulse.

The same appeal, however, pointed to other new cultural patterns as well. His rhetorical approach combined prose and poetry; indeed, Scheibler capped his case by reworking well-known biblical injunctions into a pleasing, although not particularly profound, poem. Poetry was finding a distinct place in the struggle to shape political identities and loyalties among the people newly combined into the city and dynastic states of the Germanic Confederation. The use of rhyme to evoke deep emotions accompanied the secular paeans to a new national *(deutsche Nation)* or specific territorial-state *(Nation)* identity; and such verse was recited regularly at royal entries and festivals that sought to structure bonds of loyalty favorable to dynastic legitimation.[4] For individual readers and wider audiences, poems transmit emotional symbols and sentiments in highly effective ways.

Scheibler's imagery is a case in point. He called the private charitable institutions "monuments" *(Ehrendenkmäle)*, permanent memorials on the local scene to honor the philanthropic community of patrons and clients; they were structural means to capture a vision of social activism and responsibility that would last into the future. In their daily practices of care, sponsors of these institutions passed on to subsequent generations a conception of community bound in common purpose. Although it was probably far from intended, Scheibler offers a way to think about the materiality of ideas: embedded in the very institutions on the local level were notions about charity and obligation, need and virtue, as well as authority and responsibility. Interestingly enough, this conception of philanthropy as monument was not lost on subsequent generations of dynastic leaders in Germany, who continuously drew on the same imagery.[5] In dynastic strategy, the philanthropic institute was a testimony to the living force of traditional authority and largesse.

Significantly, Scheibler's manifesto spoke powerfully of a new relationship that was solidifying between dynastic patronage and the private philanthropic "institute." In seeking to persuade his audience, he enlisted

4. For the use of poetry in the Wars of Liberation to evoke sentiments favorable to both new nationalist and dynastic identities, Karen Hagemann, "Of 'Manly Valor' and 'German Honor': Nation, War, and Masculinity during the Prussian Uprising against Napoleon," *Central European History* 30, no. 2 (1997): 190–92; and George L. Mosse, *Fallen Soldiers: Reshaping the Memory of the World Wars* (New York, 1990), 19–23.

5. Luise, duchess of Baden, evoked the identical image at the fiftieth-anniversary celebration of the Patriotic Women's Association in 1916, when she complimented Queen Augusta for building the living "monument" *(Denkmal)*. GK, Abt. 69, no. 952, Feier des 50-jährigen Jubiläums des Vaterländischen Frauenvereins in Berlin am 10 und 11 November 1916.

the Prussian crown princess Elisabeth (the wife of the future king, Frederick William IV) in his cause, expecting to capitalize on the power and prestige of the Hohenzollern court far away, even if there were serious religious tensions that made the relationship problematical in the eyes of many local Catholics.[6] But by the mid-1830s, it appears that new understandings of a wider community linked to the female dynast had been implanted in the culture at large. The tie between the female dynast (or the aristocratic woman patron) and the private philanthropic association seemed fully self-evident in Scheibler's address, which reproduced notions of community identity that were being shaped in interaction between the court and the locality. This new culture reflected processes that were making private philanthropic endeavors at the same time public and political. It demonstrates a new "public" emerging in civil society that, while it had variety of contexts and shades of meanings, was part of the effort at dynastic legitimation. At the same time, this political culture was fundamentally gendered. Unfortunately, the sources do not reveal the fate of Scheibler's appeal. It is unclear whether he founded a female philanthropic association, who its patrons might have been, or what specific clients it served. But his plea in the mid-1830s testifies to important changes in the political landscape of the states of the Germanic Confederation.

Charity, Relief, and Legitimation in Old Europe

The effort to link political legitimacy with commonly accepted notions of public welfare and the general good was not new. These ties long had been part of the very fabric of political authority in the city and dynastic states of Europe. They were expressed in institutional arrangements and communicated publicly through various ritual forms.

Renaissance Florence is a good case in point. Comprising a self-governing civic community, not an aristocratic court, Florentine elites anchored their legitimacy in a civil society of their making, at once eliding the commune and its virtues with the grandeur and power of its ruling families. Envisioned as a city of wealth and charity, the honor that inhered in communal support for the poor was part of the civic feasts and festivals giving shape to republican politics. Feeding the poor and clothing the destitute were common scenes during public celebrations, ennobling power by

---

6. A series of religious tensions had been building between Catholics and the Prussian state after the Rhineland province came to Prussia in 1815, which complicates the question of legitimacy. For an overview of the tensions, Sheehan, *German History,* 616–19; and for a more detailed analysis of one geographical area, H. Schubert, *Die Preussische Regierung in Koblenz. Ihre Entwicklung und Ihr Wirken, 1816–1918* (Bonn, 1925).

giving to the powerless and, in joining rich and poor alike, affirming communal bonds through ritual expressions.[7]

These ideas were not only ritually communicated, but embodied in institutional form as well. There was, for example, the prominent widows' asylum in Florence, the Orbatello, which was watched over by municipal officials. This quasi-private institution was a two-story apartment house for widows and their children, run by women in its daily operations and designed to insure future family formation. City fathers gave each girl a small dowry to help start a new family. Such exchange brought credit and esteem to the patronal government and the wider commune.[8] Embedded in these relationships were older values that linked fortune and wealth with sacrifice and giving. At the root of charity, or so some anthropologists argue, is an ancient moral imperative to put wealth and fortune in the service of the poor and the dependents, thereby enhancing the status and prestige of the individual donor, the particular tribe, or even the larger secular polity that afforded such largesse.[9]

Republican Florence still operated within a medieval Christian context that sanctified the act of giving alms itself and was indifferent to the nature and causes of poverty. Historians have identified two broad changes that transformed the understandings of poverty and communal responsibility for those in need. The one was the confessional Reformation and the other the rise of the dynastic state. Deeply entwined and interrelated, these seemingly distinct movements redrew the complicated ties between community welfare and political legitimation.[10]

Communities affected by the Protestant Reformation shifted responsibility for the poor from private and church hands to the municipality. In the process, they established a new relationship between poverty and work.[11] Catholic areas still maintained the older religious imperatives

---

7. I have drawn the following remarks from the exemplary study of civic life in Renaissance Florence, which is a model for its analysis of rituals in the political process, Richard C. Trexler, *Public Life in Renaissance Florence* (Ithaca, 1980), particularly part 3, "The ritual of the classical commune."

8. See also Richard Trexler, *The Women of Renaissance Florence: Power and Dependence in Renaissance Florence,* vol. 2 (Binghamton, N.Y., 1993), 88–93.   •

9. Marcel Mauss, *The Gift: The Form and Reason for Exchange in Archaic Societies,* trans. W. E. Halls (New York, 1990), 17–18, who traces the origins of alms through ancient Hebrew and Arabic linguistic forms of the relationship among gift, fortune, and sacrifice.

10. The new approach to the Reformation casts it in terms of state-building, elite formation, and social discipline. For an English summary of the new literature, R. Po-Chia Hsia, *Social Discipline in the Reformation: Central Europe, 1550–1750* (London, 1989), and his edited collection, *The German People and the Reformation* (Ithaca, N.Y., 1988).

11. Reproductions of ordinances and contemporary reports are in Sachsse and Tennstedt, *Geschichte der Armenfürsorge,* 67–80. See, as well, Peter Blum, *Staatliche Armenfürsorge im Herzogtum Nassau, 1806–1866* (Wiesbaden, 1987), 7–8.

regarding the poor, but in the heightened climate of religious fervor, they supported a whole range of new orders, congregations, and communities that affirmed the emerging principle of grace through social activism. In several Catholic lands, too, nuns and sisters provided most of the charitable and educational services in the early modern era.[12] These new institutional arrangements were powerful vehicles to structure community notions of membership and responsibility, even if such understandings always were a matter of contestation and negotiation.

Similarly, dynastic state-formation deepened these relationships in significant ways. The ongoing efforts to expand dynastic authority took place in and around orphanages, hospitals, and work- and poorhouses, even if the institutions continued to be administered locally. The provisioning of relief became an important element of political rule not only for early dynasts but also for the city "fathers" and "cousins" in the disparate territories of the Holy Roman Empire.[13]

The relationship between the Hohenzollern court and Pietist communities offers a graphic illustration of the place of poor relief and philanthropic acts in the extension of state rule itself. Conflicting definitions of community welfare and forms of relief were part of struggles to centralize power that, on the local level, were played out in good measure through the day-to-day work, and the ritual patterns, of religiously inspired models of philanthropy. Secular rule was justified, indeed, by religious scriptures to promote the "welfare of the subjects."[14]

Pietist leaders, hounded elsewhere in the territories of the Holy Roman Empire, found asylum in Brandenburg-Prussia in the late seventeenth century and established a close and mutually beneficial relationship with the Prussian court. The policy of religious toleration fit in with the

---

12. For the Christian traditions, Colin Jones, *The Charitable Imperative: Hospitals and Nursing in Ancien Regime and Revolutionary France* (London, 1989), 2–3, on the influential text by the Catholic humanist J. L. Vives, *De Subventione pauperum* (1529), which shaped European attitudes toward poverty well into the nineteenth century, and, for women's roles, 92–116.

13. For the relationship among poverty, poor relief, and political rule in a city state such as Hamburg, see Mary Lindemann, *Patriots and Paupers: Hamburg, 1712–1830* (New York, 1990). In her words, "Poor relief reform nicely illustrates how Hamburg's elites came to perceive the deficiencies of their society and how they began to rethink the purpose and redefine the range of government action" (6). In addition, Jonathan B. Knudsen, *Justus Möser and the German Enlightenment* (Cambridge, 1886), 116–32, offers insights into the place of poverty in the shaping of definitions of "public good" and "patriotism" in the case of Osnabrück, run, according to contemporaries, as a "cousin economy" (*Vetternwirtschaft*).

14. Klaus Deppermann, *Der hallesche Pietismus und der preussische Staat unter Frederick III. (I)* (Göttingen, 1961), 51, quoting the views of Jacob Spener, the most important Protestant theologian after Luther.

efforts of the state simultaneously to attract artisanal and refugee settlements in order to reinvigorate the economy after the Thirty Years' War.
As "loyal" clergy, Pietists served Hohenzollern power designs well. First,
the court used their ranks as a counterweight to the power of the nobles
(and local guilds) and their Lutheran orthodox allies, who dominated the
territorial estates. Trained at the state-supported University of Halle,
Pietists came to staff many church and government positions at the
regional and state level; they served as army chaplains and organized primary and secondary schooling in the districts. Second, Pietists helped
spearhead poor relief reform as a matter of state policy. The timing for the
changes was crucial. Society seemed to be turned upside down, or at least
this was a common complaint in reports from the local level. The better-
off groups were decrying a sense of moral decay and decline of religious
sensibilities among the common folk and noting a growing fear of beggars
on the streets, which was taking on an "ugly and violent" turn (according
to one communication) because of the number of discharged soldiers
among the poor and destitute.[15] Besides, the pest had struck Prussian
lands in 1681 and again in 1709.

Pietists addressed these fears directly. Inherent in their religious
understanding was a philanthropic imperative, a set of beliefs that supported an "active Christianity" *(tätiges Christentum)* and saw "love of
neighbor" *(Nächstenliebe)* and willingness to care for others as a way to
safeguard conversion and continuously affirm grace. Theirs was a vocabulary of the Good Samaritan *(barmherziger Samariter),* of a new dawn
breaking *(Morgenröte)* through charitable works, and of the importance
of "deeds" placed in the service of the state. These dynamic notions would
continue to resonate long into the future in a variety of contexts of social,
religious, and national activism.[16]

In its early years, Pietism inspired the renewal of official poor relief in
Prussia, which had been in disarray since the war's end. Pietist leaders such
as Jacob Spener and August Hermann Francke offered a distinct
definition of the Christian community, rooted, on the one hand, in individual Christian acts of charity and, on the other, in common commitment
to the value of useful and productive work. In their view, begging was not
tolerated (no one can live from "unearned bread"), and charity took on

---

15. Ibid., 10, for the quote; also 7–12, 21–27.

16. Carl Hinrichs, *Preussentum und Pietismus. Der Pietismus in Brandenburg-Preussen
als religiös-soziale Reformbewegung* (Göttingen, 1971), 9–12. For the relationship between
Pietism and patriotism, Gerhard Kaiser, *Pietismus und Patriotismus im Literarischen
Deutschland. Ein Beitrag zum Problem der Säkularisation* (Frankfurt am Main, 1973). And,
for the later period, Mosse, *Nationalization of the Masses,* 14–15, 50–51, and 74–75, who recognizes the importance of Pietist thought in shaping German national identity in the nineteenth century, as does Nipperdey, *Deutsche Geschichte, 1800–1866,* 304–5.

the character of work. Pietists set up orphanages and workhouses and various form of manufactories for those in need and, from their bases in Halle and Berlin, extended their model to such other cities as Darmstadt, Bielefeld, Kassel, Potsdam, Stettin, and Bunzlau. The stress on productive work in institutional settings created a harsh regime of labor regimentation and discipline, in many ways helping shape a labor force compatible with the evolving capitalist economy. But these same values of "indefatigable work" *(rastlose Tätigkeit),* self-control and productive labor became elements of statecraft, inserted into dynastic, aristocratic, or patrician strategies of rule. To the extent that governance was identified with these institutionalized values, legitimacy was enhanced, at least in the eyes of local elite groups committed to the same values. Their embrace was part of the Janus face of princely, aristocratic, and patriciate rule, at once harsh and normative, punitive yet binding.[17]

These normative ties worked to extend Hohenzollern political credit in local communities. For example, the Frederick Hospital in Berlin, founded by the Pietists and named for the newly crowned king, was supporting nearly two thousand needy people by 1704. That year alone, orphans and widows were given food, clothing, housing, and some schooling; 128 retired soldiers and soldiers' widows received regular weekly monies; a number of sick people had been provided with medicine; the institution had paid for 119 burials; and it helped a large number of migrants pass through the city by paying the exit tax. In another context, a philanthropic institute could become the backdrop for a political statement. When Frederick was crowned king in Prussia in 1701, for example, Francke arranged a festive service at his orphanage in Halle in which the community joined in prayer for the esteemed *Landesvater,* who was honored as a true Christian, committed to the care and support of the poor. Similarly, on assuming rule in 1713, Frederick William refused to receive homage from the magistrates in Halle but, rather, breakfasted with Francke at the same orphanage, which was directly under the jurisdiction of the Berlin court and not the territorial estates.[18] With the ongoing move

---

17. For the incorporation of these same values into the institutions of relief on aristocratic estates see, for example, LK, Abt. 403, no. 4420, Die Versorgung von Armen in Standesgebiet Solms-Braunfels, 1835; no. 744, Die Bevölkerung der Arbeits-Anstalt zu Braunweiler, 1823, which details the values underlying the work institute; and no. 718, den Religions-und Schul-Unterricht in der Arbeits-Anstalt zu Braunweiler, 1822.

18. Deppermann, *Der hallesche Pietismus,* 60, 141–42. Also, Hinrichs, *Preussentum und Pietismus,* 101–2, for the events surrounding Frederick William's ascension to the throne. Undeniably, poor relief and philanthropy were right at the heart of struggle for legitimacy, which always involved balancing oppositional groups. Thus, for example, the orphanages and workhouses simultaneously provoked conflict with guildsmen, who feared the competition of their labor and, at times, with the urban populace, who resented the tax burdens.

toward dynastic centralization, public relief and charitable acts became enmeshed in the political world of power, authority, and legitimation. Similar processes were occurring in Catholic Bavaria as well, where the house of Wittelsbach, for example, worked to consolidate its control by enforcing confessional conformity and welcoming new religious and charitable foundations that honored princely rule as part of their processional and festive celebrations.[19]

The Invention of the *Landesmutter* Symbol

If efforts at consolidating absolute rule had demonstrated the benefits of linking dynastic authority with normative institutional practices, the nineteenth century expressed these same relationships in an innovative symbolic idiom. New was its fundamentally gendered character, communicated in the symbol of the *Landesmutter,* who was coming to represent community well-being, obligation, and care. This distinctive female symbol of authority was being constituted partly by the act of dynastic patronage and personal involvement in the institutionalization of women's associations *(Frauen-Vereine)* on the local level; by 1835 it was a common enough connection in the political culture to impact Pastor Scheibler's manifesto. The relationship, however, was mutually constitutive—the authority and beneficence of the *Landesmutter* were communicated by the charitable activities of elite women at the local level, and the female ruler, in turn, oversaw and safeguarded women's public activity in civil society.

Equally characteristically, these ties also were encoded in a language of patriotism. Philanthropic work was named patriotic by the dynastic center, which was involved in a continuous struggle to solidify and master a definition that was, indeed, multiple and fluid. State dynastic groups sought to subsume the patriotic philanthropic activities under dynastic tutelage and, thus, link the humanitarian endeavors to dynastic legitimation and community defense. Indeed, a patriotic public was inserted right in the very heart of political and social change. The institutions and activities around patriotic philanthropy, therefore, coalesced into a "pattern . . . of meaning," to borrow a notion from Clifford Geertz.[20] Emerging from the very processes of change itself, its symbolisms helped guide and channel the ongoing nature of political change.

This new linkage of patriotism and female charitable works occurred at a precise historical juncture: the outpouring of patriotic fervor and enthusiasm that, between 1813 and 1815, sustained the mobilization of

---

19. Hsia, *Social Discipline,* 39–41.
20. Geertz, "After the Revolution," 253.

community defenses during the Wars of Liberation against Napoleon. Historians long have pointed to the famous appeal of the Prussian king Frederick William III "To My People," designed to mobilize popular support for a war seen as "decisive" for the very existence, independence, and welfare of "Prussians" and "Germans." It seemed to encapsulate the larger effort of political change sweeping the territories of the former Holy Roman Empire, reform processes that Thomas Nipperdey, in the opening of his grand narrative of *German History,* regards as laying the foundations for "modern" Germany—even if its evolution was slow, uneven, and weighted by older traditions.[21]

The king's proclamation, however, had a less well known but equally momentous counterpart: a plea by nine princesses to the women of Prussia to establish a Women's Association for the Benefit of the Fatherland (Der Frauen-Verein zum Wohl des Vaterlandes). Offered in the immediate context of the establishment of a citizen's militia *(Landwehr)* and the formation of a territorial reserve army *(Landsturm)*—the constellation of the male citizen-soldier—it enlisted women for community defense, engendering popular mobilization in ways that would become normative in the future. These female members of the royal family called on women to give freely for the cause of war and announced a weekly accounting of the public donations in the press that, they said, were expressions of "virtue" and "love of fatherland." Here was the direct construction of a patriotic public through deeds. By contributing to the outfitting of the volunteer, each woman received the right immediately to call herself *(sich . . . zu nennen)* a member of the association—and patriotic. Beyond offering monetary support, women also could volunteer to care for the sick and the wounded.[22] At its height, apparently, there were six hundred women's branch associations in Prussia alone; and similar efforts were recorded all over central Europe: patriotic associations emerged in Bavaria, Baden, and Saxony and in cities occupied by the French in the Rhineland like Koblenz and Cologne. Under royal, aristocratic, or patriciate leadership, women followed the call of the princesses and offered their sacrifices for a "new dawn" for the fatherland.[23]

---

21. Nipperdey, *Deutsche Geschichte, 1800–1866,* 31.

22. The various appeals by the Prussian royal family are republished in Ernst Müsebeck, ed., *Gold gab ich für Eisen. Deutschlands Schmach und Erhebung in zeitgenössischen Documenten, Briefen, Tagebüchern aus den Jahren 1806–1815* (Berlin, 1913), 211–12 and 216–17, specifically.

23. Heinrich Gräfe, *Nachrichten von wohlthätigen Frauenvereinen in Deutschland. Ein Beitrag zur Sittengeschichte des neuzehnten Jahrhunderts* (Cassel, 1844), 3–21, details the extensive network of Patriotic Women's Associations throughout the territories of Germany in the years 1813–15. He depicts the war as an awakening of the people, following the call of the princes, and encases the memory in a dynastic narrative. Indeed, Gräfe wrote the book at

Historic time—and social memory—entered into German political culture in new and profoundly important ways after the Wars of Liberation in 1813–15. Indeed, the growing role of "history" in political struggle points to important changes that were reshaping central European identities in part by self-conscious action that was defined by, and justified in, a memory of the past. But since memory, itself, is never fixed and can be used for multiple purposes, it entered the arena of power and struggle. Defining a precise narrative of the past was one important tool to legitimize the present political order.[24] And patriotic women's associations emerged as part of these efforts to shape memory through ongoing civic activism in the present. But women's philanthropic work assembled under the authority of a *Landesmutter* was not something that, seemingly, was predetermined, even after the successful mobilization of women in 1813. Its institutional and symbolic force in the long nineteenth century, rather, reflected a confluence of historic changes that had combined during the war in new ways to shape female patriotic service in the dynastic states of Germany.

The very term *Landesvater*—or for that matter the self-portrayal of a regime of "fathers and uncles" in cities and bishoprics of central Europe—expressed unambiguously the essential masculine character of political rule in the complex territories of the old empire. To be sure, aristocratic representations at court included women whose noble lineage naturally carried the aura of power, prestige, and authority in their person; but as an official organization of rule, *Landesmutter* does not appear as a separate entry in the lexicons or encyclopedias, nor is it part of the biographical categories of analysis of royal figures until the early nineteenth century. Then, increasingly, it became the common designation for dynastic female authority in a vast array of print media and in the ritual performances of dynastic rule.[25]

---

the request of Crown Princess (later Empress) Augusta. See Natalie v. Milde, *Marie Pawlowna: Ein Gedenkblatt zum 9. November 1904* (Hamburg, 1904), iv. For local examples, Gisela Mettele, "Bürgerliche Frauen und das Vereinswesen im Vormärz. Zum Beispiel Köln," *Jahrbuch zur Liberalismus-Forschung* 5 (1993): 31–34; and Dirk Reder, "'Im Felde Soldat mit Soldat, daheim Männerbund mit Männerbund, Frauenverein mit Frauenverein.' Der Patriotische Frauenverein Köln in Krieg und Armenpflege, 1813–1826," *Geschichte in Köln: Historisches Seminar der Universität zu Köln,* December 1992, 53–76.

24. Too often, works on nationalism reproduce its totalizing assertions when, in fact, the particular nationalist perspective silences a range of voices and interests in the national community. For this theme in its relation to gender, see Andrew Parker et al., eds., *Nationalisms and Sexualities* (New York, 1992), specifically Mary Layoun, "Telling Spaces: Palestinian Women and the Engendering of National Narratives," 407–23.

25. For the etymology of the concept of *Landesvater* see *Deutsches Rechtswörterbuch. Wörterbuch der älteren deutschen Rechtssprache,* vol. 8 (Weimar, 1984–91), 667. For *Landesmutter* see, for example, Jacob Grimm and Wilhelm Grimm, *Deutsches Wörterbuch,* vol. 6 (Leipzig, 1885), 110.

There had been important changes in dynastic representation that set the stage for this new expression of female authority. In the first place, the monarchy itself was being defined in more human terms, at times indistinguishable from the subjects at large. At least this was the case in the communications between politically powerful nobles and magistrates on the one hand and the Prussian prince on the other at key transition moments of statecraft, as on the death of a king, the ascension to the throne of the heir, or a royal entry into towns and provinces. Over the seventeenth and eighteenth centuries, the attributes of rule in these oaths of homage shifted from the once standard, classical, abstract virtues of justice, fortitude, or bravery to distinct expectations of behavior implicit in the trope of the father. While still expressed in masculine idiom, by the 1780s the "father of the fatherland" was described as a "humanitarian" of congenial personality—as *Mensch,* the greatest of kings and, as king, the greatest of men.[26]

Second, the issue of legitimate rule became tied into a new vocabulary of patriotism in the late eighteenth century, an era of intellectual ferment that brought into question many of the governing principles at the heart of the "well-ordered police state" (the Cameralist ideal in German territories). The new rubric of patriotism rearranged the older reciprocities of legitimate rule and standards of community prosperity *(Gemeinwohl)*.

Supported by enlightenment principles, a new space was emerging in the eighteenth century to complicate the already complex relationship between concepts of state rule and institutions of relief. This was a noncorporate world of voluntary, free association; its members were confident of their power to bring about reform, relied on a reading public for legitimacy, and gradually extended its influence into the larger community. In the late eighteenth century, this "public" still was male. The men who founded and ran these voluntary associations called themselves "patriots" and defined their activity as patriotic, a multivalent notion that had wide currency in eighteenth-century Europe. In the name of patriotism, supporters of enlightened absolutism argued for the need to centralize control over education to instill loyalty and obedience; so asserted the French reformer Abbé Coyer. Under pressure from the debates, enlightened monarchs, too, represented themselves as patriots, acting for "love of fatherland." In this manner, they could appeal to a public that was redefining elements of legitimate rule and at the same time couch their own paternalistic principles in new idiom.

The most common linkage in the eighteenth century, however, was the coupling of patriotism and philanthropy as a distinct, voluntary pub-

26. See the detailed investigation of shifting notions of legitimacy by Monika Wienfort, *Monarchie in der bürgerlichen Gesellschaft: Deutschland und England von 1640 bis 1848* (Göttingen, 1993), 97–128, particularly. I break company with her interpretation of charity, welfare, and philanthropy as peripheral to statecraft.

lic activity in the name of the greater good. Such work offered new opportunities for educated people in voluntary associations and clubs to demonstrate their patriotism by promoting causes that were seen to serve the wider society. Describing France in terms that could apply equally to German-speaking lands, one author astutely notes that Enlightenment "patriotism" primarily was a social norm.

> The patriotism of the Enlightenment was positively oriented toward assuring the well-being of the whole community. . . . Typically, the "patriot" . . . was a man who had done something to promote the common good, such as, for example, writing a book on agriculture, or education, or ethics, or who had performed a signal act of beneficence.[27]

In the old Empire, where the Enlightenment was more corporatist, the voluntary patriotic associations were filled by the patrician and ruling notables of the territorial, ecclesiastical, and city states (men still distinguished by the traditional criteria of birth and age). Here, patriotism represented a set of shared civic virtues of engagement such as honesty, propriety, and sincerity that bound together government and the governed. While voluntary and free, these patriotic associations were eminently loyal.[28]

Historians have identified at least sixty patriotic societies that were active in the Germanies and Switzerland between 1760 and 1820, when the newly politicized world of nationalist struggle destroyed the civic rationale that underpinned the patriotic-philanthropic connection—or so it is commonly assumed. By all accounts, the most influential association was the Patriotic Society in Hamburg, active first in the 1720s; it was a model for other organizations in cities as far away as Lübeck and Nuremberg. The association emerged again in 1765 to spearhead reorganization of the city's poor relief system, which was "the most important reform of the Hamburg Enlightenment."[29] For our purposes, its reform agenda is less important than the fact that the association had very close ties to the exist-

27. Harvey Chisick, *The Limits of Reform in the Enlightenment: Attitudes toward the Education of the Lower Classes in Eighteenth-Century France* (Princeton, N.J., 1981), 223 and 205–10 for Abbé Coyer's views.

28. R. Vierhaus, "'Patriotismus'—Begriff und Realität einer moralisch-politischen Haltung," in *Deutsche patriotische und gemeinnützige Gesellschaften,* ed. Rudolf Vierhaus (Munich, 1980), 9–29.

29. F. Kopitzsch, "Die Hamburgische Gesellschaft zur Beförderung der Künste und nützlichen Gewerbe (Patriotische Gesellschaft um 1765) im Zeitalter der Aufklärung," in Vierhaus, *Deutsche patriotische Gesellschaften,* 89. Lindemann, *Patriots and Paupers,* 205–10, argues that state and society increasingly separated after 1815, and she places charity within the "private" (nonpolitical) sphere when its work, in fact, blurred the lines between public and private.

ing power structure of the republican city. Indeed, its members, drawn from the clergy and prosperous mercantile families, were part of city government, pressing for reform of the very "state" institutions they were serving in. The Hamburg association did not represent a distinct society in opposition to the state. Rather, these patriotic *Vereine* in the late eighteenth century—and their namesakes in the next century—greatly complicate understanding of the workings of a public sphere.

A brief excursion to Schleswig-Holstein to examine the duchy's Patriotic Society between 1786 and 1829 illustrates well the protean quality of the term *patriotism* and the stakes for dynastic rulers in monopolizing its definition and energy. The case captures in bold relief the shifting fortunes of patriotic work under the impact of the French Revolution.[30]

The Patriotic Society in Schleswig-Holstein emerged on the public scene in Kiel in 1786; modeled explicitly on its Hamburg forerunner, the city's patriots and their allies were committed to the general improvement in the lives of the "less well-off" in society. Membership statutes opened the door to "all well-intended *(wohlwollende)* and working *(werktätige)* [male] citizens," shunning "title and rank" and welcoming men living in both urban and rural districts, civilians and soldiers as well as the educated and those from the business community.[31] This social intermingling represented a new departure to be sure, a break with the old corporate hierarchy, at least ideally, according to the principles embodied in the statutes.

Piecing together the early membership tells a slightly different story but one revealing in its own right. A high proportion of titled noblemen were among the founding members, as were high government officials; the patriots essentially embraced men committed to and working for an enlightened, reforming state. As importantly, in this space organized under the rubric "patriotic," nobles and educated burgers worked together even as they opposed one another in other contexts, for example over the nature, pace, and cost of agrarian reforms that were being carried out by government decrees simultaneously. What happened to this early association is unclear, for the records are incomplete.

In 1812, a successor association appeared, comprised of eighty members. By then, the political world of Schleswig-Holstein's patriots had changed profoundly; with the French Revolution, all reform seemed revolutionary. The new association now was under dynastic patronage; indeed, it received its money from a dynastic fund. Nobles continued to comprise a large proportion of the membership, which included clergy and govern-

30. I am drawing this case from Kai Detlev Sievers, "Patriotische Gesellschaften in Schleswig-Holstein zwischen 1786 und 1829," in Vierhaus, *Deutsche patriotische Gesellschaften,* 119–41.

31. Ibid., 122–23.

ment officials as well. Reflecting the territorial perspective of the dynast, intricate plans were laid (they remained unrealized) for an organizational expansion from the center throughout the land. And its work ranged widely, from securing employment for the poor to promoting the fabrication of rapeseed-oil and tallow candles to arranging institutional aid for widows and developing a statistical alphabetized compendium of all the peculiarities *(Merkwürdigkeiten)* in the duchy to promote local history. After 1815, the "patriotism" of the Schleswig-Holstein society (which continued operations until 1843) turned essentially provincial and limited. Its work centered on gathering and printing folktales and songs and preserving local customs and dress. Safeguarding "traditions" and enhancing local pride was one meaning of patriotism in the nineteenth century, a conserving impulse that reinforced local or provincial identity. Under the impact of the French Revolution and the Napoleonic occupation, this reactive patriotism had shed its ties to a broader humanistic concern with statecraft and the common good.

Most historians interested in the patriotic associations during the Enlightenment end their inquiry in the early nineteenth century, when many of the organizations gave up their wider social-reform agendas. The divide is artificial, however, and masks an important line of continuity, which the case of Schleswig-Holstein has indicated. So-called voluntary philanthropic work became increasingly tied into dynastic strategies of rule, as dynasts and their officials and promoters sought to relegitimize the principles of monarchical government threatened by the ideas and practices of the French Revolution and Napoleon's radical redrawing of the map of central Europe.[32] The French Revolution had helped crystallize distinct political positions that only had been articulated vaguely in the Old Regime. The Napoleonic occupations, in turn, heightened political tensions, adding nationalist antagonisms to the disruptions of legal and institutional innovations as well as military defeat. Their legacies continued to challenge the Germanic dynastic states long after the Congress of Vienna declared dynastic rule to be the legitimate principle of government in the new confederation. Transforming principle into legitimizing practice, however, was an imperative in this contested political age. Dynastic houses re-created rituals and supported institutions (and passed on their models to one another) that reinforced their concept of state authority and the proper relations between ruler and subject. And they increasingly relied on the female dynast as *Landesmutter* to orchestrate and coordinate a ritual and institutional world of patriotic philanthropic state service.

---

32. James Sheehan makes this important point: "Almost 60 per cent of the German population changed rulers during the revolutionary period" (*German History,* 251).

There were a number of precedents that worked to shape the early definition of the female dynast as the "true mother of the poor." That title apparently already had been given to a niece of Frederick II. But traditional beneficence of rule in the small principalities of the empire had been assuming a feminine character. In the case of Schwarzburg-Rudolstadt, for example, the crown prince founded a knitting school for poor girls in 1777, the daily supervision of which he turned over to his young wife after he inherited the throne.[33] Similarly, the conversion of many noble families to Pietism outside of Prussia—the Pietist lifestyle had an appeal among the free imperial knights and counts of the old Empire—had meant the introduction of orphanages, workhouses, and other philanthropic undertakings on their estates, often under the auspices of the woman of the household. In the correspondence, letters, and tracts on education and ethics that circulated in Pietist communities, these women were singled out as models for emulation, like Frau Henriette Catharine von Gersdorff, who also was known for her active support of Francke and the Halle orphanage.[34]

Indeed, the European aristocracy had been at the forefront of promoting philanthropic innovations both on their own estates and in administrative centers. French court and robe nobles, for example, underwrote the female character of voluntary charity in post-Trentine Catholicism, which associated women with the work of love, gentleness, and care as an evangelizing mission. These trends point to important sociopolitical patterns that were part of a movement of Europe's aristocrats everywhere on the continent to carve out roles and positions of authority in the locality in the face of political, legal, and bureaucratic challenges to their power. German aristocratic circles were no exception; as we will see, aristocratic women were the essential linchpin of patriotic philanthropic work in Germany throughout the long nineteenth century.

Understanding the formation of voluntary charity as a female religious vocation takes us briefly outside the borders of German territories to Catholic France. Only after 1815—and then only slowly and hesitatingly from their Alsace headquarters in Strasbourg—did Catholic nursing orders enter municipal service in the confessionally mixed territories of the Germanic Confederation. In contrast to the experiences of Protestant Germany that had made relief a municipal responsibility under growing state authority, Catholic France continued to rely on private and church

---

33. Rumpel-Nienstedt, "Thäterinnen der Liebe," 213, for the early title of "mother of the poor." Also, Bernhard Anemüller, *Caroline Louise, Fürstin zu Schwarzburg-Rudolstadt* (Rudolstadt, 1869), 82–83; *Handbuch für das Fürstenthum Schwarzburg-Rudolstadt, 1894* (Rudolstadt, 1894).

34. Hinrichs, *Preussentum und Pietismus,* 183–206.

initiatives. The details are available elsewhere and beyond the scope of this study except for a number of instructive points about sociopolitical power and gender relations.

The distinctive feature shaping female charitable work in France was the prominent role played by the nobility and court aristocracy. According to Colin Jones, already in the early seventeenth century, for example, robe nobles had been instrumental in founding hospitals in the municipalities. "[B]y wielding the patronage and protection a hospital afforded, local notables could build up and cement a clientele among local resident poor."[35] The feminization of charity, however, involved a struggle within the church hierarchy itself. Under the artful political wiles of Vincent de Paul and the day-to-day organizational talents of Louise de Marillac, the Daughters of Charity were constituted officially as a confraternity in 1655. The church had accepted the idea of a community of women ministering to the poor and sick in society; significantly, however, it was placed under male authority.[36]

In good measure, the outcome reflected the patronage of aristocratic families and the calculations of the French court. The monarchy profited by its association with the nursing sisters. It brought them into military hospitals and to villages to care for the poor, and it staffed newly established foundling homes with these dedicated women. Affirming the wider point about the politics of charity, Jones notes that "these were the kinds of gestures of grace and gratuity which could win public approval and remind society at large that the ruler was the fount of justice and mercy as well as a coercive and extractive agency." Furthermore, French aristocrats increasingly utilized the female nursing communities on their own estates, partly to gain honor among their peers by emulating royal practices, and partly out of self-interest and fear of unrest and discord that was accompanying the simultaneous efforts to extend seignorial and feudal burdens on the peasantry. French nobles had been the patrons of the Daughters of Charity in the first place. In time, the nursing order achieved a veritable "takeover" of poor relief in France; Jones writes that "by 1789, just about every charitable institution of any size and substance was staffed by such women," even those run by Protestants.[37]

In German territories, the profound challenge to dynastic authority posed by the Revolution and Napoleonic wars forged the royal woman into a state symbol of charity and largesse, a patriotic linking of rule to the

---

35. Jones, *The Charitable Imperative,* 9.

36. Barry and Jones, *Medicine and Charity,* 1–25; Colin Jones, *Charity and Bienfaisance: The Treatment of the Poor in the Montpellier Region, 1740–1815* (Cambridge, 1982); and Patricia Banft, *Women and the Religious Life in Pre-Modern Europe* (New York, 1996).

37. Jones, *The Charitable Imperative,* 90, 113.

feminine and the rituals of care. This new conception of dynastic authority found its way into the contemporary biographical accounts of Queen
Luise of Prussia, one written at her untimely death in 1810 and, another,
in 1814, after the battle of Leipzig assuring "German" liberation. Essentially literary creations, these early biographies reflect the purposes of the
study; for example, the 1814 work was dedicated "to the Prussian nation"
and earmarked the proceeds of its sales to the widows and orphans of the
militia troops who had died "for king and fatherland." The work was
designed to appropriate and tame ideas that were challenging dynastic
rule: in its pages, "nation" and "fatherland" were confined to the geographic borders of Prussia alone. Equally important was the novel use of
the *Landesmutter* symbol for state rule.[38]

If both contemporary biographies are read partly as descriptions of
statecraft that reflect dynastic governmental norms, they demonstrate
important changes in the rituals of rule binding the Prussian state. The
new political calculations emerge clearly in several contexts. One is the
detailed narratives of the travels in 1797–98 by the new regents—Frederick William III and Luise—to receive homage from their countrymen on
assuming rule. They contain rich portraits of "royal entries" through triumphal arches, gift giving, and stylized greetings by the powerful and the
young in performances that would be played out repeatedly on the streets
of German cities over the long nineteenth century.

What is new is the gendered script: "the oldest circles" in the population, or so we are told, "could not remember ever seeing the queen."
Prominent in these ceremonies of rule at a time of political crisis was the
"mother of the people" as a visual affirmation of rule of the dynastic family: "all wanted to see the beloved king and the new *Landesmutter*"; the
crowds shouted "welcome most beloved *Landesmutter,* offering flowers."
Her response was "I thank you, dear children."[39] The family metaphor of
rule, present in earlier concepts of monarchy, to be sure, now was linked to
justice and charity, the two muses enlisted to protect the fatherland, and
not only in the print media circulating at the time like the royal biographies themselves, but in new performances of charitable largesse in the
locality. At the time of the queen's entry into Königsberg, for example, "to
show their joy and sympathy, the merchant community generously fed the

---

38. I am drawing on the following two contemporary biographies of Luise, *Luise
Auguste Wilhelmine Amalie, Königin von Pruessen. Ein Denkmal* (Berlin, 1810); and *Die Köni-
gin Luise. Der Preussischen Nation gewidmet. Zum Besten der hinterlassenen Wittwen und
Waisen der für König und Vaterland gefallenen Landwehrmänner und Freiwilligen Jäger* (n.p.,
1814). There is a huge body of literature on Luise, who, in the nineteenth century, emerges as
a Prussian/German heroine. For general background to her era, Thomas Stamm-Kuhlmann,
König in Preussens grosser Zeit. Friedrich Wilhelm III. der Melancholiker auf dem Thron
(Berlin, 1992).

39. *Luise Auguste Wilhelmine Amalie,* 54–56, 81–82; *Die Königin Luise,* 88.

indigent and, in addition, designated a place where each resident poor could get one thaler, some linens and a three-course meal." In Frankfurt am Main, accompanied by the general of the cavalry and state ministers, Luise visited the large orphanage and "met three hundred orphans . . . who were a touching sight to the exalted *Landesmutter.*"[40]

But these dynastic ceremonies were not only orchestrated "from above" at the precise moment when the *Landesmutter* toured the municipal relief institution. They became part of an emerging political culture in towns and municipalities that maintained a momentum long after the queen had left. This pattern is seen in the origins of the *Luisenstift* in Berlin in 1806–7. A period of profound crisis for the Prussian state in light of military defeat and dismemberment, the political turmoil was matched by economic dislocations, affecting many wives and children of soldiers at the front. The biography reveals that in the depth of the winter of 1806, several "humanitarians" came together and organized a subscription for poor children for March 10 of the next year, the birthday of the *Landesmutter,* who was by then in near exile in Memmel. "Never before did the love of philanthropic work and the eagerness to give charity correspond so well to the patriotic wishes of the noble monarch and his humanitarian wife."[41] Indeed, in the account, philanthropic contributions were a mark of political loyalty. Subsequently, the birthday of the since deceased queen was remembered in new form, when the institute was named Luise and perpetuated the March 10 celebration.

Institutionalizing Dynastic Authority: Women's Philanthropic Associations

The timing of a particular turn to philanthropic work in a society is a complicated matter. Its rhythm in part reflects a mix of need and fear—contexts of deprivation and misery on the one hand and anxieties and worries about their social consequences on the other. But tracing the elevation of the *Landesmutter* as new symbol of care demonstrates other calculations of a political nature as well: efforts, in this case, to concretize the state as a wider family concerned with the well-being of its children-subjects.[42] And

---

40. *Luise Auguste Wilhelmine Amalie,* 78, 117–18.

41. *Luise Auguste Wilhelmine Amalie,* 200–203. For the emergence of new rituals in times of disorder, Robert Schribner, "Ritual and Reformation," in Hsia, *German People,* 122–44.

42. The argument away from a "need-response" model is made by Cavallo, "The Motivations of Benefactors"; and, in a different context, reinforced by Frie, *Wohlfahrtsstaat und Provinz,* 18. There was more than one notion of "family" in the patriotic rituals. Rituals around food in some public renditions mirrored notions of domesticity; in others, they affirmed a male "family" joined in a banquet of brotherhood. I develop these distinctions in chapter 6.

its institutionalization in civil society rearranged authority along new gender lines.

The dynastic symbol and its sanctioned female public were inserted into the ideological debates and assumptions about gender that were circulating in early-nineteenth-century Europe. In the 1810 literary monument, the "beloved" *Landesmutter* was honored as the most humanitarian queen, loving wife, and tender mother, in that order. This literary text placed the royal figure in a complicated gender framework that drew on a number of independent sources working to fashion the concept in the first place: patriotic practices, Christian values of charity, and bourgeois norms. But each source was distinct, with its own trajectory, and the whole was somehow greater than the sum of its parts. The emergent *Landesmutter,* as person and symbol, did not simply mirror a new bourgeois gender order that authorized a female philanthropic reform movement as an extension of the domestic sphere, although this discursive context surely played a role.[43] Rather, it also reappropriated Christian assumptions of charity and love of neighbor and patriotic notions of a voluntary space for civic activity to reenact a "public spirit" *(Gemeinsinn)* as the basis of the new polity after 1815.[44]

Somewhat surprisingly, perhaps, the model for the gendered patriotic public was the Duchy of Weimar, home of German classical humanism, and not the Prussian state. Under the patronage and tireless day-to-day supervision of Duchess Marie Pawlowna (she effectively ran the institute for forty-two years), the Patriotic Women's Institute (Patriotische Fraueninstitut) functioned as a legal person for the whole duchy. Established officially in 1817, although it drew on earlier war experiences, the organization matched the administrative divisions of the state. Its example was followed in the kingdom of Württemberg, with the near simultaneous creation of the Charity Association (Wohltätigkeits-Verein) and in Schleiz by Prince Reuss, who founded a Patriotic Women's Institute in 1828.[45]

Contemporary observers clearly connected the Weimar association with other female endeavors that, as one study put it in 1844, comprised together a network of patriotic philanthropic institutions *(patriotische,*

---

43. This is the dominant interpretation in the literature on the German women's movements, whether tracing its origins to *Vormärz* or to the founding of the bourgeois women's movement in 1865. See the essays in Lipp, *Schimpfende Weiber;* and Prelinger, *Charity, Challenge, and Change.* Also, Trentmann, *Paradoxes of Civil Society,* 18–20, underestimates the linkages between charity, ideology, and state identity in the nineteenth century—in their feminine forms.

44. As found in Gräfe, *Nachrichten von wohlthätigen Frauenvereinen,* 165.

45. Ibid., 168–71.

Map 1. Women's Associations in the Germanic Confederation, 1844. (Based on information in Heinrich Gräfe, *Nachrichten von wohlthätigen Frauenvereinen in Deutschland* [Cassel, 1844].)

wohltätige Anstalten); their visible patterns were seen as an encouraging sign of renewed life among the "German people." In this author's imagination, the shared practices of patriotic philanthropy combined to help identify a much larger German community.[46] Through dynastic family linkages, furthermore, Weimar served as inspiration for Luise, the duchess of Baden, who unified the state's *Frauen-Verein* in 1859 and also for Queen Augusta, who constituted the Prussian Vaterländische Frauen-Vereine (Women's Patriotic Associations) in 1866. Augusta was the daughter of Maria Pawlowna and, in turn, the mother of Luise of Baden. A female dynastic lineage had spearheaded a new space for women's public activity, supported by state and local interests, that found widespread dynastic and aristocratic emulation elsewhere.

What was the confluence of interests that supported the statewide female institute in Weimar and accounted for the strength of its model and message? The institute represented an appealing amalgam in this new era of bureaucratic authority after 1815: a "voluntary union of individuals" working for the "common goals of the state."[47] It addressed both "liberal" and "conservative" positions, although perhaps the year 1817 is too early to speak of these political labels; they had not yet formed into distinct political blocs.[48] Nonetheless, the more liberal-minded officials favored turning over a variety of common tasks of an agricultural, manufacturing, educational, or philanthropic nature to free associations, while aristocratic and princely interests endorsed a patrimonial model, which linked these practices to conservative social power and rule.

Government officials tied the institute directly to "state ends," as the preamble to the statutes demonstrates: the work of the women preserves and strengthens the "love of the Fatherland" *(Vaterlandsliebe)* through concern for its "well-being" *(Wohl),* which is demonstrated in the care of needy individuals. This civic activism reinforces and perpetuates those "noble patriotic sentiments," which had been awakened earlier in wartime. The last article of the statutes, too, directly relates the educational tasks to the needs of the state, "so that the state also from this side will be strengthened and preserved in its foundations." Yet, its legal "rights" *(Rechte)* and "obligations" *(Verbindlichkeiten)* defined the institute as a private

---

46. Ibid., 21. Also, Margarit Twellmann, *Die Deutsche Frauenbewegung im Spiegel repräsentativer Frauenzeitschriften. Ihre Anfänge und erste Entwicklung, 1843–1889* (Meisenheim am Glan, 1972), 47–49.

47. Gräfe, *Nachrichten von wohlthätigen Frauenvereinen,* 36.

48. For a study that complicates understanding of Prussia's *Vormärz* as the era of bureaucratic liberalism, Hermann Beck, *The Origins of the Authoritarian Welfare State in Prussia, 1815–1870* (Ann Arbor, Mich., 1995), 1–10, 125–47, 162–66.

voluntary association *(Privatanstalt)* under dynastic patronage and not as an official arm of the state *(Staatsanstalt).*[49]

As first president, the duchess was essential to the whole operation. As clearly spelled out in the preamble, her "well-known" name and aura alone elevated the institute in the eyes of the public and safeguarded the "impartiality" and "steadfastness" of its goals. Reflecting widespread concerns about arbitrary rule ("even if only in appearance"), the preamble assured both the members and the wider public that the presence of the duchess would remove all doubts about any semblance of caprice. As the embodiment of impartiality and disinterest, she would elicit the goodwill of the public, which was necessary for the success of a private association.[50] The duchess was made to embody the principles of impartiality and disinterest. Twenty-seven years after its founding, the duchess emerged also as the "benefactress and mother of the people" *(Wohlthäterin und Mutter des Landes),* a title that was activated by the very work of the institute under her active leadership. Furthermore, in a revealing passage drawing on a common image, the institute's "historian" concludes that the "noble-minded" *(edeln)* women doing the day-to-day work were keeping the association alive "from generation to generation" as a "magnificent monument *(herrliches Denkmal)* to the high-minded and beloved princess."[51] Court and institute intertwined to conserve the collective interests of the state.

The Patriotic Institute was a woman's establishment, but not exclusively. It drew on privileged social groups for its active members: estate owners, clergy, teachers, government officials, and their wives. It favored girls' vocational needs but also aided boys; it called for volunteers and, thus, relied on well-off women, whose economic background could sustain nonwaged civic duties out in public. In smaller communities, however, institute members often doubled as teachers, but the statutes prohibited them from receiving pay or gifts. Men also donated their labor.

If the position of president of the branch association was exclusively female, men served as her assistants *(Gehülfen)* and as secretaries and treasurers. These philanthropic activities worked to weld together an elite service group in the community and, by its placement in a network of similar associations throughout the land, offered a way for individuals to

---

49. "Gesetzliche Bestimungen für das patriotische Institut der Frauenvereine in dem Grossherzogthum Sachsen Weimar-Eisenach," Weimar, 1817, in Milde, *Marie Pawlowna,* 51. Art. 24 in the original reads, "damit der Staat auch von dieser Seite in seinen Grundpfeilern gestärk und gefestigt werde." For the preamble, Gräfe, *Nachrichten von wohlthätigen Frauenvereinen,* 37–39, and for its legal status, 41–42.

50. Gräfe, *Nachrichten von wohlthätigen Frauenvereinen,* 38.

51. Ibid., 40–41, 185.

imagine a larger geographical entity. Through the activities and rituals that the members shared with one another, the work also helped constitute an understanding of the fatherland (although at the time the term referred only to the Duchy of Weimar).[52]

Indeed, the fatherland became identified with the values of work, industry, and religious sensibilities that were communicated in daily practice in institutional form—in the industrial and manufacturing schools, the workhouses, rescue asylums, infant day care centers, and soup kitchens run by the institute. In turn, the members conceived of themselves as a larger community, a veritable family that bound rich and poor alike; the institute was described as substitute "parent" and also "teacher."[53] And, like family, its regime was harsh and regimented, levying fines for shoddy work and moving swiftly against begging, yet, simultaneously, sympathetic and supportive. Furthermore, social bonds were strengthened through shared festivals; the institute-run schools throughout the state simultaneously celebrated the birthday of Maria Pawlowna each February 16. In its first quarter century, 1817–42, the numbers of industrial schools and female students rose steadily, increasing more than threefold, from 20 schools instructing 813 girls to 108 schools training 3,809 girls. After completion of the studies, most girls worked as servants for a time, contributing to the smooth functioning of the households of the very elites themselves.[54]

The institute was a model for patriotic philanthropy in other areas of the Germanic Confederation, combining dynastic and aristocratic involvement with government investment. In Saxony, for example, women's associations, which emerged in Annaberg, Marienberg, and Schneeberg in the mid-1830s, reflected the joint intervention of Queen Maria and the minister of culture, von Wietersheim; similarly in Mecklenberg, inspired by the war work of the deceased duchess Caroline, a woman's institute was founded by the wives of a high-placed government minister and a councillor. These state-promoted philanthropic associations were nondenominational, as in the Weimar case, opening membership to different religious orientations; they tended to include both women and men in leadership roles; and they professed to open their ranks to members of all social orders and groupings in society. This claim to social inclusiveness was at the heart of the patriotic rhetoric. But even these pre-

---

52. This analysis fits with work on the formation of elite groups in the evolution of confessionalism, which links church and state in shared efforts to establish controls over the populace. For an overview, see Hsia, *Social Discipline*, 176–85.

53. Gräfe, *Nachrichten von wohlthätigen Frauenvereinen*, 64–68, in the regulations for girls' industrial schools.

54. Ibid., 126, for the statistical table.

sumed shared characteristics were not always the case. For example, in Freyberg, Saxony, the women's association, which had responded to the appeal of the queen and opened under the leadership of Baroness von Herder, admitted only women.[55] And the assertion that the organizations transcended social divisions was ideological, part of their own self-promotion: patriotic voluntarism was an aristocratic expression of privilege in alliance, however, with the urban patriciate and the wives and daughters of high state officials, as we will see in more detail in the next chapter. Depending on local relations, it supported different social combinations and coalitions, which often included close ties to church officials and teachers.

The dynastic model of territorially organized patriotic service, however, was not the only form of women's philanthropic work in the years following the Wars of Liberation. After 1815, not one but several "publics" emerged in German civil society, reflecting a variety of social and political patterns that were working in tandem to help fashion a female philanthropic civic mission. Other forms expressed growing urban pride and religious identity and commitments. Suggestive of this pattern, which essentially remained confined to individual urban settings alone, was the Catholic *Frauenverein* St. Barbara in Koblenz. But even this once independent association came under the patronage of the crown princess Augusta in 1852 when, after the challenges of the revolutions of 1848–49, the Prussian court sought to enhance its legitimacy through a more aggressive philanthropic strategy.[56]

The local Catholic women's association in Koblenz bore some resemblance to Weimar's Patriotic Institute; yet the differences are equally instructive. It, too, emerged in 1817, a time of serious economic crises and widespread fear of pauperism. It also was initiated from above, in this case by city officials who called on eight prominent women from the upper echelons of urban life, well known for their earlier patriotic war services, to found a women's association. They were joined by a three-man business

---

55. Ibid., 240.

56. LK, Best. 661, 23, Katholischer Frauenverein St. Barbara in Koblenz. There are several published studies of the association, particularly Petra Habrock-Henrich, "Berufung statt Beruf. Frauen in der Koblenzer Armenfürsorge des 19. Jahrhundert," in *Koblenzer Beiträge zur Geschichte und Kultur* 4 (1994): 61–78; and *Der Katholische Frauenverein St. Barbara in Coblenz. Entstehung, Geschichte und Wirken unter besonderer Berücksichtigung des St. Barbara-Waisenhauses. Zur Erinnerung an die Einweihung des neuen Waisenhauses mit Kapelle am 20. Oktober 1908* (Coblenz, 1908). I want to thank the staff of the Stadtarchiv Koblenz for sending me these two studies. After 1815, local women's associations with little formal ties to organizations elsewhere were common in the Germanic Confederation. For several examples see, particularly, Mettele, "Bürgerliche Frauen" (Cologne); and Meyer-Renschhausen, *Weibliche Kultur* (Bremen), 44–62.

committee comprised of the Prussian *Landrat* in charge of the district, a vicar, and the mayor. The local Koblenz women's association always included influential male representatives in its leadership circle.

An overview of the female members demonstrates its ongoing appeal to privileged urban groups: it drew on women of Rhenish aristocratic families and wives of high government and military circles; but it also attracted the wives and daughters of free professionals and, as the century progressed, businessmen and bankers. Despite the high proportion of artisans and small businessmen in the city, however, only a small percentage of the women of the artisanal classes joined the association. Striking, however, is the intergenerational commitment among prominent families like the Görres, Dietz, Huyn, and Wegeler clans: daughters followed their mothers and aunts and encouraged their own daughters to join; over the "long" century, many were members for over fifty years, and still others held the same position on the executive committee for decades. At midcentury, the membership stood around 190.[57] St. Barbara, undeniably, was an important vehicle for privileged women's community activism in the continuously changing political and social climate of Koblenz. It remained among the most vibrant Catholic charitable undertakings in the city until its dissolution in 1971.

The trajectory of its tasks in *Vormärz* fits well into an emerging pattern. The women initially became involved in a soup kitchen; daily contact with the poor encouraged them, in 1819, to set up a school for girls; like the Weimar patriots, Koblenz women, too, trained these young girls in the "arts of domesticity" in preparation for employment later as servants or, after marriage, as wives in "simple" orderly households. The schooling was so highly regarded by wealthy families that the association quickly attracted private donations, charitable gifts of the kind that Pastor Scheibler soon would be soliciting nearby. Money flowed so readily that, by 1826, to help secure its financial future, the Prussian government granted the association corporate rights.

In the early 1830s, the women's association had enough money to buy the former cloister of St. Barbara, which had been shut down by the French occupiers and later turned into a cholera hospital. The Koblenz women's association opened an orphanage for daughters of deceased Catholic parents and ran a school in the cloister; in 1833, it already accommodated two hundred girls. The laywomen envisioned multiple benefits in naming their association St. Barbara. Barbara was a patron saint, offering

---

57. LK, Best. 661, 23, no. 157, Verzeichniss der Mitglieder der Frauen-Verein zu St. Barbara; also Habrock-Henrich, "Berufung statt Beruf," 67; and F. C. Hell, *Adress-Buch nebst historischer Übersicht und Beschreibung der Städte Coblenz und Ehrenbreitstein* (Koblenz, 1857), 46–48, 111, 146, 215, 225.

protection for towers and fortresses, and her name was invoked to prevent natural disasters, the fever, or the pest. Besides, in popular religious practices in the Rhineland, she accompanied St. Nicholas and gave out the gifts to the children.

The association ran both the orphanage and the school. Four of its members served simultaneously on both executive boards: the vicar and treasurer of the association and two laywomen. In addition, it hired a "mother superior" to handle the day-to-day business operations. The first matron was Countess Amalia Huberta von Meerveldt, born into an old Rhenish family of imperial knights. The selection was not an isolated case; in Baden, for example, as I show in chapter 5, daughters of the mediatized nobility also found meaningful work in high administrative posts in nursing and philanthropic service.

In its origins, the local backing of the women of St. Barbara was part of an effort to reaffirm community identity, which centered on the imperative of Catholic charity and female lay service. Philanthropy allowed urban elites to articulate local values in light of the challenges to religious life of the Napoleonic occupation and the wrenching transfer of the Rhineland to Prussia. The new political overlord was responsible for many local policies, including the organization of the police, gendarmerie, and poor laws as well as the selection of mayors. While entry into Protestant Prussia had permitted Catholic renewal, it created new tensions between church and state, particularly over government oversight of church administration and finances. The distribution of urban power, however, continued to favor the propertied elites who underwrote local philanthropy; the 1845 municipal reform law prophetically introduced a three-class electoral law into local politics in the Rhineland.[58]

The urban patriciate in Koblenz used the work of the *Frauenverein* to articulate its vision of proper community relations and the social obligations of the privileged living in its walls. This is one reading of the lengthy discussions surrounding the association's activities in the local paper, the *Coblenzer Anzeiger,* in the later 1820s.[59] According to the accounts, the women's institute embodied a set of values and enforced behavioral norms that structured ideal relationships between rich and poor. In addition to the emphasis placed on industriousness, perseverance, and modesty (the dress code reflected the students' modest station in life), its educational

---

58. For the administrative and legal relations between Prussia and Koblenz, see Schubert, *Die Preussische Regierung,* 150–57, for local government. Also, Sheehan, *German History,* 485–96, for his discussion of urban life in *Vormärz.*

59. LK, Best. 661, 23, no. 98, Sammelliste, including the relevant issues of the newspaper from 1824 to 1830.

program stressed pious Christian teachings and biblical study. Six out of fourteen hours of instruction per week were religious. In addition, the house regulations imposed strict discipline on the community of children, teachers, and matron alike. As in Weimar, this institute was a stern parent, whose behavior affirmed the old adage, which reputedly was mirrored in the lives of the children of rich *Hausvater* in the city: "the more pious the children, the more our fathers are God-fearing." Indeed, both rich and poor were made the objects of the moralizing gaze. Furthermore, the fact that St. Barbara women were involved personally in ministering to the poor and sick through weekly household "visitations" reinforced a practice of care based on precise, firsthand knowledge.[60] These face-to-face relations were seen to account for the remarkable growth in charitable donations.

In contrast to Weimar, however, with its interest in a wider geographical identity, the emphasis in Koblenz was on patronage and gifts circulating in the locality alone; the community was captured best by the local patron, whose contributions were "marvelously heartening" for the association and expressed a "beautiful trust" in its ability to administer the monies for the poor fairly and equitably. If charity lay at the root of a Christian community, the personal involvement of informed women assured its fair distribution. Indeed, collaboration among the female volunteers was singled out for remarkable praise. It is worth quoting this assessment from an 1827 article.

> Such a bond between women and young girls . . . truly is an institute, which nurtures and promotes the moral and ethical education of a city. The female sex has so many tasks where it must learn care, comfort, and succor that one could call this association a preparation for many female professions *(eine Vorschule manchen weiblichen Berufs)*. The one learns from the other, and the young inspire the more experienced with their enthusiasm, from whom they, in turn, learn measured standards, goals, and dispositions. This pursuit makes the young woman secure *(sicher)* and independent *(selbständig)*, she feels she can do something for the community *(Gemeinde)*, and, through such activity, the female elements of the society grow in moral strength, while the poor, who come into daily contact with the well-off, learn trust and hope and are kept away from the seductions of crime.[61]

---

60. LK, Best. 661, 23, no. 98, *Coblenzer Anzeiger,* no. 14, April 2, 1824.
61. LK, Best. 661, 23, no. 98, *Coblenzer Anzeiger,* supplement to no. 11, March 16, 1827.

Here was a powerful acknowledgment of the intergenerational ties that bound privileged women together in public service for the sake of community stability and harmony. Philanthropy, furthermore, was expected to reinforce order, hierarchy, and deference and promote "civic and Christian virtues" at the heart of urban life. Looking back over its first thirteen years of activity in Koblenz, the women's association saw itself as an ongoing "monument" to an earlier charitable fraternity *(barmherzige Verbrüderung)* that expressed continuous pride in the city.[62]

The Circular Chain of Legitimation

Emphasis on words alone misses an important dimension of women's early philanthropic work in the Germanic Confederation: it retained the older character of *herrschaftlicher Fürsorge* (beneficence of rule), which still provided the basic expectations of behavior that bound subjects to rulers and to their officials in local communities.[63] While the discussion around the emergence of a female philanthropic public was cast variously in patriotic, civic, and religious rhetoric, much of the actual work remained traditional, demonstrating the slow process of state-building that relied on old patterns of personal intervention and immediate support. These continuities easily are overlooked when the focus is on bureaucratic reforms or the modernization of the police. The older patterns of personal concern "from above" remained part of popular expectations "from below"; one detailed study of administrative reform in *Vormärz* Baden, for example, shows conclusively that social unrest mirrored a bureaucrat's failure to meet traditional expectations of material interventions taken to insure community prosperity *(Wohlstand).*[64]

Whether the example is St. Barbara or the Weimar Patriotic Institute (or state-appointed officials in the municipality, for that matter), much of the work consisted of supporting soup kitchens and securing monies for fuel and blankets as well as food for the sick or poor pregnant women in the community. By all accounts, for example, the soup kitchens were popular and frequented regularly by poor people in need; scattered evidence indicates that in hard times the kitchens could not even meet rising demand.[65] Throughout the Germanic Confederation, then, women's char-

---

62. LK, Best. 661, 23, no. 98, *Coblenzer Anzeiger,* no. 26, March 30, 1830, quoting from *Der Frauen-Verein.*

63. Joachim Eibach, *Der Staat vor Ort: Amtmänner und Bürger im 19. Jahrhundert am Beispiel Badens* (Frankfurt am Main, 1994), 72.

64. Ibid., 71–72, for very graphic examples of expectations in local communities during the hunger years 1816–17 and 1824–29.

65. For details on the activities and importance of soup kitchens run by women see the case of Nassau in *Vormärz* (Blum, *Staatliche Armenfürsorge,* 65–68).

itable institutions insinuated themselves into more traditional fields of dynastic (or city-state) legitimation. During hard times, long winters, or famines, the dukes and duchesses as well as kings and queens (and the urban fathers) offered their subjects "immediate aid" *(Soforthilfe)*. During crises years (in 1816–17, 1829 or 1845–47), governments loaned people money to buy cattle, work tools, or equipment; they set up public works for the unemployed, offering men opportunity to build buildings, dig canals, construct roads, and renovate hospitals and poorhouses. Dynastic and other rulers bought grain on the foreign market and dispensed it at low prices, and they even gave out cash to local poor relief commissions for "extraordinary" onetime support.[66] Mere palliatives, to be sure, for such largesse only could reach a few of the needy, these interventions expressed dynastic beneficence through the ethic of personal rule; the emerging philanthropic institutions provided similar charitable interventions in the name of the dynasty, but increasingly on a much more continuous, recognized, and regular basis.

This widening sphere of philanthropic work and its institutional nexus rested on a shared vocabulary that began to circulate throughout the towns and provinces of central Europe with greater frequency after 1815. Its idioms were incorporated in the preambles of the institutes and in the statutes of the women's associations themselves; they became part of governmental rationale for the many inquiries concerning the regulations of the poor or the need to reform taxation to earmark special monies for poor relief. The same vocabulary showed up in the newspaper accounts and the published chronicles of philanthropic activities in the communities and made their way into bureaucratic correspondence, from mayor to *Landrat* to provincial governor *(Oberpräsident)* in the Prussian Rhineland, for example. This language increasingly came to impact popular usage as well, freezing a vision of care and obligation in specific vocabulary, even if the precise meaning was open to diverse and conflicting interpretations. At its base was an older religious vocabulary that, while it preserved its sacred aura and power, nonetheless was incorporated directly into the mundane realms of political debate and power brokerage. The

---

66. The following archival sources capture the importance of this traditional intervention: LK, Abt. 403, no. 4438, Die Errichtung öffentlicher Brennmaterialien Verkaufs-Anstalten für Arme, 1839; no. 796, Die bestehende resp. angerichteten Armen Speise-Anstalten, 1831, which includes detailed information on women's involvement in the Rhineland; no. 4418, Die Sr. Königlichen Hoheit dem Kronprinzen bey Höchst Ihrer Reise durch die Rheinprovinzen in Jahre 1833 gegangenen und von Höchst demselben an des Oberpräsidium abgegebenen Unterstützungsgesuche und die Vertheilung des Gnadengeschenkes von 300 rt; desgl. in Jahre 1836; desgl. in Jahre 1839.

words spoke of "purest humanitarian sentiments" *(reinste Menschen-liebe)*, the work of "Christian love," of "love of neighbor" as well as "public spiritedness."[67] While anchored in print, the rhetoric spread deep into the social fabric because it was part of the day-to-day workings of the philanthropic institutes themselves, graphic reminders that the values of care and responsibility, however personal, were linked to political rule.

This patriotic discourse comprised a circular field of causality, one in which, however, it is impossible to determine the first cause: provincial and state officials communicated "from above" the values of charity and largesse in their regulations and degrees; dynasts performed them in doling out aid. Local elites incorporated their own version "in between" in the running of philanthropic associations in the locality; their work reinforced and shaped the views from above. And, by the 1840s, similar notions were showing up as the very basis of popular understanding of legitimate rule "from below."[68]

A series of petitions by Prussian subjects, addressed to the dynast in personal terms and appealing for government subvention, demonstrate the spread of a similar vocabulary among a group of people in dire need. Admittedly, the source is biased (and limited); people petitioning for financial help would seek to structure their case in the most effective way. And that is precisely the point, because the choice of phrases reveals the assumed attributes of the legitimate ruler who, by necessity, would favor the supplicant. Furthermore, the source is not a representative sample of Prussian subjects, although it contains the voices of both men and women. It reflects the milieu of volunteer and disabled soldiers, artisans, shopkeepers, petty traders, low-level officials and schoolteachers; among the women was a widow, a shoemaker's wife, and a veteran's wife. There were no protoindustrial, mill, or factory workers in this group. And that, too, perhaps, is the point, although more detailed analysis of these types of sources would be necessary to prove it. Dynastic legitimation in the 1840s had its social contours, reflecting religious and regional dynamics, to be sure, even if the Rhine crisis of 1840 seemed to mobilize, once again, "king

---

67. LK, Best. 661, 23, no. 158, correspondence of mayor of Koblenz, August 4, 1826; and no. 153, correspondence with Princess Augusta, July 19, 1853. Also no. 98, Sammelliste, April 2, 1824. See, as well, LK, Abt. 403, no. 796, government correspondence concerning soup kitchens, Aachen, December 5, 1831. Here, the appeal is made to growing charitable sentiments affirming the good heart of the "public spirited and humanitarian inhabitants" *(gemeinsinniger und menschenfreundlicher Einwohner)*.

68. Wehler *(Deutsche Gesellschaftsgeschichte,* 3:167) dismisses these religious philanthropic sentiments "from above" and, thus, fails to see their circulation "in between" and "from below."

and people" against the French; but among the broader population, veterans, low-level bureaucrats and teachers, and petty traders were speaking a common vocabulary that was part of an emerging conservative political culture.[69]

The petitioners were true supplicants; they had nothing to give but their loyalty, with one exception. The would-be artist Johann Christian March included poems he had penned to "king, war, and fatherland" with his request.[70] Otherwise, the chips lay basically in the argument, which was remarkably similar in all cases. The royal figure—the queen mother, the king, and the crown princess—was praised as the embodiment of humanitarian sentiments *(Menschenliebe)*, benevolence *(Huld)*, and charity *(Milde)*. The veteran August Gerhard only sent his petition because he had such an "abiding trust in the humanitarian sensitivities" of the dynast. Each acknowledged in some way that the majesty was "benevolent" and "kindhearted"; for the retired teacher Franz Anton Lange, this was simply a "well-known" fact; others noted it was "generally recognized"; the Cologne resident Anna Herz went further and declared it was well known throughout the world. Similarly, Frau Schröder confessed that not she alone but the "countless masses" benefited from her majesty's immense font of mercy and benevolence.[71]

Beyond the common framework within which each described his or her specific social situation and pecuniary need, the gender differences are the most striking. Male petitioners anchored their arguments in the context of their (or their fathers') war service, stretching the bonds of reciprocity in new ways. Remarkably, in their own life story they reproduced the dynastic narrative of the wars of the Napoleonic era: August Gerhard voluntarily embarked on a military career in 1809, joining the Brandenburg artillery brigade. He described his experiences as the dynastic version of "liberation": "in the fateful years of 1813/14/15 I also had the luck to fight for king and Fatherland." August Nohl, a low level official in the land registry office, wrote that his father had been a "true volunteer and defender of the Fatherland in 1813–15," whereas Johann Hubner defined

69. The petitions are found in LK, Abt. 403, no. 4447, Die von der Frau Fürstin von Liegnitz Durchlaucht bewilligten Unterstützungen, und anderen Gliedern der König. Hauses, 1843–47. The collection contains eighteen petitions. For a compatible reading of sources, Natalie Davis, *Fiction in the Archives: Pardon Tales and Their Tellers in Sixteenth-Century France* (Stanford, Calif., 1987).

70. LK, Abt. 403, no. 4447, Bl. 1–3, Horchheim bei Koblenz, October 21, 1843.

71. LK, Abt. 403, no. 4447, Bl. 119–21, Anna Herz, Cologne, August 13, 1845; Bl. 87–89, August Gerhard, Koblenz, August 3, 1844; Bl. 85–86, Franz Anton Lange, Koblenz, August 4, 1844; Bl. 15–16 and 123–25, Chris. Brödner, invalid, Düren near Aachen, August 12, 1845; Bl. 159, Mrs. Schröder, Koblenz, August 8, 1845, addressed to the crown princess.

himself as an "old loyal Prussian soldier" who had been badly wounded in the campaigns.[72]

Women's petitions were framed by poverty, need, and despair; theirs was a tale of "death and illness," of the personal tragedies of complicated childbirths, and of landlords acting with brutal harshness *(unmenschliche Härte),* behavior that stood in stark contrast to the stated qualities of mercy and goodness attributed to the dynast. They made a direct appeal to the humanitarian side of the dynasty that, outside the context of the *Frauen-Verein,* still could be subsumed within the *Landesvater* motif, even if it were addressed to the crown princess.[73]

The groundwork, nonetheless, was laid for a specific understanding of dynastic rule in gender terms, which appealed ever more clearly to the presumed impartial patriotic context of humanitarian service under the *Landesmutter.* In the aftermath of the revolutionary crisis and civil wars of 1848–49, the patriotic rhetoric became more inclusive in its broad humanitarian claims. The insistent rhetorical appeal to a world of neighborly love gained new power in dynastic calculations at the same time as the constitutional forums opened up divisive party politics and showed unmistakably the class and religious tensions that divided the male voting public in German territories. When, after 1859, the German dynastic states sought to mobilize communities for defense and, subsequently, nation building, they drew on a complex set of symbols and rituals and an institutional culture of female patriotic service that had wide currency in the population. The successes and limits of dynastic efforts to weld together a patriotic infrastructure under the Red Cross for official state and nationalist purposes form the basis of the next chapter.

---

72. LK, Abt. 403, no. 4447, Bl. 87–89, August Gerhard, Koblenz, August 3, 1844; Bl. 21–22, Johann Hubner, Koblenz, October 24, 1843; and Bl. 5–9, August Nohl, Koblenz, October 20, 1843. The anthropologist John Borneman, in *Belonging in the Two Berlins: Kin, State, Nation* (Cambridge, 1992), makes the very important point that "national" identity is about how state narratives become part of the way in which people evaluate and talk about their own lives. This process of internalizing the dynastic narrative is seen already in the arguments given by the petitioners in the 1840s.

73. LK, Abt. 403, no. 4447, Bl. 157, Frau Schröder, Koblenz, August 16, 1845; Bl. 155–56, Frau Elisabeth Geller, Koblenz, August 16, 1845; Bl. 117–18, widow of the former invalid Wägener, Cologne, August 13, 1845. Eliding the princess with the *Landesvater* also is in the petition of the soldier Peter Theisgen, Bl. 165–66, Koblenz, August 17, 1845.

CHAPTER 2

The Politics of Philanthropy under Dynastic Patronage, 1848 to 1870–71

It once was an uncontested adage that the midcentury revolutions and civil wars in German territories were a "turning point" when German history failed to turn. The argument now is suspect, for in its original formulation it assumed a necessary and logical connection between revolution and liberal reforms on the one hand and bourgeois economic power and democratic state formation on the other.[1]

And, yet, 1848–49 undeniably was a transforming and unsettling event both to contemporaries and to subsequent generations of Germans, whose identity was being shaped by particular understandings of, as well as silences about, historical episodes. The revolution and civil war challenged dynastic authority, threatened the political sovereignty of the member states, and formulated a range of rights, from freedom of the press, of speech and public assembly, to an end to burdensome taxes and feudal services, to self-determination and widened educational opportunities for women.[2] But it also meant military battles, occupation, and, ultimately,

---

1. For the early interpretation of bourgeois revolutionary failure that set the stage for subsequent historical development, Friedrich Meinecke, *The German Catastrophe: Reflections and Recollections,* trans. Sidney B. Fay (Cambridge, Mass., 1950). The argument entered into the *Sonderweg* debate through its assumptions about the necessity of bourgeois revolution for democratic modernity. See Wehler, *The German Empire;* and his critics, David Blackbourn and Geoff Eley, *The Peculiarities of German History: Bourgeois Society and Politics in Nineteenth-Century Germany* (Oxford, 1984).

2. There is a huge body of literature on 1848. Among the classic analyses are Viet Valentin, *1848: Chapters of German History* (London, 1940); and Rudolf Stadelmann, *Social and Political History of the German 1848 Revolution* (Athens, Ohio, 1975). For a new approach that moves away from class to religion as an independent variable, Jonathan Sperber, *Rhineland Radicals: The Democratic Movement and the Revolution of 1848–1849* (Prince-

reimposition of the old authority of the conservative dynastic forces, although under changed conditions.

Reassertion of dynastic rule in German territories took place under constitutional regimes that structured the political culture in new ways. For some states, most notably Prussia, the establishment of a formal constitutional system was new, a product of the revolution itself. Only under mounting public pressure did the Prussian monarch grant a constitution in late December 1848; and, while its liberal electoral provisions were scaled back under the reaction, there was no turning back. Even the Prussian minister Manteuffel had recognized in 1849 that "the old times are gone" and "to return to the decaying conditions of the past is like scooping water with a sieve."[3] Prussia, therefore, joined the south German states of Baden, Bavaria, and Württemberg, which had received constitutions in 1818 or 1819, as well as Saxony, Braunschweig, Hanover, and Hesse, already transformed into constitutional regimes during the political upheavals shaking Europe in 1830. The documents, to be sure, were modest in restructuring authority; issued by royal decrees, their powers derived from the monarch's alone, who ruled by God's grace and not at the pleasure of the people. But they nonetheless established a parliamentary system and new forms of political expression that were notably "modern." Only Mecklenburg in central Europe abandoned its constitutional government in the period of reaction.

In the context of the new political culture shaped by constitutional and representative politics, 1848 is an important milestone, if not a veritable turning point. It unequivocally set in motion the characteristics of "modern" high politics, establishing them as normative throughout central Europe, Mecklenburg notwithstanding. "Modern" politics was understood as party and interest politics, electoral struggles, the forging of parliamentary coalitions, the transformation of the bureaucracy into an arm of the executive and, certainly throughout the long nineteenth century in German territories, as exclusively male. Not exhaustive, these were the attributes, nonetheless, that shaped contemporary discussions of political activity; as a story of the modern, they also have shaped much subsequent historical inquiry.

Indeed, recent histories of Prussian "politics" prior to the revolution focus on the origins of political parties, which emerged as distinct blocs

---

ton, N.J., 1991). For the women's side, see Prelinger, *Charity, Challenge, and Change,* 104–21, particularly.

3. Found in Sheehan, *German History,* 710. In April 1849, under mounting reaction, the king dissolved the lower house and introduced the three-class electoral law that divided the male electorate into three groups reflecting levels of wealth.

only in 1848–49; or on the debates among influential male leaders around newspapers such as the conservative *Berliner Politisches Wochenblatt* or the military organ, *Militair Wochenblatt,* that, over time, gave expression to various political factions.[4] Contemporaries after 1848, perhaps more so in Prussia since the changes were of a recent vintage and, for conservatives, wrenching, were struck by the new character of their state as a party state *(Parteistaat).* Government ministers were party affiliated, and even high-ranking bureaucrats could serve as parliamentary deputies.

Politics versus Philanthropy?

If politics was being confined rather narrowly to the contours of party life and popular attention increasingly turned to parliamentary debates and electoral struggles, this limited definition opened up considerable public space for activities that were labeled nonpolitical. All manner of philanthropic activities appeared an obvious contrast. The more clearly the presumed character of politics was etched in popular discourse, the more distinctly drawn were the boundaries of public life—and penned in ways that masked their essential permeability.

In the politics of reaction in the 1850s, dynastic houses and their supporters in government offices and army posts reclaimed the philanthropic stage for the declared collective and impartial goals of community well-being and public defense. Here, however, they met groups of active women, proud of their autonomy and accomplishments, with a strong sense of the meaning of their own labor and of their value in the community. This confrontation reshaped the female patriotic sphere of humanitarian service and forged new links to war work under a tightly knit organizational hierarchy. These new roles worked effectively in the post-1848 era precisely because the formal political sphere was defined as separate and exclusively male; indeed, the patriotic world of voluntary female service was seen as "nonpolitical" partly by its very character as female and its essential exclusion from the "modern" realm of politics. But philanthropy was not a distinct female domain; its reach covered understandings of civic actions and behavioral forms that, in fact, included both genders. Therefore, a similar veneer enveloped the veterans associations that, after

---

4. For the standard approach, Beck, *Origins of Welfare State;* Wolfgang Schwentker, *Konservative Vereine und Revolution in Preussen, 1848/49. Die Konstituierung des Konservatismus als Partei* (Düsseldorf, 1988); and Eckard Trox, *Militärischer Konservatismus. Kriegervereine und "Militärpartei" in Preussen zwischen 1815 und 1848/49* (Stuttgart, 1990). Trox, however, investigates the social basis of military power by analyzing the veterans' associations at the grassroots level; he raises important questions about formal definitions of politics and activities that were seen to fall outside "politics" but were nonetheless political.

1848, increasingly turned to philanthropic and leisure activities as well, shunning all mention of political work. Their self-fashioning also was successful; in an 1865 survey of political associations in Prussia, the veterans' groups were excluded from consideration.[5]

To lend force to a strategy that perpetuated distinctions between the political and the so-called private sides of civic activism, however, dynasts had to become the acknowledged heads of a revitalized and redirected patriotic philanthropic network. Their offensive in the 1850s and 1860s took place on two levels: in struggle over the rhetorical terrain in which people thought and spoke about public service and in the actual management and control of the local philanthropic institutions and associations themselves.

In the standard formulas of the day, patriotic service was described as "the arena of active neighborly love" *(Gebiet der werkthätigen Nächstenliebe),* which expressed the "spirit of true humanitarianism."[6] This rhetoric, however, had broadened greatly during the revolution and civil war; adherents of both royalist and democratic associations, ironically, had shared ritual forms, even if the goals contrasted starkly. Thus, both monarchical and republican women had been busy sewing flags for the royal regiments or the newly armed militias, outfitting volunteers, organizing soup kitchens, soliciting funds, arranging burials, and engaging in other types of immediate aid in hard-pressed communities. And, for both camps, the work was understood as humanitarian. Numerous democratic clubs had been founded that were called "patriotic"; and one radical veterans' group even adopted the red cross as its symbol. In the aftermath of the civil war, the rhetorical map became blurred. Listen to the words of several Schleswig-Holstein women who, in seeking support for political refugees in late 1849, appealed to women's Christian deeds and to their compassionate selves as Good Samaritans, "never mind whether the donors were absolutist or republican" in sentiment.[7]

The invocation of shared symbols with the emphasis on humanitarian service was part of the healing process after the disruptions of the civil war; as anthropologists demonstrate, by drawing potential adversaries together, symbols make it possible for the social order to survive the conflicts and

---

5. Trox, *Militärischer Konservatismus,* 286.

6. As expressed in *DRK,* 2:192; *KZ,* supplement to no. 98, April 28, 1871, and no. 282 December 1, 1880.

7. The German reads, "seien die Spenderinnen nun absolutisch oder republikanisch" and is found in Eva Kuby, "Politische Frauenvereine und ihre Aktivitäten 1848 bis 1850," in *Schimpfende Weiber,* 264. For discussion of patriotic associational life among the democrats, Trox, *Militärische Konservatismus,* 163. Radical veterans in Breslau in 1848 wore the red cross.

divisions that threaten to—and indeed at times do—tear it apart.[8] Thus, the real challenge for dynastic houses and loyal state officials was to preserve the image of an open tent—of patriotic work as humanitarian, politically disinterested, and socially inclusive—while, simultaneously, imposing on it a politically conservative agenda.

Dynastic groups never fully dominated the rhetorical field, however. Words such as *patriotism, humanitarianism,* and *selfless service* remained elusive and ambiguous, powerful sources of legitimate rule among the populace but easily attached to a range of activities that eluded dynastic authority. Dynastic rulers and their officials, therefore, developed a second, complementary strategy in their efforts to define humanitarian "politics" after the revolution. They set in motion the creation of an institutional network of civilian war preparedness—active in all manner of philanthropic work in peacetime as well—that was hierarchically organized and directed from above and rested on differentiated tasks for women and men. And they placed this organizational structure under the protection of the *Landesmutter* of each dynastic house in the different states of Germany, by now a recognized symbol of the wider community and of collective responsibility for its well-being. Significantly, this institutional network was encased in a distinct rhetorical field, which carried with it its own meanings of terms such as *patriotic, humanitarian duty,* and *sacrifice.* These meanings, then, were redeployed in the communities through print media as well as highly ritualized public performances of patriotic service-in-action. The patriotic associations were very much a part of the wider state and later nationalist struggles to shape public opinion; they were important players in the competition over mastery of meanings, which lies at the center of politics.

It is worth exploring this push toward institutional control in Prussia in the aftermath of 1848, but not to reproduce the so-called small German school of historiography, which assumes an inevitable line of historical development toward a Prussian-dominated Germany. Rather, the pattern of institutional regulation is especially clear in the politics of reaction in Prussia, which carefully prescribed the legal parameters of political organizations and associations. Prussia, however, was but one pole of a wider process of state-building. Reimposition of rule in Baden, too, reflected a concerted multipronged approach that, among other strategies, involved placing the bureaucracy under strict discipline (particularly the official representatives of the central government in the locality, the *Amtsmänner*)

---

8. Quoting the political theorist Abner Cohen in Mach, *Symbols, Conflict, and Identity,* 50.

and simultaneously encouraging an open dialogue between the local officials and the local notables over efforts to remake and control the lower orders, who anyway had proven dangerous in the revolutionary months. It was in this postrevolutionary era that the Baden *Frauen-Verein*, which had originated in the early 1840s, began to extend its operations and affiliates throughout the state.[9]

The effective organization of philanthropic politics was a complicated operation in Prussia, as elsewhere. It is not to be seen simply as a matter of co-optation or manipulation from above. Two processes coincided that helped shape the wider patriotic public. One came from the associations and organizations in civil society itself, which had found their "politics" clarified by the turmoil of 1848–49; the other involved government pressure from above on women's associations to conform to conservative policies. Successful coordination, however, only came at the price of considerable negotiation and compromise.

Typical of the changes "in between," from the institutional side, was the Prussian Women's and Young Ladies' Association (Preussische Frauen und Jungfrauen-Verein). The society had been organized in 1814 by a group of elite Berlin women to express their gratitude for the victories of Gross-Beeren and Dennewitz in the wars against Napoleon—triumphs that had saved the city from military occupation. Its avowals of dynastic loyalty also were matched by many veterans associations in Prussia.

In several respects, the Prussian Women's and Young Ladies' Association represented a new departure in social life. It was dedicated to preserving a memory of a historic event by reenacting, annually, a ceremonial banquet to honor veterans on the anniversaries of the two battles of Gross-Beeren and Dennewitz (August 23 and September 6). Yearly, the society's president—the organization was run during its first eighteen years by Carolina Knapp, a quartermaster's daughter—requested permission from the king to feed upwards of one hundred disabled veterans (the "brave defenders of the fatherland")[10] in a public display of gratitude for their military sacrifices. During the year, the organization offered charity to needy militia or volunteer soldiers who had been wounded in the battles. Initially, the support meant finding them appropriate work, giving them clothing, or insuring schooling for their children, although, in time,

9. Eibach, *Der Staat vor Ort,* 105–29. For the early women's associations in Baden, Friedrich Hündle, *Praktisches Taschenbuchlein der Residenzstadt Karlsruhe, 1842* (Karlsruhe, 1842), 83–100; Ph. Anselm, *Adresskalender für die Residenzstadt Karlsruhe* (Karlsruhe, 1846), 76–84; and Carl Reichard and J. R. Mathis, *Adresskalender für die Residenzstadt Karlsruhe, 1855* (Karlsruhe, 1855), 24.

10. GSPK, no. 15607, Bl. 4, Berlin, August 20, 1819.

the disabled veterans were offered a small monthly cash payment instead, which came from the private dues of the membership.[11] This women's association was a private response that spoke, however, to new efforts to define collective responsibility for the state's citizen-soldiers, expressed, in the words of the statutes, as "a holy duty to the invalids of the father-land."[12] From the start the association was enmeshed in dynastic patron-age; the crown princess initially served as overseer of the society's finances.

The interdependency of the association and the dynasty was revealed in time. By the late 1830s, as political factions were beginning to crystallize in Prussia, the old invalids and "comrades" themselves started to petition the king—and by 1841 Crown Princess Augusta herself—to single out and bestow the Order of Luise on the association's leaders, at the time the wives of the city councillor Saeger and businessman Müller. The medal had been established by the Prussian king, Frederick William III, in mem-ory of his deceased wife to commemorate women's war work in the strug-gle against Napoleon.

The veterans' intent was transparent; interest had slackened in their cause, and private monies were drying up at the very moment that eco-nomic conditions were deteriorating. The old soldiers hoped that "an official public recognition" of the "humanitarian" and "sacrificial" work of the two women not only would reinforce and reinvigorate the female leadership's dedication but also encourage more generous private dona-tions in the community. A formal state honor would be a crowning touch for the whole association and bolster private gift-giving. As other needy groups in other contexts, they appealed to the king as their "benefactor" and to his "love of justice," which was acknowledged "throughout Europe," indeed, in the "farthest zones" of the earth. Furthermore, revi-talization of the association would keep alive the memory of the events of 1813 and 1814.[13] That memory was precisely the issue at stake; these were militia and volunteer soldiers, whose experiences of the war might have

---

11. These were the paradoxes of patriotic relief. On the one hand, increased monetiza-tion was compatible with ongoing capitalist development. On the other, this was an aristo-cratic and military-dominated association tying contemporary memory to past wars. George Steinmetz, "The Myth of an Autonomous State: Industrialists, Junkers, and Social Policy in Imperial Germany," in Eley, *Society, Culture, and State,* 257–318, links relief to formal bour-geois power but misses the contradictions.

12. GSPK, no. 15607, Bl. 2, Statutes of the Association, Berlin, August 29, 1814.

13. GSPK, no. 15607, Bl. 30–31, Berlin, June 13, 1838, petition by the loyal and old invalids of Gross-Beeren and Dennewitz, Johann Jacob Heilmann and five veterans; also Bl. 37, July 9, 1841, petition addressed to the crown princess of Prussia. The criterion for the Order of Luise was war service in 1813–15, and, apparently, Mrs. Saeger did not qualify. Also, Bl. 40–41, Berlin, June 16, 1841, soldiers and invalids, describing the work of Mrs. Saeger in the effort to convince the king to award the medal to their president.

been remembered as part of an insurrection of "the people" united in a larger nationalist cause; while loyalty to "king and fatherland" became the watchword of the dynasty, some gravestone placards to fallen militiamen had emblazoned "freedom and fatherland" and ignored the king.[14]

It was the commemorative work of organizations like the Prussian *Frauen-Verein* that was structuring a memory of history in ways favorable to dynastic legitimacy. And in this expectation, the dynasty was not to be disappointed. Clarification came gradually. For example, the association's 1842 request for permission to arrange a public feast did not commend the specific invalids themselves but spoke, rather, of the "praiseworthy" Prussian army in general. In the words of the president, however, it was the "many sad and tumultuous" events of the years 1848–49 that worked most forcefully to weld this women's association to avowedly conservative politics, the politics themselves being clarified simultaneously. In its 1851 request, the leaders acknowledged the painful trials of the revolutionary months and the loss of many privileges, including free postage. But their honorable association had persevered to "celebrate the most memorable days in Prussian history." The Wars of Liberation had become a permanent monument to a dynastic glory that was inserting itself into the very center of political life. By 1863, the women's association had been invigorated once again, this time by the wife of Lieutenant von Markatz, with the purposeful goal of supporting, through gifts and loans, "monarchically loyal" *(Königstreue)* worthy veterans. Significantly, the evolution and specificity of language in the petitions are indicative of a maturing conservative politics. At the time, the Prussian Women's and Young Ladies' Association had come under the protection of the princess Frederick Charles, wife of the nephew of the Prussian king, William I.[15]

In certain respects, the "political" evolution of the Prussian Women's and Young Ladies' Association paralleled the politics of many Prussia's veterans' associations, which had sprung up throughout the territory from the campaigns of 1813–15. They, too, in the main were loyal to the Crown. As male organizations, however, these groups could have taken a more active part in political life. But they elected to remain officially "neutral" and "independent of the parties" *(Parteilos)*, even after formation of the Conservative faction in 1848, with which they had much in common. Under the censorship restrictions of *Vormärz,* many veterans already had turned to philanthropy and supported a rich festive culture, often overseen

---

14. Mosse, *Fallen Soldiers,* 19–28, concerning the ambiguity of the memory of the wars against Napoleon.

15. GSPK, no. 15607, Bl. 55, Berlin, May 1, 1851, Mrs. Saeger to the king; also Bl. 71, Berlin, June 13, 1867, describing the association's revitalization in 1863. The documents show that Mrs. Müller later was awarded the Order of Luise.

by the military pastor; in the aftermath of revolution, they began to institute new popular social provisions like the burial fund and oversee more
traditional forms of charity, such as doling out bread and meat to poor
veterans and veterans' widows. After 1851, this older form of beneficence
was organized by a statewide foundation of National Thanks *(National-
Dank)*, formed in the various administrative districts of the monarchy. Its
military leaders were determined to link the "gifts" unmistakably to
dynastic legitimacy: veterans were told to remember the compassion of the
king and his household, who had been so thoroughly disrupted by the
unfortunate events and the emerging party system in that unhappy year of
1848. Within a few years, the state organization also had authorized the
formation of affiliated Women's and Young Ladies' Associations. These
groups raised money to support soldiers' widows and orphans, arranged
nursing for wounded veterans, and often ran soup kitchens. Apparently,
in the late 1850s and 1860s, the women's branches had some success in
Breslau, Stettin, Minden, and Erfurt.[16]

These philanthropic efforts on the ground, furthermore, dovetailed
with debates among Conservative Party leaders such as Lorenz von Stein,
Carl Rodbertus, and Hermann Wagener, who pushed simultaneously for
the establishment of a social monarchy—reinforcing the presumed linkages between king and loyal populace sustained by social provisions—as
the most effective basis for conservative power in the new Prussia. These
parallel moves in the "distinct" spheres of state life testify to the intersec-
tions between philanthropic and party political domains.[17]

A dense network of philanthropic activities for veterans had emerged
in the aftermath of the revolution; indeed, the project of the older Prussian
Women's and Young Ladies' Association in Berlin was hardly distin-
guishable from other work on behalf of veterans going on around them.
This philanthropic milieu speaks to a royalism from below, a key ingredient of the social basis of monarchical rule in the new constitutional state.
The extent of the support is difficult to gauge, however; already in April
1849, there were 120,000 requests for invalid pensions; and in 1853, on the
fortieth anniversary of the battle of Gross-Beeren, forty thousand Berliners showed up at the battlefield to hear patriotic speeches, including an

---

16. Trox, *Militärische Konservatismus,* 214–17, for information on the National
Thanks and the military-run women's associations. For more details on veterans' politics in
a slightly later period see also Dieter Düding, "Die Kriegervereine im wilhelminischen Reich
und ihr Beitrag zur Militarisierung der deutschen Gesellschaft," in *Bereit zum Krieg. Kriegs-
mentalität im wilhelminischen Deutschland 1890–1914. Beiträge zur historischen Friedens-
forschung,* ed. Jost Dülffer and Karl Holl (Göttingen, 1986), 99–121.

17. For examples of emerging social conservative voices, see Beck, *Origins of Welfare
State,* 66–78.

address by Prince William himself, and to sing war songs.[18] These enthusiasts were turning the festival into a mass demonstration of remembrance of a victory that could serve well conservative dynastic state goals.

Women's Associations and State Authority in the Decade of Reaction

A second potential institutional source of royalist support on the ground were the local *Frauen-Vereine.* In the 1850s, the Prussian state increasingly turned its intrusive bureaucratic eye directly onto their domain. Ironically, intervention partially reflected growing willingness of local donors throughout the monarchy to bequeath considerable sums of money to their town's women's association. Acceptance required corporate rights; that is, the organization had to obtain the rights of a juridical person. In return, government officials meddled into organizational life and sought to force changes in the statutes.

The legal debates initially took place against the backdrop of political reaction. Prussian officials had closed down the more radical women's clubs of 1848; barred women from formal participation in party life in 1850; and moved against individual women seen as a threat to the established order. They also instituted revisions in the legal codes that made divorce and remarriage more difficult for Prussian subjects.[19] Now, in the 1850s, they were rethinking women's place in the structure of corporate rights.

In the climate of reaction, it was the legal status of the married woman that had become problematical. Debate centered specifically on whether a wife could administer the capital that was bequeathed to her association and, as an elected officer, whether her word was legally binding in financial and administrative dealings with the outside. For those women's associations with male advisors serving in financial and secretarial posts, the issue was less acute. But as we have seen in chapter 1, there were plenty of local philanthropic organizations that were run exclusively by women; these were the first to come under state scrutiny.

In some instances, the government's insistence that the statutes be

---

18. The description of the festival at the battlefield is in Trox, *Militärische Konservatismus,* 226.

19. For the impact of the reaction specifically on women see Prelinger, *Charity, Challenge, and Change,* 159–64; and for similar changes in Baden, Isabel V. Hull, *Sexuality, State, and Civil Society in Germany, 1700–1815* (Ithaca, N.Y., 1997), 382. For the definition of juridical rights, *Brockhaus' Konversations-Lexikon,* vol. 16 (Leipzig, 1898), "Vereinswesen"; and *Illustriertes Konversations-Lexikon der Frau* (Berlin, 1900), 639–41, which lays out clearly the legal characteristics of public and private associations and their rights.

revised to include a male advisory board was adopted with no opposition. This was the case in 1853 in Neuwied, a Rhineland city that had been founded as an asylum for all manner of religious adherents after the Peace of Westphalia. The princely family zu Wied still was powerful in the area, and the local all-woman *Frauen-Verein* was under the protection of the princess. The *Landrat* spoke positively of its considerable successes and predicted that, given the continued patronage of the frau princess and her contacts among other wealthy families, the association would have "the necessary means to pursue its goals" of nursing the sick among the poorer classes. Because of the anticipated flow of cash, the *Landrat* recommended that the association establish a male advisory board for its business affairs, but warned against "compulsion" *(keinerlei Zwang)*. Indeed, he rejected the efforts of local officials and the police to force the association presidents to hospitalize patients in certain cases. "We cannot recognize such an interference into the private rights *(Privatrecht)* of the association." Women's associations were finding legal space for autonomous decision-making about professional matters at the same time that they were being pressured to bring local officials and clergy into advisory positions to deal with the outside in financial matters. In the Neuwied example, the statutes were changed to reflect the desired organizational standard: the female executive committee was to elect yearly two male officers and a secretary who, together, would represent the association in its business dealings with other officials.[20]

The government, however, had to agree to a draw in the case of the *Frauen-Verein* in Saarbrücken and St. Johann. Since 1835, this women's group had been affiliated loosely with the Prince Wilhelm and Princess Marianne Institute, a philanthropic organization coordinating all manner of public welfare and educational endeavors in the Saar region. The leadership was exclusively female and included a female treasurer; as it turns out, its members had a strong sense of pride in their accomplishments. The association came to the attention of the provincial governor in 1857, when it received a large legacy of three thousand thaler from a widow, Henriette Korn. To permit the monetary transfer, the governor's office, however, rewrote the group's statutes, in effect subordinating the women to the larger institute, and called for a general assembly to ratify the new regulations.

---

20. LK, Abt. 403, no. 7363, Bl. 111–16, Koblenz, May 18, 1853; Bl. 117–18, March 9, 1853; Bl. 119–24, reporting the finances of the organization; Bl. 127–33, September 9, 1853, Statutes of the Neuwied Women's Association. For information on the family zu Wied see *Neues allgemeines Deutschen Adels-Lexicon,* vol. 9 (Leipzig, 1870), 565–66; and *Coblenz und seine nächsten Umgebungen. Ein Wegweiser für Reisende* (Koblenz, 1838), 38–39, on the city itself.

The strategy was a typical legitimizing tactic used by the Prussian *Rechtstaat:* it demanded changes in the statutes and had them approved at a general assembly to give the appearance of "popular" consent by the members. But it backfired, and differences in opinion among high government officials gave the women some maneuverability.

Under the able voices of the two presidents, Ida Roechling and A. Sello, as well as fifteen women officers, the members turned the general assembly into a forum in defense of women's autonomy and competency. They forcefully rejected the suggestion that their organization join the institute "because such a union would be an absolute *(vollkommen)* subordination of the women's association to the executive committee of that institute" and undercut women's "independence" and "autonomy," which has existed in financial matters for twenty-three years. Women had proved perfectly capable of managing alone this laudable "work of love" *(Liebesthätigkeit)*. If the political climate in Prussia now seemed to dictate new forms of public presentation, the leaders declared their willingness to appoint a (male) secretary *(Schriftführer)*, who would work alongside the president and female treasurer. "However, he would be a member of the *Frauen-Verein* and chosen by it, would be fully cognizant of the prevailing facts and personal relationships that existed, and would be someone regarded by the association as suitable to represent it in legal matters . . . without the mixing in by strangers." Gender difference could be bridged for organizational strength. And the meeting ended with a threat by the women that if their proposal, which was the "simplest and most desirable from the point of view of the independence of the association," were not accepted, they would withdraw their request for corporate rights and seek other means to secure the bequest from their own position as a valued charitable institute *(Wohlthätigkeitsanstalt)* in the locality.[21]

The provincial governor, by contrast, had different ideas; a secretary alone, he wrote after the meeting, was insufficient to represent the association. It needed a male executive committee to administer the capital, although, bowing to the women's desire for independence, he acknowledged that the actual decisions about distributing the revenues would remain in women's hands. His tone was unmistakably paternalistic. The government administration would "instruct" *(belehren)* the women's association in the proper relationship between the new male and female committees and, at the same time, "take the necessary steps" *(veranlassen)* to see that the male board would be comprised of a minimum of three persons, elected from those who long had been members of the association.

---

21. LK, Abt. 403, no. 7363, Bl. 195, April 16, 1858, for the effort to obtain juridical rights; Bl. 217–36, for the original statutes of the association; Bl. 333–41, protocol of the meeting, August 5, 1858.

But the governor also expressed pleasure that the activities of the women's association now would expand due to the monies flowing into its coffers.[22]

The outcome was a victory of sorts for the women; the new statutes of 1859, signed by both presidents, provided for a secretary only. While the reasoning behind the governor's concession is not clear, disagreement existed among Prussian officials concerning women's legal right to act on behalf of the association. At the time, the ministers involved in the dispute consulted the executive secretary (the *General-Prokurandar*); while he supported in principle the election of a separate male committee to administer the capital, he added a host of other considerations, which may have prompted the governor's willingness to compromise. Married women, he argued, needed the consent of their husbands to administer money; with sizable sums, however, men would be hesitant to give their wives such authority because of their own liability; but even the asking of permission *(blosse Anfrage bei dem Ehemann)* would be regarded by the women as an irritation *(Störung)*. Essentially, and now striking at the heart of the matter, the philanthropic associations relied on the voluntary labor of women who, he admitted, will not be shackled lightly nor reduced to "subordinate work tools" *(untergeordnete Werkzeugen)*.[23]

This was a revealing set of sentiments that provided the backdrop for subsequent discussions among Prussian ministers; debate in Prussia over the proper structure of female philanthropy continued, although in more muted form, into the 1890s. By then a normative standard had been established that created a protected legal space for women—the legal person of the *Verein*—from which elected female members could act administratively and financially on its behalf in the community: they could raise and disburse money, accept bequests, organize lotteries, run bazaars, and negotiate in business matters with local artisans, shopkeepers, and merchants. At the same time, the "norms" were flexible enough to accommodate local traditions and idiosyncrasies, which helped promote the work of branch organizations in a specific community.

The executive secretary had recognized early on that state and municipal officials were dealing essentially with a leadership of volunteers made up of privileged and well-born women, often aristocrats or those with ties to the nobility or officer corps, and wives of magistrates, many of whom communicated an aura of authority "naturally." These women sought and obtained a legal setting that gave them a protected place for impressive managerial ventures in public; in turn, their prominent efforts on behalf of the organization attracted public attention, which translated into private

---

22. LK, Abt. 403, no. 7363, Bl. 343, October 22, 1858.
23. LK, Abt. 403, no. 7364, Bl. 33–34, March 5, 1858.

donations. The statutes set the parameters to this necessary reciprocity between local philanthropy and private financial support; at the same time, a normative push by officials facilitated an organizational "takeover" from above for state purposes—but one that accommodated privileged women's understanding of the depth and importance of their voluntary services.

Patriotic Women's Associations and the German Red Cross, 1859–69

In Prussia, the founding of the Patriotic Women's Association (Vaterländische Frauen-Verein) was a new departure for the state, although it was based on the Weimar forerunner. The association was constituted formally by the queen on armistice day, November 11, 1866, which marked the end of the Prussian-Austrian war. Through model statutes, it drew local philanthropic groups into a centrally administered association and integrated them into the heart of public displays of dynastic power and rule. These rituals increasingly turned public attention to the emerging institutional network, which now unmistakably linked philanthropic practices to patriotic defense and conservative state goals.

The leaders of the Patriotic Women's Association pulled into their orbit all related (and sympathetic) women's philanthropic groups in the monarchy; the executive committee from the start encouraged the provincial governors to target the relevant organizations for immediate membership.[24] Within the first year, forty-four branch associations had been newly founded or incorporated, including the women of Saarbrücken and St. Johann. The timing partly reflected the international context of the Wars of Unification raging in the background as well as growing humanitarian concern with the fate of wounded soldiers in wartime—these female patriotic associations became the mass base of the future German Red Cross. As we just saw, however, coordination also took place in the context of struggle between government officials and privileged women over the extent and nature of voluntarism. Protection of the Prussian queen meant just that—legal protection so that the female leadership could manage the complex financial transactions that underwrote the continuously evolving tasks in light of equally complex socioeconomic change. At the same time, the imprimatur of "patriotism" and "humanitarianism" and the close, personal ties to the *Landesmutter* legitimized the women's growing public presence in local communities. Local women could call on a repository of

---

24. LK, Abt. 403, no. 7364, Bl. 177–78, June 16, 1867; and Bl. 179, May 21, 1867, the appeal of the executive committee. Also, Bl. 181, May 25, 1867, circular to government officials publicizing the goals of the women's association.

values and symbols that reinforced a complex—although often tense—gender alliance for patriotic purposes.

The statutes of the Central Committee of the Prussian patriotic association solved the issue of legal representation by its original four-woman and four-man executive committee, half appointed by the queen.[25] But the branch organizations made room for alternative patterns, reflecting the earlier compromises that had set the institutional framework of women's philanthropic work in Prussia. In the Rhineland, for example, the "model" statutes were those of Elberfeld, adopted in 1873, and then flexibly extended to other groups in Cologne, for example, in 1877 and Crefeld in 1882. In these negotiations, the Ministry of the Interior distanced itself from the position that married women needed their husbands' authority to handle money matters in the first place. Rather, as elected presidents, women were authorized to represent the association legally under the following conditions: their election was accepted formally *(durch Attest)* by the office of the mayor; as far as third persons were concerned, their mandate in legal matters was "unrestricted"; and they could be served legal papers either personally or in their homes.[26] Associational life, therefore, extended to women a wide range of responsibilities in the community; we will see in chapter 4 the types of work that qualified a woman for a state medal to honor her service.

Who were the women and men who lent their names to the reorganized Patriotic Women's Associations? Table 1 presents an overview of the social backgrounds of the individuals who signed the original call to organize or were founding members of the state associations centralized from above between 1859 and 1868. With one exception—the Mecklenberg state women's association was established only in 1880—the patriotic work of "German" women in later decades was facilitated through these seven (and later eight) state organizations of the Red Cross.

The table reveals the significant place of central European aristocratic groups among the early leaders and of high government officials, who often were noblemen themselves. Among the professionals, there was a preponderance of medical doctors and wives of medical personnel. The

---

25. The statutes underwent numerous revisions, increasing the members of the women and men on the executive committee. For an overview of the evolution of the statutes, *DRK*, 2:199–237.

26. LK, Abt. 403, no. 7364, Bl. 193–202, for the Elberfeld example, which, from June through August 1873, was the subject of considerable discussion; Bl. 231–35, May 11, 1877, for Cologne, in which the Ministry of Interior rejects the position of the *General-Prokurator;* also Bl. 347–49, March 13, 1882, concerning Crefeld. The example of Crefeld is revealing, for it both fit the norm and deviated by permitting a four-woman committee of elderly members to continue to advise the official executive committee, as had been stipulated by the original donors.

TABLE 1. Social Backgrounds of Founding Members of Women's Associations, 1859–68

Organization	Date of Founding	Founding Members Total	% Female	Aristocracy Estate Owners	Aristocracy Titled[a]	High Government Officials and Estate Owners	High Government Officials	Military Officers	Municipal Officials and Clergy	Business Professionals
Baden Women's Association[b]	1859	19	95	5(2)[c]	4	0	1	1	0	2(1)[c]
Prussian Patriotic Women's Association	1866	22	41	3(2)[d]	1(1)[d]	3	4	3	2(1)[d]	6(6)[d]
Bavarian Women's Association	1859[e]	8	75	3(3)[c]	1	0	1	1(1)[c]	0	2
Saxon Albert Association	1867	15	67	2	0	0	4	5	0	4
Hesse Alice Association	1867	11	63	2	1	0	1	0	1	6(1)[d]
Württemberg Charity Association[f]	1817	21	57	—	—	—	—	—	—	—
Weimar Patriotic Institute[g]	1817	3	66	—	—	—	—	—	—	—

Source: DRK, 1: 998; 2: 72–73, 137, 200, 624; GK, Abt. 233, no. 2848, Statuten des unter dem Protectorate Ihrer Königlichen Hoheit der Großherzogin Luise stehenden Badischen Frauenvereins, Karlsruhe, June 6, 1859; 125 Jahre Rotes Kreuz, 1863–1988 (Stuttgart, 1988), 30; Heinrich Gräfe, Nachrichten von Wohltätigen Frauenvereinen in Deutschland (Cassel, 1844), 45.

Note: Social background of female members is measured by husband's or father's occupation.

a Granted the right to use *von* in their name.

b Precise information is not available for six women signatories of bourgeois background.

c Number in parentheses represents those who simultaneously held offices in the court (*Hofstaat*).

d Number in parentheses represents those who held the honorific state title *Rat*.

e Founded in 1859, but data for social backgrounds comes from those active in 1866.

f Data is from the 1864 Women's Committee of the Württemberg Sanitäts-Verein. Württemberg was the only Red Cross organization not to have a separate women's association.

g The Central Board of Directors in 1817 consisted of the dutchess as president, one female (the wife of a minister of state), and one male (baron and high judicial official) advisor.

table captures, too, the gendered nature of patriotic service, which in each case rested on collaboration and negotiation between and among women and men. In Baden, for example, eighteen prominent women signed the call to organize in 1859 and only one man; in Prussia, nine women and thirteen men had underwritten formation of the state's patriotic group in 1866. These broad generalizations would prove remarkably long-lasting.

But a more in-depth look at the social composition of early supporters in the territorial states finds other revealing patterns. After all, the so-called German aristocracy was a complex group. At the time in Prussia alone, it was comprised of old Silesian and Rhenish magnates, often Catholic, and the more provincial Lutheran East Elbian Junkers. Among the noble male signatures in Prussia were Junker families such as Count Behr-Negendank and the estate owner Schwerin-Putzar; both, however, were active in provincial and state administration. On the committee, Junker perspectives per se were offset by the more cosmopolitan worlds of the Catholic prince Radziwill and Eberhard zu Stolberg-Wernigerode, whose wealthy family owned extensive properties in Hesse, Prussian Saxony, and Silesia. Stolberg-Wernigerode, a military officer, served as head of the Knights of St. John, a volunteer aristocratic medical brotherhood that became an important component of the German Red Cross. The one Prussian titled nobleman, von Langenbeck, was a medical doctor with the honorific title of *Medizinal-Rat*. The remaining six professionals, who brought their own sense of rank to the working group, also had been singled out by the state for special commendations.

For women, an identity that derives essentially from husbands' or fathers' status draws attention to the importance of family and kin, birth and marriage, as well as "proximity" to power in the workings of power.[27] It downplays, however, the sites and nature of women's own exercise of authority and influence, themes taken up later in this study. By the former criterion, nonetheless, a case can be made for important business, financial, and ideological ties around the von Itzenplitz family, which arguably attracted other individuals to the association. After all, it was the daughters of Count von Itzenplitz, "an old Junker favorite of the king," who took the leading role in the Prussian Patriotic Women's Association. Luise was the first president, but after her marriage in 1867 she turned the office over to her sister, Countess Charlotte. Never marrying, Charlotte served as president of the Central Committee for nearly a half century. Inclusion of Frau Borsig, wife of Berlin's "locomotive king," and the wives of other

---

27. For rethinking "politics" before female suffrage to include women's informal networks and proximity to power, see Siân Reynolds, *France between the Wars: Gender and Politics* (New York, 1996), 156–80.

financiers and businessmen arguably reflected Charlotte's father's position as minister of commerce in the 1860s and his key role in granting railroad concessions.[28] The Ministry of War, represented through Frau von Roon, had an equivalent stake in building and laying railroads.

In Baden, the wives of the once most powerful aristocratic families—the mediatized imperial aristocracy—remained aloof from incorporation into a state women's association, which stood under the personal and public patronage of Duchess Luise. As their husbands, they shunned state "service" and affiliation with the Court. It was only much later, around 1900, that a number of single daughters of these old aristocratic clans—for example, among the Leiningen lineage—would affirm a female patriotic identity through medical training, volunteer nursing, and sociability in associational life, a theme developed in chapter 5. Similarly, some unmarried daughters of old Catholic Rhenish noble families found meaningful work as matrons of orphanages or private girls' schools. Table 1 demonstrates, therefore, that the early aristocratic leadership of the Baden Women's Association was nearly evenly divided between estate owners' (*Grundherren*) wives, who maintained ties to the land through agriculture and scientific management of forestry, and the wives or daughters of titled (*unbegütete*) aristocrats, who owed their livelihood (and, typically, their elevation into the nobility) to state service.[29] Together, they outnumbered their bourgeois counterparts.

The table also shows that two estate-owning families held official positions at the Baden court. Indeed, the close integration into the dynastic court (the *Hofstaat*) was striking in Bavaria, where the leadership of the early women's association was dominated by court ladies (*Palastdamen*). Through the continuous contacts with associations at the various state administrative levels, court and civil society stood in constant, mutually profitable interaction. One prominent leader and lady-in-waiting, the wife of the Bavarian general Count Tann-Rathsamhausen, often fre-

---

28. Henry Vizetelly, *Berlin under the New Empire,* vol. 2 (1879; rpt. New York, 1968), 212. For information on social background I consulted E. H. Kneschke, ed., *Neues allgemeines Deutsches-Adels-Lexicon* (Leipzig, 1860–70; rpt. Hildesheim, 1973) and numerous volumes of "Der Gotha," the genealogical records of the German "high" and "low" aristocracy (for "Der Gotha," see the bibliographical essay at the end of this volume).

29. The backgrounds of Frau von Gulat-Wellenburg, Ida von Kettner, and Countess Emma von Gemmingen are particularly illustrative. Fr. Cast, *Historisches und genealogisches Adelsbuch des Grossherzogthums Baden* (Stuttgart, 1845), 87–91, 122, 258. Also, Martin Furtwängler, *Die Standesherren in Baden (1806–1848): Politische und soziale Verhaltensweisen einer bedrängten Elite* (Frankfurt am Main, 1996). For the aristocratic matron of St. Barbara in Koblenz, LK, Best. 661, 23, no. 136. Vermächtnis der Gräfin Amalia von Merveldt, 1853–1859.

quented Berlin high society, renewing contacts and reaffirming shared commitments across the state divides.[30] A number of high military officers or officers' wives also were part of the early leadership in the different states. And Hesse testifies to a developing union between public health and charity; there, all the professionals were drawn from the field of medicine.

The gender alliances that coalesced to redesign women's charitable activities were part of a wider set of simultaneous developments in Europe giving rise to the founding of the International Red Cross in 1864 and the initial Geneva Conventions covering the war wounded.[31] Early leaders were responding to growing public outrage at the senseless loss of life in wartime and the plight of sick and wounded soldiers. A new "humanitarian" public was coming into being against the backdrop of war. Seen through the eyes of Baroness Spitzemberg, whose diary reflects these sentiments, the image of human intervention through the military ambulance *(fliegendes Lazarett)* or the brave stretcher-bearers and nursing sisters seemed reassuring, somehow, to a public horrified by war's inevitable "grief, misery, tears and horror."[32]

Public opinion had been galvanized first by Henri Dunant's searing memoir of the battle of Solferino in 1859 in the wars between Austria and France over Italy, which had resulted in nearly forty thousand casualties. He and other humanitarian figures toured the German dynastic courts in the early 1860s to gain support for their project of coordinating voluntary relief societies throughout the world to alleviate the suffering and misery of war and of natural and other disasters in peacetime. Dynastic supporters, thus, could reappropriate this heightened "humanitarian" sentiment and redirect women's philanthropic organizations toward war work, establishing an essential place for women's work in new planning for war. Through the ongoing efforts on the ground, followed by an avid reading public, they consistently defended the case for voluntarism, solicited public money to finance the training of nurses and provisioning of hospitals, and—because of the weight of women's advocacy of their earlier philanthropic activities—envisioned multiple relief and medical interventions in peacetime. Indeed, these principles became the hallmark of the German Red Cross—a combination of voluntarism and tight, disciplined organiza-

---

30. *Das Tagebuch der Baronin Spitzemberg,* ed. Rudolf Vierhaus (Göttingen, 1960), 127, 198.

31. For a critical overview of the International Red Cross, Hutchinson, *Champions of Charity;* for its role in contemporary crises, Nicholas O. Berry, *War and the Red Cross* (New York, 1997), 7–20, which contains a brief history. For an assessment of its historic ties to militarism, Gerhard Müller-Werthmann, *Konzern der Menschlichkeit. Die Geschäfte des Deutschen Roten Kreuzes* (Hamburg, 1984).

32. *Tagebuch der Baronin Spitzemberg,* 100–101, 108, 116.

tion, which relied on public backing not new state taxes. Through these combinations, war planning extended ever deeper into civil society.

In the International Red Cross, however, the German pattern was only one possible model; the "international" relief community held together because each "national" component was free to develop its own institutional patterns and forms. French officials and philanthropists, for example, long remained skeptical of the principles of voluntarism (and of women's place in war work), and in England, Florence Nightingale, while carving out new roles for women, consistently advocated state responsibility alone for soldiers and their families. Similarly, Russian leaders feared diluting the wartime measures by including public health planning in peacetime, a venture strongly advocated by the Hessens.[33]

The reality and tragedy of war, and the philanthropic responses they elicited, influenced the timing and course of institution building in central Europe. A recent study of the Red Cross—admittedly from the perspective of the male International Committee in Geneva—credits Queen Augusta for her role in shaping developments outside of Prussia.[34] The date of founding shown in table 1, however, reveals a different dynamic and set of interactions. The war scare of 1859 provided the immediate context to the restructuring of women's associations in both Baden and Bavaria. In the conflict with Austria over Italian unification, Napoleon III of France threatened to extend his borders to the Rhine River again, reawakening fears of French aggression and occupation. Luise of Baden and the queen mother of Bavaria responded swiftly by calling on women to mobilize for the impending crisis. Within a few months in Baden alone, ninety-five local associations had been constituted, although not all continued their work once the fear of war abated. Only in 1866, influenced by her own daughter and by the overwhelming numbers of wounded at the battle of Königgrätz, did Augusta sanction women's patriotic mobilization to overcome a perceived gap in civilian war work. The Prussian move, in turn, reinvigorated the then languishing efforts in Bavaria and also directly stimulated the founding of the Albert-Verein in Saxony. Both the Weimar and Württemberg associations were reinvigorated by events in Geneva, which created the International Red Cross. Württemberg was the first German state organization to affiliate with the international in 1864; the Baden *Frauen-Verein* joined in 1866. The international movement in Geneva encouraged the duchess of Hesse to form her own dynastic-supported Medical Care Association (the forerunner of the Alice-Verein), which, however, in its manifesto, paid a direct debt to the Baden model of

---

33. A clear discussion of these diverse patterns is in Hutchinson, *Champions of Charity,* 37–45, 98–102.

34. Ibid., 119–20.

nursing care. And, in 1866, the older Weimar Patriotic Women's Institute made Queen Augusta an honorary member.[35]

If events in central Europe had distant echoes in the international community, they had profound implications for power and rule at home. The gender alliance capitalized on the name, status, and aura of aristocratic authority; participation in philanthropic projects was part of the way many central European aristocrats adapted to socioeconomic changes that were challenging their place as the natural ruling class. They formed associational alliances, however, that were not based on birth alone but on shared patriotic identities and religious and humanitarian commitments.

Women's Associations and German Unification

The timing of these dynastic interventions offers a clue to their importance also for state and, subsequently, nation building. The period 1859 to 1871, as German historians readily acknowledge, was a pivotal one in terms of nation building. This is not to say that there necessarily was a predetermined outcome. But the numerous options for political organization that seemed to be available in 1815—a small Prussian- or larger Austrian-dominated Germany, some form of dual hegemony, or a confederation in which the German middle states would be powerful—gradually dissolved as unification proceeded through "blood and iron" under Prussian leadership and design. The women's associations were not peripheral to, but embedded in, these events, reflecting state needs and, in turn, constituting an element of dynastic strength that was part of the difficult diplomatic negotiations and eventual military struggles affecting German unity.

Many historians of the German nationalist movement in the nineteenth century also see 1859 as a pivotal moment. Defeat in Italy revealed Austrian weakness and, significantly, its isolation; neither Russia nor England intervened to uphold the still powerful principle of dynastic sovereignty. Abstention convinced nationalist leaders like those who founded the German Nationalist Society in 1859 that only Prussia could achieve the goal of national unification. These same historians argue, too, that the pressure of nationalists "from below" forced the liberal principles of man-

---

35. For these details see the separate histories of each state's women's association affiliated with the Red Cross in *DRK,* 2: Baden, 23–70; Bavaria, 71–132; Hesse, 133–79; Mecklenberg, 180–90; Prussia, 191–368; Saxony, 623–38; Weimar, 639–49; Württemberg, 650–64. Also, for the early years of the Baden associations, GK, Abt. 233, no. 2848, Armensachen (Der badische Frauenverein), Statutes, June 6, 1859; correspondence with The Hague, August 1866; Munich, August 12, 1867, in which the Bavarians solicit information about the Baden women's organization.

hood suffrage and parliamentary rule on those conservative government and military officials constituting the new nation-state in war "from above." But it is not fully accurate to say, as the historian Schulze does, that after 1859 political legitimacy derived solely from the idea of the nation-state.[36] The dynastic state did not disintegrate in central Europe; German unification, which constituted the *Reich,* represented a federal alliance of dynastic states *(Länder),* with Prussia as the dominant state power.

Bismarck's so-called white revolution was made at the state level—an alliance among dynastic houses—partly reflecting the powerful connections between dynastic authority and civil society that worked to sustain a royalism from below. Expansion of dynastic patronage over women's associations after midcentury was part of a wider move toward political integration at the state level that was occurring simultaneously through constitutional, administrative, and police reforms. Therefore, there was an equally powerful, older loyalty in 1859 that was attached to the very person of the *Landesmutter* and *Landesvater,* who were palpable symbols inspiring monarchical loyalty and identity through extensive institutional and associational bonds. Allegiance was enhanced by the disciplinary power of the state—embodied in the police, the military, and even philanthropy.

Patriotic women certainly were not formative players in the struggle for German unification, directing events in the manner of generals commanding the troops at Königgrätz or Sedan, for that matter. But they were part of a dynastic world rooted in associational life that was responsible for communicating a particular memory of these same battles, which worked to strengthen conservative loyalty and identity and continued to do so even after unification. The shared commitments of the women's associations to nonpartisan relief services that accompanied affiliation with the International Red Cross laid the foundation for coordination across state lines well before the proclamation of German "unification" in January 1871. Their institutional forms helped promote the place of the *Land* in the new *Reich.* Foundation of the North German League in 1868 brought the member states' women's groups into close contact. And, as war with France loomed on the horizons, the major state Red Cross affiliates in north and south Germany formally established an all-German Red Cross Association in 1869. Affirming the "closest ties" based on "common tasks," it established a Central Committee, headquartered in Berlin, that, in peacetime, served only in advisory capacities but, in wartime, became the "unified" representative of the associations in their

---

36. Schulze, *Course of German Nationalism,* 100.

dealings with the military authorities.[37] The German Red Cross was being incorporated into the German military chain of command; with its unique gender structure and its anchor in a war culture, which it continuously reproduced, the women and men in patriotic service became seductive players in dynastic antiparty "politics" of imperial Germany. Furthermore, its prestige was rooted in its activities during the Franco-German war, 1870–71, the first major historical event shared by all Germans alike. Red Cross ritual work later kept alive the memory of this war and, thus, of its own valued services to national defense and unity.

The Franco-German war involved an extensive tapping of human and material resources for the war effort and drew in civilians in ways that transformed military calculations toward planning and strategy.[38] The earlier wars against Denmark and Austria had not met with much popular enthusiasm in German lands. By contrast, there was an outpouring of patriotic display in this war against Germany's old enemy across the Rhine; and that the issue at stake was German unification was central to cultural production.

Poetic voices in the patriotic associations formulated an image of unity that became widely popular. In this phrasing, unity was forged purposefully over and above difference; distinctions were acknowledged but harmoniously balanced in a unified whole. Opposites, too, were linked together in ways that produced a comprehensive and orderly synthesis for the present and the future. In one poem written in the context of patriotic women's war work, the fatherland was likened to a brotherhood, linking the distinct areas of the north and south together; another praised common German bonds, which transcended differences in social origins, religious confessions, and levels of wealth. Crown Prince Frederick, too, in his move to establish a National Invalid Fund in September 1870, arranged his appeal around similar metaphors. As he put it, he felt empowered to address "all Germans" because he had led an army in which the Baden, Bavarian, and Württemberg soldiers fought side by side with the Prussians: "In the same way as the war has created a uniform and united German army in which the sons of all the social orders fought in brotherly

---

37. "Gesammtorganisation der deutschen Vereine vom Rothen Kreuz," agreement of the state Red Cross associations of Prussia, Bavaria, Saxony, Württemberg, Baden, and Hessen on April 20, 1869. Found in *Handbuch der Deutschen Frauenverein unter dem Rothen Kreuz* (Berlin, 1881), 101–3.

38. For a more detailed examination of the specifics of women's war work in the Franco-German war and their place in later memory see Jean H. Quataert, "German Patriotic Women's Work in War- and Peace-Time, 1864–1890," in Förster and Nagler, *Road to Total War*, 449–77.

expression of bravery, the care for the invalids and helpless whom the war leaves behind must become the common business of Germany, the north and south of our fatherland taking a like share in it."[39] The language of national sacrifice and care was being enclosed in an idiom of equality and brotherhood, reflecting powerful notions that were helping shape a new nationalist discourse.

Other poems memorialized women's work for the common cause of victory, linking the home front to the battlefield as well as the work of civilians to the soldiers. And, significantly, the symbol of the cross—blood red—was inserted artistically into this effort of national defense. One poem addressed to the unnamed German soldiers, who were being "forged as one people in the knowledge of its strength," elevated the Red Cross women "not as spectators" but as active players, "together in alliance with our sons. . . . We join the battle."

> We dress each bloody wound
> and bring comfort with soothing hands.
> The red cross against a white background
> fights for humanity's German fatherland.[40]

From the start, the Red Cross was an international symbol—of non-partisan, humanitarian, and neutral service—and, as such, it linked Germany to other nations in the international community bound by common legal conventions governing treatment of soldiers and medical practices in war. At the same time, the "red cross" was being absorbed into a distinctly German domestic political landscape that centered on the dynastic houses and their military apparatuses. Although the institutions of the Red Cross were tied directly into dynastic political and military rule, the symbol cloaked their work under preexisting and time-honored notions of humanitarian service for the common good, now tied into an emerging national-

---

39. Frederick's call was printed in *KZ*, no. 217, September 17, 1870. For the poems, see, among other collections, *Deutsche Gedenkblätter, 1870–1871. Herausgegeben zum Besten des Vaterländischen Frauenvereins* (Berlin, 1871), particularly "Ein deutsches Kriegslied," 21–22, in which Bavarians, Saxons, and Schwabians are welcomed into a united Germany; and one entitled "Nord und Süd," 93.

40. *Deutsche Gedenkblätter*, "Das rothe Kreuz auf weissem Grunde," August 1870, by Emilie Heinrichs, 51. The key phrase in German reads, "kämpft für der Menschheit Vaterland." For other poems in the same collection hailing women's "noble" contributions, see "An die deutschen Frauen," by A. Stobbe (37), and one by the same title written by Luise H. (57–59). What is important is the linkage of women with blood and, therefore, with nationalist sacrifice. Chapter 6 develops the theme more fully.

ist rhetoric of sacrifice. Dynastic voices successfully played both sides of the symbol to their own advantage.

Civilian war work relied on distinct gender roles, and it also separated war and peace—but in ways that produced meaning by the one anticipating the other and vice versa. In the discourse of patriotic service, war and peace were a continuum in time and space. Thus, in the midst of war, the poems spoke of victory and peace. And, while peace followed the war, the peace itself was not devoid of war; war lived on in collective memory and in the multiple measures taken to safeguard the peace by preparing for military victory in the inevitable cycles of war and peace. Significantly, dynastic patriotism defined the normative services of men and women, linking their work in war and peacetime. These gender roles are captured graphically by the certificate given by the queen to each new affiliate of the Patriotic Women's Association, which was mushrooming throughout the North German Confederation under war conditions and, later, in the Prussia of imperial Germany.[41]

The diploma opens with a statement that "God's blessings bring together the groups that are put at the service of the fatherland," offering a religious sanction for patriotic endeavors. It calls for unity, despite confessional and social differences, and, rhetorically, aligns the "dynastic" association with "popular" mobilization. In its own formulation, the association during war serves the people in arms and, in peace, those people in need. And it declares women's philanthropic work to be the highest expression of the "love of fatherland," through which "men are victorious, women are consoling, and, as an inheritance of German sentiments, the duties of a sacrificial love of neighbor are affirmed." Men as victorious soldiers and women in the role of consolers are the two complementary poles of a gendered patriotic sacrifice. In practice, the evolving gender patterns of service and the public accounting of sacrifice were much more diverse than these simplified and formulaic sentiments indicate. But taken together, they were designed to mobilize an ethic of care for military and state purposes. Sara Reddick writes perceptively that neither the practice nor the perspective of care assures an antimilitaristic politics.[42] These same sentiments, furthermore, appealed to an essentialist quality in the woman, which underwrote her voluntary labor but disconnected it from any necessary feminist reforms or expanded state expenditures or entitlements.

---

41. *DRK*, 2:233.

42. Sara Ruddick, "The Rationality of Care," in *Women, Militarism, and War: Essays in History, Politics, and Social Theory*, ed. Jean Bethke Elshtain and Sheila Tobias (Savage, Md., 1990), 249. Ruddick also makes the important point that peace is inside a frame with war and not outside of it (258).

War in the Experiences and Memories of Patriotic Women
and Reform Feminists

Immediately at the outbreak of war in July 1870, the patriotic associations launched a well-orchestrated campaign in their states to mobilize women for the war effort. Long prepared in daily practice, it met with considerable success. The appeal stressed the direct danger to the "fatherland," left purposefully vague and indeterminate, and affirmed women's practical "duty" to defend the state, whether by sending goods immediately to the Rhine or by organizing local philanthropic services for soldiers and civilians in need. Everywhere, patriotic associations initiated greater organizational coordination, concentrating and centralizing decision making and supporting alliances across state lines. At the same time, as stressed by the predominantly female executive committee of the Berlin Victoria-Bazaar, an ad hoc relief society, they anchored the work in the "spirit of 1813," appealing to a longer historical tradition of "national" defense that, in the official narrative, drew in its wake old and young, rich and poor, as well as aristocrats and plebians.[43]

Women's war work was integrated into the larger military strategy of medical care and hospital support services; at least this was true of the activities of the state women's associations loosely tied to the Central Committee of the German Red Cross in Berlin. Thus, there was a common pattern to much of the war work at the state levels. Patriotic women organized fund-raising campaigns—for example, they coordinated a house collection for December 7, 1870, in "all parts of the German fatherland"— helping integrate through common endeavor the imagined political community. In many locations, they sponsored bazaars and earmarked the money for wounded soldiers, and, to raise cash for the families of reservists, they ran lotteries. They also gathered supplies and sent them to the designated depots in Germany and France. When the troops passed through their area, they set up refreshment stations. In return, the women received considerable official backing. Members wearing the red cross armbands rode the trains free of charge; affiliate associations were given free postage and telegraph usage and could transport freight at no cost as

---

43. *KZ,* no. 165, July 19, 1870, for the appeal of the Prussian Patriotic Women's Association; supplement to no. 165, July 19, 1870, for the address to German and Prussian women by the Committee of the Victoria-Bazaar. And also the report of the Baden Women's Association in the war, Rechenschaftsbericht der vereinigten Hilfskomite's des badischen Frauenvereins, *Die freiwillige Hilfsthätigkeit im Grossherzogthum Baden im Kriege 1870/71* (Karlsruhe, 1872), 16, which, in retrospect, linked the efforts of the diverse groups together in common cause of "national defense."

well; and the matériel procured for war work was exempt from tariffs and duties.[44]

Success depended on the energies at the local level. It was the individual members in each locality who produced the medical supplies, procured work for the soldiers' wives and paid the wages, and also cared for the wounded in military hospitals or municipal clinics. What began at first as a purely military effort to support nursing training and to care for wounded soldiers and soldiers' families moved inexorably into a wider philanthropic mission for all manner of needy people in the municipality in general—a commitment that, based as it was on the older pattern of women's municipal philanthropy, continued after the armistice.

While it shared notable characteristics, patriotic women's war work also exhibited a number of surprising patterns. In Baden, the *Frauen-Verein* provided the institutional support for the founding of a Men's Relief Association (Männer-Hilfsverein), belying the common assumption in the literature on German nationalist associations that women's groups were auxiliary only.[45] In the case of Baden, it was the reverse; women consistently outnumbered men in patriotic relief and municipal philanthropic services. The appearance of men's associations in Baden and elsewhere, however, introduced an increasingly differentiated gender division of labor into civilian war work, although the specificity of the gender roles became more clearly defined only in the long years of peace after the Franco-German war. Men operated essentially as relief workers, organized in sanitary corps *(Sanitätskolonne)*, who transported wounded soldiers from the field of battle to the military trains and then to the hospitals. They also organized the depots, kept the records and correspondence, and were prepared to help needy families of soldiers and reservists as well as minister to the wounded and the sick.[46] Care was a patriotic duty that defied simple gender typecasting.

Furthermore, women's war work was not confined solely to the borders of German lands. Women "served" in France, following the invading German troops from Sedan to Ravon L'Elappe to Paris; aristocratic women in particular supervised much of the nursing operations and

---

44. Details are drawn partly from my reading of *Kreuz-Zeitung* during the war years and partly from the rich details in Gotthold Kreyenberg, *Mädchenerziehung und Frauenleben im Aus-und Inlande. Mit einem Anhange: Deutsche Frauentätigkeit während des Krieges, 1870–1871* (Berlin, 1872), 313–73.

45. Chickering, "Casting Their Gaze," 167, and his *We Men Who Feel*, 169–72.

46. Rechenschaftsbericht der vereinigten Hilfskomite's des badischen Frauenvereins, *Freiwillige Hilfsthätigkeit*, 2–3, 13; also GK, Abt. 233, no. 2848, the reports of the Landes-Hilfs-Verein (the state Red Cross).

administered ambulance services and war front hospitals in enemy territory. And a few, like Rosa Behrends-Wirth, nurse-administrator of a mobile German medical team behind enemy lines, added their own recollections about women's wartime experiences to the steady stream of veterans' accounts that were an essential part of the memory of war in imperial Germany.[47]

The state Patriotic Women's Associations, the largest and best coordinated in the German territories, never had the field of care to themselves, however. During the war, a range of other women's clubs assisted and supplemented their work; many of the smaller organizations, however, dissolved after the war or were absorbed by the patriotic organizations. There was, for example, a Berlin association, headed by the Baroness Wrangel and Countess Bismarck, with the title of Central Relief Committee for Needy Families Whose Breadwinners Were Called to Arms, an 1866 ad hoc club recalled to life in July 1870 with the outbreak of the war. Active, too, was the Women's Club of the Lazarus Hospital for the Care of Wounded and Sick Soldiers and the women of the Stuttgart Medical Association. The list is hardly exhausted.

There also were the nursing sisters of both Catholic and Protestant denominations, and a more secular version of a nursing order, the Red Cross sisters, officially instituted in 1859–60; the Baden *Frauen-Verein* was able to field two hundred of its nurses for the war effort. The religious revival of *Vormärz*, as we have seen, had supported a wide range of philanthropic endeavors; the Sisters of Charity and other Catholic nursing orders joined a revitalized charitable movement in Catholic areas, helping to establish medical prevention as a distinct part of municipal and parish poor relief. Similarly, with the emergence of a Protestant deaconess movement under Theodor Fliedner in Kaiserswerth in the 1830s, a network of Protestant mother-houses had spread in German areas, which also supported nursing training.[48]

There was another group of women active in local communities dur-

---

47. Rosa Behrends-Wirth, *Frauenarbeit im Krieg. Selbsterlebtes aus den Jahren 1870–1871* (Berlin, 1892), 43, 87, who describes encounters with aristocratic women; and Mary Olnhausen, *Adventures of an Army Nurse in Two Wars: From the Diary and Correspondence of Mary Phinney, Baroness von Olnhausen*, comp. J. P. Munroe (Boston, 1903).

48. Prelinger, *Charity, Challenge, and Change*, 165–69, describes the place of the Protestant nursing sisters in the era of reaction and their increasing alignment with conservative monarchical forces. Also see Sachsse and Tennstedt, *Geschichte der Armenfürsorge*, 227–32, for a discussion of Catholic and Protestant charity in the nineteenth century. See also Helene Lange and Gertrud Bäumer, eds., *Handbuch der Frauenbewegung*, vol. 2, *Frauenbewegung und soziale Frauentätigkeit in Deutschland nach Einzelgebieten* (Berlin, 1901), 51–76, on the nursing orders in Germany.

ing the war: reform feminists[49] in associations like the Berlin Lette *Verein,* who advocated the expansion of women's access to education and training, or Lina Morgenstern's People's Kitchen, also based in Berlin, which had been in operation ever since the Prussian-Austrian conflict in 1866. Indeed, the organizational landscape framing women's associational life had become complex with the founding of the German Women's Association (Allgemeiner deutscher Frauenverein), an umbrella body of the emerging bourgeois women's movement, which had been constituted by Louise Otto-Peters and Auguste Schmidt in Leipzig in 1865. It, too, represented an effort at coordination and ideological demarcation; but its affiliated *Vereine* were working to promote and expand women's educational and employment opportunities in social and economic life. And, in principle, the member associations were organized and run exclusively by women.

Reform feminists, however, had been receptive to the patriotic appeal in 1870; many bourgeois feminist leaders implicitly accepted the existence of the state and the need to maintain it. They, too, had inherited a memory of the Wars of Liberation, although their reading, arguably, stressed the thwarted democratic and constitutional ideals of the struggle against Napoleon I and not the dynastic narrative.[50] Middle-class feminists understood well, however, that women's patriotic involvements in the earlier wars had not been solidified by concrete educational and occupational gains for women, and they expected to win meaningful reforms after the Wars of Unification; similar demands were raised forcefully again in 1917.

These reciprocities between sacrifice and rights were part of feminist calculations from the early foundation of the women's movement. For example, a lecture in Berlin in 1867 on the "woman question" by Dr. Franz von Holtzendorff linked women's medical services during the

---

49. I prefer the term *reform* feminists to the more standard "bourgeois" feminists because, of course, there were women from bourgeois (professional and government service) backgrounds in the Patriotic Women's Associations. Information on bourgeois women's societies is found in Helene Lange and Gertrud Bäumer, eds., *Handbuch der Frauenbewegung,* vol. 1, *Geschichte der Frauenbewegung in den Kulturlandern* (Berlin, 1901), 34–62; and, also, Margarit Twellmann, *Die Deutsche Frauenbewegung. Ihre Anfänge und erste Entwicklung. Quellen, 1843–1889* (Meisenheim am Glan, 1972), 149–51. For an overview of the later period, Barbara Greven-Aschoff, *Die bürgerliche Frauenbewegung in Deutschland, 1894–1933* (Göttingen, 1981).

50. Lange and Bäumer, *Handbuch der Frauenbewegung,* 1:27; Twellmann, *Die Deutsche Frauenbewegung im Spiegel repräsentativer Frauenzeitschriften,* 2–3. Also, Ann Taylor Allen, *Feminism and Motherhood in Germany, 1800–1914* (New Brunswick, N.J., 1991), 100–103. Allen broadens the debate on German feminism but lays an implicit claim to antiwar sentiments among bourgeois feminists in the Wars of Unification. She fails to assess women's wartime roles, however; nor does she account theoretically for an ethic of care that is militaristic.

Austrian-Prussian war to demands for better education for women; similarly, during the Franco-German war, the Lette Association pushed for improved training of nurses and supported hospitals like the Queen Augusta Hospital in Berlin, where both female professionals and volunteers could receive instruction. In the immediate postwar era, the association justified its efforts on behalf of women's professional advancement by their sterling performances during wartime. Pushing the logic of patriotism their way, feminists also made the case early on that girls' curriculum had to be redesigned so women, better educated and knowledgeable in history, could fulfill their duties as wives and mothers, a position that reinforced their anticipation of reform in the near future as well.[51]

German women, therefore, embarked on war work with quite different assumptions and motivations. In this respect, the war and the particular shaping of its memory helped differentiate among the women who were active in seemingly similar philanthropic activities in local communities. Scattered evidence indicates that patriotic and reform feminist associations involved in war work at the local level remained organizationally distinct. The example of Braunschweig is revealing. The city's patriotic association, founded in 1869, had 195 members at the end of the war; it was headed by the wife of the state minister, Auguste von Campe, and its secretary was Frau Elisabeth Thiele, the wife of the court preacher. During the war it had been busy soliciting funds and, from its own revenues, had set up a hospital with seventy-four beds. The city's (bourgeois) women's association also originated in 1869; it had 146 members at war's end and was headed by Frau Dorette Sack; the secretary was Fräulein Marie Selenke. Its members had been busy gathering needed war materials and caring for the wounded in a hospital for reservists. The report pointedly noted, however, that the feminist club had functioned more as an educational institution, supporting a continuing school, which offered instruction in the use of the sewing machines, and organizing evening entertainment.[52]

The existence of two umbrella organizations—the German Patriotic Women's Associations on the one hand and the General Women's Association, reorganized into the League of German Women's Associations (Bund deutscher Frauenvereine) in 1894 with its own print and institutional apparatuses on the other—in later years reinforced distinct identi-

51. Twellmann, *Deutsche Frauenbewegung Quellen,* 11, for proposed curricula that included patriotic literature and history; 157, for the lecture; also Lange and Bäumer, *Handbuch der Frauenbewegung,* 1:35–36. A similar argument is made in the context of republican motherhood in North America by Nancy F. Cott, *The Bonds of Womanhood: "Woman's Sphere" in New England, 1780–1835* (New Haven, 1977).

52. Local report in Kreyenberg, *Mädchenerziehung und Frauenleben,* 319–20.

ties and practices. But the differences were inherent in the memory of the war itself.

The official institutional "histories" of the Patriotic Women's Associations stressed their extraordinary growth in wartime: "The war years, 1870–71, gave the cause of the women's associations a powerful boost." In subsequent years, their commemorative work centered partly around celebrating the war and honoring individual and community sacrifices. In contrast, the war decade was seen as an impediment to feminist associational life. Only after the wars, according to the leadership, did feminist organizations develop and prosper.[53] By then, the feminist community itself had coined separate labels for women's "work." As formulated in an 1872 study, patriotic women were engaged in work for the "general good" *(gemeinnützige Unternehmungen);* in comparison, the bourgeois feminist flagship supported remunerative "work" and "education" *(Arbeit und Bildung)* for middle-class women, and it pointedly distanced itself from all forms of "charity."[54] In later years, these distinctions became standard stereotypes within which bourgeois feminists spoke and wrote about women's social lives and activities; subsequent chapters will offer other ways to think about the differences between patriotic women and the moderate reform feminists. Throughout much of the *Kaiserreich,* many members of both groups, indeed, found part of their own personal and political identity in the symbol of the *Landesmutter.*

The process of differentiation was not one-sided, however; dynasts and their government and military supporters had their own conceptual "framework," part of their efforts to define the transition from the *Land* to the *Reich* after 1871. Significantly, voluntary philanthropy played an important role in the emerging ideology and praxis of "official nationalism." At a conference in Würzburg in August 1871, the state Patriotic Women's Associations were welded into a Union of German Women's Associations (Verband der deutschen Frauenvereine), under the patronage of the newly elevated empress Augusta, who was the patron of the German Red Cross as well. This institutional arrangement, too, permitted considerable autonomy at the state level even while it elevated the Prussian association to a position of de facto leadership in the whole structure by virtue of its proximity to the Central Committee of the Red Cross in

---

53. *DRK,* 2:30. In contrast, Lange and Bäumer, *Handbuch der Frauenbewegung,* 1:52, 61, write that the effort to found women's associations had been "thwarted" *(vereitelt)* by war.

54. These distinctions are drawn by Kreyenberg, *Mädchenerziehung und Frauenleben,* 305, 309.

Berlin.[55] The institutional reorganization of the women's associations in 1871, therefore, accommodated the new political reality of nation building on the basis of the old constituent dynastic entities. Leaders also sought to rewrite the philanthropic services for the new political context, in effect binding the rhetoric of nationalism and national service to conservative state ends.

In a revealing address to the general assembly of the women's association in 1872, Dr. Friedenthal, at the time a member of the Prussian parliament and *Landrat* and one of the most prominent spokesmen for the women's group, put a premium on the benefits of organizational life. He redesigned the principle of "organized voluntarism," which blended self-administration and discipline, and linked the volunteer to the care and support of the state. Significantly, the organizations themselves became the defining characteristic of the "nation" (indeed, its very embodiment), expressions of collective commitments and loyalties. He drew his inspiration from the recent military campaigns that taught the necessity of organization. As he put it, "[Patriotic] work meant inserting the nation, expressed by the independent activity of associations and corporations, right into the organism of the state and particularly the army."[56] Through a proper balance of autonomy and discipline, "organized voluntarism" could be harmonized with state and military needs, insuring "centralization when unity of action required it; and autonomy when an individual course of action was called for." These principles alone would insure the necessary institutional continuity in peacetime so that, in case of war, the state would have at its disposal adequate personnel and material. In the patriotic imagination, indeed, national energies were disciplined, organized, and turned to the needs of the state.

Dr. Friedenthal's remarks suggest that the conclusion of war was

---

55. For the Würzburg conference, GK, Abt. 233, no. 2848, *Dreizehnter Jahresbericht des Vorstandes des Badischen Frauenvereins, Abteilung Karlsruhe über seine Thätigkeit während des Zeitraums vom 1 Juli bis 31 Dezember 1872.* From the Prussian side, GSPK, no. 15609, Bl. 100, *Bericht über die zwölfte General-Versammlung des Vaterländischen Frauen-Vereine am 24 März 1878,* 75–78, the protocol of the conference. Additional information is in *KZ,* first supplement to no. 98, April 28, 1872, for a report by the undersecretary of state, Heinrich Achenbach, on Würzburg; and for confusion about the women's associations operating in German political life, see *KZ,* supplement to no. 84, April 11, 1875, "Die Frauen Hülfe- und Pflege-Vereine."

56. Found in *KZ,* first supplement to no. 98, April 28, 1872. Some of his ideas are reminiscent of conservative notions of a social mission proposed, for example, by Ludwig von Gerlach and Viktor Hubner in the late 1840s. For the earlier conservative debates, see Beck, *Origins of Welfare State,* 79–86, on leaders with ties to the Protestant social mission and Johann Wichern.

forcing association members to rethink their social mission. If their institutional life had been assured, the organizational purpose was not immune
from uncertainty. Association leaders, therefore, turned to two additional
tasks in their move to "name" and "frame" patriotic service for the future.

One worked to shape memory by characterizing the previous war
work in ways that would sustain future state service in the new nation-
state. It was launched by the empress herself, at a meeting of the German
Red Cross and its women's associations in Nuremberg in October 1871.
Augusta continued in the public limelight a process that had been tested
earlier in poetic form. Her greetings layered a nationalist vocabulary on
older familiar images of social and confessional inclusion. The association,
a tightly knit symbol of unity embracing all social groups and creeds,
inserts "the organizational power of humanity for the first time into our
national life. Here it is guaranteed a permanent abode, where it weaves the
experiences of war into the tasks of peacetime" and "fulfills the expectations that the fatherland has a right to demand of us," she wrote with
words designed to bring the diverse audience clearly into her imagined
fold. Continuing, Augusta speculated what a "realistic review" of the
"work of humanity" over the last year might contain and offered her own
list of accomplishments. She portrayed the "donations" of the rich as well
as the "offerings" of the poor, "which were no less valuable," stressed the
willingness to care for friend and enemy and evoked the spirit of humanity
embedded deep in the cross.[57] Through these personalized images of service to the fatherland, Augusta could appeal to aristocratic groups, who
otherwise might be alienated from the political nation and its then powerful National Liberal leadership in the Reichstag.

The second task was to set an agenda for the immediate future. Let us
pick up again Dr. Friedenthal, who provided a detailed blueprint of action
at the general assembly meeting. Delegates were drawn from all corners of
Prussia and included a representative from Baden. On one level, the
speech was a statement of official expectations, outlining the work to be
done in war and peacetime. Friedenthal's analogy with the army was striking and prescient, and he spoke about mobilization orders that soon
would be extended to the Red Cross organizations. On another level, it
revealed a powerful gender component, laying bare the implicit assumptions of the male leadership about the feminine rituals of care. (Later
chapters examine women's own understanding of this work.)

Peacetime operations, Friedenthal said, involved an extensive philanthropic mission: educating orphans, running homes for neglected youth,

---

57. *KZ*, no. 250, October 26, 1871, written remarks to the meeting of the German Relief
Societies comprised of representatives throughout Germany.

providing nursing services and public health, and promoting domestic industry, among others. The key, however, was not simply the need to solicit private funding to underwrite such extensive activity (although private donations apparently were necessary since he failed to mention additional state expenditures to cover the new services). Rather, he stressed the "friendly and loving manner" in which these services were to be rendered personally to each individual in need, characteristics, he claimed, that were female at their very core. Peacetime philanthropy rested on a sphere of care that was inherently female, and he cast it dramatically against the male sphere of politics. His was, indeed, a male discourse in which the other (the mother) represented the unifying public community *(Volksnation)* that overcame the social, political, and confessional divisions among her sons. His imagery is forceful and worth quoting.

> At a time when social, political, and religious divisions threaten to split the whole nation into enemy camps, when the passions of the call to battle of all the political parties drown out everything else, the German women's associations . . . offer a place of tranquility where those parts of the polity that are in opposition can be reconciled in common work for the love of neighbor and in the feeling that we all are sons of one mother. . . . Just as in the old German Reich, where all conflict ended with the emperor's peace, so in our resurrected Reich may the symbol of peace reign over the activity of the Union of German Women's Association: its elevated patron, the German empress.[58]

The gendered language is striking: from the perspective of the son, at odds with his brothers, the unifying elements binding the social, political, and religious divisions in German life were seen as female. Indeed, the true national community was characterized as feminine—caring and motherly—in contrast to the masculine political world with its divisions, tensions, and conflicts. His words redeployed the ideological distinctions between philanthropy and politics. Furthermore, the patriotic public joined in service offered men elsewhere in conflict a space to reconcile their differences and work to support common national goals, which were necessary for the survival of the state. Any notion of women's agency is lost in the musing, but Dr. Friedenthal, nonetheless, described a space for women and men that could be envisioned as unifying in the face of political and religious conflicts. And it held out a highly visible public persona for patriotic women that they could mold to their own personal and social advantages.

---

58. *KZ,* first supplement to no. 98, April 28, 1872.

The work of the Red Cross continued to be closely tied to the dynastic courts in imperial Germany. The relationship between the dynast and the association, indeed, remained close and interdependent. The continued successes of the Red Cross kept alive the words of William I, who had praised the war relief associations for preparing the ground for unification: "German unity," he declared in March 1871, "was carried out successfully first by the humanitarian work of the Central Committee [of the Red Cross] at a time when the political unification of our fatherland remained but an ambition."[59] In the narrative of patriotic acts, which prescribed the hierarchy of values, humanitarian work had preceded the political. And memory, as its theorists remind us, is selective, reflecting relations of power and their institutional structures.[60]

In subsequent years, the kaiser's words lent authority to the Red Cross itself, reinforcing its own sense of place as a vital yet nonpartisan institution. And the state offered an unequivocal affirmation of its worth when it placed the organization's original charter in the final stone that completed construction of the Cologne Cathedral in 1880. In circular fashion, the extensive publicity surrounding the ceremony reminded readers of the kaiser's earlier assessment.

The celebration in 1880 capped over forty years of festivities around the rebuilding of the Cologne Cathedral, which stood, as the empress put it succinctly, as a "monument to the completion of German unity."[61] Through the actions of the *Landesmutter,* imperial officials affirmed the importance of the Red Cross for national life. A telegram from Augusta sent to the delegates of the German Red Cross, who were meeting just days before the festival in October, announced her intent. As their patron, she was inserting into the cornerstone the charter of the organization's predecessor, which would be rolled and encased in leather. The document, which had established the unified, national Red Cross, in her account expressed the organization's "inner connection to the unity of the German Reich, as a precious gift of the past and as a guarantee for the future."[62]

---

59. For the kaiser's speech, which was given in Nancy on March 14 prior to his return to Germany, see *KZ,* no. 68, March 21, 1871. For institutional use of the remarks, *Handbuch der Deutschen Frauenvereine unter dem Rothen Kreuz,* 9–10.

60. A classic formulation of the social context for memory is Maurice Halbwachs, *On Collective Memory,* ed. and trans. Lewis A. Coser (Chicago, 1992).

61. For details on the gesture in the conservative press, *KZ,* supplement to no. 230, October 1, 1880, at the meeting of the German Associations of the Red Cross.

62. *KZ,* no. 236, October 8, 1880, comments on the note that the queen sent to the Central Committee; no. 240, October 13, 1880, describes the artistic encasement of the document, bound in leather, with one side in gold emblazoned by the *Reich* eagle and the kaiser's crown. The original statutes are in *Handbuch der Deutschen Frauenvereine unter dem Rothen Kreuz,* 104–9. For a general discussion of Cologne Cathedral celebrations over forty years, Leo

The linkage of the Red Cross to this potent architectural symbol of German unity sought to raise the organization to the level of a quintessentially German institution. It was a powerful nationalist gesture with its appropriation of historic time and assurances for the unfolding future.

The institutional, rhetorical, and ritual worlds of dynastic-sponsored philanthropy became an important vehicle for the implementation of official nationalism after 1871. Through its gender symbols and roles, it drew into its orbit an expanding institutional network of women's and men's associations. The main lines of activity were set gradually, over time, reflecting the ways that work for the needy and endangered proved a testing ground for facilitating the transitions from times of war to peace and peace to war. The rhetoric, however, distinguished the one from the other. Following this strategy, the next two chapters turn to women's peacetime endeavors in the new German nation-state. They combine institutional history and ritual and symbolic analysis to locate the Patriotic Women's Associations in the interstices between patterns of municipal relief and consolidations of national power and identity.

Haupts, "Die Kölner Dombaufeste 1842–1880 zwischen kirchlicher, bürgerlich-nationaler und dynastisch-höfischer Selbstdarstellung," in Düding, Friedemann, and Münch, *Öffentliche Festkultur,* 191–211.

CHAPTER 3

Civic Voluntarism and Gift Giving in the "Caring" State

Women who volunteered their patriotic services in imperial Germany entered a distinct cultural world that managed the day-to-day relief work at the community level. The evolving nature of these charitable interventions—from poor relief *(Armenfürsorge)* to social welfare services *(Sozialfürsorge)*, as they usually are called in the literature[1]—was part of the contradictory processes of social change in the "long" nineteenth century.

This world of voluntarism was "seen" in the community through its symbolic practices that were part of the daily performances of its tasks as well as its distinctive festive time. The force of these well-known symbolic forms worked to dramatize the invisible—for example, the presumed altruism and selfless sacrifice of the scores of women who were giving their services freely—and communicate the complicated conservative messages of gender and power that were at the heart of its services. Its annual festive calendar, furthermore, linked distant communities together in shared ritual time. This volunteer work under the rubric "patriotic" encouraged the public to interpret the same activities of the separate local associations as expressions of the personal concern of the *Landesmutter* and, by implication, as concern of the state itself for the well-being of the wider national community.[2]

---

1. This is the typical framework within which changes in relief measures are analyzed. For details, Sachsse and Tennstedt, *Geschichte der Armenfürsorge,* and *Fürsorge und Wohlfahrtspflege.* While fascinating and informative, the study does not connect charitable work to the political realm; it also privileges the bourgeois women's movement and the move to professionalize social work.

2. For the ways organizations represent themselves symbolically, and the implications for identity, see Kertzer, *Rituals, Politics, and Power,* 15–16; also for the importance of naming, Firth, *Symbols,* 48, 171–73.

Over the years, the availability of a continuous supply of volunteer labor reflected the complex values that underpinned dynastic patriotic service. Generations of privileged women were committed to volunteer work precisely because its value system combined—in ever-changing proportions, however—both "modern" and "traditional" elements.[3] It captures, therefore, some of the paradoxes that were constitutive of the efforts at state-building on the ground.

The voluntary, nonwaged nature of the philanthropic labor appealed to women whose social backgrounds favored a conservative gender order that was hostile to women's gainful employment. Simultaneously, however, this volunteer work demanded considerable abstract thought and, in turn, taught numerate and literate skills. A striking example of these combinations is seen already in a Prussian survey of the activities of local soup kitchens in the 1830s. At the time, government officials were concerned about a cholera outbreak and sought to improve nourishment as a preventive measure. If the preparation of the meals came under the supervision of a doctor, who controlled for calories and fat, women's association members oversaw the running of the kitchens, exercising "modern" supervisory and financial skills as well as implementing the new nutritional standards.[4] Indeed, over time, despite its voluntary nature, the philanthropic activities increasingly came to rely on specialized training in continuing educational courses that were sponsored by the network of women's associations itself. Voluntarism became linked to modern science and advances in public health. But it also sustained an ethic of care that was personal and, at least on the surface, nonbureaucratic. These personal ties to the dynastic house were the point for the service elites, who acquired and expressed their conservative political identities in self-conscious activities sanctioned by the dynasty.

The World of Circulating Gifts

Voluntarism enveloped its practitioners in a world of circulating gifts. Money, time, labor, and food all were deemed to be "freely" given in the institutional life of philanthropic service. The gift *(die Gabe)* was the paradigmatic expression of a personal commitment to improve the plight of

---

3. There is a current debate whether "traditional" is a valid notion because so-called traditional practices are transformed in the ever-changing present. For these ambivalences, Dipesh Chakrabarty, "The Difference—Deferral of a Colonial Modernity: Public Debates on Domesticity in British Bengal," in *Tensions of Empire: Colonial Cultures in a Bourgeois World*, ed. Frederick Cooper and Ann Laura Stoler (Berkeley and Los Angeles, 1997), 380.

4. LK, Abt. 403, no. 796, Die bestehende resp. angerichteten Armen Speise-Anstalten, 1831, Bl. 3–6, 29.

neighbors and others. Private money largely underwrote the philanthropic associations, which were places for elites to exercise patronage. Money was bequeathed in wills and testaments, donated at specific moments for commemorative purposes, and solicited more widely through lotteries, bazaars, and house-to-house collections. In addition, dynastic families "generously" supplemented these funds through all manner of gifts and bequests. At times as well, monies came from state coffers, earmarked through parliamentary debates and deliberations.[5] Much more than just money was exchanged in these settings, however. There were reputations to be made and authority and power affirmed in the very act of giving. Significantly, too, the new world of empire gradually was incorporated into the public appeals for donations, refashioning through older forms of solicitation in a seemingly natural way the very definition of patriotic service and sacrifice in Germany.

The power relationships of Germany's evolving social structure were embedded in the exchange networks that linked dynasts, service elites, and clients together. The so-called gifts circulating within the patriotic associations fashioned ties of reciprocity that functioned both vertically and horizontally. On the one hand, they expressed the power of the donor over the recipient, representing a compelling acknowledgment of the social hierarchy. In practical terms, they affirmed the power and authority of the *Landesmutter* over her "subjects," including the members of the women's associations and, in turn, the power of association members—who often referred to themselves as mothers—over the poor and needy clients. The apparent one-way transfer of money and services from dynastic court to the elites and, in turn, to the clients served to reinforce bonds of dependency and foster loyalty. But on the other, the ties were more complicated, both in terms of the dependency of the *Landesmutter* on the daily workings of the local associations and in the ability of clients to modify the bases of care. Furthermore, the bonds of gift giving also worked horizontally to create communities of elites tied together by common Christian service. The shared patriotic commitments bridged, however imperfectly, the confessional, gender, and social divides that might, indeed, separate activists

---

5. Baden legislators, for example, increasingly were willing to invest public monies in private institutes for medical training. For details see Arleen Marcia Tuchman, *Science, Medicine, and the State in Germany: The Case of Baden, 1815–1871* (New York, 1993). Gift giving runs through the archival sources. Among others, GSPK, no. 15609, Bl. 202, Berlin, June 23, 1886, discussion of the deceased pensioner Wilhelm Heinrich Willems's bequest of twenty thousand marks for the branch Patriotic Women's Association in Emden. Or, LK, Abt. 403, no. 7364, Bl. 53–54, *Geschäfts-Bericht des Aachener-Zweigvereins des Vaterländischen Frauenvereins für das Jahr 1901,* thanking donors for their generous gifts.

and donors in their other walks of life. Solidarity need not express consensus, as anthropologists remind us.[6]

Gift giving, above all, was a public event designed to broadcast the social relationships and patriotic values that the gift symbolized. Mary Douglas aptly notes, "Gifts are given in a context of public drama, with nothing secret about them. In being more directly cued to public esteem, the distribution of honour and the sanctions of religion, the gift economy is more visible than the market."[7] Her comments were written with an eye to demonstrating the complementarity of the gift and capitalist economies; both offer individuals incentives to collaborate in patterns of exchange. But the gift economy operates under explicit assumptions that its transactions are undertaken freely and with no thought of return. It veils the necessity of obligations in a language of selflessness, charity and care. In the milieu of philanthropic services under dynastic patronage, the central symbol of the gift, indeed, constituted an image of the state as caring; nonetheless, it carried implicit understandings of reciprocal responsibilities that bound each of the constituent elements together.

Participation in philanthropic work in municipal life, then, was sustained by the personal nature of the relationships that developed between the volunteers, other local patrons, and donors as well as clients. Individual reputations were very much at stake. Fame was reinforced by the rituals that tied the philanthropic associations to the person of the dynast. In turn, these rituals were opportunities to assert associational identity and perpetuate the memory of exemplary individual leaders and activists. Deaths were opportunities for ritual dramas, commemorations designed to shape the future by celebrating a particular vision of the lived past. Local politics in imperial Germany—whether of the right or the left—were built partly on the memory of individual achievements, and women's exploits were no exception.[8]

---

6. Kertzer, *Ritual, Politics, and Power,* 67–69.

7. Forward to Mauss, *The Gift,* xiv. Some gifts were given anonymously; however, they were sent to the Patriotic Women's Association and thus intended to support a known set of relationships and values. For a discussion of anonymity see Firth, *Symbols,* 379.

8. The political world was suffused with commemoration of individual exploits on the local as well as the national levels. For example, among socialists the death of Lassalle was celebrated (August 31) in public ceremony, and it was increasingly common to turn the burial of a "comrade" into a public event. See Lüdtke, "Trauerritual und politische Manifestation," 128. Also, the memory of patriotic women was kept alive at ceremonies, which placed flowers at their graves. GK, Abt. 69, no. 951b, Das 50-jährige Jubiläum des Badischen Frauenvereins am 16. und 17. Juni 1909, for list of deceased members whose graves received wreaths on June 16.

Death in the Patriotic Community

A funeral oration—for it was artfully crafted as a political document with an eye to the future—in the industrial Rhineland town of Düren captures well the power of these ritual dramas in the political life of dynastic service. In 1903, Frau Eberhard Hoesch, president of the local Patriotic Women's Association, died. By all accounts, she must have been a remarkable, charismatic figure. Her eulogy was extraordinary in length and detail, and great effort was made to assure its literary life. It was inserted in its entirety into the annual report of the branch association, which circulated widely among patriotic groups in imperial Germany.[9] Its perspective from the institution on the ground reveals the distinct local flavor that gave the shared patterns of dynastic philanthropy their living force.

In the second half of the nineteenth century, Düren was a booming industrial town; its goods had been included already in the first World Industrial Exhibition in London in 1851. The population grew nearly threefold between 1871 and 1910, from 12,858 to 32,500 inhabitants. The 1910 census recorded ninety-one factories, employing around six thousand workers. Local power and authority were matched by public gift-giving, or at least the chroniclers honored the memory and largesse of individual industrial families who had donated parts of their wealth for philanthropic projects. Frau Hoesch was the wife of a leading industrialist, owner of metal factories and iron foundries, and known in business and civic circles for his generosity; he had endowed the city theater, among other charitable acts that found their way into the town's histories.[10] The Hoesch family was Protestant, although Protestants represented only a small minority (around 11 percent of the population in 1885) in a city that was overwhelmingly Catholic.

The Düren branch of the Patriotic Women's Association had been formally constituted several years after the Franco-German war by women who had been active in war service. It languished until 1886, the year Mrs. Hoesch took over the presidency. Local leaders correlated the subsequent "takeoff" and organizational successes of the branch to her leadership skills; but its flowering both reflected and, in turn, reinforced the easing of religious tensions that slowly followed suspension of the discriminatory laws passed against Catholics during the Prussian *Kul-*

---

9. LK, Abt. 403, no. 7365, Bl. 119–20, *Jahresbericht des Vaterländischen Frauenvereins Düren pro 1903,* Düren, n.d.

10. Wilhelm Bruell, *Chronik der Stadt Düren* (Düren, 1895); Erich Keyser, ed., *Rheinisches Städtebuch* (Stuttgart, 1956), 96–103. For a case of gift giving in Düren, GSPK, no. 15611, Bl. 60, April 3, 1897, concerning the bequest of the widow Emma Schull in Düren, who gave twenty thousand marks to support the school for domestic arts.

turkampf in the previous decade. The Düren Patriotic Women's Association, as was true of the model everywhere in the *Kaiserreich,* was interconfessional—open to women irrespective of their religious backgrounds—and, in principle, represented a powerful "political" statement of Christian collaboration in confessionally mixed areas like the Rhineland and, as we will see, Baden.[11] One main characteristic of official nationalism, at least seen through the philanthropic prism, was its interconfessional character and its consistent sponsorship of "Christian" service and sacrifice for the fatherland. Its relationship to Jewish participation was complex and contradictory, however. In the 1880s and 1890s, Prussian officials tried to halt statutory changes that explicitly excluded Protestants and Jews from certain Catholic parish relief organizations in the Rhineland, but they essentially were powerless because these groups already had left the Catholic associations. Similarly, as we will see later in this chapter, the rise of political anti-Semitism made many small independent patriotic organizations inhospitable to Jewish members, who also dropped out of the collaboration. And, yet, there were no official prohibitions to membership in the state women's associations, so a few young Jewish women joined Baden Red Cross activities, as chapter 5 demonstrates.[12]

The funeral oration, therefore, offered local philanthropic leaders an opportunity to affirm the common bonds of patriotism at a moment of public grief and experience of loss. Assuring the continued vitality of the shared principles binding peoples of different religious backgrounds in philanthropic service in the future was the intent of the message to the audience and the wider reading public.

Preceded by a more intimate gathering for immediate association members and the young student nurses, the funeral service was a public ceremony, held in the association's headquarters. The building itself on the Holtzstrasse had been donated to the *Verein* by the Hoesch family. According to the account, the throngs of mourners spilled out beyond the designated rooms, a testimony to the breadth of the deceased president's influence. People came from far and near, including powerful city and provincial figures, among them the *Landrat,* a high government official from Aachen, and the mayor. The secretary of the group, Superintendent

---

11. LK, Abt. 403, no. 7364, Bl. 553–54, "Statutes." In 1902–3, the membership stood at 1,236 and 1,130 respectively; while I do not have information on confessional distribution, the large proportion of women from the outlying rural districts was arguably Catholic. *Handbuch des Vaterländischen Frauen-Vereins* (Berlin, 1910), 688–89, Kreis Düren. In 1910, there was one city member for four members from outlying districts.

12. LK, Abt. 403, no. 7364, Bl. 463–68, Düsseldorf, August 29, 1891, concerning statutes of women's associations in the district. The correspondence and various handwritten exclamation points reveal how sensitive high government officials were to the statute changes.

and Pastor Müller, gave the main address; his "we" arguably represented the perspective of the association, and his address sought to communicate its values to the wider audience.

The pastor's eulogy interwove four themes. He began by reminding the audience of the specifics of the association's history under Mrs. Hoesch's guidance. He included a year-by-year chronicle of memorable events, which described the increasingly complex nature of the welfare services and the organizational growth throughout the hinterlands. Membership had risen from 137 to 1,236 over the sixteen years of her leadership, and wealth skyrocketed from a paltry 1,000 marks in 1886 to an impressive 405,000 marks in 1902, testifying to the cumulative impact of private donations and support.

The story of institutional growth offered the pastor a chance to praise the dedicated members of the association who, in his account, formed a tight community of activists welded together under the inspired leadership of the deceased president. It was her person, however, that stood at the center of attention; Pastor Müller went to considerable lengths to pen a vivid portrait of the personal attributes that so successfully had guided her life's work. His choices had much to say about issues of gender and service at the heart of patriotic voluntarism.

Mrs. Hoesch as public persona was foreground; the pastor essentially neglected the other roles of wife and mother, although at one point he turned to the audience and rhetorically questioned if *Verein* employees remembered how motherly *(mütterlich)* she had been toward them. Perhaps this was an extreme case; ascribed attributes of motherhood were central metaphors in patriotic discourse, even though they were slippery images that worked uneasily in public places. On another occasion, Mrs. Hoesch was described as a "shining example of true German womanhood" in startling similarity to the standard, oft-repeated descriptions of the *Landesmutter* who, invariably in the language of patriotism, was hailed as the "model" of an ideal German woman.[13] In this 1903 eulogy, the gender norms of female patriotic service and care had become part of civil society itself, operating independently of the dynastic context that had supported and spread them in the first place. Indeed, the institutional and cultural identifications associated with the monarchy were taking on a life no longer fully dependent on the person of the monarch herself.

---

13. *KZ,* no. 282, December 1, 1880, an anniversary ceremony of the Jülich women's association, where the *Landesmutter* was called "a true model of a German woman." Also, LK, Best. 661, 23, no. 156, Erinnerungen, Notizen, Quittungen, ceremony where the Conservative Reichstag member Albert von Levetzow called Augusta the "model of German womanhood" at her death, January 7, 1890.

As revealing, the pastor took considerable pains to distance Mrs. Hoesch from the wealth of her husband. To be sure, through the goodness of her spouse she had available the ample funds that she had used so generously to strengthen and support the association. Her portrait would soon join his on the walls of the *Verein* reception hall as a permanent tribute to the family's largesse and as an inspiration for the future. But the pastor stressed that her work began before "this source [of money] flowed freely" and exemplified "the ease and noblesse of giving" *(Leichtigkeit und Noblesse im Geben)*—the true source of her service—that had made her so irreplaceable. She was "a working woman, to whom doing her duty was a holy matter" *(eine arbeitende Frau, die es heilig ernst nahm mit ihrer Pflicht)*. Although unsalaried and a volunteer, nonetheless, in this milieu, she was described as a hardworking woman.

Pastor Müller praised other qualities, for example, the freshness and warmth that she brought to her work and, perhaps with a tinge of unease, described her own style of doing business. She was fearful of the typical bureaucratic approach of men—or so we learn from the eulogy—as critical, restrained, and bound by rational calculations. In contrast, she employed her own methods that the pastor admitted, perhaps here reflecting a male perspective, "we found amusing at times" but nonetheless remarkably effective. Through her approach, the association was not a "soulless machine but a living organism, indeed a community of the most distinct and diverse people *(eine Gemeinschaft verschiedenster Menschen)* bound together by personal respect, love, and friendship, and shared commitments to the common good."

Turning, then, to the third theme and central political message, the pastor artfully arrived at the point by quoting Mrs. Hoesch herself. She had kept the association's "protocol," a daily reckoning of the purposes and goals of this "pure humanitarian" organization. He chose to read her last entry, a description of the annual festival (which she had instituted) that linked the different members from the city and countryside in ritual and festive exchange. Recurring festivals, she had written, were opportunities to bring together very different groups of people committed to the same principles and weld them as members of *one* association (the emphasis is in the original) through face-to-face contacts in time set aside from daily routines. According to the pastor, the bonds that were forged through common humanitarian service was "her favorite idea *(Lieblingsgedanke)*, yes," he added, "it was part of her religion, her personal belief system, to find ways to bridge the divisive barriers of religious affiliation and encourage people to good deeds *(zu guter Tat)*." In worldly terms, humanitarian acts expressed deep-seated religious imperatives that helped create a wider sense of community linked in service. The ritual spaces, in turn, served to span differences, mediate misunderstandings, and, as importantly, reinvigorate the routines of administrative life.

The specific physiognomy of "difference" was understood by speaker and audience alike. Patriotic philanthropy, which drew on values of female service and sacrifice deeply rooted in the Christian tradition, appealed to people of diverse religious backgrounds precisely because it joined groups who had a common social grounding in privilege and power; its horizontal stretch reached the well-off groups in the industrial city and towns of the Rhineland—wives of successful businessmen and professionals and those of state and municipal officials as well as adjacent aristocratic estate owners and other titled noblemen. Poor working-class wives were clients not members, and, certainly, there were no advocates of socialism in the ranks; indeed, partisan politics and party affiliations were kept veiled and muted.[14] The "community" through ritual commemoration and daily exchange was rhetorically inclusive, in practice socially limited and formally placed outside the sphere of politics. It was linked, however, directly to the dynastic state. Coming full circle, the pastor ended his address by invoking the sanctions of the state, which had acknowledged and rewarded the multiple patriotic efforts in Düren; Mrs. Hoesch had been the recipient of various Prussian honors, including the Order of Luise, the Service Medal for Women and Young Ladies and the Red Cross Medal of the second and third class.

A commitment to personal gift-giving was the central value of dynastic philanthropy—its self- and projected image. The funeral oration in Düren, not surprisingly then, framed its commemoration around the pervasive symbol of giving—enclosing the life's work of Mrs. Hoesch in a vocabulary that sustained and shaped "reality" for those involved in patriotic services. These values worked for those on the outside looking in, as well as for those serving on the inside, cementing relationships among the women and men donating their labor and money and linking them to the power and aura of the dynastic court.

Ritual Correspondence between Court and Civil Society

While overlooking the specific appeal of the gift metaphor in patriotic service altogether, many recent German historians have tended to dismiss these forms of ritual interactions and commendations as either irrelevant for understanding politics or blatant examples of ideological manipulation

---

14. LK, Abt. 403, no. 7365, *Jahresbericht* (1903). These social divides are clear in the protocol: clients are working women *(Arbeiterinnen)* and association members are ladies *(Damen)*.

from above.[15] The assessment, however, misses the significant psychological appeal of the power of personal relationships to women and men in dynastic service, which added a vitality and emotional content to the otherwise bare, rational institutional nexus that connected the associations to one another throughout Germany.

Political identification was expressed through the various grammatical transformations of *Anteilnahme* (interest and sympathy) and *Teilnahme* (collaboration), the two most common words in the syntax of patriotism. For many association members, the *Landesmutter* was neither remote nor abstract. As the president of the Koblenz charity society St. Barbara put it in the mid-1850s, Augusta was its "most active patron" *(thätigste Beschutzerin)*, embodying the virtues of "charity" and "mercy" . . . to ease not only the suffering of the poor and abandoned but also ward off the whole fount of calamities." In turn, the association members offered their profound "veneration" and "gratitude."[16] Similarly, the duchess Luise of Baden, patron of the state's remarkably successful Women's Association during the imperial era, was so involved in the daily life of the Karlsruhe central association *(Hauptverein)* that she helped build up its library, regularly offering suggestions for books to purchase and sending members copies of works for possible adoption; when in town, she attended the final exams of the Red Cross nurses' aides *(Helferinnen)* in the years before World War I.[17]

The political implications of these mutual relations are revealed in the correspondence that flowed behind the glare of the public limelight: the exchange of letters between association members and the dynast. The example takes us back to the most powerful and prestigious philanthropic organization in Koblenz, the St. Barbara Association. Its leadership maintained regular contact with Augusta from 1852, when she became its patron, until her death in 1890. The ties then were established with her daughter Luise of Baden, who took over protection of this Prussian *Verein*

---

15. There has been little work done on the politics of royal patronage in nineteenth-century "Germany," even though John Röhl correctly points out that it is difficult to understand the Wilhelmine era, for example, without the court (*Der Ort Kaiser Wilhelms II,* vii–viii). For his persuasive account of the mechanism of monarchical rule, "Der 'Königsmechanismus' im Kaiserreich," in *Kaiser, Hof und Staat,* 116–40. A recent exception is Margaret Jarchow, *Hofgeschenke: Zwischen Dynastie und Diplomatie* (Hamburg, 1998).

16. LK, Best. 661, 23, no. 153, Correspondence, Koblenz, June 5, 1854, president of St. Barbara to Augusta.

17. GK, Abt. 69, no. 889, Berichte der Abt. III des Frauenvereins und Antworteten, May 21, 1901, concerning an exchange of books with the Central Committee of the Red Cross. Also, no. 1117, Mitteilungen (communiqué), Karlsruhe, June 6, 1908, and February 24, 1908.

until her death in 1923. These years reflected the shifting fortunes in the tense relations between Catholics and Protestants in Prussia and Germany. Mutually beneficial relationships were cemented through the correspondence, however; the rhetoric of sympathy and collaboration both expressed these values and at the same time created them.[18]

Over the many years, association letters were penned by Mrs. Luise Huyn and subsequently her unmarried daughter of the same name, reflecting the longevity of leadership and intergenerational ties that bound associational women together in local communities like Koblenz and Düren. The association was a model of Catholic charity in the Catholic Rhineland. And that was the point for the Protestant Hohenzollern dynasty after the turmoil of 1848. The court's philanthropic strategy never simply proved to be integrative but was part of political struggle and negotiation that revealed powerful fissures and pressures at court as well as in society. Augusta herself became the lightning rod for radical Protestant wrath against any accommodation with Catholics, antagonisms that were particularly virulent during the Prussian *Kulturkampf* (1871–78). In addition, from the early 1860s on she had an exceptionally poor relationship with Count Bismarck, who disdained her religious inclinations and opposed on principle any semblance of a woman's involvement in the affairs of state.[19]

Her name, nonetheless, elicited considerable loyalty, cemented by the practice of institutional patronage and involvement. After moving to Koblenz with William, who had been named military governor of the rebellious province in 1850, the crown princess Augusta became more active in philanthropy: that step rounded out a Hohenzollern strategic triad, which offset the unmistakable power and authority of the Prussian army with conciliatory efforts at economic growth and attention to charitable undertakings. Augusta immediately presided over a ceremony in 1852 that transferred the administration of the orphanage and the girls' school to Catholic nuns. The change permitted the women of St. Barbara, who previously had run the institution, to turn to all manner of welfare for the families of the poor students; each family came under the exacting "support" *(Schutz)* of two association members. Through regular monthly visitations, they personally oversaw the life situations of poor

---

18. The analysis is drawn from the letters in LK, Best. 661, 23, no. 153, correspondence with Augusta; and no. 154, Dank-und Grüssadressen der Grossherzogin Luise, 1861–1918.

19. Political tensions swirled around Augusta's memory, mobilized in the context of publications of biographies of her life. For example, GK, Abt. 69, nos. 191–94, Biografie der Kaiserin Augusta von Frau von Adelsfeld, 1900, 1902–4, contains clippings of numerous reviews. Bismarck made no effort to hide his difficulties with Augusta. Otto von Bismarck, *Gedanken und Erinnerungen,* vol. 2 (Berlin, 1900), 101–2, 132, 147–49, 183, 195, 320–22.

clients and hashed out the extent and nature of the support at monthly meetings.[20]

The ties cemented by the correspondence between the Hohenzollern dynastic house and the Catholic St. Barbara *Verein* in Koblenz demonstrate the mutual advantages to both sides. Otherwise, the intense and intimate nature of the exchange between the leadership on the one hand, and Augusta and, subsequently, her daughter Luise on the other, would not have been sustained for over half a century. For *Verein* members, the dynastic house was an alternative source of identity and power—if need be distinct even from the Prussian bureaucratic state. Paradoxically, the dynastic presence sustained old personalistic values and influence in the ongoing evolution of political relations and state activities in Germany.

Augusta's continued support of Catholics during the *Kulturkampf,* including the women of St. Barbara, was an obvious source of solace to the organization at the time and an important component of institutional memory, which helped shape the association's ongoing work in Wilhelmine Germany. As Augusta expressed it to the executive committee in April 1879, her "care" *(Fürsorge)* for the orphanage compelled her to respond to the dismissal, under the harsh anti-Catholic laws, of the sisters, many of whom sought refuge in Holland. She offered her personal thanks for their "selfless, successful, and blessed work," gave a cash gift to the mother superior and, as a common symbol of remembrance, a cross as well.[21] Between 1879 and 1898, when a new Catholic order of nuns took over the orphanage and school again, lay association women had to administer the institutions. The orphanage continued to support its "free school," which, however, was put under the authority of the municipality; the women teachers all were licensed by the Prussian state. The city entered into a contract with the association to rent the rooms for the girls' classes. At the start, these were held in the old familiar building, but demand was so great that there soon was an "overcrowding" and the city had to make other provisions.

It was precisely the reputation of St. Barbara that had encouraged

---

20. Here is revealed the harsh regime in which association mothers were authoritarian figures, dispensing gifts in return for proper behavior and intervening directly into the lives of the families who sent their children to the school. The visit was carefully orchestrated to match "gifts" with scrutiny about the deportment of the children. *Verein* members were instructed to offer "advice, consolation, and encouragement" but also administer "warnings" and "reprimands." The school also was organized hierarchically, with clear prescriptions about deportment and behavior for matrons, teachers, and students, alike. For details, LK, Best. 661, 23, no. 95, Verhandlungen über die Übernahme der Mädchenfreischule, particularly January 7, 1853, the rules and regulations establishing the sisters' and association women's roles.

21. LK, Best. 661, 23, no. 95, Dankadresse der Kaiserin Augusta, April 5, 1879.

poorer Koblenz families to send their girls to the "secular" school, indirectly overseen by the elite Catholic women. To be sure, religious affinities never fully dampened class antagonisms in Koblenz, or elsewhere; at the time, there was grousing about the "rich women" who were concerned mainly with their bazaars and collections, leaving the deserving poor "out in the cold." But the Prussian anti-Catholic legislation encouraged community support of the girls' school, so closely tied into the Catholic charitable tradition.[22] Besides, the type of instruction was popular; the young orphans and students received specific training for low-level, white-collar jobs like telephone operators and sales clerks that were opening up for women in the evolving urban economy. Furthermore, there never was a break in relations with Augusta; when in town in the 1880s, she attended the association's regular Friday meetings.

Indeed, the correspondence expressed an intimacy that was sustained by face-to-face contact as well as by the memory of the personal connections, kept alive by the exchange of letters itself. It had a rhythm that was partly calendrical: the mutual greetings at the new year or the regular solicitation and response for the *Verein*'s annual auction. And it followed the emotional moments of the life cycle as well: the death of Augusta's father (1853), the birth of her grandson (1859), or a letter from Luise at the death of the long-standing member of the executive committee, Frau Rottmann (1903). These ties were cemented by gifts, and many letters were written on the occasion of gift giving and receiving. In the 1860s, for example, Augusta augmented the money made from the annual benefit concerts to the tune of six gold Frederick coins; she gave the association extra clothing at Christmas with an understanding that the clothes, in turn, would be given out to the poor and needy. This custom of gift giving was taken over by Luise.

The women of St. Barbara felt "empowered" by Augusta's involvement in *Verein* affairs to give her gifts as well, partly to assure the continued "protection" from above. In 1854, for example, at the time of a statewide celebration of Augusta's wedding anniversary (July 11), they sent her a small token *(eine kleine Gabe)* of their "veneration" and "gratitude." The gift was a picture of St. Barbara herself, "mother of the poor." The members, too, had joined the celebration as "loyal inhabitants of the monarchy" for whom their secular and religious mothers essentially were one in common concern for the suffering of the poor and the destitute. From her side, Augusta interpreted the correspondence as proof of loyalty

---

22. LK, Best. 661, 23, no. 95, August 24, 1881, chief mayor of Koblenz, and March 21, 1882. Also, Petra Habrock-Henrich, "Berufung statt Beruf," 66, mentions the social tensions that appeared in a novel by the Koblenz writer Bertha Augusti, *A Fateful Year (Ein verhäng-nisvolles Jahr),* in 1879.

(die treue Anhänglichkeit) and faithfulness *(Treue)*, expressions of political legitimacy that extended into the Catholic community of Prussia. Her letters regularly began with pleasure in *Verein* loyalty (and the contact reinforce it). The exchange opened venues to articulate joint values of a common Christian nature that linked dynasty and association in "gentle" *(zarte)* deeds: their shared "work of Christian love," commitment to piety, faithfulness in fulfilling one's calling, indeed, would be consummated by God's blessings.

At Augusta's death, the Verein immediately established contact with Luise, insuring her "participation" and patronage. They called themselves the most subservient subjects *(unterthänigsten)*—a vocabulary employed throughout the period by Patriotic Women's Association members elsewhere when addressing the monarchy. Ironically, the trope was the avenue for these elite groups to enter into a realm of equivalence with the dynast. The letter was filled with deep pathos and empathy that identified the members and Luise as one: "your Majesty lost your precious mother, but wasn't our noble empress mother of the poor and needy? So we feel we are able to join our pain with the pain of the noble daughter and mourn with you."[23]

The correspondence with Luise lasted throughout the Wilhelmine period. It, too, was personal and intimate; for example, at the fiftieth wedding anniversary celebration for Frederick and Luise in 1906, Luise Huyn inquired how the aging duchess was feeling and whether the festivities had tired her out. For both sides, the letters were a chance to reminisce about Luise as a child attending *Verein* meetings with Augusta. These stories kept alive and meaningful the memory of Augusta's patronage and direct involvement in the affairs of the association.

From her side, the letters of Luise willy-nilly reflect the changing values that, in effect, were overwhelming the old dynastic houses in late Wilhelmine Germany. To be sure, she used every opportunity to affirm her pleasure in the "old proven custom" *(alte bewährte Gewohnheit)* that the exchange of letters still embodied. Indeed, this exchange was so important to the duchess precisely because of the institutional growth that was outstripping the monarchical reach in civil society. The old form of personal "collaboration" was at stake and was perpetuated consciously in the correspondence with the associations under dynastic patronage. But even if a growing number of social and relief organizations conducted business with no reference to the dynasty, monarchical groups were not fully out of touch with social change, either. In the early twentieth century, the corre-

---

23. LK, Best. 661, 23, no. 153, Koblenz, "Aller unterthänigsten Vorstand des Frauenverein von St. Barbara," n.d. (around 1890).

spondence shows that old "proven" customs could accommodate new content. Luise was kept informed of thoroughly "modern," if equally moderate, approaches to the "woman's question," for example. In 1910, St. Barbara members were encouraged to attend a lecture in Koblenz by a representative of the Association of Catholic Women and Girls, a politically moderate women's organization concerned with the necessity of appropriate training and wage work for girls.[24]

The ties that had been reinforced through long years of mutual exchange proved politically beneficial for both parties. In 1910, St. Barbara faced a crisis, or so Fräulein Huyn claimed in seeking an immediate audience with Luise. In effect, the "women and men" of the executive committee sought the personal intervention of the duchess of Baden, with whom they had maintained a long, successful relationship, to do an end run around the Prussian bureaucracy.

St. Barbara was in financial trouble; after considerable time and effort, the association had obtained funds to build a more modern orphanage, which had opened with considerable fanfare and much celebration in 1908 (the details were disclosed to Luise in letters because illness had kept her away). According to a report prepared for the Baden court, the new building accommodated two hundred orphans, but currently only one hundred were in residence. The *Verein* wanted to supplement its income temporarily by opening up its empty rooms to young professional women (precisely the types it had been educating over the years). These reputable girls, then, could find a safe haven in the *Verein* walls. However, local inns and private lodging establishments regarded the move by St. Barbara as "an unwelcomed competition." The Prussian Cultural Ministry, indeed, had turned down the request, even though it was elegantly crafted to downplay the role of the nuns, highlight the laywomen members and stress the association's long commitment to educating the young German women in "Christian and patriotic sentiments."[25] But the intervention of Luise with the kaiser, who in war and peace still held ultimate authority for all manner of political decisions in Germany, was the critical factor. The ministry reversed itself. Needless to say, the subsequent letters were effusive in their thanks and in reaffirming the ties that had been so effective.

But the benefits to the dynasty were not inconsequential, either. The

24. LK, Best. 661, 23, no. 154, Koblenz, October 21, 1910, artisanal chamber to the executive committees of the women's associations.

25. GK, Abt. 69, no. 940, letter from Luise Huyn, January 31, 1910, including a copy of the petition to the minister of culture, August von Trott zu Solz in Berlin, as well as the report for the Baden court prepared by the president of the Rhine province, Koblenz, January 23, 1910.

Catholic association affirmed its loyalty, and letters assured the royalty that the students and orphans in their charge "prayed" for them and that the young children were reminded daily of dynastic generosity at the heart of legitimate rule. In World War I, St. Barbara unequivocally joined the war effort and placed its building and personnel at the service of wounded soldiers. Like the many philanthropic groups in Germany that had been preparing for war under dynastic supervision, the members' nationalist identity and service for the fatherland continued to be framed by identification and collaboration with the dynastic houses. Furthermore, this form of exchange was not an isolated case; for example, clusters of letters from local Baden state women's associations to the duchess celebrating dynastic family events such as births, marriages, christenings and deaths are preserved in the archives under the rubric "good wishes."[26]

Growth of the Women's Associations in Imperial Germany

The correspondence that continuously flowed between dynastic house and associational headquarters expressed the volunteers' self-understanding of philanthropic service, an identity that was shaped, however, by the ties of patronage and the sense of personal involvement of the *Landesmutter.* From whatever vantage point or motive, it reveals much about the values that sustained a voluntary civic activism in the imperial period.

Participation in what increasingly was understood as "national" life had a powerful attraction for generations of privileged women from the centers to the remotest corners of the newly unified nation. In the early twentieth century, reform feminists even gave patriotic women a backhanded compliment, although they distanced themselves from the conservative gender implications of charity. The feminist *Handbook,* edited by Helene Lange and Gertrud Bäumer in 1901, offered the following assessment of Patriotic Women's Associations: "for a long time [they have] occupied a leading place in women's social work," the editors wrote. "Germany has no other equivalently large women's organization serving poor relief and municipal welfare."[27] And the statistics bear out the judgment, even if the statement casts patriotic women's activities much too narrowly in the framework of municipal social services alone. It therefore masks the significance of charity for cultural politics as well as the tragedies of war and nationalism.

Table 2 offers a statistical overview of the growth of women's associ-

---

26. GK, Abt. 69, no. 169, Glückwünsche verschiedener Frauenvereine, clustered in 1878 and 1882.

27. Alice Salomon, "Die Frau in der sozialen Hilfstätigkeit," in Lange and Bäumer, *Handbuch der Frauenbewegung,* 2:28.

ations in the states of Prussia, Baden, and Bavaria in select years between 1870–71 and 1916, the three most important states sustaining women's Red Cross activities. The table shows that in Prussia, for example, the most significant institutional growth occurred after 1880, increasing 42 percent in the decade and nearly doubling between 1890 and 1908. The rate of growth slowed to 18 percent between 1909 and World War I. In wartime, however, membership again increased significantly. Among a population of roughly 37 million in 1908, there was one Patriotic Women's Association member for every ninety-eight inhabitants of Prussia. The table does not include the many local philanthropic groups involved in patriotic work as, for example, the Prussian Women's and Young Ladies' Association in Berlin.

TABLE 2.   Development of Women's Associations in Prussia, Baden, and Bavaria in Select Years, 1860–1916

	Baden		Bavaria		Prussia	
	Branch Associations	Membership	Branch Associations	Membership	Branch Associations	Membership
1860	24	—	—	—	—	—
1865	59	—	—	—	—	—
1866	—	—	—	—	44	—
1870	63	7,980	131[a]	—	364[b]	36,740
1875	91	7,233	—	—	—	—
1876	—	—	—	—	383	32,219
1879	—	—	—	—	493	50,000
1880	103	11,618	—	—	—	—
1885	112	15,170	—	—	—	—
1890	152	20,983	—	—	700	90,000
1891	—	—	—	—	772	105,958
1895	224	31,671	—	—	—	—
1896	—	—	278	31,097	—	—
1900	294	46,007	289	35,783	—	—
1905	359	66,582	334	47,069	—	—
1907	—	—	340	50,346	1,321	395,054
1908	391	75,000	345	52,352	1,393	420,726
1909	398	76,893	346	55,154	1,455	450,269
1913	—	—	—	—	1,647	557,000
1916	—	—	—	—	2,330	800,000

Source: DRK, 2: 69, 74, 90–91, 94–96, 214, 242, 260, 297, 350, 364, 410–11; GK, Abt. 69, no. 951b, Das 50-jährige Jubiläum des Badischen Frauenvereins am 16. und 17. Juni 1909, Literarisches Bureau, clipping of *Deutscher Reichsanzeiger,* Berlin, June 19, 1909; GSPK, Zivil Kabinett, no. 15613, Bl. 17–19, August 21, 1916.

[a]Composed of 1 central, 8 district, and 122 branch associations.

[b]With the outbreak of the Franco-German War, the number of associations rose by 74 adding 13,124 new members at the end of the year.

Similarly, the statistics for Baden embrace only the formal member-ship of the state's *Frauen-Verein*. The table reveals more steady growth over the period, from a membership of nearly eight thousand in 1870 to nearly seventy-seven thousand in 1909. That year, the fiftieth anniversary celebration of the association's founding, newspaper accounts show that nearly one in seven Baden women over twenty-five was a member of the *Frauen-Verein,* while one in four municipalities had an active branch asso-ciation.[28] These are impressive statistics, testifying to the depth and breadth of the association's appeal. In Bavaria, growth reached a plateau in the decade prior to World War I.

In the smaller affiliated states in imperial Germany, women's patri-otic voluntarism typically was more specialized and increasingly tied into the medical sides of war preparation. The Alice-Verein in Hesse, for exam-ple, concentrated on nursing training; in 1908 in addition to its main asso-ciation in Mainz, it had seventeen branch and two affiliated organizations and a membership of forty-seven hundred. Similarly, in Saxony, members of the Albert-Verein had devoted their organizational and financial efforts to establishing the Carola House, a hospital for nursing training named after Queen Carola, who had been instrumental in supporting the work of the association. It opened in 1878. Figure 2 is a Saxon poster from the First World War raising money for war work by appealing to the old polit-ical legitimacies that had welded imperial Germany together, however imperfectly, as a monarchical nation of dynastic states.[29] It honors the memory of the queen, whose care and concern are evoked by the cupids gesturing toward her. Red Cross strategy clearly sought to solicit public donations by an appeal to this dynastic institute, which had been such a familiar landmark in the local landscape. The memory of its ministerings made it a useful rallying point. So did the promise of the wealth to be won in the lottery; this, too, was an older instrument, marking the emerging consumer culture of late-nineteenth-century Germany. And use of the complementary red and green colors on the original poster added to the emotional force of the poster. In 1907, the Albert Association had forty-four affiliates and a membership of nearly eight thousand.

In the Duchy of Weimar, the Patriotic Institute maintained its older philanthropic profile. In 1908, it supported 8 main and 197 branch associ-ations, with emphasis still on industrial and domestic schooling for girls, cooking classes, nursery schools, and soup kitchens, but it also was spon-soring nursing stations throughout the state. In Württemberg, after the

---

28. GK, Abt. 69, no. 951b, Das 50-jährige Jubiläum des Badischen Frauenvereins am 16. und 17. Juni 1909, Literarisches Bureau Clemens Freyer, June 19, 1909.

29. GE 222, HIA. I want to thank the Hoover Institution for giving me permission to reproduce these posters. Also, DRK, 2: Hesse, 158–60; Saxony, 630–31.

Fig. 2. Lottery to support the Queen Carola Foundation honoring her memory and the Red Cross, 1915. (Courtesy Hoover Institution Archives, Poster Collection, GE 222.)

state's relief association, Wohltätigkeits-Verein, affiliated with the Union of German Women's Associations, the focus of women's work, too, centered on nursing training. In 1880, even the Duchy of Mecklenberg founded a small women's association (the Marien-Frauen Verein). Membership grew slowly but steadily, rising over 60 percent from 1,281 members at the outset to 3,340 in 1908.[30]

By numbers of members alone, women's patriotic organizations under the Red Cross had a significant place in German associational life. In some cases, most notably Prussia and Baden, the relationship of member per inhabitant was striking, made doubly so because voluntarism attracted a distinct group of privileged women. The diary of Baroness Spitzemberg, which she kept faithfully over the latter half of the nineteenth century—from 1859 to 1914—offers a vivid portrait of patriotic philanthropy in the life of a well-heeled and connected woman.[31]

Born Hildegard von Varnbüler, the baroness grew up in the aristocratic milieu of Württemberg before finally settling in Berlin. Her father was a prominent estate owner (von und zu Hemmingen, located west of Stuttgart) in a state that had few old landed noble families; he was involved in dynastic state service until 1870. While the family's wealth remained in land, he helped manage a machine factory of his in-laws in Vienna and over the years also dabbled in investments in banking and other enterprises, which reinforced his ties to wider economic and political circles, as the diary shows. The baron also was a passionate "humanitarian" who, in 1866, had formed one of the earliest wartime voluntary medical units *(Sanitätsverein)*; but rumors surrounding his so-called personal regiment led to his dismissal from state service in 1870.[32] The family was Protestant, and although Hildegard married a Catholic—Carl Hugo von Spitzemberg, a Württemberg diplomat in St. Petersburg, Bern, and, after 1866, in Berlin—she raised her three children Protestant.

To be sure, the baroness was a more typical follower than a leader, although she served on the executive committees of several prominent philanthropic organizations in Berlin and, as such, was granted formal audiences at court. But she also was part of Berlin high society by "birth" and "marriage" and a keen observer of its life, manners, morals, and secrets. A close supporter of Otto von Bismarck and his wife Johanna (and her life's work, the charitable Frauengroschen-Verein), in later years she fell in with the circle around the foreign minister Friedrich von Holstein

30. *DRK,* 2: Mecklenberg, 185; Württemberg, 650–64; Weimar, 642.

31. *Tagebuch der Baronin Spitzemberg.* Since the diary was long and detailed, by his own admission (35), the editor Vierhaus omitted many of the references to charitable undertakings and lectures; what remains, nonetheless, is revealing of their importance in her life.

32. *Tagebuch der Baronin Spitzemberg,* 19–21, 100–101, 103–6.

through close family ties to Klotilde von Wedel-Malchow, wife of a Junker *Rittergut* owner, who served on the Central Executive Committee of the Patriotic Women's Association in the early twentieth century. As high society, furthermore, she often joined prominent patriotic association leaders at public ceremonies; for example, she accompanied the state minister von Boetticher and his wife to the Augusta Stiftung in March 1887 to help "test" the young pupils. Willing to lend her good name to the cause, these traditions "for show" (and she uses the English words) seemed misplaced somehow, given "all the real work done" in these institutions by the ladies. Over the years, too, she socialized with various bourgeois members of the Central Committee of the Patriotic Women's Association at private dinners and gatherings: the director Eck and the banker Krause and his wife as well as the wealthy Hansemann and Borsig families.[33] These social alliances were never simple; in Berlin, patriotic committees opened working spaces for collaboration distinct from, yet intertwined with, high society, although many were never simultaneously regarded by the old Prussian nobility as *Hoffähig*—no matter how many times they had been at court—which left them "livid" *(bitterböse)*.

Consistently conservative—the baroness was uncomfortable with the turn to mass politics of the Agrarian League—she was nonetheless cosmopolitan, well-read, loved history and delighted in the company of artists and intellectuals. Despite her long sojourn in Berlin, her perspective remained decidedly hybrid—blending an abiding identification with her Württemberg *Heimat* with what was becoming Deutschland. Within the new territorial borders, furthermore, she wanted to reconcile south German Catholics with Protestants. In this regard, her personal politics matched well the official nationalist effort to create patriotic subjectivities through an interdenominational emphasis on Christian "deeds." If she betrayed a visceral anti-Semitism—the diary is filled with nasty stereotypes about Jewish influence and behavior—she became a committed Dreyfusard; significantly in the early 1880s, with the rise of grassroots anti-Semitic political mobilization in the streets of Berlin, she attended synagogue with her sons and like-minded Christians as show of support. Her racial stereotyping, however, was matched by an equally pervasive antifemale rhetoric: the ills of the age were dismissed as *weibisch,* a shorthand critique that she leveled against opponents of her father or those who failed to honor Bismarck's memory, the socialists in general—indeed, even against "modernity" itself.[34] With no apparent contradiction as woman, she often joined a normative male Christian voice, reproducing the mas-

33. Ibid., 132, 137, 146–47, 229 (for the excursion with the von Boettichers).

34. Ibid., 100–101, 194, 327–28, 389, 436, 520, 526.

culine perspective within which women had to negotiate their own place. Her work with other women in patriotic service was one such space.

Her organizational apprenticeship began in St. Petersburg, where her new husband was stationed as diplomat in 1864. Immediately she entered, and apparently ran for a time, a so-called German Charity Association (Deutscher Wohltätigkeits-Verein), holding regular meetings with the ladies' committee, raising money, and attending benefit events. On foreign soil, this work—modeled on the Württemberg state relief association— nonetheless served to forge "German" community identity. It testifies to the psychological linkages between self-conscious activity and the acquisition of identity.

The many references over the years to the time and energy that she put into volunteer service made this work a conscious part of her life. Her membership in the Prussian women's association was noted by a simple statement on July 29, 1870: "several days ago I joined the Patriotic Women's Association."[35] The entries also show the social mechanisms that prompted self-reflection: the various medals that she received from the state for philanthropic service and the annual festivals and commemorations prompted her to think back and evaluate the evolving present in light of an imagined (indeed, often frozen) historic past. And they reveal the security of routines: the monthly women's meetings held during the winter season in Berlin to accommodate the lifestyle of aristocrats, many of whom spent summers on their estates or at spas, to return to the capital only with the opening of parliament and the Prussian chambers. This rhythm also organized the parallel work of the "Sewing Society" (Nähverein) under the direction of Mrs. Noedelchen, wife of a Berlin city official, and Patriotic Women's Association Executive Committee member for over forty years; for decades also during the winter season her group met every Thursday between 10:00 A.M. and 2:00 P.M. to coordinate the making and stockpiling of medical bandages and other hospital supplies, later adding undergarments and clothing for infants and the sick that were given away at Christmastime as well. The members subcontracted part of the work to poorer widows and other women in the city.[36] Significantly, this was an all-woman enterprise; it had been formalized in 1866, when the Patriotic Women's Association emerged through collaboration with men, and it was sustained over the years as a space for women alone to gather outside their homes and develop, organize, and finance a set of relief activities.

For Baroness Spitzemberg and, arguably, the women of the Sewing

---

35. Ibid., 96.

36. *Handbuch des Vaterländischen Frauen-Vereins,* 6. A long report on the work of the Sewing Society is in *KZ,* supplement to no. 493, October 20, 1893.

Society as well, there were the planning and staffing of booths at charity bazaars, the pleasure at successful strategies to raise money, and regular attendance at ad hoc benefit events responding to natural disasters. At times, the baroness took her daughter Hanna along, turning participation into a family event. The diary reveals personal choices, for example, deliberations in 1887 whether to join the executive committee of a new women's association to provide baths for ill children at the seaside; despite, as she puts it, a mounting "burden of work" *(Arbeitslast)* she does so. But outside these formal institutional structures, too, acts of charity were a regular part of domestic life. We learn from the diary that Countess von Itzenplitz, for example, had opened her house to a young well-born woman whose family had fallen on hard times.[37]

Through the eyes of the baroness, philanthropy reflected a deepseated religiosity and helped fashion an identity rooted in "goodness through deeds" *(Gute in Taten)*, a striking echo to the words spoken at the funeral in Düren. The pulls of this orientation inform her emotional responses to the lectures that she attended over the years and to her detailed observations of social and political life around her. "Inactive" *(tatenlos)* was a word of derision.[38] In the secular milieu of patriotic philanthropy—seemingly above the fray of politics—she could practice her religious ideals, keeping them alive and vibrant as a fundamental definition of self. This commitment to action gave meaning and purpose to life. It forged bonds among women through time spent together but linked them inextricably to like-minded men, with whom they collaborated, socialized, corresponded, and traveled—and whom they observed from a distance as well. Her numerous references to sitting in the audience witnessing intense moments of parliamentary debate and speechmaking bring home the point. Hildegard von Spitzemberg used philanthropy as a stepping stone to a wider community, rooted in gendered service and committed to a Christian ethic of care through purposeful charitable acts.

These gender ties remained a common feature of patriotic philanthropy throughout the *Kaiserreich.* Thus, for example, the Directory of the Saxon Albert Association in 1909 was divided evenly between eight women and eight men. In Prussia that same year, the numbers were weighted slightly toward women, and, significantly, there was a much greater continuity among the female as opposed to male leaders in the tight inner circles that did the day-to-day administrative and conceptual work. As we have seen, Charlotte von Itzenplitz, president of the Central Executive Committee and her representative, Marie Noeldechen, had

37. *Tagebuch der Baronin Spitzemberg,* 220, 232, 235, 359–61, 269, 391.
38. Ibid., 361, 413–14.

assumed their leadership posts already in the mid-1860s; and while this was true also for the treasurer, the banker Krause, the two other male members of the inner circle, Dr. Kühne (as secretary) and imperial minister von Müller (speaker of the assembly) only had come on board in 1909. Dr. Kühne's professional career, which landed him a state government post in the judiciary *(Oberverwaltungsgerichtsrat),* had been accompanied by a parallel rise in the institutional hierarchy of the Patriotic Women's Association. He had been a member of its executive committee in Danzig and served as provincial secretary in West Prussia before his election to the Central Executive Committee in Berlin. He had been a member of the committee twelve years before becoming its secretary in 1909.[39]

In all, women comprised 59 percent (for a total of twenty-two) of the Prussian Central Executive Committee membership in 1909, all titled, and a full half were from Germany's old hereditary estate nobility: countesses and princesses, including several wives of entailed East Elbian estate owners but also Princess zu Wied and Countess von Berckheim, whose husband was part of the Baden mission at the Berlin court. Their presence brought geographic balance, as did Dr. Sieveking, who came from Alsace-Lorraine. Five other members simultaneously held official appointments at court. Occupationally, seven were wives of former or present ministers of state, and two were bankers' wives: Ottilie von Hansemann and Sophie Henschel. Sophie Henschel also was plugged into the state's honorific infrastructure: together with Charlotte von Itzenplitz, she served on a committee that gave out the Order of Luise, second class, Prussia's highest decoration for women's state service. Two additional members, Elizabeth zu Hohenlohe-Schillingsfürst and Marie von Ratibor, were from great aristocratic Catholic families that had sided with the liberal state in its cultural policies against Catholics. Of the male members, five were medical doctors, one was a major in the army, and three were simultaneously members of the German Red Cross (and Baron von dem Knesebeck also was chamberlain to the empress). The heart of this Prussian committee, then, lay in its ties to state service and medical expertise; it reflected a diverse geographic base; and, in its bow to interdenominationalism, the alliances reproduced the growing Catholic accommodation to the state.[40]

---

39. *DRK,* 2:336, 350–52, 637–38.

40. Information on occupational and social background is derived from *Handbuch über den Königlich Preussischen Hof und Staat für das Jahr 1909* (Berlin, 1908), 46, 57, 73, 297, 340; John C. G. Röhl, *The Kaiser and His Court: Wilhelm II and the Government of Germany,* trans. Terence F. Cole (Cambridge, 1994), 138, 148, 252, 269; *Tagebuch der Baronin Spitzemberg,* 568–612, short biographical sketches; and Radziwill, *Memories of Forty Years,* 129–42, on the "upper 10" in Berlin society.

Table 3 presents the Baden leadership of the Central Women's Association and Men's Relief Society in Karlsruhe, 1872–73. Several observations are in order. Women leaders came from decidedly higher social status than men in the separate, equivalent societies. The table shows that of the heads of the four sections, three were baronesses and, in one case, Betty Molitor, her husband was a state official. In three of the four cases, they had been part of the original eighteen-woman committee that had founded the state *Frauen-Verein* with the duchess in 1859; the one new participant, Countess von Berstett, had married into an old aristocratic landowning family in Baden.[41] Six of the active members of the subcommittees also were original founders. Aristocratic women were no mere figureheads. For the past thirteen years they had been setting policy, overseeing personnel, and tending to the day-to-day administrative details that kept the sections running smoothly.

The table also shows the gender balance in the early years of the Baden State Red Cross organization. Men comprised a significant proportion of the leadership as directors and advisors. On the executive committee of the women's association, for example, was a councillor in the Department of Justice, another in Commerce, a retired medical military official, and a penal official. Significantly, Section III, Nursing (the code word for the medical side to war planning), had four male members, the largest of any section, and three of the members served simultaneously on the State Relief Association (Badischer Landes-Hilfs-Verein) of the Red Cross, the organization tied into the army and responsible for coordinating civilian war preparation work throughout Baden and with the other states in imperial Germany. No woman served as delegate on this important state committee, even though its composition was divided between representatives of the Women's and the Men's Relief Associations, although Duchess Luise regularly attended the meetings.

Membership lists for branch associations in Baden offer another perspective from which to assess social composition and confessional ties, although they do not provide the rich texture of personal meanings found in diaries and letters. But in several cases, unexpectedly, archival sources included handwritten notes on confession in the more standard information on social and occupational backgrounds. Baden was a confessionally

---

41. *Gothaischer Genealogischer Hofkalender nebst Diplomatisch-statistischem Jahrbuch 1872,* vol. 109 (Gotha, 1872), 337–39; *Gothaisches Genealogisches Taschenbuch der freiherrlichen Häuser,* vol. 22 (Gotha, 1872), 36, 247; Ernst Heinrich Kneschke, ed., *Neues allgemeines Deutsches Adels-Lexicon, im Vereine mit mehreren Historikern,* vols. 1–9 (Leipzig, 1860–70, rpt. Hildesheim and New York, 1973), vol. 3: 562–63, 479–80; vol. 4: 85, 99–100, 197–200; vol. 5: 177–79; A. J. B. Heunisch, *Das Grossherzogtum Baden, historisch-geographisch-statistisch-topographisches beschrieben* (Heidelberg, 1857), 292–95.

TABLE 3. Baden Leadership of the Women's and Men's Associations of the Red Cross, 1872–73

Committee	Leaders
Karlsruhe Men's Relief Association	
Executive Committee	Dr. von Weech, archivist[a]; Dr. Prof. Emminghaus[a]; Dr. Cathiau, architect; L. Voit, cdr. of volunteer firemen; H. Stutz, furrier
Women's Association	
Executive Committee	Luise, duchess of Baden, *president. Section heads:* von Kettner, Molitor, von Berstett, von Hardenberg. *Directors:* Women's Association Secretary Dr. A. Bingner,[b] Dr. Spemann,[b] Penal Official Szuhany,[b] Medical Doctor Hoffmann,[a] Herr von Stösser.[b] *Advisors:* Financial Councillor E. Vierordt,[b] Treasurer von Delaiti[b]
Section I: Female Domestic Arts	Baroness Ida von Kettner, *section head*[c]; Mrs. District and Court Judicial Officer Wielandt; Miss Johanna Jolly; Council Minister Dr. Bingner
Section II: Child Care	Mrs. Betty Molitor, *section head*[c]; Mrs. v. Gulat-Wellenburg[c]; Mrs. Sophie v. Porbeck, Excellenz[c]; Mrs. Sophie Weylöhner[c]; Miss Chr. von Delius; Baroness A. von Göler-Seldeneck[c]; Mrs. Hack; Dr. Spemann
Section III: Nursing	Baroness von Berstett, *section head;* Mrs. Keeper of the Stalls Sachs[d]; Miss Emilie v. Bunsen; State Medical Doctor (retired from military) Hoffmann[a]; Penal Official Szuhany[b]; State Assembly Deputy Kimmig (replaced K. v. Stösser)[b]; Bookkeeper Wenz, *treasurer*
Section IV: Supply (changed later to Poor Relief)	Baroness von Hardenberg, *section head*[c]; Baroness Emma Taets v. Amerongen[c]; Mrs. Government Surveyor Land; Businessman's wife Ida Weill[c]; Dr. Spemann[b]
State Red Cross Relief Association	
Executive Committee:	
Representatives of the Women's Association	E. Vierordt; Szuhany; Dr. Spemann; Dr. Bingner; von Stösser; bookkeeper von Delaiti
Representatives of the Men's Association	Dr. von Weech; Prof. Dr. Emminghaus; Dr. Hoffmann; Treasurer Heidenreich; Dr. Omelin, archivist; Military Pharmacist (retired) Ziegler

Source: GK, Abt. 233, no. 2848, Armensache (Der Badische Frauenverein), *Dreizehnter Jahresbericht des Vorstandes des Badischen Frauenvereins* (Karlsruhe, 1873); Verzeichnis der Mitglieder des Gesammtvorstandes des Badischen-Landes-Hilfs-Vereins im Jahre 1872, supplement.

[a]Simultaneously representative of Men's Relief Society on the state level.
[b]Simultaneously member of State Red Cross Relief Association for the Women's Association.
[c]Original founding member of the association in 1859.
[d]Replaced Miss Marie v. Froben, who married and moved to Zurich.

mixed state that had experienced a veritable "cultural war" prior to the outbreak of the Prussian conflict, and, like Prussia, its dynastic house struggled actively thereafter to define a common basis for a Baden-German identity. In 1905, furthermore, a grand coalition of liberals and socialists was constituted against the Catholics in the state parliament, the first such move to incorporate socialists in a ruling coalition. Equally to the point, the forces of grassroots anti-Catholic sentiments worked to push the Catholic Center Party toward reconciliation with the state.[42] In patriotic philanthropy, Catholics could affirm their loyalty in an interdenominational space. Indeed, by drawing Catholics and Protestants together in festive time, for example, it forced them to commit to a public show of solidarity.[43]

On the local level, the gendered patterns of social interaction were the stuff of daily life and, thus, of festive time. In 1890, for example, the mayor of Baden-Baden sent the Karlsruhe court a detailed listing of the advisory board of the local *Frauen-Verein;* a gala event was to take place in the presence of the duchess, and the court wanted a full accounting of who would attend, their official function in the organization, and their particular religion. Protestants made up around 27 percent of the population of the city (which stood at 15,718 in 1905); for all intents and purposes, the rest were Catholic. Only a few Jewish families resided in the town, which was a popular resort, known in the nineteenth century as "the pearl of the Black Forest" because of its healing waters; Augusta had frequented the spa as queen and empress.[44]

On the advisory board, women outnumbered men two-to-one (thirty-one to fifteen in total). Protestants were 38 percent of the women and 33 percent of the men, a slightly higher proportion than in the population of the city as a whole but an indication, at this early date, that local Baden state women's associations—if a generalization is possible—were places of interconfessional interaction in actual practice. Significant, too, were the numbers of titled aristocrats, demonstrating that aristocratic presence was more than "for show" at the top, as Baroness Spitzemberg fully understood. Twenty-five percent of the women on the committee had the title countess or baroness or otherwise *von* in their names; with three exceptions, each served on one of the working subcommittees. Among the men was Baron von Lüttwitz, who joined his wife on the committee. The family long had ties with the women's association. In the early 1870s, for

---

42. Smith, *German Nationalism,* 138–40.

43. This important insight into the power of rituals is from Trexler, *Public Life,* 270.

44. GK, Abt. 69, no. 932, Der Frauenverein in Baden-Baden, 1888–92. In 1905, of the total population, there were 4,215 Protestants and 192 Jews in the city. *Deutschlands Städtebau: Baden-Baden* (Berlin-Halensee, 1923).

example, Helene von Lüttwitz had been sent to study nursing in London, Leipzig, and Würzberg before assuming her post as matron *(Oberin)* of a local Karlsruhe hospital.[45] There were few business people on this committee, although a number of the women appear only with their given and family names, making social identification difficult. In a city with a lot of forest-based activities and a number of important metalworks, names of owners of prominent firms do not appear on this list. The businessman Alois Schweigert was in hatmaking, and the retiree Koch, presumably, was once in the jewelry business. Otherwise, the occupations were mayors and other city and district officials, teachers, pastors, and medical doctors (including several associated with the state Red Cross, as Dr. and Mrs. von Corval) and several other military officers. Four of the women were single.

In the day-to-day running of the sections, Protestants and Catholics worked in close quarters. For example, in Section II, responsible for women's schooling, the Catholic wife of the mayor, Frau Gönner, two Catholic daughters of school councillors (Marie Gruber and E. Jung), a Protestant wealthy aristocratic woman, Frau von Plessen, and a Catholic retiree, Josef Koch, shared leadership tasks. Similarly, work for the Martha House, a sanatorium for single girls and women, brought the two groups together. In charge of oversight were the Protestant baroness Hanna von Goeler and her husband Ernst August, a wife of the district doctor, also Protestant, as was the Countess Ysenburg and the wife of General von Kluber. They were joined on the committee, however, by a Catholic baroness, Freifraulein von Roeder, and the wife of the city councillor Zabler, also Catholic. And the volunteers also collectively organized theater and concert performances; the pieces included selections written by the members themselves, as the children's play, the "Christmas fairy tales," by E. Jung, performed in 1892. From the proceeds, around one thousand marks were raised and donated to the women's association's day care center.[46] Festive time was an integral part of patriotic service, a chance to broaden contacts beyond the intimate work environment.

Delegates from local women's associations along the Lake of Constance (Baden *Seekreis*) regularly attended a reception at the Mainau Castle, hosted in their honor by the duchess, who often spent time away from Karlsruhe at this peaceful island retreat. In select years from 1897 to 1913, lists were kept for those attending; the numbers of guests ranged from 94 to 106 and, at minimum, they included the core leadership of twenty-six

---

45. GK, Abt. 233, no. 2848, *Dreizehnter Jahresbericht des Vortandes des Badischen Frauenvereins* (1871–72).

46. GK, Abt. 69, no. 932, theater program for Sunday, February 21 1892; also, the letter of the city councillor, Hermann Weber, Baden-Baden, February 29, 1892.

branch associations. In 1905, to acknowledge an important extension of *Verein* activities, a group of rural nurses employed in the area was added; and, periodically, influential women attended, such as Frau Anna Lauter, good friend of the duchess and head of the Association of Red Cross Sisters in Karlsruhe.[47]

The extent of official government presence in the life of local associations in Baden (as elsewhere in Germany) by now should come as no surprise: from notes on these lists, men in advisory positions were mayors, local and district state-appointed officials *(Ober-Amtsmann)*, and members of state councils. Impressive, too, was the extensive involvement of local clergy: in small Protestant-dominated communities, these were the pastors; in Catholic towns, the priests; and several high officials (monsignors) of the Catholic Church were also on the list. But here, in Mainau, the clergy intermingled, sharing festive time on behalf of the values of a common cause. In addition, many husbands and wives worked in the same organization and appeared together as guests. The occupations of the men outside of government and pastoral service centered on teaching, medicine, and pharmacy. Women members typically were married, although there was a sprinkling of single women and widows in their ranks. Reflecting the wider social milieu, there were baronesses and wives of the nontitled landowners (the *Landgraf* of southwest Germany) among them as well.

The duchess affirmed her superior status as hostess—it was, after all, her party—and the recurring festival perpetuated the values of intimacy and personal collaboration at the center of dynastic service. It stood as a moment to recognize an elite in constant formation, a group sharing common status as servitors of the *Landesmutter,* although some participants, clearly, were elevated and honored to be in the presence of such exalted company. Its pomp and ceremony, however, was an equalizer and part of an ongoing process of desacralizing and demystifying the titular aristocracy while simultaneously drawing on its "aura" to create a new social formation. If in the moment of celebration it could downplay distinct Protestant and Catholic identities by recognizing the common work for the public good, it simultaneously grew out of diverse confessional communities on the ground. But the affirmation of common goals linked them to a wider secular space beyond the immediate community, reaffirming the shared values in their cyclical reenactment and, arguably, in the memory of these performances. The gatherings, similarly, helped consolidate gender alliances. Women and men together had been singled out and honored

47. GK, Abt. 69, nos. 942–44, Versammlungen der Frauenvereine des Seekreises am Schloss Mainau, 1897–1902, 1904–7, 1909–13. The more detailed lists of participants begin in 1904.

for their work for the state, however much the need for negotiation over the evolving boundaries of gender roles and divisions might have disrupted the daily philanthropic activities in practice.[48]

Patriotic Women in Municipal Service

The steady growth in the numbers and members of Patriotic Women's Associations in the states of Germany misleadingly suggests inevitability. The foundation for the "takeoff," however, had been set in the late 1870s and, then, only after considerable attention and concern among the highest levels of dynastic state patrons. The decade was one of stagnation and in some instances, as the empress worriedly wrote her daughter Luise, of "actual decline" in numbers *(verschwindende Zahl)*.[49] High government and court officials needed to reformulate a powerful ideological raison d'être for continued state support of philanthropic work in the new united Germany. In the years of peace to come, they sought to promote and protect a vital role for organized voluntarism in order to assure its disciplined presence in wartime.

Patriotic peacetime philanthropy was set on a new course in 1880, and the ground was very carefully prepared in the highest political circles. A series of national congresses in 1880–81 recommended that women's association members be given official authority in poor relief administration in volunteer capacities.[50] This proposal seemed to solve multiple needs. It certainly offered the *Frauen-Vereine,* languishing in the previous decade, a new rationale and legitimacy, which reinvigorated their peacetime occupation. The call, however, simultaneously opened the field of activity to reform feminists, and feminist organizations also quickly moved into this terrain, for example, overseeing the training and development of a new profession for women as social workers.[51] The focus on

---

48. There were mounting gender tensions and rivalries, despite the effort to create a public image of unity and harmony. These groups employed what Chickering calls "Vereinsdeutsch" (*We Men Who Feel,* 155), a public voice of unity and cohesion, masking the internal divisions. I deal with these tensions as they surface in the documents.

49. *DRK,* 2:262–65, reproduces the exchanges between Empress Augusta and her daughter, Luise.

50. For details on the planning by government officials associated with the Red Cross, see Albert Döll, "Über die Theilnahme der Frauenvereine an der Armenpflege," in *Handbuch der Deutschen Frauenvereine unter dem Rothen Kreuz,* 322–35. Also, reports in *KZ* in 1880: no. 279, November 27; no. 280, November 28; no. 281 and supplement, November 30.

51. For an informative local study of this process, Reagin, *A German Women's Movement,* 71–97. For a description of the interaction of patriotic and reform feminists activities over nurses' training and social relief in Bremen, see Meyer-Renschhausen, *Weibliche Kultur,* 114–26. The study is not connected to patterns outside of Bremen and, thus, misses the wider political implications of the activities.

women dovetailed with renewed debate over state poor relief policy and the place of voluntarism in charity, itself set against the backdrop of increased concern with poverty, wageworkers, and worker insurance.

By 1880, it was clear even to liberal municipal officials in the localities that the influential Elberfeld model of poor relief, which since 1853 had relied on the personal visitations of male volunteer relief officials, was being overwhelmed by expanding definitions of social needs. Infants, children, youth, and rural people essentially were outside the existing system of care, as were various forms of medical and social services, such as infant nursing and housing, for example. Most agreed that salvaging poor relief required expanding the system of voluntarism; and the agenda sequence at the Congress of Poor Relief Officials *(Armenpfleger)* in November 1880, which established guidelines and a national organization to coordinate the integration of private charity into official welfare administration, was carefully orchestrated, with support from the empress, by high government and military officials.

The November congress had been preceded one month earlier by a special conference of the German Red Cross, which had passed a unanimous resolution encouraging its patriotic women's organizations to enter official welfare posts; a second, follow-up conference continued to press the discussion on the local chapters by soliciting their views. Furthermore, Empress Augusta saw to it that a well-known representative from the Executive Committee of the Prussian Patriotic Women's Association (Dr. Friedenthal) was a delegate and speaker at the congress, as was another participant with close ties to dynastic service, the Bremen editor Dr. Lammers.[52]

The debate had its own logic that led, seemingly naturally, to a spotlight on the state Patriotic Women's Associations. First came a more abstract discussion about the relationships between private philanthropy and official municipal relief work. Consensus readily emerged on the need to safeguard the practice of individual oversight of each specific welfare case, which remained at the heart of Germany's public poor relief services. That commitment turned attention to women, who were seen as an important source of volunteer labor.

Item 3 on the agenda dealt with "women's participation in poor relief and charity." Here, the discussion was more contentious, however. The delegate from Oldenburg, City Councillor Beseler, totally dismissed any role for women "because they belong in the home"; Professor D. Böhmert

---

52. For the role of the empress and her patron organization, the Red Cross, see R. Osius and P. Chuchul, "Die Heranziehung von Frauen zur öffentlichen Armenpflege," in *Schriften des deutschen Vereins für Armenpflege und Wohltätigkeit,* vol. 25 (Leipzig, 1896), 2, 15–16, 31, 41–42.

from Dresden thought it best to include women only if they were the wives
of male relief officials; other delegates, while supporting women's official
participation in principle, nonetheless spoke about the need to demarcate
the precise areas of women's and men's competencies. It was partly the
direct intervention of Drs. Lammers and Friedenthal as well as a general
of the infantry, von Etzel from Berlin, that carried the day, at least as measured by audience response of clapping and shouts of "Bravo!" All three
spokesmen made it eminently clear that their model of women's participation was the proven dynastic-supported women's associations. These loyal
and well-off women would become, as Dr. Friedenthal put it, "voluntary
officials of the commune" *(freiwillige Beamte der Kommune)*, ideally
suited—by their very nature in fact—to undertake the sensitive yet necessary personal visitations needed to learn about conditions of life in the
homes of the poor and to win their trust.

The manner in which official administrative posts would be opened to
women was left entirely to each municipality, depending on local conditions and historical practices. But the end goal was explicit: to dampen
class tensions and stem the tide of "social misery," and Dr. Friedenthal's
nationalist rhetoric stressed an imaginary unity of "all social energies"
drawn together for this common purpose. Indeed, his solution did not rely
on legislation *(die Gesetze)* but rather on civil society *(die Gesellschaft)*,
although simultaneously he placed the anticipated national mobilization
against poverty in a decidedly authoritarian framework. There was no fear
of "dilettantism," Friedenthal assured the audience, slipping into military
analogies that were so powerful in the imagining of women's peacetime
philanthropic work by those in dynastic state service.[53] Women's volunteer labor was based on discipline—the discipline of associational life—
and had the same invisible force at its core as the army, which offered a
powerful model. Discipline assured a collective response to the misery of
poverty's death toll, which Friedenthal compared to the agony of the
bloodiest battle.[54] And the vision enlisted the older vocabulary of "active
love of neighbor" in its mobilizing appeal. But it was unmistakably clear
to all that voluntarism for state purposes never was intended by its official
promoters to be the autonomous expression of civil society. The patriotic
public was being shaped more fully as official authority, while maintaining
its face as the embodiment of widespread private responsibility, concern,
and care.

The overwhelming sense of the congress to admit women into local
welfare agencies as volunteers and, over time, as paid officials infused new

---

53. *KZ*, no. 281, November 30, 1880.
54. Döll, "Über die Theilnahme," 324, 331–33.

life into local Patriotic Women's Associations in the years after 1880. It partly explains the expansion of their numbers reflected in the aggregate statistics for the states of the *Kaiserreich.* In turn, this growing voluntary sector helped transform and reshape the very nature of social services in the locality and guaranteed the viability of a model of municipal relief based on personal visitation and case-by-case assessment. Germany as *Wohlfahrtsstaat* expressed a Janus face, an admixture, on the one hand, of an insurance-based entitlement system (emerging also in the 1880s) reflected by economic activity based on a classically liberal definition of work as wage and salaried labor.[55] This system privileged regularly employed workers who, given the interpenetration of the capitalist labor market and gender household realities, most typically were male. On the other, it perpetuated the more familiar, face-to-face public relief system and the asymmetrical relations that it embodied, even as it was "modernized" by increasing attention to public health measures and other medical and social interventions. An expansion of the secular and religious voluntary sectors also accompanied changes in state and local social services and provisions.

Volunteer work multiplied along with growing state welfare interventions to deal with the many problems of family welfare, increasingly at the heart of municipal relief services.[56] Some of the local relief efforts maintained their old familiar character as benevolence of rule with its rhetoric and rituals of care coupled with harsh social discipline: soup kitchens, orphanages, and girls' asylums; industrial, work and Sunday schooling; and gift giving to poor children and young confirmees shared the stage with the workhouses and punitive measures against door-to-door begging. Dynastic and aristocratic figures who gave out food and fuel to the poor during hard times, furthermore, were the daily fare of news in the estab-

---

55. Jean H. Quataert, "Workers' Reactions to Social Insurance: The Case of Homeweavers in the Saxon Oberlausitz in the Late Nineteenth Century," *Internationale wissenschaftliche Korrespondenz zur Geschichte der deutschen Arbeiterbewegung* 20, no. 1 (March 1984): 17–35. Also, Paul Weindling, "The Modernization of Charity in Nineteenth Century France and Germany," in Barry and Jones, *Medicine and Charity,* 190–206. Weindling misreads the broader chronology of German philanthropy and the forces shaping the ties between state and voluntary charity, which go back earlier than the "liberal" era of the 1870s; however, he makes a number of important observations on the alliance of state and voluntary associations in the era of imperialism.

56. Blum, *Staatliche Armenfürsorge,* 47–52, 134–42, offers several thoughtful passages on the gender structure of poverty in the first two thirds of the nineteenth century. Also, Steinmetz, *Regulating the Social,* 163–69, on the gender profile of indoor and outdoor relief. Steinmetz looks to women's place in the formal structure of poor relief. In his schema, issues surrounding women, gender, and family are important for the emergence of "scientific social work" after 1890. However, he has not adequately followed women's incorporation into the municipal relief hierarchy nor their complementary place in the world of private charity.

lishment press during the *Kaiserreich.* So were the public banquets for poor people that now worked to intertwine key moments of dynastic and nation-state history.[57]

After 1880, women's associations joined local poor law and municipal offices through a variety of formal relationships: some associations "loaned" several of their members to the municipality for specific bureaucratic posts; in other cases, the municipality contracted with the association so, as a group, the women were responsible for "female" tasks such as care of infants or needy pregnant women; in still other cases, the association functioned as an intermediary, securing its trained nurses or the religious sisters (both Catholic nuns and Protestant deaconesses) paid positions in municipal service.[58]

The post-1880 model for the expansion of municipal relief by reliance on patriotic women's labor and expertise was Cassel, which also influenced social programs in cities like Frankfurt, Düsseldorf, Wiesbaden, and Magdeburg. Copies of its statutes were sent outside of Prussia, for example, to Baden as well. The annual report of Cassel's Patriotic Women's Association for 1888 demonstrates a wide range of undertakings that was supporting and continuously reshaping the municipality's relief commitments in the years after 1880.[59]

In 1888, the branch had six distinct sections; and every Friday at 11:00 A.M., there was an information meeting for the presidents of the association, the (male) secretary, the women overseeing the training of nurses, and the medical doctors employed in the association's nursing training institute, the Kaiserin Augusta-Stiftung. Under its authority, for example, impoverished pregnant married women were given foodstuffs, including meat and wine, and coal, as well as shirts, jackets, and diapers;

---

57. *KZ,* no. 480, November 24, 1888, a report on the duchess of Weimar feeding nearly one hundred needy people warm "healthy" soup; no. 584, December 13, 1889, in connection with the visit of the kaiser to Worms, Baron Heyl zu Herrnsheim gave the magistrates five thousand marks for dispensing coal and one thousand marks for free suppers. Also, *Berliner Tageblatt und Handels-Zeitung,* no. 259, May 24, 1889, and no. 277, June 4, 1889, for charitable bequests.

58. Lange and Bäumer, *Handbuch der Frauenbewegung,* 2:24–27, develop the different models of women's integration into official poor relief; as does Dr. Friedenthal's blueprint speech, "Die Theilnahme," 327–31. For the slow movement toward implementation, Sachsse and Tennstedt, *Geschichte der Armenfürsorge,* 1:241–44. The authors show that by 1895, for example, Patriotic Women's Associations in seventy-eight municipalities supported "sisters" who had official *(amtlich)* authority.

59. GSPK, no. 15610, Bl. 33. Geschäftsbericht für das Jahre 1888. Also, GK, Abt. 69, no. 887, reports of section III, 1890–92, containing pamphlets of women's associations for comparative purposes, including Cassel, *Statuten des Vaterländischen Bezirks-Frauen-Vereins zu Cassel* (Cassel, 1881). See, as well, Sachsse and Tennstedt, *Geschichte der Armenfürsorge,* 1:243.

that year, the association was helping 121 women (Section III). Another section (IV) aided the "shameful poor," augmenting official public support by keeping destitute families off the dole. In 1888, 201 needy families were receiving cash payments and food supplements behind the scenes. Section V worked directly with the official poor relief agencies. By the late 1880s, the association had placed sixteen of its members into the city agency in official posts *(Armenpflegerinnen)*. And the women seemed to be making a difference; they turned bureaucratic attention for the first time to temperance issues, and the head of the section had been brought into the process of annual review of foster care for the area. In 1888, this section of the women's association was being funded by the interest from a small bequest that had been willed to the city for poor relief and by gifts of wool from the executive committee of the local association against begging. The gift circulated in the form of wages paid to poor women to knit children's wool socks that, in turn, were doled out to other poor families. The women's association's interventions into the urban economy were not without their impact on the gender character of the labor market.

A variety of interests had coalesced around these domestic and family undertakings, which reveal much about the wider place of Patriotic Women's Associations in the evolving industrial economy of imperial Germany. The determined effort to remake poor women's domestic and home management skills emerged as a central concern of voluntary philanthropy, a key part of the relief package of support that increasingly accompanied official intervention into the life situation of poor people in Germany.[60] These peacetime undertakings resonated in ways that simultaneously linked civil and court society.

In the first place, girls' training in domestic skills and home management was relatively popular with working-class families, as seen by the continued expansion of educational institutes designed to teach cooking, ironing, and sewing to poorer girls of confirmation age. In both artisanal and working-class calculations, these were the very skills seen as necessary to keep daughters out of the factories. Even the soup kitchens, the more classically charitable form of largesse, were widespread and heavily used in hard times.

Second, the preoccupation with household management also forged new and effective links between growing numbers of municipal officials

---

60. The empress Auguste Victoria put the issue of "girls' domestic education" on the agenda of the ninth annual meeting of Poor Relief Officials, *KZ,* supplement to no. 325, August 26, 1888. In Baden, too, the state women's association was involved in promoting the education and training of women for wage employment. GK, Abt. 233, no. 2848, *Vierzehnter Jahresbericht des Vorstandes des Badischen Frauenvereine Abteilung Karlsruhe* (Karlsruhe, 1874), for the report on Section I.

and women volunteers: many relief officers recognized that well-run domestic households supported orderly municipal communities and that women's domestic situation was important for social stability. They accepted elite women's claims to special "female" domestic knowledge in carving out these new municipal welfare services. In circular fashion, by drawing on the resources of patriotic associations with their broad institutional networks and ties to the dynasty, these patterns of municipal services helped fashion a wider understanding of the state. The duchess of Baden, for example, regularly attended the celebrations throughout her land commemorating the opening of a new school for domestic arts or a hospital, as the next chapter shows in detail. Her presence reaffirmed a set of values tested on the ground designed to enhance legitimacy through ongoing identification with a state that, in the philanthropic act, was seen as "caring."

The Radical Nationalist Challenge

At the very moment of its first formulation on the national scene in the early 1880s, however, the official commitment to the philanthropic component of municipal relief came under searing attack by angry voices on the right. In effect, the "caring state" of official nationalists fractured even before it could work to bind fully national life. It immediately was forced to enter a terrain of battle over the very definitions of German national identity that were fought out in the debates and practices of community responsibility and obligation. These tensions would plague political life in imperial Germany to the bitter end of the regime.

The 1880s were a time of heightened nationalist fervor "from below," a radical expression of growing social and economic discontent among urban artisans and workers as well as peasants in the context of the depression years, 1873–96.[61] At stake were alternative visions of state organization at the very heart of national life. Pastoral groups like the old Inner Mission found renewed purpose in an expanded program of re-Christianization of urban society through charitable works, while other

---

61. Peter Pulzer, *The Rise of Political Antisemitism in Germany and Austria,* rev. ed. (London, 1988). Eley, *Reshaping the German Right,* 10, and elsewhere, argues that the key moment in the breakdown of the Bismarckian synthesis is the decade of the 1890s, signaling the end of the anti-Socialist laws. This marker overlooks the extraordinary turmoil of the 1880s around state obligations and responsibilities. The nationalist challenge in the late 1880s was forcing clarification of official nationalist policies and principles. For the radical challenge to Conservatives, see his "Anti-Semitism, Agrarian Mobilization, and the Conservative Party: Radicalism and Containment in the Founding of the Agrarian League, 1890–93," in Jones and Retallack, *Reform, Reaction, and Resistance,* 187–227. Also, Richard Levy, *The Downfall of the Anti-Semitic Parties in Imperial Germany* (New Haven, 1975), 72–90.

distinctly political groups emerged to mobilize and channel the discontent for electoral battles specifically. In the 1880s, the dominant idiom still was religious and turned on a Christian vision of community but now with the added menace of the proven political attraction of anti-Semitism. Indeed, in the countryside, politicians emerged to mobilize rural discontent using anti-Semitic appeals against the elite nature of notable politics.[62] In urban areas as Berlin, the continuous influx of new migrants seeking work and the loss of community and identity that seemed to be a part of industrial transformation, too, fueled distinctly anti-Semitic politics, which were expressed in the "Christianization" of the "social question." These radical Christian groups, like the Christian Social Party around the court preacher Adolf Stöcker or the short-lived German Women's Association (Deutscher-Frauen Verein) that he helped spawn in Berlin in the summer of 1881, proposed alternative definitions of national identity. They demonstrate the explosive potential in the concept of the social state.

On one end of the nationalist pole was the radical anti-Semite Stöcker, political leader until his death in 1909, who early in the 1880s had turned to the plight of urban wageworkers, including women. He coupled a loyally monarchical position on state rule with a frontal attack on private philanthropy and the paternalist model of care behind voluntary service, which was being reformulated at the time for poor relief. In many ways, his arguments were compatible with the traditions of dynastic rule: he, too, employed the analogy of a "large family" to describe the state's responsibility for its members, and he drew on an old familiar vocabulary of Christian community and charity as well. To those above, he spoke a welcomed language of patriotism, holding up the monarchy, which spread its "eagle wings" as protection against misery and want, as a model for emulation.

But his definition of "Christian" was dangerous and disturbing; it excluded Jews in principle and admitted into the "true" *Volk* community only those who accepted his own notions of Christian service and politics. For a time he broke company with the conservative dynastic commitment to intermediary associations and institutions in national life, not the least for their importance as private sources of funds for social relief. A proper Christian state, he declared on the offensive in February 1881, "owed" its workers social services and benefits as a matter of "right," not "alms." He redeployed the pietist image of "new dawn" to describe the dawning of a system of national support under the authority of the state. This expansive system of state welfare provisions inaugurated "a completely new age," a reign of Christian rights and culture against all odds and opposition. He

---

62. Eley, *Reshaping the German Right,* 21–24, 34–35.

even attacked by name the old philanthropic state institutes, such as Kaiser Wilhelm Solicitation and its coordinator, Councillor Staemmler.

At the same time, Stöcker thanked God for a Christian monarchy and reintegrated his radical nationalist critique into the dynastic framework. His ended an inflammatory address to the Deutscher-Frauen Verein, for example, an artisanal group that had been formed primarily to boycott Jewish stores, with a "salute" to the German empress, whom he hailed as a "model" for women's patriotism, symbol of "devotion," and the incarnation of women's "participation" in state affairs.[63] In time, Stöcker was forced to shift his appeal to artisans and other *Mittelstand* groups in the Berlin economy; urban wageworkers proved unreceptive to his message. The radical nationalist critique that gave rise to his politics in the first place, however, was redefining the terms of debate, heightening, in essence, a Christian identity and inexorably linking it to the very basis of German national identity.

These linkages were reinforced by other forces that also profoundly shaped German self-understanding as it was tested in the evolving nature and character of philanthropic services in the *Kaiserreich:* the transition to empire. Already in the same decade of radical nationalist "awakening," missionaries returning from work in Africa or Asia became a regular addition to the public lecture scene in cities like Berlin. As invited speakers at festive family evenings sponsored by nationalist and distinctly political associations, they put on slide shows and brought their personal experiences with the "exotic" back home to people in the metropole. Many of these same religious groups long had been active in ministerings in Africa; but after the acquisition of colonies in 1884, with seeming ease, their work was placed in a different context: it no longer was a matter of private Protestant (or Catholic) missions. Now, evangelicalism was an essential ingredient of a larger "German national cause," as an article in the conservative *Kreuz-Zeitung* concluded in August 1888.[64]

These missionaries also strengthened the ties between German and Christian identities, although the apparently straightforward correlation

63. *KZ,* supplement to no. 38, February 15, 1881, "Christlich-Soziale Partei." Also, the paper covered the few months' existence of the Deutscher-Frauen Verein, first supplement to no. 135, June 12, 1881, and first supplement to no. 136, June 14, 1881. For a further assessment, Wanda Kampmann, "Stöcker und die Berliner Bewegung," *Geschichte in Wissenschaft und Unterricht* 13 (1962): 558–79.

64. Reports on missionaries in Berlin associational society are found in *KZ,* supplement to no. 41, February 17, 1888, and no. 294, August 8, 1888, in particular. There is a recent new body of literature that connects Europe and empire as one integrated analytic whole. I have profited from its perspective. Particularly useful is Frederick Cooper and Ann Laura Stoler, "Between Metropole and Colony: Rethinking a Research Agenda," in *Tensions of Empire,* 1–56.

of "Christian" and "German," which was at the basis of Stöcker's radical nationalist message and lurked in the allure of a Christian mission at home and abroad, never was simple, given the confessional divides that were powerful sources of distinct identities and affinities in Germany. Empire helped reshape German identity, however, not only by providing a continuous contrast with "others" that was part of the discourse supporting orientalist missionary societies, but also by authorizing a critique of religious apathy and indifference at home. It was more than one missionary who decried the heathen practices that shocked him in Berlin itself in the late 1880s. The normative mode of behavior could come from either side of the ocean. The context of empire, itself, blurred the lines between a Christian mission to strengthen Germany's power and national vigor within its borders and one to support and advance its power position in world affairs.

But the radical Christian upsurge in the 1880s in some cases destroyed the older model of philanthropy, which had brought into leadership positions women of high social standing, irrespective of their religious backgrounds. Critical here in shaping leadership had been social status, government connections, and wealth. So, for example, the old independent Berlin organization the Prussian Women's and Young Ladies' Association had Jewish women on its executive committee until 1880. In June, however, the Jewish members resigned in protest because for several years running Adolf Stöcker had been invited to give the yearly "festival" address; they objected to his offensive "smear campaign" and "rabble-rousing," but a resolution calling for his removal had failed to find support among the majority of the members.

The tensions spilled out into the press, and the *Kreuz-Zeitung* reports offered a revealing defense of Stöcker in its highly sarcastic rendition of the controversy: "The court preacher was very much aware that he was speaking at a patriotic celebration of a charitable institute . . . and hardly uttered a word on politics, religion, or confession." The editorial employed the useful fiction of distinct arenas of life, claiming for philanthropy an imaginary space above and beyond the divisive pulls of politics and religion. In the face of mounting political anti-Semitism on the streets, however, the old, independent association of elite women no longer defended its bridging role; and, after the Jewish women resigned, what remained in miniature was the very homogeneous Protestant "Christian national" community espoused by elements of the Prussian radical Right.[65]

The radical critique in the 1880s also forced an immediate response by

---

65. *KZ,* no. 140, June 18, 1880, includes the reports from the rival press as well and provides a description of the association's annual celebration "with God for king and fatherland."

government officials designed to reclaim the work of philanthropy for conservative ends. Their reformulation was fashioned through four interrelated arguments that, later, themselves, were subject to continuous evolution. In official publications, it became standard fare to dismiss the label *alms,* which had been repoliticized as an object of scorn, and constitute charitable activities, again, around hard work and training.[66] At the same time, official praxis perpetuated gift giving in a distinct symbolic economy of honor and obligation of the propertied, privileged groups.

This play of idiom and performance was facilitated by a second response that cast philanthropy and poor relief as eminently "modern." In contrast to the activities of states in antiquity or the Middle Ages, or so voices in the quasi-official government organ, the *Provincial-Correspondenz,* argued in January 1881 during the heated debates over social insurance, expanding and safeguarding the legal regulations governing relief was an appropriate task of the modern state. This made the modern state not only "a necessary but also a charitable institution." While the development of the "modern state idea" grew organically from Christian "civilization" *(Gesittung)* and bore no resemblance to socialist principles, it was anchored in a larger context than simply the old duty of humanity and Christian service; it had an added political rationale in modern life. In circular fashion, welfare and relief services worked to aid the propertyless and thus uphold the state itself *(staatserhaltende Politik).*[67] The state had both a defensive and a protective core.

This formulation fed in seamless fashion into the third, and self-evident, strategy of official nationalists, which involved personifying the state through its dynastic body. Its essential twofold nature as defensive and charitable institution was embodied in the dynastic family. In October 1881, celebrating the seventieth birthday of Augusta, "our beloved *Landesmutter,*" the same semiofficial newspaper praised her patriotic women and young ladies "as the complement to the ever-ready army"; indeed, their formal involvement in social relief and welfare provided not only a rich source of volunteer nurses for war but also "guarantee[d] the state a national foundation *(volkstümliche Grundlage)*". Time and again, dynastic rulers provided a distinct gender framework for their nationalist vision. In a publicized exchange of greetings with the Central Committee of the Red Cross at the new year in 1888, for example, William honored its "ded-

---

66. *KZ,* supplement to no. 103, May 4, 1880, a report of the official Relief Committee of the Unified Patriotic Women's Associations. Also, supplement to no. 161, April 5, 1892, meeting of the Patriotic Women's Association and no. 540, November 17, 1892, for a report on an auction.

67. The semiofficial "Provincial-Correspondenz" article is reprinted in *KZ,* no. 234, October 6, 1881, "Die Kaiserin Augusta und das Rothe Kreuz."

icated" work for the "welfare of my army"; Augusta singled out for praise its medical services in peacetime, which symbolized the "patriotic tasks" at the root of national life.[68] Indeed, in the persuasive field of gender symbols, dynastic nationalists artfully defined the state through the women and men in the associations working on its behalf. The practices of the organized patriotic public gave living form to the state, identified by the mobilized national energies as its base.

Fourth and finally, the appeal to a Christian identity ran like a leitmotif through official nationalist discourse on state obligations and women's place in philanthropic service. The Christian values of "love of neighbor," as well as "humanitarian" sacrifice and service, continued to feed official patriotic messages. Protestant and Catholic individuals and associations could join together on the basis of a common patriotic mission that remained rooted in a vision of a large supportive Christian family. Interconfessionalism was the official policy underwriting dynastic-led *Frauen-Vereine,* and it remained so even in the face of mounting radical national competition or, later, the reinvigoration of the Protestant and Catholic inner evangelical missions. In this sense, the decade of the 1880s did not so much transform as reaffirm the official norm.[69] In response to the pressures from below, then, dynastic and high government leaders continued to advance the older norms, although the new climate of racist thinking in some arenas closed the doors to Jewish membership. As Ute Daniel notes, however, generalizing from her case study of Westphalia, by the end of the *Kaiserreich* women's patriotic associations were "fully established as a . . . model of interconfessional conservative charity, responsible to and dependent on the state."[70] If her formulation misses the

---

68. For the ritual greetings, no. 15, January 18, 1888, "Vom Rothen Kreuz." Here the distinct tasks in war and peace divide nicely by gender, but the categories are more fluid. "Male" could be invested with stereotypically "female" attributes.

69. A routine press report in March 1888 on a local (Prussian) Patriotic Women's Association in Iserlohn is paradigmatic of the norm: that year, among its considerable expenditures, the patriotic association had "given" the town's Catholic and its Protestant women's associations an equal subvention of thirty marks. See *KZ,* second supplement to no. 77, March 30, 1888. These practices took place in the context of ongoing confessional conflicts and continuous tensions with Jews, however. At a benefit concert for the fleet and the army, the Conservative paper pointedly noted the absence of Jews, referred to as the "oriental element," no. 52, January 31, 1893; and, also, for anti-Semitic remarks in the context of the Sedan celebration, no. 412, September 2, 1893. For anti-Semitism in confessional conflicts, Smith, *German Nationalism,* 154–61; his statement that "the [German] nation was made in the province" (204) excludes Jews from that formulation. Willy-nilly, it reflects the significance of "Christian" in the formation of German national identity.

70. Daniel, "Vaterländischen Frauenvereine in Westfalen," 171. For Daniel, it is a question of Catholic and notable women's integration into the state; for me, it is a question of how this participation works to construct understandings of the state.

crucial reciprocities that constituted state identities through patriotic acts, Daniels nonetheless recognizes that the official goal, to bridge the large confessional Christian divide, gradually was being realized, even if it continued to operate in a context of religious antagonism and suspicion.

The contradictory paths, indeed, were the stuff that dynastic state philanthropy had to negotiate throughout the imperial period. In time, former enemies could become new allies; for example, radical nationalist groups hostile to private philanthropy in the 1880s for supporting the so-called unfit, by the turn of the century advocated cooperation with the state for imperialist-driven eugenics projects to manage population size, strength, and health.[71] The political positions were fluid and malleable, and the ongoing evolution of class society enforced the power of its conceptual categories on social identities, partly reconfiguring the clients. Potential clients had a range of linguistic frames through which to express their interests, only one of which was the imagined patriotic and caring Christian family of official nationalist discourse. In the contested terrain of the nation-state after 1870–71, however, the struggle over German national identity was not only a battle of words, political platforms, or programs. A set of cultural performances were working to reenact the benefits and largesse of the "caring" state for the wider German public, helping to constitute, in turn, images of the national community. The next chapter examines the sites of official nationalist performances of the imagined community and the struggles over its definition.

---

71. Weindling, "Modernization of Charity," 201–3, has a short discussion of the new face of Social Darwinism, which led to "solidarism," his term for the interdependence of state and voluntary charity.

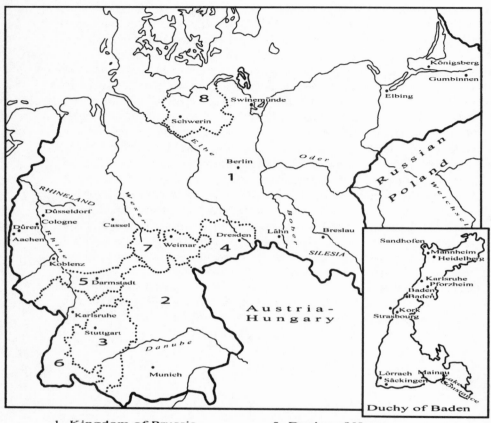

1. Kingdom of Prussia
2. Kingdom of Bavaria
3. Kingdom of Württemberg
4. Kingdom of Saxony

5. Duchy of Hesse
6. Duchy of Baden
7. Duchy of Weimar
8. Duchy of Mecklenburg

Map 2.   State Associations of the Red Cross in Imperial Germany, 1871–1918

CHAPTER 4

Cultural Performances in the Struggle over National Community after 1871

The dynastic center of official nationalist politics in Germany came under intense public scrutiny in the year 1888. William I, already revered in nationalist lore as the "beloved old" unification kaiser, died in March 1888. After three months as emperor, his own son, Frederick III, also died and was succeeded, in turn, by his son, William II, on June 16. While loyal monarchists could feel secure in the smooth workings of legitimate hereditary succession, these transitions nonetheless introduced elements of deep uncertainty over policy and purpose from above.

Frederick's speech "to my people" on March 14 had confirmed his father's military reputation, evoking one pole of dynastic rule in the "untiring sovereign concern *(landesväterlicher Fürsorge)* for the Prussian army." Prussia's strength had, indeed, paved the way for the "victory of German weapons" in war and laid the foundation for the unification of the German nation.[1] Assured of its power position in world affairs, the new *Reich* subsequently turned to "the work of peace," as Frederick phrased it, a coded reference to the complementary pole of dynastic rule, anchored in a concern for community well-being. At the time, official nationalists were embroiled in serious controversies over state obligations and responsibilities, as the last chapter has shown. While Frederick's rendition of dynastic history found applause in official circles, his pointed reference to "religious toleration" as a fundamental principle of "[his] house" evoked considerable tension and debate over its practical meaning for social life among the same loyal groups.[2] On careful examination, the Conservative

---

1. Reprinted in *KZ,* no. 63, March 14, 1888.

2. For controversies over Frederick's memory, among others, *KZ,* no. 380, October 3, 1888; and Emil Ludwig, *Wilhelm Hohenzollern: The Last of the Kaisers* (New York, 1927), 48–64.

triad of monarchy, army, and Christendom proved elusive and ambiguous even for its most vocal proponents.

In the midst of the uncertainties of death, political transition, and conflict, a devastating flood of unparalleled ferocity inundated areas in east and central Germany, affecting the lives of tens of thousands of people along the Elbe, Oder, and Weichsel (Vistula) Rivers. In late March 1888 the "shocking news" of a community in danger hit the newspapers throughout Germany.[3] The situation was serious, indeed. In the province of Posen alone, nine cities and eighty rural communities were under water; eight thousand people were left homeless in the city of Posen itself. Twenty thousand were affected in the province of Hanover, and thousands of families were in dire need in East Prussia. The flood immediately activated the dynastic states' philanthropic associations throughout the nation and, specifically, the Red Cross–affiliated women's groups.

In the glare of the public limelight, the disaster permitted the *Landesmutter* to demonstrate what had been merely glimpsed in Frederick's speech: the force of a mobilized nation responding with a dramatic performance of relief for a community in danger—a drama that, however, was political rather than aesthetic. If in nationalist circles, controversies over definitions and meanings of words might divide adherents, official nationalists also used the power of cultural performances to create community and solidarity, which they did time and again when natural disasters struck. While this effort to "tame fear" was not a secular ritual in the strict sense, it had a highly developed structure and a set of symbols that were reenacted repeatedly in moments of natural calamities. For authorities, such moments invariably are charged with danger.[4] These performances

---

3. To assess the effects of the patriotic public, I have read not only the Conservative *Kreuz-Zeitung* but also several newspapers of the "bourgeois" public that also were "national" in scope: the *Vossiche Zeitung* and the *Berliner Tageblatt.* In 1911, at the time of a disastrous railroad accident in Müllheim, Baden, I added the main socialist organ, *Vorwärts,* to the sample. While future research is needed to demonstrate greater nuances of politics and region, my reading reveals the power of civic relief practices to transcend distinct public realms, working, indeed, to shape common concerns, public responses, as well as wider national identifications. For the importance of these national papers, see Mommsen, *Imperial Germany,* 190.

4. The idea of secular ritual is taken from a discussion in Mach, *Symbols, Conflict, and Identity,* 76–77. Disasters bring a breakdown of the routines and the existing forces of order, permitting outbursts of pent-up tensions and hostilities. For several examples, *VZ,* third supplement to no. 366, April 7, 1888, "daring thefts" in Elbing, one of the hardest hit areas of flooding; *KZ,* supplement to no. 214, September 13, 1874, on a fire in Meiningen (Weimar). There were 199 houses destroyed, twenty-four hundred persons left homeless, and, reputedly, widespread looting. Also in 1911, *Berliner Tageblatt und Handels-Zeitung,* no. 362, July 19, 1911, on the use of the military to contain the threat of public disorder during the railroad disaster.

expressed in dramatic time cultural messages about the nature of community life in the new Germany that were as powerful as the official ideological formulations of nationalism.

Disaster relief work had been incorporated into the original charters of the state women's associations that had joined the German Red Cross after 1869. As the earliest Prussian statute expressed it, the association would "provide relief in one or another part of the fatherland at times of extraordinary emergency caused by contagious diseases, rising prices, flooding, railroad disasters, or other kinds of crises."[5] Over the years disaster relief increasingly took on the character of a national mobilization campaign simultaneously affecting all parts of the expanding "fatherland," which it was helping to construct. Assuaging the fear of danger was very much part of the way Germans came to imagine themselves as members of the nation. But the image was hardly preordained; nor was it "neutral," despite the veneer of neutrality that lay at the heart of Red Cross service. This "nation" was a creature of the very groups that were leading the relief services in the first place. The complex process of forming national identity can be followed in some detail at this moment of disaster relief in early spring, 1888.

As in other emergencies, the coordination of relief from the dynastic center integrated four distinct elements to communicate a powerful emotional message. But each crisis was played out at a specific historic moment, which deepened the emotional impact. For example, an extraordinary session of the Patriotic Women's Association's business committee in late March summarized the ongoing Red Cross relief measures, which were directed "from the center." The report assured the readers that modern communications technology was at the organization's disposal: instructions had been dispatched to the flooded areas by telegraph, and monies already had been dispensed to two hard-hit communities. The committee appealed for donations, however, by drawing on the memory of the recently deceased kaiser: charitable contributions to defend a threatened community in which house and possessions *(Haus und Habe)* had been destroyed were a "noble tribute" to his honor. It linked the dynasty directly to community defense.[6]

It was through a combination of print media and the performance of relief services at the points of danger that new identities were created and reinforced. The process reveals much about the way the dynastic-led philanthropic infrastructure communicated its messages to all corners of the

---

5. In *DRK,* 2:207–8.

6. *KZ,* no. 75, March 28, 1888. Also, *VZ,* no. 155, March 29, 1888. The Patriotic Women's Association's communiqués easily caught the readers' eye because of the large cross placed between the words "Patriotic" and "Women."

nation, simultaneously integrating them through a common focus. Patriotic philanthropy persuaded through dramatic performances that concurrently were reported in a variety of print sources. The strategy is appropriate for complex industrial societies with growing literacy and reliance on words; it centered the work, nonetheless, on performing the rituals of care in "dramatic time" set apart from the routines of daily life. As Victor Turner recognizes, no one fails to notice the shift from "routinized social living" to "dramatic time."[7] What Turner leaves unspoken is the political significance of these social dramas.

Four interrelated elements joined to give living form to the mobilization in the face of the tragic flooding. Each had its own logic and independent momentum and, in other contexts of nationalist drama, would reappear either singly or in some combination with the other patterns.

The first brought about a "coalescence of the nation" at the moment of danger and reflected the centrality of communications technology and print media in the complex organization of dynastic philanthropic service. To the liberal *Vossische Zeitung,* Berliners, indeed, were first "in all of Germany" with their generous contributions to the needy elsewhere.[8] The second element was the actual performance of relief by the "agents" of the state. It involved the specific implementation of collective concern, which shaded into political work. The third was political and highly partisan, indeed. It was the official reporting of the relief endeavors—the effort to shape wider understandings of events and bend notions of community to conservative dynastic purposes.[9] Fourth and finally, dynastic groups stressed the human responses, and not the natural event itself, as living proof of the swift and successful mobilization of the "home front" in the face of sudden danger just as it would be mobilized in times of war. But, as we will see, dramatic time carried with it dangers of breakdown, unfulfilled promises, or even subversion. Despite the best efforts of official nationalists to control the event, it could be transformed into a moment of protest. It is to the workings of these interlocking elements in 1888 that I now turn before examining the importance of theatrical performances in dynastic endeavors to concretize the image of a unified national German community.

The state women's associations had access to a wide array of publica-

---

7. Victor Turner, *From Ritual to Theatre: The Human Seriousness of Play* (New York, 1982), 9.

8. *VZ,* no. 157, March 31, 1888.

9. Despite remarkable similarities in newspaper coverage, there were distinct differences in reporting. Significantly, in late March the liberal press downplayed the women's role in relief, giving voice to the appeals of all-male ad hoc committees. By early April, the work of women's patriotic associations emerged more prominently, and, when reporters followed the tour of Empress Victoria to the devastated areas, they no longer could neglect women's relief services on the ground. *VZ,* no. 170, April 10, 1888.

tions spanning much of the political spectrum from left-liberal to conservative. This contact insured broad exposure to its activities by the reading public. In times of natural disasters, of course, even the socialist press would report the tragedy, offering its own interpretation of its cause and course and assigning blame; but, at times, even these papers partly reproduced the official response.[10]

From their inception, the state women's associations had to announce their general assembly meetings in the local press and provide readers with yearly reports. Thus, for example, the Berlin Central Women's Association from its earliest statute (1867) was required at a minimum to publicize its work in five Berlin papers: the *Spenersche Zeitung, Vossische Zeitung, Neue Preussische Kreuz-Zeitung, National-Zeitung,* and the *Fremdenblatt.*[11] The associations were granted free postage by simply noting on the correspondence "affairs of the . . . women's association." Most had arrangements with government printing offices, which published their protocols and reports free of charge. In addition, the administrative bulletins (the *Amtsblättern*) of the state governments regularly included reports detailing the work of the women's associations for their bureaucratic readership. In 1888, this complex print nexus assured considerable coverage of the relief measures.

Through the public call for support, communities everywhere were mobilized simultaneously to provide relief for the flooded Prussian provinces. The response, indeed, was a coalescence of the nation: outside of Prussia, people all over raised and gave money, organized benefit concerts, ran lotteries, and gathered and sent off materials, including clothing, to the provincial relief organizations. And they read about similar efforts going on at the same time in other communities. In April, the two German royalty, Augusta and Victoria, gave three thousand marks to the Executive Committee of the Patriotic Women's Association for support of the victims. As they put it, "the present calamity essentially has found no parallel in peacetime," leaving unspoken the need for similar coalescence for its victims in wartime. Six months later, in October, the Patriotic Women's Association had raised over 3.4 million marks, a staggering amount of private money for relief, which still was in full swing.[12]

---

10. In 1911, at the time of a train wreck in Müllheim, *Vorwärts* reported self-evidently about the military's role in relief as well as the medical stretcher-bearers (the *Sanitätskolonne*). As I show in chapter 5, these units were key vehicles for communicating militaristic values in society. At the time, socialists were involved in serious antimilitarist struggles. See *Vorwärts,* second supplement to no. 165, July 18, 1911, and no. 166, July 19, 1911.

11. *DRK,* 2:204; also LK, Abt. 403, no. 7364, Bl. 177–90, correspondence between the executive committee of the Prussian Patriotic Women's Association and Prussian provincial presidents, May 25–June 16, 1867.

12. *KZ,* no. 100, April 14, 1888. Details of the mobilization efforts were reported later in *DRK,* 2:288–94. For similar coverage, *VZ,* no. 157, March 31, 1888, and first supplement to no. 158, April 1, 1888, on various benefit concerts throughout Berlin.

In Prussia itself, the package of relief measures was funneled through the multiple relief committees, including the provincial women's associations in the affected districts. Coverage of events offered an opportunity to break down for the readers the full complement of state "agents" at work: various state and municipal officials, private ad hoc relief committees, the Order of St. John,[13] as well as members of the well-connected Patriotic Women's Associations. In May, civilian relief workers were joined, as the *Kreuz-Zeitung* headline noted, by "our troops" (a pointed reference to an imagined "we"). A military battalion of young pioneer-trainees had been sent to the stricken area near Drewenz, establishing a model of joint civilian-military operations for public health and emergency measures that would be reenacted in subsequent times of emergency in the *Kaiserreich*.[14]

For official nationalists, whose own power requirements favored the mix of private charity alongside municipal relief measures, the crisis seemed to demonstrate the efficacy of their principles, at the time under attack in the meeting halls of Berlin and other urban areas by radical nationalist unrest and worker mobilization. Disaster relief combined state-supported medical provisions such as disinfecting the flooded areas to prevent epidemics and setting up provisional hospitals on the one hand and quintessentially traditional philanthropic models on the other: feeding and clothing the homeless, replacing household effects, and providing makeshift employment. Much of the work later was institutionalized as well: permanent knitting schools were established in the buffeted areas, as were places for clients to obtain baths, and a number of new local women's chapters of the patriotic association also were founded.[15]

Equally important was the imagery that jumped out of the press: patriotic voices described the emergency not just as a flood—it was a war. Posen had not been merely inundated; it resembled a bombed-out city. The war analogy ran like a leitmotif through the speeches and editorial commentaries, in essence, linking the effectiveness of peacetime emergency mobilization at home to the promise of successful community mobilization in wartime.[16] Just

---

13. These were the Knights Hospitallers of the Order of St. John, an old religious, military order active in medical service, who worked with the women's associations under the army's inspector for civilian medical services. In this crisis, they set up provisional hospitals to deal with possible outbreaks of epidemics (*KZ,* supplement to no. 150, May 16, 1888). For more on the knights, see the obituary of Countess Marie zu Stolberg-Wernigerode, whose husband was the head of the order in 1864 when it joined the Red Cross (*KZ,* no. 594, December 19, 1893).

14. *KZ,* no. 131, May 4, 1888. A similar report was in *VZ,* no. 157, March 31, 1888.

15. *DRK,* 2:288–92.

16. See the report on the delegate conference of the Patriotic Women's Associations, *KZ,* supplement to no. 90, April 9, 1888. The war analogy is repeated in the "bourgeois" press (*VZ,* third supplement to no. 168, April 8, 1888, which described the cities on dry land inundated by "refugees").

as war had provided the context for national unity, so all Germans were coming together in this crisis for common purpose, or so cooed the *Kreuz-Zeitung* on April 10, in the middle of the empress's tour of Posen. To celebrate her visit, so the paper said, even the Polish houses had been dragged into the public world and decorated as their German counterparts in the city. The liberal *Vossische Zeitung* saw her tour, too, as a "triumph . . . in which national and confessional differences all but disappeared." But the enthusiasm quickly soured when word spread that the empress had been slighted by a group of aristocratic Polish women who had greeted her at the railroad station. Apparently, they addressed her in French, not in German. In this affront, the Conservative paper angrily noted, they showed their true colors, behaving not as Prussians but as *Polonaises*.[17] At the very moment of the consolidation of national unity, the fragile creation was disaggregated by the display of unmistakable difference that could not be suppressed. The hostile reaction by nationalists forced to confront the voice of the "other" rhetorically constituted the nation by imposing an extremely exacting set of conditions for membership.

This moment of tension had disrupted a cultural strategy that was an essential ingredient in official nationalist politics: a ritual performance of the imagined national community mobilized in self-defense. Within the emergency ad hoc relief operations were highly scripted ritual forms that structured the tour of the empress through the provinces of Posen and West Prussia and along the Elbe River in April and June.[18] These performances were modeled on the old familiar dynastic rituals of rule, representing up-to-date versions of "royal entries" and other forms of visitations that, as we will see below, regularly punctuated the routines of social life in Germany. As happened in Posen, however, they could backfire and reveal deep social fissures rather than affirm community.

The tour in June, however, went according to plan; the river had not yet receded, and the personal visit of the empress was designed to articulate to the homeless themselves and the wider reading public the concern and care of the dynasty for the innocent victims. At the same time, backed by the force of state and private emergency measures and the generous donations from all corners of the national community, her visit sought to assuage fear: "everything will work out well in the end," she promised with words meant not only for the refugees within hearing range but to assure others that the dynastic state would provide similar relief when and where it was necessary.[19]

---

17. *KZ*, no. 91, April 10, 1888, and no. 99, April 14, 1888; *VZ*, no. 170, April 10, 1888, and no. 178, April 14, 1888. The liberal paper was equally disturbed by the allegations but called for the facts before drawing any conclusions.

18. The detailed report is found in *KZ*, no. 191, June 10, 1888; and *VZ*, April 9, 1888, April 10, 1888, as well as third supplement to no. 172, April 11, 1888.

19. *KZ*, no. 191, June 10, 1888.

The choreography surrounding the tour was a familiar one and patterned to legitimize state authority. Triumphal arches, which were described as "unpretentious" given the tragedy, nonetheless had been set up. In Elbing, the empress was greeted by columns of schoolchildren and corporate groups lined up along the route. In one account, thirty-two hundred girls, who threw flowers in her path, were on "display" from the girls' schools in the area; at one of the stops the daughter of a city councillor recited a poem and gave the empress a bouquet. The female workforce of a local cigarette factory, Loeser and Wolff, also appeared en masse in their white aprons and high caps, flanked at both ends by the male workers and the factory craftsmen and supervisory personnel. While assuredly not a spontaneous demonstration of support, their official assignment as audience added an industrial dimension to the presentation of "community" that, typically in dynastic ritual time, remained corporatist in structure, highlighting gender and age.

A face-to-face meeting of local notables also was part of the script. Victoria honored the women of the patriotic associations involved in relief work, who were elevated in the ceremony to the status of the other familiar representatives of power and authority: the clergy, the magistrates, and members of the business community. Pointedly, she walked through the festively decorated streets accompanied by two military generals from the area. The next month, now as widow, Victoria sent each of the schoolgirls in the flooded environs a gift as a token of her visit: a small latched box filled with sewing materials to serve as a "cherished" memento and a "spur to serious and useful work."[20] To be sure, more was being tamed than fear itself! The gift was meant to domesticate the future by a symbolic gesture that affirmed the proper household gender order and the values of hard work that upheld the status quo.

In this flood tragedy, constellations of dramatic performances had become intertwined to affirm the legitimacy of dynastic rule through its "taming of fear"; these dramas were scripted actions imposed on the actors themselves, in this particular instance at a moment of natural disaster in the context of political uncertainties raised by dynastic succession. They were meant to reassure a community threatened by sudden unpredictability and support the reaggregation of the group as a normative gendered community in the larger national family in the future.

Cultural Performances and Identity

Cultural performances and ritual forms stand in a complex relationship to traditions. In turn, this linkage is vital to the political process. Each per-

---

20. *KZ*, no. 191, June 10, 1888, and also no. 236, July 6, 1888.

formance has a living force to the extent that it upholds a tradition, which is kept alive in the very cycle of enactment; if the tradition is broken, the identity of the group is threatened (and new ritual forms are required to consolidate and reaffirm group solidarity). Alternatively, the socioeconomic fissures that undercut group cohesion challenge the power of traditional rituals to maintain identity and to do their work of persuasion.

This shifting and slippery terrain of negotiation between ritual forms, group cohesion, and tradition underlies the fabric of political rule, manifest most vividly in revolutionary breaks, such as those occurring in France in 1789 or in Iran in 1979. In both cases—separated by nearly two centuries and by vastly different political cultures—consolidation and legitimacy required their ritual enactment. In the case of France, these were the revolutionary symbols of color, dress, gesture, and ceremony; in Iran, it meant the Islamic co-optation of the ritual life of its main left-labor opposition. Similar processes were at work in the *Kaiserreich* and, to maintain the parallelism across time and culture, in the newly emerging nations in Asia and Africa in the throes of decolonization after 1945.[21]

For the dynastic groups in the political establishment after German unification, ritual performances of rule were powerful vehicles to intertwine dynastic legitimacy and national identity. These rites perpetuated the dynasty as a familiar tradition itself, which carried an aura of authority within the "natural" social hierarchy and, in turn, reaffirmed and reinforced the very principles of the hierarchy. To be sure, dynastic rule stood in stark contrast with a new locus of political authority in the male citizen, which was the basis of the political nation-state in Germany after 1871. Citizenship at home had a powerful if uneven logic in the notion of rights and entitlements, which was not, however, incompatible with subject peoples in empire. Nor could it at once transform older identities in the new political order.

Dynastic "subjecthood"—traditional understandings of individual identity and loyalty in terms of the royal figure—remained an integral part of the vocabulary of self in certain contexts for a wide range of peoples in imperial German society. These groups included the poor in need, who petitioned for "immediate help" as loyal subjects, however much that

---

21. In this study, I am modifying the idea of cultural performance found in MacAloon, *Rite, Drama, Festival, Spectacle.* For the importance of ritual consolidation of rule in the French case signaling the end of the initial revolutionary process, see Lynn Avery Hunt, *Politics, Culture, and Class in the French Revolution* (Berkeley and Los Angeles, 1984); and Mona Ozouf, "Space and Time in the Festivals of the French Revolution," *Comparative Studies in Society and History* 17 (1976): 372–84. For Iran, Ervand Abrahamian, *Khomeinism: Essays on the Islamic Republic* (Berkeley and Los Angeles, 1993). An example of socioeconomic change that destroys the power of rituals to bind social groups is Clifford Geertz, "Ritual and Social Change: A Javanese Example," in *The Interpretation of Cultures,* 142–69.

"identity" was imposed on them; all manner of veterans, who continued to identify as dynastic state subjects; members of associations like shooting societies, with old ties to the dynastic center. It also comprised part of the patriotic service elite's self-description in civil society—in "free" associational life—in contrast to the bureaucratic elite in administrative posts, who did not identify themselves as *Untertanen,* however loyal they might have been.[22]

For elite women excluded from political citizenship, dynastic loyalty structured a complex performative identity in public service. It formed a powerful source of female identification that was at once hierarchical and leveling. It permitted traditional deference toward those above and demanded it from those below; at the same time, it assumed an elite of equals based on its expressed understanding of shared attributes of femininity (which extended to the person of the royalty) as catalysts in shaping the national community through the female rituals of care. However much in flux, this identity expressed intermediate solidarities that upheld conservative social and political power—a power best served by reinforcing such clusters as families and communities as well as religious and philanthropic associations.

These institutional bodies—familiar architectural "monuments" to care in the locality such as hospitals, sanatoria, asylums, and orphanages—became the sites of ritual performances of rule. The actors themselves were the members in their corporate and associational identities. Philanthropy remained an ideal stage for dynastic performances—with or without the person of the dynast—because it was a familiar vehicle to embody the "state" in its traditional side of care as well as its evolving modern medical and scientific side. These theatrical performances, furthermore, had a familiar form and patterned structure. If the structure seemed to maintain its old shape throughout the *Kaiserreich,* the messages changed over time, which lent a dynamic quality to this expressive political culture.

---

22. Traditional identities were maintained in a range of places in civil society. For shooting societies, for example, LK, Abt. 403, no. 8819, Schützen-Feste, 1832 (although the collection has materials into late 1870s); and Bruell, *Chronik der Stadt Düren,* who has a long section (in a short chronicle) on the shooting societies and their dynastic patrons. Also Düding, "Kreigesvereine im wilhelminischen Reich." The literature on bureaucratic reform stresses the spread of rational and normative thinking with ongoing modernization. For a useful summary, Beck, *Origins of Welfare State,* 125–47. A caricature of the "Untertan" comes from Heinrich Mann's novel of the same name (1918), translated as *Man of Straw* (London, 1984), which, indirectly, reflects the importance of associational ties in the life of the wife of Dr. Hessling.

The concept of "theatrical" politics is not simply a product of the historian's gaze or that of an observer trained in the interdisciplinary readings of culture. It was the explicit vocabulary of the "new politics" in the dynastic philanthropic associations after 1871. Facing an uncertain future in the new nation-state, dynastic groups early on described novel performative strategies, which they took into the public arena in their efforts to shape public opinion. For example, in the protocols of the Baden state Red Cross organization recounting its activities for 1875, the exercises of the stretcher-bearers were described as "a fully new theatrical performance" *(ein vollkommen neues Schauspiel)* for the public audience. The organizations drew on and popularized a new world of visual display in addition to their reliance on print capitalism. The same groups in Karlsruhe in 1873 had arranged the first of many exhibitions, in this case a sample of diverse medical equipment needed to sustain a "modern" war, showing it in the garden castle in the Herrenstrasse. They also published and circulated a catalog of the show.[23]

These performances were understood by their "producers" in part as instrumental and were inserted into the political struggle for money and power. They were aimed primarily at "the public" and, over the course of the *Kaiserreich,* partly forced therefore to accommodate shifting expectations and standards of community care. The public audience always was an explicit object of concern as the source of much of the financial support for these quasi-private organizations in the first place. Money was the bottom line, and the leadership devoted considerable time and attention to the details of each financial campaign.

Daily life in the patriotic culture, which spilled out into the community, was infused with lotteries, auctions, benefit concerts and theaters, prize competitions, as well as door-to-door and street-corner solicitations. Organizing and executing these events brought a variety of groups together: for example, military bands were a regular part of benefit concerts, and theatrical companies used veterans to sell tickets, earmarking a small proportion of the profit for the ex-servicemen's organizations. In addition, these performances extended down through society to become a very "natural" part of middle-class expressive culture, affecting, for example, the private lessons of a piano teacher. In 1909, Anna Söhnlin-Wettach, pianist in Karlsruhe, received permission to hold a recital on the day of the fiftieth-anniversary celebration of the Baden Women's Associa-

---

23. GK, Abt. 233, no. 2848, *Bericht über die bei Gelegenheit der ersten Versammlung des Landesausschusses am 31. Mai und 1 Juni 1875 gepflogenen Verhandlungen* (Karlsruhe, 1875); also, Badischer Landes-Hilfs-Verein, *Rechenschafts-Bericht für das Jahr 1873* (Karlsruhe, 1873).

tion. Preceding the works of Schumann, Mendelssohn, Wagner, and Brahms was a prologue written by the music students that honored the dynasty and the noble work of its women's association. The proceeds of this modest patriotic festival were earmarked for needy children to take a cure at the brine baths in Dürrhein.[24] In this way, patriotic and dynastic values accompanied the aesthetic charm of the classical tune.

The extent to which dynastic festivals and performances shaped political consciousness, however, is a complicated question. Individual reminiscences were biased by those who had much to gain from their ties to the dynastic court and its rituals. The celebration of the fiftieth anniversary of the Baden Women's Association in 1909, nonetheless, occasioned much reflection, particularly among the recipients of a commemorative publication and brooch from the duchess. It brought back memories of a shared past—of the beneficiary's own life experiences or those of her father or mother.

Marie Bissinger of Pforzheim, for example, recounts her father's and mother's work for the *Frauen-Verein* in a letter of thanks to the duchess.

> The gracious thoughts of Your Highness in those past years . . . awaken the most precious memories of the time in which my father had the pleasure to work (as advisor) in the association, spurred on by the blessed activities and under the patronage of Your Majesty Luise. . . . But also the work that my mother did for Section III . . . is an indelible part of her memory.[25]

For Marie Burgner, by then a resident in Leipzig, the celebration allowed the reexperience of her Baden identity, which had not been extinguished in the move to Saxony.

> My most precious memories are those that take me back to the time when I was permitted to work on the tasks of the Baden Women's Association, the heart and soul of which was our beloved *Landesmutter*. . . . Even after fate forced me to leave my *Heimat,* I continued to participate in the ongoing development of this creation that . . . through God's grace spread beyond the borders of our beloved state.[26]

---

24. GK, Abt. 69, no. 951b, Das 50-jährige Jubiläum des Badischen Frauenvereins am 16. und 17. Juni 1909, report to Duchess Luise, Friday, June 18. For an example of Berlin theaters using veteran associations to sell tickets, *KZ,* supplement to no. 284, December 4, 1873.

25. GK, Abt. 69, no. 951b, Pforzheim, June 20, 1909.

26. GK, Abt. 69, no. 951b, Leipzig, June 17, 1909. For a more detailed analysis of *Heimat* in the context of German national identity-formation, Applegate, *A Nation of Provincials.*

Indeed, her willingness later to volunteer in dynastic patriotic service in another German state had been shaped by her formative experiences as a young women and her enthusiasm for "our then young princess."

For others, the anniversary celebration in 1909 was the medium to reexperience and reaffirm loyalty. Listen to Anna Kuhlenthal, supervisor of the Friedrichstift, a girls' school and home in Karlsruhe under the auspices of the Baden Women's Association. While she interprets the meaning of the festivities at the castle for the schoolgirls, she also describes its importance for herself and the other adult members of the foundation. Apparently, the older students had helped set up the benches outside in the garden, and two in the group had been chosen by lottery to serve at the duchess's table.

> Our schoolgirls were extraordinarily happy to be able to participate in something so beautiful and ennobling: the singing, the festivities in the garden, and the reception in the castle, where they ate scoops of ice cream with golden spoons. . . . They rarely had experienced anything as splendid. [It is] a sacred memory for a lifetime, and many seeds that were planted here will blossom and bear fruit later.[27]

Kuhlenthal unmistakably alluded to sowing loyalty early on among the young. Employing a metaphor straight out of the conservative lexicon, she proffered her own florid assessment.

> We members of the Friedrichstift are thankful that our house owes its origins . . . to the creative care *(schöpferische Fürsorge)* of Your Majesty and is now part of the deep-rooted and fully canopied tree that is the Baden Women's Association. . . . For myself and the sisters, the festival is a wonderful memory and, at its center, is our noble duchess and *Landesmutter,* resembling a precious jewel, radiating to all sides generously and from all sides receiving.

These excessive expressions of loyalty nonetheless fed into a ritual exchange that reinvigorated the bonds between dynast and subject.

In Mannheim, Major Max von Seubert also expressed his gratitude in a letter to the duchess, in which he, on his own, turned to the formative place of ritual experiences early in life. In his case, the 1909 medallion was but a continuation, as he put it, of the "graciousness" he had received during the fiftieth wedding anniversary celebration of the duke and duchess of Baden in 1906. His letter centered on "the important years, 1856 and 1906." This was a reference to the "joyous entry" of Frederick and Luise into Mannheim at the time of their marriage and the exact duplication of

---

27. GK, Abt. 69, no. 951b, Karlsruhe, June 20, 1909.

the ceremony fifty years later—down to a replica of the large triumphal arch and reactivation of the steamship *Hohenzollern* to transport the royal couple. In von Seubert's words, "In the first mentioned year I stood in Karlsruhe at the entry parade of the exalted newlyweds and God's grace permitted me to participate in the jubilation and together with the other loyal Baden subjects join in the festival of their marriage."[28] The historic reenactment fifty years later was a memorable expression of continuity and unity. For von Seubert, the 1909 gift was a "splendid keepsake," reactivating a memory that centered on dynastic celebrations. Through its effects, he could relive the experiences of his youth and the feelings of past solidarity and community. These were powerful emotions that later, arguably, helped define his own work and political commitments. Von Seubert spent his career in loyal dynastic service. Still active in the army in 1909, he served as well in the Mannheim branch of the women's association. He had joined in the early 1880s, from 1883 on worked as advisor to Section II (overseeing women's industrial schooling), and for the past twenty years served also as advisor to the whole chapter.

As anthropologists show, many rites reinforce and celebrate the status quo. These are the dramatic moments when the establishment becomes, in Geertz's famous phrase, a "theater state," a form of "organized spectacle" in which the power structure of a community is expressed, interpreted, and reinforced. Considerable interdisciplinary work on popular culture in early modern and modern Europe also has uncovered multiple forms of celebrations and popular festivities that affirm—although often by apparent transgression—the dominant gender and power hierarchy. In northern Burgundy at Mardi Gras time, for example, cross-dressing and other types of mock reordering of private life and property relations regularly accompanied a reordering of the social order at the new agricultural season. Equally to the point in this French example, a larger national identity as French increasingly became connected to these symbolic practices of community membership, such as the right to free firewood in the act of cutting wood. As one woman informant in the village of Minot put it as late as 1962, "The first year [after moving to the area] we were not given the right to free firewood. So I didn't go to vote that year because I said if I am not French enough to keep warm, I'm not

---

28. GK, Abt. 69, no. 945, Der Frauenverein Mannheim, 1909 and 1912, Mannheim, December 13, 1909. For information on 1856 and 1906 celebrations, see no. 572, Allerhöchster Besuch in Mannheim, 1856–99, *Extra-Beilage zum Mannheimer Anzeiger,* no. 42, September 17, 1856; and no. 575b, Allerhöchster Besuch in Mannheim, 1906–7, October 7, 10, 1906, letters of the mayor.

French enough to vote, either."[29] National identity is "seen" in its symbolic forms in daily life partly as it insinuates itself in older community rituals and practices.

Most studies of nationalism in imperial Germany have missed its integration into dynastic power and rituals, although the extent of coverage of these royal celebrations in the press should have occasioned more historical reflection. A wide range of print media eloquently speak to the importance of public display in the day-to-day life of German communities.[30] Some historians, among them Lynn Abrams, have concentrated on an emerging working-class culture "from below" and argue that festive life in imperial Germany increasingly became class divided. Truly integrative *Volksfeste* remained illusory, and, Abrams concludes, the German state essentially failed to win over the working masses through its nationalist celebrations. Following Mosse, the argument is based in the main on analyses of the presumed key nationalist rituals instituted "from above": Sedan Day, September 2 (an official national holiday commemorating the decisive Prussian/German victory in the war against the French in 1870) and the kaiser's birthday, March 22 and, in Wilhelmine Germany, January 27. Mosse himself concludes that these festivals were a "failure," although his own evidence of mass indifference is somewhat contradictory: socialist gymnasts by the early twentieth century were unable to keep many of their colleagues away from the state-inspired celebrations.[31]

The early implementation of the Sedan Day festival, however, reflected local circumstances and mirrors the complicated interaction between the locality and the center that is at the heart of my analysis. The new holiday, in effect, was co-opted for local purposes by various powerful groups. In the case of communities in Posen, for example, the Protes-

---

29. Geertz, *Negara*. The French quote is in Tina Jolas and Françoise Zonabend, "Tillers of the Fields and Woodspeople," in *Rural Society in France: Selections from the Annales,* ed. Robert Forster and Orest Ranum (Baltimore, 1977), 148.

30. Wolfgang Kaschuba, "Von der 'Rotte' zum 'Block.' Zur kulturellen Ikonographie des Demonstration im 19. Jahrhundert," in Warneken, *Massenmedium Strasse,* 86, makes a similar point.

31. Mosse, *Nationalization of the Masses,* 91–93, 170; and Lynn Abrams, *Workers' Culture in Imperial Germany: Leisure and Recreation in the Rhineland and Westphalia* (London, 1992), 57. Abrams notes that "respectable" workers shunned the nationalist festivals but many other types of workers did not (52–53). The complicated receptivity of dynastic festivals and images among the populace requires careful empirical attention, however. For a detailed case of how dockworkers' own patriarchal values enhanced their receptivity to the paternal image of the emperor, see Marina Cattaruzza, "Das Kaiserbild in der Arbeiterschaft am Beispiel der Werftarbeiter in Hamburg und Stettin," in Röhl, *Der Ort Kaiser Wilhelm II,* 142.

tant churches and the synagogues underwrote the celebrations, which were turned into popular festivities for schoolchildren; coordination of activities in the denominationally distinct schools, apparently, reflected a shared commitment to communicate a particularly Prussian version of history to the young students. In other instances, veterans used the event to dramatize their memory of sacrifice in war and instruct Germany's sons for the future.[32] And the former territorial sovereigns *(Standesherren)*—many of whom were deeply ambivalent about the newfangled notions of nation in the early years of the empire—bent the ceremony to affirm their own authority. Thus, in 1872, Count von Hochberg-Fürstenstein in Wirschkowitz in Silesia also arranged the memorial to German victory around activities for schoolchildren in the area. According to the report, thirteen hundred children joined in the music and dancing, games and pole climbing as well as eating and drinking in three wooded locations set up for the events. The count and countess personally made the rounds accompanied by two Evangelical sisters *(Diakonissinnen)* and their young charges. This commemoration, however, spilled over into a more traditional harvest celebration six days later. But in the new context of war and unification, the count now invited 164 veterans to his castle for a midday meal as a testimony to fellowship and community. As in older times, the man and maid servants *(Dienstleute)* of the count's nine domains lined up before the castle in "their fine attire" to present a harvest wreath to the lord. A *Hoch* to king and kaiser transformed the ceremony into something different in its very familiarity. And the day culminated in an evening of dance and general merrymaking.[33]

These locally molded "national" celebrations were a new source of memory, in this German case filtered through the festive expressions of the old social and military hierarchy. They added a new identity to an already complex field of values that affirmed deference as it supported autonomous village space. Since it could escape class and religious moorings, in the right circumstances it could be mobilized in defense of an order that was inherently unequal and hierarchical. Or, as the French example shows, this identity could become attached to the practices of popular resistance and notions of social dignity. This is why the politics around the formation of national identity are so hard for historians to pin down.[34]

---

32. The nationalist celebration throughout Germany was followed closely by the *Kreuz-Zeitung,* which carried many local reports. For the veterans and the Posen example, supplement to no. 213, September 12, 1872.

33. *KZ,* supplement to no. 216, September 15, 1872.

34. Anderson's initial study was prompted by the nationalist wars between two Communist countries (a "theoretical" impossibility); it is why he turns his analysis from "ideology" to the cultural forms of meaning and identity (*Imagined Communities,* 1–4). For primary texts that demonstrate the place of nationalism in liberal, conservative, socialist, fascist, as well as anticolonial visions, see Dahbour and Ishay, *The Nationalism Reader.*

Whatever role Sedan Day—or the kaiser's birthday—played on the local level in the constellation of power and its contestation, it is the perspective "from above" that speaks to its meaning for dynastic rule. Its precise choreography—the minutely scripted use of specific texts, the repetitive refrains of patriotic songs, hymns, and music that made the tunes more and more familiar in the cultural landscape, the careful attention to actors and audience—all demonstrate what Benedict Anderson has called the fictional "meanwhile," the narrative trope that expressed a growing consciousness of actions occurring simultaneously, elsewhere.[35] It is from the dynastic center that this simultaneity of political activity was orchestrated and its impact best observed. Similarly scripted patterns of "invented" celebrations also shaped the character of political life in the new nation-states around the globe after 1945: there, too, rulers recognized the efficacy of standardized presentations not only to involve local groups with central authority but to provide expressive means for the locality to identify with others living elsewhere. To employ an apt formulation of Kertzer: "In simultaneity lies political communion."[36]

Criteria other than Mosse's, then, are needed to evaluate these and other nationalist celebrations. In the first place, as official nationalist rituals, they could not, as Mosse would have it, "break through to be genuine rites," expressing a dynamic mass participation; but the *Vormärz* examples of nationalist festivities used by Mosse as contrasting models were equally limited—in this case essentially to the educated, young, male elites. From the start and in its core, to be sure, official nationalism sought to limit the democratic potential inherent in nationalism; its mix worked to thwart overt expression of the ongoing transformations of modern industrial class relations and struggle.

Official ceremonial spaces drew on and displayed a particular constellation of "community" that was rooted in "real"—albeit partial—identities.[37] In addition to the representatives of the political and military power structure, these spaces privileged in carefully gendered scripts the members of corporate work groups, people in their leisure and recreational roles, those in philanthropic and veterans' associations as well as schoolchildren and young people. Beyond the invited participants, of

---

35. Anderson, *Imagined Communities*, 22–36.

36. Kertzer, *Ritual, Politics, and Power*, 23.

37. For new thinking on the construction of identity, Denise Riley, *"Am I That Name?" Feminism and the Category of "Women" in History* (Minneapolis, 1988); and Belinda Davis, "Home Fires Burning: Politics, Identity, and Food in World War I Berlin," Ph.D. diss., University of Michigan, 1992, 53–58, who shows how different identities were constituted and redeployed in wartime. For persuasive evidence for the complexity of hybrid identities, Antoinette Burton, *At the Heart of Empire: Indians and the Colonial Encounter in Late-Victorian Britain* (Berkeley and Los Angeles, 1998).

course, were the "mass" of onlookers—through the windows and on the balconies of the houses along the route as well as those milling about on the streets—who could form their own understandings of the festive time. Vigilant police oversight and the constant threat (and systematic use) of force continuously maintained the semblance of order and authority. For the time of the ceremony, too, the streets lost their character as places of economic exchange, of class interaction, or as transit venues.[38] As part of the ongoing struggle for power, these dynastic performances appropriated various manifestations of identities; to that extent, I argue, they structured a tangible understanding of the national community that was ambiguous enough in its symbolic formation to permit multiple readings.

Mosse's perspective is limited in two other ways. He claims, ultimately, that the official celebrations came to express a form of "bourgeois sociability," an argument that encases German nationalism—in a way that is repeated in the literature—in a limited class framework. His perspective also reflects a stark male bias—also repeated—in which women do not figure in the nationalist project at all.[39] But the ritual and performative worlds of official nationalism utilized gender in multiple ways to help constitute (conservative) "reality."

In the struggle to define the normative German community, official nationalism did its best performative work as part of a wider set of public roles for the dynast—the *Landesvater* and the *Landesmutter.* Not only was this public space inhabited by patriotic women at all levels of political administration and associational life, but these same women were part of public performances designed to communicate conservative messages about power and national identity. To be sure, conservative nationalist writing throughout most of the *Kaiserreich* remained deeply ambivalent about women in public life.[40] But this same conservative political culture was shaped inexorably by the gendered rituals and celebrations of rule. Their performative spaces were open to many women, not the least the "reigning" *Landesmutter,* an aspect of nationalist struggle too easily missed if nationalism is seen merely as political program or bourgeois ideology. These insights shift the focus away from Sedan Day, for example, or the official holiday on the kaiser's birthday, and onto the gender dynamics of national identity-formation in other sites and locations.

---

38. This point is made in an analysis of a military parade, Roberto Da Matta, "Carnival in Multiple Planes," in MacAloon, *Rite, Drama, Festival, Spectacle,* 218–19.

39. Mosse, *Nationalization of the Masses,* 93, 100.

40. The conservative organizations acknowledged a "woman's question" but not a feminist response. For an historian's understanding of the discrepancy between official rhetoric and actual behavior, Lipp, *Schimpfende Weiber,* 7–13, 270–72.

Genres of Nationalist Cultural Performances

Cultural performances come in a variety of forms. Each is a distinct mode of communication that itself is evolving and dynamic. I have coined four genres of official nationalist performances in imperial Germany through which vivid images of membership in a larger national community were expressed. Each illustrates the continuing importance of dynastic figures and patronage, institutions, and identity in structuring understandings of such abstract notions as "state" or "national community." Identity-formation is not a linear process in which a national identity magically displaces state or local identities; similarly, while nationalism might be a code of modernism, the evolution of the German nation-state nonetheless was mediated by traditional loyalties, practices, and award systems. Paralleling the nationalist debate over German identity in language and words, these rites and ceremonies were terrains of struggle in which political meanings were tested and contested. As Geertz states with his usual perspicacity, these ceremonies of self-definition are about "power, place, privilege, wealth, fame, and all the other so-called 'real' rewards of life."[41]

The first genre is the national mobilization for the "community in danger"; we have followed one example of its unfolding already in some detail in the devastating 1888 flood. Second are the visitation ceremonies that repeatedly brought the *Landesmutter* to a village, town, or city in her domain for an inaugural celebration, which marked the opening of a new hospital, for example, or an exhibition. These ceremonies took place in and around concrete buildings, recalling Pastor Scheibler's conception of philanthropy as a monument, which I quoted in chapter 1. In point of fact, over time the specific building consecrated in ceremony was a visual tie to the past as it was reexperienced in each present moment, keeping alive a memory of events and practices and, simultaneously, summarizing collective values.[42] No wonder dynasts associated their rule with ceremonies that centered on such "stable" material foundations; in this festive time, rooted in a specific locality, various layers of community identification commingled and interacted. The third genre is the public ceremonies in which the dynastic state conferred its ranks and honors for public service as well as normative family living. Fourth, and finally, is the widespread practice of linking patriotic associations' leisure and festive time with the

---

41. Geertz, "After the Revolution," 252.

42. For a fascinating philosophical treatise on architecture and time, see Aldo Rossi, *The Architecture of the City,* trans. Diane Ghirardo and Joan Ockman (Cambridge, Mass., 1982; rpt. 1997). Despite the appearance of stability, architecture also falls into ruin and, thus, serves as a metaphor for tension and unease in the process of state-building, a theme I return to in chapter 7.

dynastic life-cycle calendar. In most cases, these official performances were designed to communicate their messages well beyond the avowed circle of dynastic associations, seeking, in essence, to enlarge the patriotic public. In other instances, the ceremony was for the service elite itself, designed to reinforce loyalty and group cohesion. In a class-divided society, not all ritual expressions are meant to be inclusive.

The Rituals of Disaster Relief

Nineteenth-century chronicles of villages, towns, and cities throughout central Europe offer poignant testimony to the vulnerability of human life and livelihood in the face of sudden, unpredictable natural disasters. Their systematic record of the annual events "worthy" of note invariably included the fires, floods, and famines, too often accompanied by deadly epidemics, that seriously disrupted community routines and threatened life, livelihood, and property.[43] Over time, the territorial states and urban magistrates invested in modern technological infrastructures, implementing public health regulations or works' projects such as dams and levies— components of central planning partially justified by the human susceptibility to the idiosyncrasies of nature. Technology seemed to offer a key to locking up the forces of nature. Technological change, however, brought with it new hazards. Space in local papers was taken up as well by other calamities riveting the public such as train wrecks, which also seemed to call for energetic official responses.

Reflecting a centralizing imperative as part of state-building itself, disaster relief became increasingly coordinated from above, reinvigorating the very center in the process. Because of its choreographed script and organizational networks, this moment of relief service mobilized widespread support and generated, in the language of the day, "patriotic" responses throughout the land.[44] The pattern was tested early on in a particularly severe famine that hit East Prussia in 1867; there was serious

---

43. The observation of the content of village chronicles comes from my earlier work on the protoindustrial transformation of the Saxon Oberlausitz. Among others, Ludwig Engelmann, *Geschichte von Reichenau* (Reichenau, 1904); Johann August Ernst Köhler, *Bilder aus der Oberlausitz, als ein Beitrag zur Vaterlandskunde* (Budissin, 1855); Christian Adolph Pescheck, *Handbuch der Geschichte von Zittau,* 2 vols. (Zittau, 1834–37).

44. Several documents show how wider identities were created in the local responses to the flooding in 1872. GSPK, no. 15609, Bl. 38, Bericht des Vorstandes des Vaterländischen Frauen-Hülfs-Vereins zu Hamburg. Here is the imaginary "we came together" to help those in need. Also, for Baden, GK, Abt. 233, no. 2848, *Dreizehnter Jahresbericht des Vorstandes des Badischen Frauenvereins, Abteilung Karlsruhe.* The Baden group organized an exhibition of slides and a benefit concert and sent 1,625 Floren to the Executive Committee of the Prussian Women's Association.

flooding on the North Sea coast in 1872; a cholera outbreak threatened East Prussia in 1876; a disastrous flood inundated parts of mountainous Silesia in 1897, the effects of which reverberated in local communities for six years; towns in Baden experienced serious fires (Breton, Dinglingen, Donauschingen) that drew the duchess of Baden into the center of relief measures; a train wreck in Müllheim made headlines for days in 1911; and, in January 1914, the public again was mobilized in the name of "love of neighbor" to supplement state aid measures for flooded victims in Pomerania. The list of large-scale disasters, here picked at random, is practically endless. The 1888 flood was but one of many calamities that focused simultaneous attention from far and wide onto the communities in need.

At its foundation, rooted in the unpredictable, this mobilization seems to be the opposite of ritual; given the politics of dynastic service, however, it took on the character of a patterned, repeated "ritualized" performance. Two illustrations, in addition to the discussion of the 1888 flood, demonstrate the "politics" of disaster relief for shaping nation-state identities in Germany. The first is the ad hoc public mobilization by patriotic women in the famine conditions in 1867 in Prussia, which fashioned the behavioral precedents; the second, drawn from an extraordinary set of archival letters, traces the gendered politics of identity from the perspective of a community in danger, in this case, the town of Lähn, Silesia, which was flooded in 1897.

In patriotic lore, the 1867 famine relief was the original "trial by fire," the first (and effective) step onto the public stage by the newly founded Patriotic Women's Association in Prussia. Not surprisingly, a retrospective rendering of women's services at the twenty-fifth anniversary celebration of the association drew an analogy to military battle in its assessment of the effects: a precedent had been established, and "the first campaign was won."[45]

The politics surrounding this early "campaign" are unmistakable. Famine hit the districts of Königsberg and Gumbinnen with extraordinary force, bringing in its wake a typhus epidemic; estate owners, fearing contagion, dismissed their day laborers. The numbers of unemployed and destitute people multiplied and estate owners as well as state officials saw increasing numbers of women and children begging "from farmstead to farmstead and from village to village." In the face of serious social unrest and disorder, official response was swift and two-pronged. Reflecting the constellation of power in Prussia, state tax and relief measures favored the

---

45. GSPK, no. 15610, Bl. 122, Festrede . . . April 5, 1892, speech by Dr. Paul Hassel of Saxony. For more details, *DRK,* 2:215–21.

landlords "to maintain their base of livelihood," whereas public relief was instituted through the model of patronal largesse, overseen by Queen Augusta.

Three components of voluntarism were tested. First, a widespread, simultaneous, and effective mobilization of philanthropy throughout the whole monarchy was orchestrated by the women's association networks. This mobilization had long-term effects: 174 local chapters of Patriotic Women's Associations were founded in East Prussia in the aftermath of the crisis. Second, traditional forms of beneficence were instituted on the spot: soup kitchens, over the course of the crisis, dispensed more than 3 million portions of food; clothing and fuel, which had been acquired elsewhere, also were doled out. It was estimated that nearly thirteen thousand people were beneficiaries of this charity. Third, there was a sustained effort to secure alternative work for the unemployed beyond the makeshift jobs (for men) in railroad construction and other forms of public works that state officials quickly arranged. Designed in particular for women but also for (old) men who could not leave their communities, association members brought work contracts and materials—in hand spinning, which had no real economic potential as a source of permanent livelihood—and they also organized consumer cooperatives to buy provisions more cheaply. The final aspect of choreographed relief concerned its interpretation. Augusta herself sought to define the message in a letter to the association's advisor. In her words, "Above all we must found new chapters and present their work not only as a model of private philanthropy but also as state-supported relief."[46] Through this humanitarian work of "love of neighbor" and "patriotism"—the linguistic frame of choice placed on voluntary service—the dynasty clearly intended to reinforce the identity of its state as "caring."

The Prussian examples of famine and flood relief demonstrate a key mechanism of identity-construction—the simultaneity of action that mobilized the whole "nation" around the needs of a threatened locality. Its work deployed a particular form of state responsibilities, which remained limited in intent and supplemented by philanthropy. At its heart was a gendered script in which the *Landesmutter* oversaw her patriotic female disciples in sanctioned public service to insure community renewal. To be sure, the wider public could draw its own conclusions about the nature of this relief effort, but it undeniably served to link members of disparate communities to one another at precise moments of crises, broadening horizons and helping expand borders.

A complementary perspective comes from the locality and its ties outward to the larger territory. In point of fact, the envisioning of a national

---

46. Reproduced in *DRK,* 2:217, December 13, 1867.

community developed directly out of the very institutional growth of the dynastic associations themselves. This change in consciousness can be traced through the correspondence of leaders of a local women's association in Lähn, a town on the Bober River, in a poor, remote agricultural district of Silesia. Archival sources have preserved yearly reports of the association's presidents in the form of letters to the *Landesvater* for over forty-seven years.[47]

The local branch was run throughout the period by three powerful and articulate aristocratic women (with only one year's interruption in leadership): Marie von Haugwitz, 1870–83; Marie von L'Estocq, 1883–1901; and her daughter, Countess Fanny Pfeil, 1902–18. Basing themselves in each case on inheritance of a landed estate, these women transformed the foundation of aristocratic rural power into a leadership role of a modern voluntary association. The unique source—the letters are handwritten and deeply personal, while also self-serving, to be sure, for the supplicants are out for money—demonstrates the subtle processes whereby nationalist identification grew in the context of traditional loyalty and ties to the monarchy.

The women's association in Lähn had been founded in July 1870—in war—to care for wounded soldiers; immediately in peace, its first president exercised the old feudal subject right to petition the king/emperor for an immediate subvention—and continued to do so, as did her successors, for the next forty-six years. The small association had taken over administration of the old hospital (founded in 1575) in return for acquiring the deed to its property. Now it wanted to employ a nursing sister (a *Diakonissin* trained at the Lazarus Hospital in Berlin) to run the hospital as an enclosed "refuge" for disabled and impoverished inhabitants who, apparently with local official and police connivance, until then had been allowed to beg for their livelihood. But in the immediate aftermath of war, the women's association and the local power structure were allied in appealing to the "generosity" of their *Landesvater* to provide a dynastic subsidy for this project of incarceration.[48] The king complied.

The tone of the requests was formal and deferential yet also intimate,

47. GSPK, nos. 15609–13, 1867–1919, reports on Lähn throughout these documents. The ties to the *Landesvater* were an older pattern of "immediate help" linked to the sovereign and not easily gender typed. Remarkable, however, are the obituaries of men active in dynastic philanthropy. They used the same tropes as those characterizing women leaders: self-sacrificing and tireless in working for love of neighbor. See GK, Abt. 69, no. 1175, Tod des Frh. v.d. Knesebeck, November 6, 1911. For more on men who were attached to qualities coded as feminine, Judith R. Walkowitz, *City of Dreadful Delight: Narratives of Sexual Danger in late-Victorian London* (Chicago, 1992): 59–61.

48. GSPK, no. 15609, Bl. 23, Breslau, September 29, 1871, the supporting letter of officials; Bl. 24–25, Liegnitz, September 16, 1871, the immediate request of Countess von Haugwitz.

taking pleasure in the dynastic family events that were such an important matter of public record. The letters utilized many of the same tropes as urban Catholic women in Koblenz did in reaffirming their ties to Queen Augusta, although these intimacies, as we saw in chapter 3, had been built on a close working relationship with the then crown princess when she lived in the city and participated in St. Barbara affairs. They were bonds of female identification as much as affirmations of political and social hierarchies.

Power in this confessionally mixed Silesian region rested with aristocratic families. The leadership profile of the women's association duplicated the apex of the local social hierarchy. Into the twentieth century, its executive committee still had a preponderance of estate owner wives *(Rittergutsbesitzer)* in its ranks.[49] The appeals were couched in prescribed and reverent idiom. As loyal "children" of the territory and as Silesian *Untertaninnen,* they invoked the old feudal attributes of legitimate rule: the territorial monarch's fatherly good-heartedness *(landesväterliches Herz),* benevolence *(Huld),* and grace *(Gnade)* would assure a positive response to their request (which, indeed, it did, reinforcing the bonds of dependency). Over time, they conjured up threatening images of modern social tensions and class conflicts to contrast with their own declarations of loyalty and support.

In the midst of the passionate identification with the dynasty was an accommodation to the German fatherland, experienced partly through the dynastic lens. In 1881, for example, Marie von Haugwitz wrote the kaiser from the resort town of Bad Boll, where she had gone for a cure—a mark of upper-class status, leisure, and wealth. She asserted her happiness at the birth of his grandchild and described a festive gathering at Pastor Blumhardt's residence to celebrate this moment of dynastic family joy. "From the most varied part of the German fatherland" *(aus den verschiedensten Theilen des deutschen Vaterlandes),* she exclaims, "we all [presumably aristocrats and other worthies] gathered in reverence and thanksgiving."[50] Dynastic family celebrations had structured an identity as a wider national community.

---

49. GSPK, no. 15611, Bl. 199, Lähn, January 12, 1903, "Verwaltungs-Bericht des VFV zu Lähn für das Jahre 1902." Also, *Handbuch des Vaterländischen Frauen-Vereins,* 421. In 1902, the women's chapter had 637 members; the vice president had married into the powerful von Haugwitz family; von Haugwitz himself, who was a lieutenant in the army, served on the executive committee. The male secretary owned a watch factory, and the treasurer was an architect and master builder. Two of the three women on the executive committee were wives of estate owners. The other two male members were the mayor of Lähn and a pastor. For confessional information, Franz Schroller, *Schlesien. Eine Schilderung des Schlierlandes,* vol. 2 (Glogau, 1887; rpt. Frankfurt am Main, 1980), 11. The district of Löwenberg had between 25 and 49 percent Catholics, demonstrating again the importance of patriotic women's associations in confessionally mixed districts.

50. GSPK, no. 15609, Bl. 125–26, Bad Boll, March 8, 1881.

The yearly letters of the presidents reveal the slow and steady evolution of Lähn's women's association: over the ensuing two decades, it hired two more sisters from Berlin, who provided medical services in the homes of the sick and poor in town and in the countryside; with a financial gift from the kaiser's fund, it bought the building next to the hospital and enlarged the medical facilities, affecting the architectural landscape of the small town. And there are glimpses of natural disasters in the correspondence: mention of a year of bad harvests and another of drought. But a serious flood inundated mountainous Silesia in late July 1897, wreaking havoc in Lähn. Water stood two meters high in the local hospital, and it did extensive damage, too, to the area's farmlands involved in fruit and vegetable cultivation.

The letters of the presidents reveal the significant financial backing provided by the wider patriotic network itself. Despite their grousing about the yearly dues funneled upward, in this tragedy money flowed downward. According to the report, the provincial association had been especially generous and so too, in the crisis, was Berlin. In addition, aid had come from "all corners of the fatherland." The letters from this eastern spot on the German map demonstrate a very strong sense, in the words of Duchess Fanny Pfeil in 1903, "that the eyes of the whole, large, and expansive fatherland are watching."[51]

Relief efforts took a complicated turn in this collective work of flood assistance, offering an unusual glimpse into the nature of gender negotiations, which were becoming increasingly necessary to the continued smooth functioning of dynastic philanthropy—against the backdrop of the moderate feminist project that was bringing about real improvements in the lives of educated and privileged women in imperial Germany. Serious gender tensions over jurisdictional boundaries forced the Silesian provincial women's association to reign in women's relief activities; or, at least, it did so in several public pronouncements of "proper" gender role divisions, which read almost like a chastisement. The provincial association was run by powerful women; its president, Charlotte, was the crown princess of Sachsen-Meinigen and a princess of Prussia. But it clearly accepted—and in turn prescribed—limits on the extent of women's relief endeavors. Self-evidently not proper female tasks were the efforts to rebuild destroyed houses and torn-down dams, or reclaim ravaged farmland and silted-up fields: "Our work must have clear boundaries." These included care for the daily needs of the victims; the restoration of living quarters; and a replacement of household implements such as beds and clothing, "so that where possible a modest domesticity can again become

---

51. GSPK, no. 15611, Bl. 155, report "Thätigkeit" (1898), and Bl. 197–98, letter Matzdorf, March 11, 1903, in the context of state efforts to control flooding.

a livable hearth." And it proposed a new motto for this female "work of love": "ever ready to offer support but never in a rush to act."[52] The official statement confined patriotic women's public roles to the restoration of the private household.

But the work on the ground—reflected in the private letters to the kaiser, which described with great pride the ongoing relief work of Lähn women—demonstrates more fluid boundaries in practice. According to the president, association women secured seeds to promote agricultural redevelopment, and they oversaw the rebuilding of the nursery school as well as the renovation of the damaged interior of the hospital. Yet even acknowledgment of this work was conveyed in contradictory messages, a reflection, perhaps, of a deepening ambiguity about women's public roles, even if "protected" by the *Landesmutter*. These contradictions reflected the continuous need to renegotiate the nature of women's services, which were acknowledged as such important components in dynastic-sanctioned patriotic work. Women's work, after all, was essential to the reproduction of the state as "caring."

The uncertainty is refracted in different usages of the German verb *stillen* (to nurse, to silence, to quiet), which reappeared in the correspondence and increasingly intruded into the public discourse around women's patriotic service. In an 1898 letter requesting the yearly subvention from the kaiser's fund, for example, Marie von L'Estocq chose to describe the hospital work as continuing along its "steady soothing way" *(stetig stillen Weg)*; several years later, she also mentioned the more controversial renovation work that was being overseen by the women.[53]

Duchess Pfeil, her daughter, was much more political and direct. In 1903, construction on a large dam project began in a valley near Lähn to regulate the flow of the Bober River. It attracted a large number of migrant workers, many of whom, for one reason or another, found their way to the Lähn hospital. The construction work also was straining resources because the patriotic association had sent one of its sisters to tend to the migrants' daily needs at the work site.

To the countess, the dam itself became the ideal metaphor in which to cast her ongoing requests for dynastic aid (in this case, to hire a fourth sister). As she put it baldly, "From our perspective as Christians and from a political standpoint, it seems best to have nursing sisters serve the municipality, not only to help care for the bodily needs of the ill, but also to work

---

52. GSPK, no. 15611, Bl. 86, "Ein Dankeswort," Breslau, August 28, 1897, makes reference to two earlier circulars on August 8 and 16 that established the norms for women's activities.

53. GSPK, no. 15611, Bl. 155, "Thätigkeit" (1898), Bl. 174, "Thätigkeit" (1900).

against serious damages done by dissatisfaction."[54] Redeploying the notion of *stillen* in a way that expanded its possibilities, she described her duty as "never to stand still but bravely show the colors for all requirements. Let us hope that it is within the contours of women's tasks to serve the people and to work as a dam against the tide of dissatisfaction." The next year, her words were even more precise as she explained those borders: through women's "work of love," she wrote the kaiser, "all the more energetically do we build the foundation against all forms of . . . disorder and contribute our modest part to help defend throne and fatherland."[55] Legitimate rule, in her eyes, was associated with laying solid foundations to control the irrational forces of nature and those of social unrest, both equally unpredictable and threatening.

The work of the Lähn women's association, indeed, was transforming the physical landscape of the town as it was simultaneously contributing to its definition. In and around the old municipal hospital was a growing clustering of activities, a spatial location for an imagined patriotism that at the same time claimed to embody the public spirit. Association work on behalf of the municipality gave a public character to the very buildings under its administration. In 1875, at the three hundredth anniversary celebration of the hospital's founding, beds also were endowed for old people and invalids who lived outside of Lähn, extending the radius of institutional charity. The hospital became at the same time an old-age home, while most of the daily nursing care continued to take place in the houses of the poor and the sick. A year later, a local association that had run a nursery school joined the patriotic women's chapter, adding its buildings and garden to the property. In 1880, the hospital was enlarged for the first time; and again, in 1916, in the midst of war, when the medical and philanthropic facilities had been turned over to the care of wounded soldiers, a dynastic fund earmarked ten thousand marks to buy an adjacent building for further expansion. This construction project—and the myriad functions around the hospital—proved a foundation that continued long after the end of dynastic rule.[56]

Inaugural Rituals and Visitations

The state women's associations were very much involved in promoting building projects in their local communities—some civic and others pri-

---

54. GSPK, no. 15611, Bl. 189–90.

55. GSPK, no. 15611, Bl. 197–98, Matzdorf, Silesia, March 11, 1903. Also, Bl. 209–11, "Thätigkeit," April 11, 1904, Lähn.

56. GSPK, no. 15612, Bl. 123, Berlin, March 17, 1911, concerning expansion of the old-age home; Bl. 198–99, June 8, 1916, concerning wartime renovations.

vate; the Lähn chapter was no exception. Even a cursory reading in the archival and printed sources after 1871 reveals the considerable time and energy that went into raising money for construction projects to "house" the various patriotic functions: nursing services in hospitals, clinics, and sanatoria, for example, or infant and day care centers. Members also raised money to build, buy, or renovate their headquarters and, after the turn of the century, there was a move to construct various "homes" for their own administrative personnel for recreational purposes as well as convalescence. As part of new notions about social provisions that helped to create a sense of community among the service employees themselves, the home served as well as a refuge for single women in their old age. Typically, these buildings and grounds were located in rural settings.[57] Furthermore, the patriotic associations joined local efforts to organize exhibitions in public spaces, drawing audiences to specific sites.

The opening of an exhibition and the inauguration of a new building invariably were marked by public ceremony—and many of these inaugural rituals involved the *Landesmutter* herself or a representative of the dynasty. These events were important moments of community celebration, acknowledged as such by the serious attention given to the planning of the event. Each involved elaborate negotiation between the dynastic center and local officialdom, which shaped the spatial arrangements of the ceremony down to the smallest detail.

There was much to be gained by the two parties. Their interaction highlights one attribute of power in the dynastic "center" in the *Kaiserreich:* its reliance on negotiation, persuasion, and awe. In the ritual celebration, the dynast linked her rule with a community's decision to invest resources in a "monument," which expressed esteemed public functions of a medical, educational and training, or religious nature. The building, constructed at a specific moment in time, became a site of memory, part of the local lore preserved in chronicles and association "histories" that collectively helped write the dynastic narratives as an important source of the wider German identity.[58]

---

57. Among other examples, GK, Abt. 69, no. 938, Die Einweihung des Frauenvereinshauses in Heidelberg am 26. August 1911, betr., description of renovations of the headquarters by the architect F. Kuhn, and no. 933, Die Einweihung des Frauenvereinshauses in Blankenloch am 30. Juni 1905. Also, *KZ,* no. 277, June 17, 1913, reports on the provincial Patriotic Women's Association's "home" in upper Bavaria, which in peacetime served the convalescent needs of the nursing sisters and, in war, would be used exclusively for the recovery of officers.

58. These dynastic narratives were once powerful sources of German identity. For the ubiquity of dynastic events, holidays, and family time in associational history, for example, Werner Wilhelm Weichelt, *Casino Coblenz, 1808–1908. Ein Gedenkbuch zur Hundertjahr Feier* (Koblenz, 1908); and Bruell, *Chronik der Stadt Düren.* After the reunification of

By the same token, the ability of the material object to embody values made it an equally useful symbol for the articulation of opposition and dispute. Indeed, political struggle was played out in daily life not only in the arenas of party mobilization—membership drives, meetings, and lecture tours—but at building sites and monuments in the environment. By the early twentieth century, for example, socialists placed their newspapers and pamphlets in the waiting rooms of women-run "patriotic" clinics, which "enraged" the nationalists; so, too, the feminist doctor Adams-Lehmann performed abortions in the clinic run by the Munich Patriotic Women's Association. Compounding the tension, red flags were hung above nationalist monuments on May Day, bringing down the full force of the police state on the left-wing perpetrators. Cemeteries, too, became battlegrounds over commemorating the war dead. Beginning in the late 1880s, for example, young radical Christian groups tried to appropriate the memory of "nationalist" struggle for evangelical purposes, handing out printed sermons at the "festival of the dead"; at one cemetery in Berlin, they took up an annual collection for the poor. Within several years, however, members of "free religious communities" *(Freie-Gemeinde)* appeared to protest dispensing such "trash" *(Zeug)* and even called in the police.[59] Clearly, the built landscape was as much a location of conflict as a symbol of national consensus.

For local officials, however, the consecration of a public building in a joint ceremony with the dynastic center offered distinct advantages, despite the possibility of disorder and subversion that lurked beneath the surface. For a brief moment, in the glare of publicity surrounding the dynastic tour, the locality, with its own routines reflecting multiple combinations of more intimate forms of community life, was pulled into national life. To the extent that the nation is a community of numerous communities, the celebration, indeed, was a moment of nation building.[60] The local community was projected onto larger spatial levels through the dynastic medium: it was insinuated into older state identities as well as new nation-state definitions. The dedication rituals highlight an important but elusive aspect of the construction of national identity:

1989–90, for example, Berliners again are addressing the dynastic heritage in the urban setting. See Brian Ladd, *The Ghosts of Berlin: Confronting German History in the Urban Landscape* (Chicago, 1997), 41–79, particularly.

59. For the complaint against socialists, *KZ,* no. 25, January 16, 1913; and Weindling, *Health, Race,* 183, for the case of the feminist doctor. On the Festival of the Dead, among other accounts, *KZ,* no. 482, November 26, 1888, first supplement to no. 547, November 22, 1892, and supplement to no. 161, April 7, 1904. Mosse, *Nationalization of the Masses,* 76–77, deals briefly with the festival, although shorn of any recognition of contestation.

60. The reference is from Turner, *The Ritual Process,* 142.

its integration in, and coexistence with, multiple, often competing, identities. In the *Kaiserreich,* indeed, national identity was framed partly by performances in which local, associational, and dynastic loyalties all mixed together.[61]

It is the politics of nation building, however, which complicates this process of identity-formation. Official nationalists had to keep the various identities aligned for conservative purposes. The negotiations, therefore, were about inclusion in the ceremony—and exclusion. They were opportunities for local officials to structure the public representation of "community" in ways that spoke of solidarities yet simultaneously worked to reinforce existing power relationships—and, in the flow of exchange, affirm as well those ties that were deemed compatible with dynastic interests. Through negotiation, then, this public ceremonial time was purposefully gendered: indeed, privileging and legitimizing women's voluntarism in local communities was part of the calculation.

Local officials readily acknowledged the centrality of the state's women's associations in the public ceremony with the *Landesmutter.* In this context, it simply was a matter of how many executive committee "ladies" to invite and how wide a territorial net to cast among the neighboring branch chapters.[62] In the dynamics of conservative politics, the ceremony graphically expressed the interdependency of dynasty and women's association: these women's groups were the axis in civil society around which notions of the state, personified by representations of the *Landesmutter* as "caring," were played out.

Dynastic participation also imposed on the participants an exchange of gifts, services, food, and sociability, solidifying the personal bonds of loyalty through the transactions. Officials opened up their homes and

---

61. For theoretical work recognizing the coexistence of politically distinct spatial identities see John Agnew, "Representing Space: Space, Scale, and Culture in Social Science," in *Place, Culture, Representation,* ed. James Duncan and David Ley (London, 1993), 251–52; and for a German case study, Applegate, *A Nation of Provincials.* Archival sources offer many examples of the interplay of multiple identities. A prime example is the celebration of the birthday of Frederick of Baden in 1904 by a Baden organization in Koblenz that blended German, Baden, and dynastic identities. GK, Abt. 69, no. 227, Den Besuch in Koblenz und Düsseldorf vom 18–20 September 1904. For historians, the key is to access the multiple identities at any moment of time beyond the standard modern measure of voting behavior, a compelling project in light of the reemergence of regional parties and identities in the move toward European integration since 1989.

62. GK, Abt. 69, nos. 556–87, Besuche in einzelnen badischen Orten (e.g., Adelsheim, Badenweiler, Bruchsal, Heidelberg, Lörrach, Säckingen, Oberkirch). In addition, the ceremony unveiling the monument to victory in 1873 in Berlin (the Sieges-Denkmal) included representatives of the Prussian Patriotic Women's Association. See *KZ,* no. 201, August 29, 1873.

arranged a small meal or tea with select guests, or the meal would take place at women's association headquarters.[63] The wealthy often provided private transport for the royal guest in remote areas that were outside the state's modern transportation system.

Gifts later flowed down from the center, too. For example, after Duchess Luise visited the Baden village of Kork in 1904 to inaugurate a new epileptic sanatorium, a pastor wrote effusive thanks for the many gifts that had been sent to the institute, "unexpected but welcomed proof of the beneficence of the female side of dynastic rule *(landesmütterlicher Gnade)."* The mother superior had received a portrait of the dynastic pair that, in the pastor's optimistic language, "will keep alive for us and our descendants always a grateful memory of our most noble couple." He passed on the appreciation of two nurses and a young woman teacher who had received books from the duchess, thanked her for the flowers she arranged to be sent to the patients' rooms, and assured her that he had communicated her thanks to Christiane Kraft, a rose cultivator, for the beautiful bouquet presented to the duchess at the ceremony.[64] Clearly, these gifts trickled down to many different elements of town society, the sick and the healthy, the educator and petty entrepreneur.

At the same time, a visit by the dynast invariably meant a special cele-bration in the institute itself. If the residents were not invalids or the seri-ously ill, it involved an elaborate cultural performance, typically a recita-tion of poetry or a one-act play, often written by one of the volunteers of the institute and performed with the royalty in the audience. In other cases, popular poems were gathered, rearranged, and recited. In this context, too, institute authorities could insist on a display of patriotic values. But draw-ing on popular culture as a source meant a recitation of "loyalty" fashioned "from below," one that spoke of popular expectations of rule that were not unequivocal. Popular conceptions of philanthropy demanded dynastic state economic performance.

The complex interplay of expectations and multiple identities that surfaced around a dynastic visit is best illustrated by concrete example. The Baden state archive has preserved the private papers of Duchess Luise over her entire reign. They document in rich detail the nature and extent of her travels to many points throughout the realm. Visitations were older types of rituals of rule—at one time in the past, too, expressions of royal

---

63. GK, Abt. 69, no. 571, Besuch in Lörrach am 25 Mai, verlegt am 25 September im Jahre 1900, where the duchess took a late breakfast in the women's association headquarters.

64. GK., Abt. 69, no. 1161, Besuch der Grossherzogin in der Pflegeanstalt in Kork am 29 Oktober 1904, letter, Pastor Niederkehr, November 12, 1904. Her transportation was donated by a widowed factory owner, Trick.

domination over subject peoples and urban subjects.[65] But ongoing political evolution in central Europe increasingly favored municipal self-rule, and the ritual itself, perpetuated in its external form, took on new meaning, reflecting and re-creating the ties that bound local interests to those of the dynasty.

There were many reasons why the Baden duchess would visit a city or town in her realm—the "joyous entry" at the accession to the throne in 1856, for example; a tour of a city's philanthropic institutions to coincide with a military maneuver nearby; or an expression of concern during natural calamities, as we have just seen. By the late nineteenth century, inaugurating buildings and opening exhibitions increasingly drew the dynast into distinct urban spaces, a product of the quantum leap in building construction that strikes architectural historians of the modern period.[66]

And the invitations, too, increasingly were initiated from the side of the town. The reasoning was expressed eloquently by Pastor Ludwig Hofmann, advisor to the local women's association in Blankenloch, a small, predominantly Protestant village near Karlsruhe. He could be speaking for many other communities, however. Writing the duchess in 1905, he asked her to attend the inaugural ceremony of a new set of institutions that were being built under the women's association auspices: a nursery school with crèche, a home for the nursing sisters, and public baths. His "most reverential request" was that she "baptize" the building with her "exalted name." And he offered his case. "The reason . . . is the wish to bestow on the public welfare establishment a majestic dedication to assure its inviolability for all time."[67] The stability inherent in the institution of dynastic succession, it appears, became a guarantor of the sanctity of community welfare practices in the future. The petition sought to utilize this longstanding female symbol of collective obligation, drawing on and replenishing the reservoir of monarchical legitimacy through the female line.

Dynastic participation at the ceremony heightened the sense of dra-

---

65. For discussion of older ritual entries, Geertz, "Centers, Kings, and Charisma." For the more traditional dynastic rituals marking territorial rule through an exchange of gifts see, for example, Nikolaus Schüren, *Die Jubel-Huldigungsfeier der Vereinigung der Rheinlande mit der Krone Preussen am 15. Mai 1865. Blätter der Erinnerungen* (Aachen, n.d.); and A. J. B. Heunisch, *Das Grossherzogtums Baden, historisch, geographische-statistisch beschrieben* (Heidelberg, 1857), 564–66, "Huldigungsgaben" offered from the provinces at the time of the marriage of Frederick and Luise. Significantly, the gifts were earmarked for purposes of the general good *(wohltätigen Zwecken)*.

66. Carlo Olmo, "If the Architectural Historian Came to Marmusha," in *Architecture and Legitimacy*, ed. Hans van Dijk and Liesbeth Janson, trans. D'Laine Camp (Rotterdam, 1995), 69. The collection includes discussion of architecture and modernism.

67. GK, Abt. 69, no. 933, Einweihung des Frauenvereinshauses in Blankenloch am 30 Juni 1905, letter, May 1, 1905.

matic time: it suspended mundane routines and imposed a carefully chore-ographed script that drew on community resources and involvement from the moment of arrival to the moment of departure. Buildings were deco-rated; arrangements were made for public viewing along the route; select individuals were formally presented to the royal figure, transforming them for the moment into celebrities; and a time was set aside for serious speech-making. For many speakers, indeed, the presence of the dynast forced an evaluation of the relationship of the local community to the wider polity, in effect, working to shape a complex identity that blurred traditional and modern imagery. This juxtaposition of old and new was part and parcel of the contradictory processes of "modernity" in Germany, which dampened the pressures of rational disenchantment in the everyday. It affirmed the dynastic context as relevant to conceptions of community welfare and the medium to think about the place of the locality in the flow of history.

   The pull of these alternating visions of time was reflected in two for-mal speeches at a ceremony in which the duchess consecrated a hospital in Sandhofen on December 19, 1904; at her request, copies of the addresses by Pastors Klemk and Ehrler later were sent to Karlsruhe.[68] For both speakers, it was the hospital that was new ("although much had come and gone in the community"), and its very building seemed to symbolize a new era of "progress" that was affecting even this remote village in Baden. Since Sandhofen had become Baden territory in the early nineteenth cen-tury, it never had hosted a dynastic visit. There were, therefore, many rea-sons to celebrate in 1904.

   Pastor Klemk placed the festivities in a precise moment in time; his words, in effect, defined "history," linking his community to its teleology in a way that established a common German identity. This identity had all the attributes of "modernity" itself, but it was shaped and sanctioned by dynastic authority and the personal exploits of dynastic leaders. "The extraordinary political and economic ascent of the German people" had been set in motion (with God's help, of course) by the "economic activity and trustworthy efforts of the first German kaiser, his territorial lords and military officers." Time even "pulled our community into the maelstrom of progress. It drew in manufacturing and industry and created much that was new." And proof was the construction of the hospital not merely to reflect present needs but as a statement about security and well-being in the future. The *Landesmutter,* as embodiment of the active Christian spirit, too, lent the whole festival and the building itself more dignity and

---

68. GK., Abt. 69, no. 1166, Besuch der Grossherzogin in Sandhofen am 19 December 1904. Pastor Klemk sent her his speech, "Zur Einweihung des Krankenhauses in Sand-hofen," as did Pastor Adolf Ehrler, "Ansprache gehalten am 19 December 1904 bei Einwei-hung des Krankenhauses in Sandhofen."

worth. For the moment of the ceremony, in the pastor's eyes, the community of Sandhofen had become the center, encapsulating in the "building that stands before us" the very forces that comprised the essence of a collective German nation. Adopting first a normative tone, he described the ideal work of doctors and nursing sisters that was needed to heal the sick; shifting to the declarative tense, however, he ended the speech on a divisive note. The hospital, he said, "is an abode of faith and patience *(Geduld),*" but he defined the latter against projected negative female qualities, testifying to deep gender tensions and divisions that in reality continuously subverted the imagined collectivity in the discourse on nation-state identity.[69] Pastor Klemk mirrored, indeed, an unresolved contradiction between an idealized feminine community and the actual place of women in it, which included the efforts of feminists of various stripes to change the basis of community life.

Pastor Ehrler, in turn, offered a different version of the same theme. In one respect, his was a more familiar gloss. Claiming to speak for all of Sandhofen ("I know that I am one with the thoughts and beliefs of the whole community [*die ganze Gemeinde*]"), he acknowledged that his small collective might not be able to provide the same external glitter in the festival as the "richer communes in our beautiful Baden land," but he assured the duchess that "we excel in devotion, loyalty, and affection." For this speaker, the ceremony was a moment to affirm a Baden identity by proffering fidelity to the dynastic house ("we are loyal monarchists," he asserted simply) for its efforts on behalf of the welfare of all the people. If this were the extent of the message, it would be noteworthy still as a calculated expression of notions of legitimacy that, with their own rhetorical power in public, served partly to reinforce the bonds of loyalty. But in Ehrler's version, Sandhofen long had been the recipient of dynastic attention for the "weal and woe" of the community. Its fate had been shaped by the imperatives of "active Christendom" and the commandment of "love of neighbor," which he acknowledged as the life task of the duchess. His understanding of community, significantly, was the wider values of dynastic patriotism that were being implemented through the work tying women's associations to the royal patron. Noting that it was her first time in the community, he nonetheless said, "You do not come to us as a stranger but as a deeply concerned mother, who always was in our hearts." In this ceremonial setting in a Baden village, the work of patriotic philanthropy had become the very definition of community well-being.

---

69. The pastor offered negative comments on women's so-called patience *(jene weibliche Geduld),* which was "sullenly" tendered, and went on to define the concept as Goethe had understood it, as a matter of will.

Other types of documents follow the inaugural celebrations into the buildings themselves, highlighting the multiplicity of performances in different settings that announced the royal figure in a local community. This festive occasion punctuated the otherwise somber and regimented life in public welfare institutions. But it also reveals a complex cultural dynamic that speaks as much about popular visions of dynastic rule as about the efforts of institutional authorities to instill obedience and loyalty through theatrical vehicles. Besides, it demonstrates a pervasive female voice on patriotism in a set of tales that transformed the *Landesmutter* into a figure of hope and solace for the common folk anywhere, no matter how wretched or miserable. It touches on a popular female patriotic subculture that was reinforced also in economic exchange. At key moments of dynastic celebration—at marriages or christenings, for example—the women of the royal house would commission the necessary ritual objects and clothing exclusively from women-run artisanal businesses in the land.[70] This linkage, which the monarchy used cumulatively to instill patriotic values through the many female mediums, also is a process of identity-formation unrecognized by historians of "modern bourgeois" nationalism.

Several different types of institutional "performances" are preserved in the Baden archives. They include, for example, a one-act play, "In the Spinning-Room," performed by the residents of a girls' home in Lörrach when Duchess Luise visited an exhibition of industrial crafts in the district in 1900, as well as a set of poems that were to be recited by orphans in Säckingen under the title "Queen Luise of Prussia and the Ugly Child." The duchess took a tour of the Rhine in 1892, visiting a wide range of philanthropic institutes in the different towns in the area; she stopped in Säckingen in September.[71]

These two examples in no way do justice to the complex festive worlds that, elsewhere, also transformed "inmates" into theatrical "players" and the institutional personnel, local patrons, volunteers, and the dynastic entourage into "audience." Previously untapped in the literature, these dramas are an important site for the shaping of conservative identities, a place of "organized play," in which the script, created under certain con-

---

70. *KZ,* no. 528, November 11, 1889, reports that the empress sent cash gifts to the seamstresses who did the special needlework for her daughter's marriage; no. 324, July 14, 1892, notes that Princess Margaret of Prussia, for her dowry, ordered items from Martha Hoppe's Silesian Lace-Making school; also no. 260, June 6, 1913, the seamstresses of the same school were asked to make the wedding veil, handkerchiefs, and lace for the daughter of the empress.

71. GK, Abt. 69, no. 586, Der Allerhöchste Besuch in Säckingen, Buchen und Sinsheim, 1892. The time frame was shortened so that the recitation did not take place; but it was fully choreographed, arranged, and rehearsed and sent later to Karlsruhe as a testimony to her aura and authority. Also, no. 571, Lörrach visit, 1900.

straints, to be sure, conformed to the symbolic types that reinforced legitimate authority. The setting became a real theater, replete with actors and audience, organized around the *Landesmutter* symbolically as well as in person.[72]

The performance by the residents in Lörrach comprised women's stories about intergenerational sharing and solidarities across the social divides. The short play centered on an old grandmother, sitting before a portrait of Duchess Luise, the typical background prop for many of these ad hoc "theaters," as we will see also in chapter 7. Deep in thought about her youth, she is interrupted by three young girls who have come with their spinning gear and ask to hear her life story as she instructs them in the arts of spinning. Her memory is of the time her own son was ill and she was nursing him; she heard that the *Landesmutter* Luise herself was coming to the area to "console and uplift all those who are suffering," and Luise, indeed, appeared at her doorstep. The grandmother says to the audience, "I stepped aside and the exalted princess arrived. I saw how she sprang to my child's bed, how lovingly she took his hand, how he smiled." Here, the *Landesmutter* becomes every mother through the eyes of the poor mother. While the story stressed the power of "caring," not a magical quality of "touch" that once adhered in some forms of royal authority, the son, indeed, recovered.

The grandmother's intent is to reinforce loyalty, and her message is transmitted across the generations in a conservative vision that passes wisdom on from the old to the young; it is set in the once popular village institution of the "spinning evening," a place of sociability and gossip (doubling often as a marriage market) where skills, indeed, were transmitted through intergenerational ties. In the historic past, rather than the theatrical present, however, dynastic and religious authorities had moved hard to discipline and censor activities in the spinning bee; but here, the village gathering was appropriated for dynastic purposes.[73] The play ends with the young girls' personal testimony of their veneration for the *Landesmutter,* who in the script and in the audience was the center of reference. For the duration of the play, a sense of community was created among those present, while at the same time the whole performance worked to enhance the "sacred" status of the ruler.

"Queen Luise," carefully scripted to be performed by the orphans in

---

72. For a useful discussion of theater in the everyday, Turner, *From Ritual to Theatre.*
73. On the "spinning evening," Hans Medick, "Village Spinning Bees: Sexual Culture and Free Time among Rural Youth in Early Modern Germany," in Hans Medick and David Warren Sabean, eds., *Interest and Emotion: Essays on the Study of Family and Kinship* (Cambridge, 1977), 317–39. For the medieval royal touch for scrofula, Weindling, *Health, Race,* 163.

Säckingen, is a poetic verse narrative also of a dynastic visit; it opens with preparations in a town for a "joyous entry" in which the queen is met by twelve girls, among the others in the delegation. However, one girl is ugly and ashamed and hides. The queen reaches out to her, stills her tears, and shows herself to be what the common folk always knew she was: a refuge for the weak, the helpless, the poor. The orphans-turned-actresses re-created and experienced the queen's solicitude and love in rehearsing the poems.

The choice of the dynastic figure, the Prussian queen Luise, testifies to the breadth and longevity of her appeal as mythic, unifying German figure. Säckingen was a town in southern Baden, and yet Luise was as much a folk heroine there as in Prussia. Indeed, she was a highly malleable figure in nationalist lore, whose life and meaning, because she died so young, could have a number of endings depending on the narrator. For the orphans in Säckingen, the queen facilitates an inversion of the normative social structure only to reaffirm it again in the end. Part of the recitation included the musings of a young orphan girl imagining wealth and power. Speaking to the *Landesmutter:*

> Mother, if I were rich and exalted *(gross)*, I would put everything in your lap *(Schoss)*. If I had white lambs, I would give you the most beautiful pair; if I had an apple, sweet and red, I would give it to you. . . . If I sat on the king's throne, I would give you the crown: I would give you everything that you wanted.

The poetic theme ended with a return to the "real" social hierarchy: "But because I do not have these riches, I will pray every day for God to protect our noble lady," implying that only the ruler can implement the fruits of the orphan's wishes.

These words had a double meaning, however, for they established a set of expectations about power, responsibility, and authority that put the monarchy under obligation. Even the "orphan girls" expected care, food, and comfort day in and day out, in peace and war. The philanthropic imperative had created its own constraints. The words of the superintendents of an orphanage that had burned down in the town of Dinglingen in 1908 were both obsequious and expectant: the duchess's solicitude had been "proof of royal benevolence."[74] The question that lurked in the back-

---

74. GK, Abt. 69, no. 934, Brand im Lahrer Waisen-und Rettungshaus in Dinglingen, 1908, letter of Marie und Wilhelm Lenz, headmasters, September 22, 1908. In this case, the official response was slow and halting, and local authorities also had turned to the Central Women's Association in Berlin for help.

ground concerned the bonds of popular loyalty if the expectations were unmet.

Participation in the inauguration ceremony or at the theatrical performance was by invitation only. Lists were drawn up purposefully. Listen, for example, to the calculations of the Baden state official Herr Rech in Bühlerthal at the consecration of the new hospital in that Black Forest town in 1903. He refused to invite one of the owners of a flower factory: "he commands little respect here, and I believe to honor him with a presentation to Your Highness could be misinterpreted in this city." Or follow the classifications of the mayor in Mannheim at an unveiling ceremony of a war monument: he targeted "officials" and "corporate groups," to be sure, yet the category trade *(Beruf)* allowed him to tap representatives of local industrial workers: "There will appear also five workers who [recently] had been decorated" by the state. An inquiry with the local women's associations revealed no similarly "honored" industrial-wage-earning women, although the mayor was pleased to note that a selection process among the working women was well under way.[75] Indeed, official audiences often included wage-earning women, servants, and midwives who had been recipients of state awards. Ceremonial time was part of the award structure that drove the dynastic state.

Medals and Award Ceremonies

From the start, the system of awards and honors in the form of medals and medallions was elaborated in the dealings of the dynastic state with women in philanthropic service. The recognition of women's valued activities in public ceremonies represents a graphic statement about the importance of gendered service and sacrifice for dynastic rule and its principles. In a society obsessed by rank and title, these honors were coveted markers of official esteem; and they raised a woman's status and her bargaining power in the day-to-day affairs of associational life in the community. The medals were prominently featured in the obituaries of the elites; used by the recipients to enhance the authority of petitions fired off to local and state officials; and, as we saw in chapter 2, even pushed by "clients" in the expectation that state recognition of the work of the leaders of a philanthropic association would enhance their credibility and encourage generous financial giving among the populace.[76] In circular fashion, the central-

75. GK, Abt. 69, no. 1147, Den allerhöchsten Besuch in Bühlerthal zur Errichtung des neuen Krankenhauses betr. 1903, November 4, 1903. Also, no. 572, Mannheim, letter, September 20, 1896.

76. Remember, the pastor who gave the funeral oration to Frau Hoesch in Düren (chap. 3) had referred to her many state honors; also *KZ*, no. 218, September 19, 1871, obit-

ity of philanthropy to the state system of honors provided a context, too, for wealthy patrons to bequeath money; their status rose with the fortunes of the patriotic association so closely identified with state authority.

The recipients constituted a community of the service elites—in some cases defined by the territorial state borders only *(Land)* and in others, after 1871, as German *(Reich)*—that had its own gradations but worked to dissolve the social distinctions among aristocrats, officials, patricians, and professionals. Honorees were recognized for their work and commitments in various patriotic projects, not for their origins, religion, or in some cases even gender, since several of the medals were given to both women and men for valued services.

Among the most coveted state medals were the Prussian Order of Luise for women and young ladies and the Baden Frederick and Luise Medallion, given to women and men in volunteer capacities; after 1871, there was also the German Distinguished Service Cross for the Wartime Services of Women and Young Ladies and various Red Cross medals (in three grades) singling out exemplary women and men for their "sacrifices" on behalf of Red Cross activities, including peacetime services.[77]

The medals and honors were given at public ceremonies, the third meticulously orchestrated genre of performances. They represented a public accounting of the valued labor that was part of the maintenance of political legitimacy. Honors also were given to individuals and couples in the wider population for their normative gender behavior, which also was deemed to underpin conservative rule and identity. Dynastic intent here was to signal out and reward neighbors as a model for household living in a specific community.

Civilian service medals were political awards while simultaneously substituting for political rights. Their origins lay in the linkages forged in the early nineteenth century among army, civilian, and state to support "modern" national war, although increasingly their criteria broadened to embrace peacetime service as well.

This evolution is reflected in the Order of Luise, established on August 3, 1814, by the King Frederick William III of Prussia in memory of his deceased wife. It consisted of a small cross, with a sky blue medallion

---

uary of Frau Caroline v. Normann, recipient of the Order of Luise. Supplicants were emboldened by their honors to enter into a correspondence with the royalty in the first place. Among others, see GK, Abt. 69, no. 175, Teilnahmebezeugungen zum 100-jährigen Todestag der Königin Luise von Preussen, 1910, letter of Friedrich Dondler.

77. A detailed description of the history of the Order of Luise on the one hundredth anniversary of its creation (August 3) was designed to remind readers of women's long tradition of supporting war work (*KZ*, supplement to no. 358, August 2, 1914). Also, *Illustriertes Konversations-Lexikon*, 276–80, for a full description of the various service medals for women.

in the center; surrounding the golden letter *L* at its heart were seven stars for her seven children; on the back were the dates 1813–14. It was worn on the left side of the body, hanging on a white-and-black ribbon (the Prussian colors). The medal initially recognized only women's wartime services in the struggles against Napoleon; in 1850, the order was restructured and refinanced by Frederick William IV to honor the "patriotic" work of women in the difficult years of 1848–49; therefore, it was inserted into the political struggle to define revolutionary/civil war memory. In 1865, it again was redesigned. Adopting the same language that was enveloping the state Red Cross, the order now honored Prussian women for their "humanitarian" services in war and peace. It stood for the "purest expressions of love of neighbor," qualities needed to support the army at the front, their families in the home front, and communities torn by natural disasters and calamities.[78] In effect, the medal sanctioned the cultural messages of disaster relief going on while simultaneously the minting of a single form expressed the state's view of the equal value of service given in times of peace and of war. But what kind of activities qualified as exemplary day-to-day "humanitarian" work in peacetime? Just how public was the work of these volunteers decorated by the state?

A particularly telling case is a nominee for the Friederick and Luise Medallion in Baden. In 1907, the mayor of Mannheim proposed the wife of a local lawyer, Frau Dr. Martha Kahn, for her efforts in "founding, organizing, and developing" a reformatory in the nearby village of Neckerau, which recently had been incorporated into Mannheim's metropolitan borders. The mayor wrote glowingly of Mrs. Kahn's "rich service," which practically single-handedly had sustained the whole project. Of the required ten thousand marks for the building, she raised eight thousand marks alone and contributed fifteen hundred marks from her own pocket. In a "particularly energetic" fashion, she oversaw the actual construction of the house, working closely with the architect, Noll, himself, and she negotiated with several Baden firms to obtain free of charge the kitchen stove, the bathtubs, and the toilets. In keeping with the values of her station, she saw to it that the young inmates obtained "regular work" at a local company making waterproof clothing. She was the institute's treasurer and kept its books. If this were not enough, Frau Kahn served on the Executive Committee of the Mannheim Women's Association for Section 7 (overseeing the training of domestics); the district committee for the protection of children, youths, and prisoners; and the Legal Aid Society for women and girls. In short, her well-known and influential place in

---

78. *KZ,* no. 358, August 2, 1914.

Mannheim's municipal welfare structure made her an excellent candidate for special recognition, a public model for others. State officials agreed.[79]

Rewarding exemplary behavior in local communities drove state honors of normative gender and household relations as well. The awards also worked to shape German identity in a number of unanticipated ways beyond their manifest intent to reward "pious, moral, and irreproachable" living as a "model for the community" *(Vorbild der Gemeinde)*. In one case, a cash award made possible anniversary celebrations for poor couples who had been married fifty or, after 1899, even sixty years in Prussia. Given the differential mortality figures by social class in the nineteenth century and the difficult moral hoops that the poor candidates had to go through to qualify, the numbers affected were limited.[80]

In official calculations, the cash was not a subsidy *(Unterstützung)*— it was not intended as a payment of support—but a gift *(Geschenk)* from the king—and later kaiser—for a specific purpose: to help poor and needy celebrants "gain an understanding" of the "festivities around golden anniversaries" *(die Feier der Jubelhochzeit aufzufassen)*. The money was a small, onetime payment of ten to fifteen thaler in the early 1860s, rising to fifty marks by 1905 for the purposes of hosting a family celebration in the community. It was designed originally to popularize such cultural forms among the common people in the body politic, to deepen, perhaps, the meaning of the simultaneous celebrations of dynastic family events. Along with other state measures, however—for example, child labor laws and those on compulsory education, protective legislation, laws regulating women's work, and pension provisions—willy-nilly these initiatives were important forms of homogenizing the individual and family life cycle, even if access to health insurance and education and many other rewards of life remained unequal and differentiated by class.[81] The provisions created shared patterns of living and a vocabulary to speak about them. In their

---

79. GK, Abt. 69, no. 875, Die Verleihung des Friedrich-Luisen Medailles betr., Mannheim, January 12, 1907.

80. LK, Abt. 403, no. 10041, Allerhöchst Gnadengesuche an Jubel Ehepaare sowie Auszeichnung weiblicher Dienstboten für treue Dienste, 1861–1909. As of January 24, 1891, the state called for statistics on the number of couples eligible to receive the award. The document contained a rough penciled table for the period 1898 to 1906, with an average of 127 couples per year.

81. For life cycle changes shaped by welfare legislation see Jean H. Quataert, "Demographic and Social Change," in *Imperial Germany: A Historiographical Companion,* ed. Roger Chickering (Westport, Conn., 1996), 97–130; and also Reinhard Spree, *Health and Social Class in Imperial Germany: A Social History of Mortality, Morbidity, and Inequality,* trans. Stuart McKinnon-Evans (Oxford, 1988).

own way, too, the investigations fed the process of defining membership in the German "nation": eligibility was empirically tested on the ground.

Other aspects of state-formation are revealed in the documents on the anniversary ritual, which cover over forty-six years in Prussia. The original initiative, reorganized in 1862, dispensed devotional literature to the selected couples, not only cash; it was remarkably inclusive, acknowledging religious diversity (relevant Protestant, Catholic, and Jewish texts were handed out), available in German, Polish, and French translations as well as Sorb and Slavic languages. Whether due to heightened religious tensions, the rise of political anti-Semitism, or growing radical nationalist hostility to minority rights, these provisions simply were dropped by the state in the mid-1880s, the decade that first pitted "official" and "radical" nationalists against one another. The revised regulations, however, added a silver medallion for couples who were financially better off. That is, the state turned to honor its own low-level civil servants and propertied families, extending its ritual distinctions to groups already benefiting materially from state service.

Remarkable, too, was the growing bureaucratization and standardization of the whole process of selection in this "ceremony of passage"; it captures well the paradoxical face of the German dynastic state, which operated according to bureaucratic norms while also relying on the values of charismatic rule. For the bureaucrats involved, the background checks increasingly were standardized in model forms and formulas that required ever more precise flows of information across and between administrative offices. And careers were on the line as well. In 1894, the police commissioner in Cologne, for example, had to defend himself against charges of sloppy work. Although he pulled the state medal at the last moment, it nearly had been awarded to a person who, apparently, had spoken publicly against the sacrament of marriage and refused a church celebration.[82]

In this example of state-initiated life cycle celebrations, the bureaucratic details were a prop that maintained only the facade of dynastic involvement; the kaiser was as distant from the lives of these couples as they were alienated from any meaningful dynastic solicitation and concern. But to speak of this celebratory moment solely as manipulation misses its potential appropriation as a genuine family festival by couples with a conservative bent. The celebration planned by the tiller Nikolaus Meier and his wife Magdalana in Trier in 1887 is a case in point. They had organized a special church festival for the community to coincide with the anniversary date of the defeat of the French at Gravelotte in August 1870,

---

82. LK, Abt. 403, no. 10041, Bl. 169, Cologne, July 14, 1894.

which had set the stage for the Prussian victory at Sedan.[83] Meier had fought with a Prussian Guards regiment in the war.

Association Festivals and the Dynastic Life Cycle

The fourth type of cultural performance worked to keep alive the interconnection between the dynastic court and civil society. Patriotic associations timed their annual festivals to coincide with a key life cycle event in the royal family saga. This genre drew on an old tradition of sacralizing dynastic time in ritual celebrations of what were, indeed, dangerous and uncertain moments for the perpetuation and continuity of royal power: deaths, successions, births, and marriages.

These older life cycle rituals, however, had a particular salience in the "long" nineteenth century, capitalizing on the slow secular changes that transformed the dynast into *Mensch* and worked to popularize the royal couple as mother and father. The power of these celebrations and ceremonies, too, reflected changes in the very heart of family life among the privileged groups of women and men who were finding their way into dynastic service, as well as among the common people. As extensions of increasingly widespread yet ordinary family rituals, the celebration of dynastic family time exercised a compelling pull on the spectators— whether on the streets, in the quiet of the association's meeting halls, or at family gatherings in the community.[84] Besides, the continuous celebration of the life cycle ritual added an important emotional prop to the emerging nationalist message of the state as one large family.

Patriotic associations were tied directly into the dynastic life cycle. For example, the annual festival of the Baden women's associations all over the state occurred each December 3, the birthday of Duchess Luise; the Baden Nurses' Aides League, as we will see in more detail in the next chapter, arranged its yearly gala holiday on the same day; under Augusta's patronage, Prussian patriotic women and the German Red Cross celebrated each September 30. Nationalist tensions, however, could also be played out over these very ceremonial markers. In 1888, Christian men of the Inner Mission and the evangelical city mission in Berlin, for example, pointedly began to celebrate Auguste Victoria's birthday (October 22),

---

83. LK, Abt. 403, no. 10041, Bl. 83–86, Trier, June 24, 1887. As it turns out, the government did not contribute to the festival because the couple had celebrated earlier, but the plans, arguably, show how people could turn the state-initiated events into something personal and meaningful.

84. This discussion of the relationship between state rituals and ordinary experience draws on Cannadine and Price, *Rituals of Royalty*, 8, 16.

with the expectation that German national identity would be properly Protestant under her patronage.[85]

Dynastic cultural performances were at the center of struggle to shape national identity in the new Germany. Relief measures, inaugural rituals, and award ceremonies for public service as well as celebrations tied to dynastic family time communicated powerful messages about community cohesion and identity. They helped give shape to an annual patriotic calendar, providing continuity and security of form in a changing geopolitical context; and alternative dates both expressed and contained the tensions within the patriotic community itself. At the same time, these rituals were activated in moments of natural disasters, eliciting a wider sense of national solidarity to "tame fear." The genres reveal multiple sites for the construction of patriotic identities in the *Kaiserreich* beyond the manifestly "nationalist" celebrations, such as Sedan Day, or the political debates swirling around the navy or other imperialist projects that have interested historians to date.

Patriotic philanthropy, however, also worked to support a civilian war preparedness infrastructure in imperial Germany; indeed, the celebrations around community health and welfare were equally about warfare, as the next two chapters show. The women and men in the associations of the Red Cross were placed under direct military authority after 1878 and subject to the army's mobilization orders. War preparedness, the second pole of dynastic legitimation, entered the new terrain of medical science, expanding the understanding of the dynastic state from "caring" to "curing."

---

85. *KZ,* no. 420, October 20, 1888, and supplement to no. 499, October 25, 1889. In contrast, the Kaiserin-Augusta Stiftung continued to celebrate September 30. See *KZ,* no. 459, October 1, 1892.

CHAPTER 5

Gendered Medical War Services in the "Curing" State

A detailed set of notes published in English in 1891 introduced the various establishments affiliated with the "Ladies' Association" (the *Frauen-Verein*) in Karlsruhe to the English reading public.[1] The broadsheet was designed to advertise the city as "an important center for the development of female art, industry and learning" and attract well-off British families or other foreigners who wanted to live abroad and educate their children. Assurances were given, too, that "comfortable" housing was available with respectable families and in boarding homes.

The descriptions captured the educational and charitable aims of the Baden Women's Association, couched squarely in the language of upper-class gentility and refinement. They highlighted the association's formative role in the evolution of women's continuing education in Germany and its acceptance of the "modern" educational needs of socially diverse women. And the use of select words such as "blessing" reproduced the official rhetoric of the basic humanitarian and beneficial impact of its philanthropic mission. It was an appropriate "face" to present to wealthy foreigners interested in sojourning in Karlsruhe for a while.

Significantly, the portrait masked another face. Omitted from the description was the association's wartime goals and the extensive preparations for war going on in peacetime. These war-related activities had become the central rationale for the women's association after its enlistment in the German Red Cross in the 1860s. In anticipating war, however, the association appealed to the same humanitarian rhetoric that enveloped its philanthropic side, appending to it, however, a new language of medical science. The war face of the association, indeed, was a public persona, but

---

1. GK, Abt. 69, no. 1179, Karlsruhe Associations, 1891.

one clothed by the players in the old, familiar veneer of care, now infused by the new promises of modern science and technology.

This powerful combination of humanitarianism and science had underwritten construction of the Ludwig-Wilhelm Hospital in the Kaiser-allee, which had opened in 1890, one year before the English communiqué. As central headquarters of the Baden Red Cross nurses and later the nurses' aides, it was the main staging ground for many of the patriotic ceremonies and rituals that brought Duchess Luise together with the women's association volunteers and personnel. To supplement the building fund that had been solicited from private donors over the past several years and a loan from the duchess, the women's association had sought permission to arrange a lottery in 1889; its justification demonstrates the centrality of war services to its mission and the persuasive appeal of the argument with both officials and the wider public audience.

The secretary, who prepared the case, reminded the readers of all the association's activities "in the public interest." High on the list were the education and support of a nursing staff *(Krankenpflegerinnen)* and the administration of its own division for medical services (Section III, *Krankenpflege*). Its activities included sending out nurses in times of natural disasters, often with little or no remuneration; providing free medical care to patients; and arranging for the theoretical training of rural nurses *(Landkrankenpflegerinnen),* who were given free room and board in its small clinic. But in the formulation, working for the "common good" meant, in essence, preparing for the national defense: "When it comes to the common good, let us stress above all the fact that our nurses are sisters of the Red Cross and the end goal of our whole enterprise is to train the largest number of nurses possible in case of war and keep them ready and prepared."[2] Section III was an integral part of a wider network of state and imperial organizations serving civilian war preparation.

To meet the evolving medical needs of war in peacetime, the Baden association had bought land at a reasonable price ("thanks to the gracious support of the duke") and was building its own hospital, which specialized in optometry and surgery in addition to serving as the central headquarters of the nursing institute. The hospital had a one-hundred-bed capacity, sixty for the patients and forty for the nurses and student trainees; in addition, several rooms were designated as benefices and available as a temporary refuge to nurses who might become disabled or, later in their life, for their old age.

---

2. GK, Abt. 69, no. 1158, Bau des Ludwig-Wilhelm-Hospitals in der Kaiserallee in Karlsruhe durch den Frauenverein, 1889–90. In the calculations, war was a permanent feature of modern life, and war preparation required no further justification beyond the humanitarian claim to ease its misery.

This *Verein*-hospital was an exceedingly complex institution, testifying to a process of medicalization of German society that had been accelerating from midcentury. Increasingly centered around the professionalizing male medical practitioners were the patients, whose life condition was being defined by medical science, and a cadre of nurses, who were being subordinated by the same process. But for the nurses, the hospital also was a place of community, an alternative family reinforcing conservative loyalties through close, personal bonds with the Baden royal house. The nursing personnel at the time stood at 173, and the lottery was seen as a way to expand operations safely without taking on a debilitating debt. Success of the lottery, indeed, guaranteed that the new hospital would open its doors on a solid financial footing. Growing societal attention to medical themes and practices—a product of the gendered professionalization of medicine—was having a powerful effect on preparing the civilian populations for war.[3] Section III was responding to, as well as shaping, these changes.

The German Red Cross and Civilian Medical War Preparation

The German Red Cross coordinated the drive in peacetime to prepare men and women for civilian war work. Through continuous testing on the ground, an elaborate gender division of labor was arranged, which reflected the transferability of women's peacetime municipal philanthropic work into defined home front services as well as the training of male volunteers for support services at or near the front. In this context, "patriotic duty" became identified with participation in the medical operations of war—a commitment that ranged from actual training in medical science to merely dropping pennies in a solicitation cup for nursing education or to support the colonial troops—undoubtedly an appealing definition to a public that was encouraged to see war as an inevitable part of "modern" life, let alone the glorified context of German unification in the first place. The historian John Hutchinson has characterized these transformations as "the militarization of charity."[4] Its effects, however, spread well beyond the philanthropic acts.

At the end of the Franco-German war, the state Red Cross organizations were determined to implement detailed civilian war mobilization orders. Listen to the leaders of the Baden State Relief Association as early

---

3. The theme of medicalization is complex. For the period before the professionalization of medicine in midcentury Germany, see Francisca Loetz, *Vom Kranken zum Patienten. "Medikalisierung" und medizinische Vergesellschaftung am Beispiel Badens, 1750–1850* (Stuttgart, 1993); also Tuchman, *Science, Medicine, and State.* For an exhaustive study of medicine, health, and eugenics in the period after unification, Weindling, *Health, Race.*

4. Hutchinson, *Champions of Charity,* 103.

as 1873: "modeled on the army, the unified executive committee (of the women's and men's associations) takes on the task already in peacetime to prepare as completely as possible a full mobilization plan *(Mobil-machungsplan)* for the state's voluntary medical services in war and to renew it yearly."[5] While transforming intent into reality on the ground was a slow process in all the states of Germany, it was aided by the incorporation of the Red Cross directly into the military chain of command.

In Red Cross narratives of its history, passage of the Kriegs-Sanitäts-ordnung in 1878 stands out as the key transition moment in the evolution of *Freiwillige Krankenpflege,* the shorthand term for the voluntary civilian activities to support military medical services in war.[6] These statutes regulated the medical services for the troops in wartime; they contained an additional twenty-two paragraphs outlining the principles and guidelines under which the admittedly murky sphere of civilian voluntary war services would be organized and coordinated "from above." However much imperial and state leaders predicted a natural outpouring of patriotism among the people in case of war, there was no premium on spontaneity.[7] The watchwords were organization, training, and discipline.

Civilian war work continued to rely on voluntarism, a principle that, simultaneously, was kept alive and normative in municipal poor relief and private charity. Paragraph 206, however, purposefully subordinated the mobilized energies to state interests: "volunteer medical war work cannot operate independently of the state; its field of activity is opened only as part of the state organism, overseen by state officials."[8] Organizational integration hinged on the central figure overseeing the voluntary medical hierarchy, the imperial commissar and military inspector of civilian war services, who was based in Berlin. The position was filled by Count Eberhard zu Stolberg-Wernigerode (1866–70), who had helped found the Prussian Patriotic Women's Association; Duke Hans Heinrich XI von Pless (1870–92); Wilhelm Prince zu Wied (1892–97); and Prince Friedrich zu Solms-Baruth, the last representative before World War I. Drawn from the ranks of the "highest" German nobility—old Silesian aristocratic industrialists and former territorial sovereigns—these *grand seigneurs* were members of Germany's wealthiest families, powerful and well con-

---

5. GK, Abt. 233, no. 2848, Badischer Landes-Hilfs-Verein, *Rechenschafts-Bericht für das Jahr 1873* (Karlsruhe, 1873).

6. *Handbuch der Deutschen Frauenvereine unter dem Rothen Kreuz,* "Auszug aus der durch Allerhöchste Kabinetordre vom 10. January 1878 genehmigten Kriegs-Sanitätsord-nung, die freiwillige Krankenpflege betreffend," 110–26.

7. The opening paragraph of the regulation predicted an outpouring of popular patriotism due to "past experience" but nonetheless stressed disciplined planning and training for it (110).

8. Ibid.

nected abroad. The Silesian coal mines owned by the von Pless family, for example, employed over eight thousand miners before 1914.[9]

On the one hand, the commissar worked with the Ministry of War and the head of the Frontline Medical Service (*Chef des Feld-Sanitätswesens*) and, therefore, was plugged into the daily affairs of the military sanitary bureaus (*Sanitätsämte*) that, on the ground, brought the army into contact with Red Cross women's and men's associations in the careful planning for war. On the other, he oversaw a civilian federal and state bureaucratic structure that simultaneously was part of the hierarchy of the Red Cross associations, the members of which were being trained to undertake the day-to-day war work. Military and civilian perspectives increasingly blurred.

The chain of command was complicated, indeed. It moved from the army into the civilian bureaucracy and down the organizational ladder to the voluntary associations active in the municipalities of Germany. And it mirrored the army's medical corps as well. As early as November 1870, the medical services of the German armed forces became the exclusive jurisdiction of the *Reich*. This new arena of medical science was coordinated by the head of the Medical Division in the Ministry of War, the *Generalstabarzt,* who was the chief frontline medical officer. He served at the same time as director of the Military Medical Academy in Berlin. Under the ministry's guidance, furthermore, the bureaus developed close working ties with the Imperial Health Office, which had been established in 1876 to gather and publish scientific and statistical information on public health, much of it of interest to the army.[10] The growing connection between medicine, public health, and war, too, accounts for the visible shift to doctors and doctors' wives on the executive committees of the state women's associations, a pattern I looked at in chapter 3.

The command structure for civilian medical service established in 1878 was geared to implementing at the grassroots level the army's projections of its need for front and home front medical services. It moved down from the imperial commissar, who received his instructions from the Ministry of War, to the Central Committee of the Red Cross (headquartered in Berlin as well) and from there to the "territorial" delegates to this national organization—one from each Prussian province, one from Berlin, and one from each member state. In turn, these delegates communicated

---

9. *DRK,* 1:32–42. Also, Dominic Lieven, *The Aristocracy in Europe, 1815–1914* (New York, 1992), 30, 57, 65, 145–46.

10. Weindling, *Health, Race,* 161–62, 172. Also, GK, Rep. 456, F 113, no. 17, Schriftwechsel über Vereinswesen, Sammlungen in militärärztlichen Kreisen, clippings of *Deutsche Militairärztliche Zeitschrift* and publications of the Imperial Health Office.

directly with the executive committees of their state or provincial Red Cross organizations.[11]

The average civilian training for war work had most contact with his or her state (or provincial) Red Cross executive committee; in daily life, this leadership body was the vital force organizing and overseeing the whole war preparedness effort. Quite possibly, the complicated structure was lost on the typical volunteer, even though state officials on an ongoing basis made sure that each local affiliate had an up-to-date copy of the whole Red Cross organizational hierarchy and its evolving tasks. These linkages certainly extended military influence and wartime calculations in peacetime down to the lowest level of the extensive philanthropic nexus, which was well positioned in local communities.

The army came into direct contact with civilians in both planning for war and supervising the current medical needs of military personnel. These interactions took numerous forms, as several examples drawn from the Baden case, home of the Fourteenth Army Corps, demonstrate. The army's projection of its medical needs in a given locality spurred local women's chapters to found, supply, and administer a small hospital *(Vereinslazarett)* or a reconvalescence home through funds raised privately. In this fashion, a good portion of medical provisioning was privately organized and financed, obviating public debates over policy or onerous tax burdens. By 1901, for example, in twenty-four towns in Baden, local women's associations had arranged for rest and recovery of soldiers and officers through private care. Furthermore, in an effort to raise money for hospital renovations or for the running of sanatoria, men and women in military and civilian life hobnobbed at charity theaters and balls; and military medical doctors were invited guests at the annual festivals honoring the Baden nursing sisters. The day-to-day running of the military in peacetime, however, did not utilize the voluntary services of the Red Cross personnel.[12]

The 1878 regulations did not specify which organizations were part of the civilian war readiness structure; rather, they stressed the guiding principles of "sacrifice," "coordination," and "discipline." In a subsequent public appeal by the Prussian Ministry of War, the relevant associations and cooperatives were invited to apply to the imperial commissar for for-

---

11. Details are in GK, Rep. 456, F 113, no. 13, Ausbildung freiwilliger Krankenhelfer . . . durch den Korpsarzt, 1875–1914, pamphlet "Die deutsche freiwillige Krankenpflege."

12. GK, Rep. 456, F 113, no. 13, correspondence of the state delegates with the commanding general, Karlsruhe, January 28, 1901; GK, Abt. 69, no. 889, Karlsruhe, July 3, 1907, Militär-Intendantur of the XIV. Armee-Korp, and no. 890, letter from Anna Lauter to the duchess, May 11, 1912, as well as flyer announcing a celebration to raise money for the Ludwig-Wilhelm Hospital on June 7, 1913.

mal inclusion. This call set in motion a flurry of meetings by the Red Cross to identify the organizations under its wing. The national executive committee had not called a general meeting since 1871, a clear indication that the Red Cross itself—as was true of its women's associations in the 1870s—was searching for a viable identity in the new political arena of imperial Germany. But the subsequent meetings—the first important one took place in late September 1880—began to link the organizations more tightly together in a process that was defined as a national effort.[13] In time, the so-called reliable *(zuverlässig)* organizations became clarified: only then could they use the name and symbol of the Red Cross.

Table 4 presents the major organizations that made up the German Red Cross in 1912. Many of them had been incorporated already in the decade of the 1880s. It shows the number of branch associations for each distinct category of activity, as well as total membership. The German Red Cross, as the table indicates, had a diverse organizational profile that mirrored the malleability of the gendered patriotic messages of care: as old-fashioned benevolence, specialized social work, and modern medical science and hygiene. There were, for example, the older Red Cross samaritan organizations, among them the Kaiser Wilhelm Foundation for German Invalids and the German Sanatorium for the Sick and the Invalid at Loschwitz (Saxony), essentially a veterans' training hospital. Since the mid-1890s, there also was the People's Sanatoria Association sponsoring clinics, children's "open air" camps, and sanatoria for cure, rest, and recovery. Under a controlled environment—testing new theories of diet and hygiene—Red Cross endeavors were helping to justify new patterns of medical interventions for purposes of national strength and health. In addition, a women's organization that supported a small nursing staff for the German colonies in Africa and Asia eventually joined the Red Cross. As part of its daily practice, the milieu of patriotic philanthropy was infused with new notions of empire and concerns about public health and hygiene, obscuring, perhaps, the standard distinction in the literature between a "new" radical nationalism and the "old" dynastic patriotism.[14]

There also were very close connections between these Red Cross organizations—including the women's associations—and veterans'

---

13. For these meetings, *KZ,* supplement to no. 229, September 30, 1880, supplement to no. 230, October 1, 1880, and also no. 164, April 6, 1892, in which new organizations were added.

14. For distinctions between the old and new nationalism, Jost Dülffer, "Einleitung: Dispositionen zum Krieg im wilhelminischen Deutschland," in Dülffer and Holl, *Bereit zum Krieg,* 15–17. Also, Nipperdey, *Deutsche Geschichte, 1866–1918,* 2:252–53, 257–64, for his analyses of "Reich nationalism," in which he uses "official" nationalism as an empirical description (260).

groups, an interpenetration of activities, ideology and festive time that has escaped attention by most historians interested in nationalism and associational life. Veterans, including those who fought in Germany's brutal colonial wars, were given free access to the range of Red Cross medical services at home and abroad, in special veterans "homes" constructed for that purpose in resort areas; some surely had been nursed by Red Cross sisters in the colonies. In turn, veterans often outfitted and helped rehearse the stretcher-bearer units (so-called veterans' *Sanitätskolonne*), although by 1905 the Ministry of War tried to transfer sole responsibility to the Red Cross, provoking a serious turf war in Baden.[15] The organizations under the Red Cross, however, had little formal ties with the national associations *(Nationalverbände)*, identified by many German historians as the driving force of the nationalist debates in imperial Germany: the Pan-

TABLE 4. Participation in German Red Cross Organizations, 1912

	Branches	Membership
State Associations	26	174,000
Voluntary male stretcher-bearers	2,009	65,000
Cooperatives of male volunteers in wartime	77	11,100
Good Samaritan associations	9	1,300
Women's associations	2,840	680,000
Red Cross nursing orders	49	5,489
Red Cross nurses' aides	—	8,462[a]
German Women's Association for the Colonies[b]	146	15,099[c]
Peoples' Sanatoria Association	13	1,472[d]
Total	5,169	961,922

Source: Fünfzig Jahre Deutsches Rotes Kreuz, 1864–1914 (n.p. 1916), 7–8, 12–16; GK, Abt. 69, no. 892, Die Abteilung III des Frauenvereins betr., 1914–18, Oberinnen-Konferenz, March 20, 1914, and no. 1133, Jahresversammlung, 1909; *DRK*, 2: 665–70; 704–24; *DRK*, 3:47–49.

[a]Figures are for Prussia and Baden (Karlsruhe) only.

[b]Supporting 65 sisters in the German colonies.

[c]Membership figures are from 1909 and do not include numbers from Baden or Anhalt, which that year together had 11 branches of the association.

[d]Estimates of patients and children in "fresh air" camps in 1909; that year 170,000 men, women, and children sought medical help from the association's 6 clinics in Berlin.

---

15. By 1905, the army was trying to promote uniformity in the sanitary corps throughout the country. It sought to transfer them to the jurisdiction of the Red Cross, but the veterans' associations in Baden were opposed to the loss of authority. For the controversy, GK, Abt. 69, no. 1117, Mitteilung, Marine-Oberstabsarzt z.D. Ratz, Freiburg, February 3, 1910, and February 12, 1910. For Red Cross care of veterans, *Fünfzig Jahre Deutsches Rotes Kreuz, 1864–1914* (n.p., 1916) 12, and GK, Abt. 233, no. 2848, Badischer Landes-Hilfs-Verein, *Rechenschafts-Bericht für das Jahr 1873* (Karlsruhe, 1873), collaboration with the Kaiser Wilhelm Foundation for German Invalids.

German League, the Navy League, the German Society for the Eastern Marches, among them.[16] But Red Cross philanthropic practices, seemingly above and distant from the clashes among interest groups, worked just as powerfully to shape nationalist messages and did so in gendered idiom.

At the center of civilian war preparation stood the state *(Land)* associations. Table 4 shows that by 1912 these influential organizations had enlisted around 175,000 members. The daily activities at the state level were working to fashion the gender alliance, which was at the root of Red Cross humanitarian patriotism. There was, however, nothing simple nor automatic about the gendered allocations of tasks: they were being proposed, tested, implemented, and refined over time.

In the first place, they relied on the older philanthropic women's associations that, as the table shows, had the largest membership by far, accounting for the mass grassroots appeal of patriotic voluntarism. The imperial leadership was forced to acknowledge already in 1881 that the success of its women's organizations was giving the Red Cross its domestic "boom."[17] Encased in a language of philanthropy and women's continuing education, as the English broadsheet reveals, each local women's association had a separate section for war work, supporting nurses' training and the founding and provisioning of clinics, homes, and hospitals. Second, there also were distinct men's organizations. In 1912, the largest were the stretcher-bearer units, followed by male cooperatives providing medical services in war *(Verbände der Genossenschaft freiwilliger Krankenpfleger im Kriege)*. Despite their original efforts at municipal relief and philanthropic activities after 1871, the Red Cross male volunteers increasingly were being trained for frontline services *(Sanitätsdienst im Felde)* alone, including aid in the colonies. As early as 1889, for example, nine members of the cooperatives applied to work in a Protestant mission hospital in Zanzibar under the command of the chief medical doctor of the colonial troops, and numbers of stretcher-bearers also began a tour in Africa starting in the late 1880s.

The growing division of labor between men's and women's associations, however, reflected earlier failed gender experiments. In the early 1870s, for example, the Men's Relief Association in Karlsruhe had set up a soup kitchen with much fanfare in the former wartime barracks near the train station, entering the more standard philanthropic field of the "caring" state. Within a year, the undertaking was defunct: interest fell off, and

---

16. Eley, *Reshaping the German Right;* Chickering, *We Men Who Feel.*

17. As expressed in a very long analysis of the Red Cross in *KZ,* first supplement to no. 237, October 9, 1881.

poor people stayed away.[18] Urban patriotic women, in contrast, were able to sustain the soup kitchens. Arguably in the case of women, societal assumptions about gender roles made their place in food preparation seemingly natural, more easily masking, perhaps, the class and other social divides that threatened to disrupt the ties of community created through a sharing of food. In time, the male volunteers in Baden also gave up their efforts at popular education and turned to equip medical compartments on hospital trains and administer model depots that stockpiled medical supplies. As stretcher-bearers, they combined a theoretical study of medicine under the guidance of a doctor with lots of hands-on practice in applying bandages, for example, or in trotting and exercising in "military style" *(militärische Bewegung)* on command. Indeed, the versatility of this exercise encouraged the Breslau provincial school council in 1889 to replace the standard course in gymnastics with this type of "Red Cross praxis" for boys of the upper grades.[19]

The apparent clarity of table 4 cannot hide the tensions that continuously required negotiation on the living substance of these arrangements. The powerful rhetoric of patriotic unity dampened any move toward outright secession, but it hardly guaranteed internal harmony over the shape and extent of the division of tasks. Preparing for war was a complicated business, even if the widely shared bottom line put a premium on hierarchy, obedience, and loyalty. Fissures appeared in overlapping patterns.

Serious disagreements strained relationships between the unified state women's associations and the Central Committee of the Red Cross, particularly over the proper relationship in wartime. Here, it was not so much a question of the gender of the delegates to the Central Committee, who, in any case, would be male, but whether representatives of the women's associations—the largest constituency in the Red Cross hierarchy, after all—would be on the Central Committee in wartime at all. Would the civilian home front—imagined in the women's organizations crisscrossing the territory—have a place in the deliberations of war? Tough negotiations in 1878 gained the women's association delegates a formal seat on the committee at the moment of wartime mobilization. Similarly, divisions continuously strained the relationship among representatives of *Land* and *Reich,* expressing the powerful pulls of dynastic state loyalties that sustained the work of this "German" relief association. The state women's associations continuously jockeyed for influence in a series of maneuvers that often saw four of the states joining to curb Prussian influence. Furthermore, these

18. GK, Abt. 233, no. 2848, *Rechenschafts-Bericht* (1871–72).

19. GK, Abt. 69, no. 1117, Mitteilungen, "Aus dem Vereinsleben," no. 3, March 22, 1910; Abt. 233, no. 2848, *Rechenschafts-Bericht* (1873); *KZ,* no. 492, October 21, 1889, for the change in curriculum.

tensions spilled over to other arenas, as in the refusal for nineteen years running of the Baden, Bavarian, Saxon, and Weimar Red Cross nursing orders to join the Prussian (Cassel)-run Association for German Nursing Institutes.[20]

Expansion of the civilian side of war preparation through medical training in the 1880s was paradoxical for the dynastic state. The leaders needed to extend into "society" to recruit medical personnel. In doing so, however, they brought into the organization the same tensions between official and radical nationalists that simultaneously were exploding on the streets, in the meeting halls, and at electoral campaigns; conservative dynastic groups had to tame and contain this potentially more radical base. Similar challenges came with the continued professionalization of nursing and, starting in the early 1890s, the turn to nurses' aides, well-off women volunteers who, nonetheless, were being educated in the science of medicine. The leaders, indeed, were forced to confront a "woman question," but they did so not from a feminist perspective but by grudging acknowledgment of ongoing changes affecting the lives of privileged aristocratic and bourgeois women. Successfully negotiating the gender frameworks, which anchored service in normative notions of masculinity and femininity, helped reinforce conservative power and authority.

Red Cross leaders had clear expectations about the proper functioning of their social base, which they articulated in a gendered language of state service. After all, it was partly through the medical practices of the Red Cross—in tandem with the professionalization of medicine, to be sure—that a gender hierarchy came to dominate the emerging new field of medical science. As an institutional force, the German Red Cross was as much a "catalyst" as a "mirror" of the gender assumptions coming to structure the medical profession and influence public discussion and understanding of civilian war work.

Listen to the crystallization of the images around 1907, a time of renewed attention to the specifics of civilian wartime mobilization because of mounting international tensions. In describing the "rigorous" *(kräftig)* stretcher-bearer units, the Central Committee called them a "powerhouse" of men who were tightly organized together in "military discipline, systematically trained, fearless of death, and willing to sacrifice."[21] The work was designed to instill military discipline and order among young (potentially disruptive) male civilians and touted as appropriately masculine, with its emphasis on strength in the face of death and sacrifice for fellow members

---

20. These details are in a chronological overview of the negotiations, GK, Abt. 69, no. 889, Die Ausbildung freiwilliger Pflegerinnen, notes and protocols, 1871–1905.

21. GK, Abt. 69, no. 1117, Mitteilungen, Baron von dem Knesebeck, Berlin, June 4, 1907.

of the nation. Real men also were actively patriotic. Similarly, the statement of principles in the mobilization orders for the "experienced" *(bewährte)* women's associations reflected essentialist notions about women's nature and the values they would bring to their work, in this case, in hospital administration. While the doctors self-evidently provided the medical care, according to the author, the presence of a superintendent *(Vorsteherin)* and her female colleagues "would add a spirit of peace and collaboration, which not only assures the necessary order but also has a comforting and soothing effect on the sick, so essential for recovery."[22]

For its medical providers, then, the Red Cross leadership extended its reach deep into civil society. It tapped into social groups with potentially diverse and challenging conceptions of national service. Among the young middle-class men and university students who typically joined stretcher-bearer units or volunteered and trained as orderlies, conservative authority was imposed by strict organizational control, an extension, in effect, of military discipline, hierarchy, and loyalty into the volatile corps of volunteers. Besides, the attributes of service were defined as masculine and incorporated into the image of the self. Red Cross leaders basically were working with a set of norms that elided masculine virtues and military values.[23]

In contrast, the move to recruit the cadre of women employees who would work as Red Cross sisters and aides brought the conservative dynastic organization face-to-face with a set of complicated gender contradictions. In seeking to harness women's work for patriotic causes, the aristocratic leadership was challenged on both its right and left and forced to negotiate a middle ground that defined the contours of official nationalism. The turn to gainful employ incorporated all the ambiguity of the "woman question" and debates about femininity into the heart of the conservative patriotic war culture.

The Patriotic Community Confronts the Woman Question

Two historians of the evolution of Germany's public relief services, Christoph Sachsse and Florian Tennstedt, claim that the Red Cross women's organizations spearheaded the transition from religious to lay nursing with its cadres of "nursing sisters" readied for wartime but

---

22. GK, Abt. 69, no. 1117, "Muster-Pläne fur den Übergang zur Kriegstätigkeit," no. 1, January 27, 1909. The loaded gender adjectives to describe the two organizations were General Limberger's vocabulary. He was the head of Baden's state Red Cross organization at the time.

23. For a particularly clear formulation of the relationship, although for an earlier era, Karen Hagemann, "Of Manly Valor." For thoughts on masculine identities and military values, Elshtain and Tobias, *Women, Militarism, and War.*

engaged in gainful employ in the years of peace.[24] The situation was more complicated, however. The women's association, as we have seen, actively drew on the services of religious sisters as well, keeping alive the central Christian charitable imperative as an ideal of feminine behavior: ennobling but self-effacing acts expressing care and concern for others. Simultaneously, the Red Cross organization supported its own cadre of certified nurses, welded together into a tight community of sisters under a motherhouse, who worked in civic and military hospitals and clinics as well as in private practice *(Privatpflege)*. Their numbers rose steadily and reached a total of 5,489 by 1912, as table 4 shows. This figure represents around 10 percent of the more than fifty-five thousand vocational nurses counted in a 1909 special census on nursing; together with other communities of nurses associated with the Red Cross, for example, the Sisters of St. John, the orders of lay nursing sisters made up 16 percent of the total and the only groups kept in a state of readiness for war.[25]

These statistics, however, mask the considerable transformation in the field of nursing that influenced the evolution of the Red Cross sisterhood in the *Kaiserreich*. There was a steady decline in confessional nursing from its high of 87 percent of the total in 1876 to 61 percent in 1909 and a concomitant rise in the numbers of "free" wage nurses, many of whom were organized in professional associations. Professional nurses comprised 22 percent of the total nursing contingent in Germany in 1909.[26]

The nursing components of the Red Cross represented a concession to the complicated forces of feminist "modernity" that willy-nilly were affecting women's lives in the *Kaiserreich*—for example, the demographic changes reducing average family size, the spread of education and literacy among women, an emerging consumer culture, and, above all, new life expectations among the young.[27] But they did so on their own terms,

---

24. Sachsse and Tennstedt, *Geschichte der Armenfürsorge*, 233–35.

25. *Fünfzig Jahre,* 13. For the 1909 census, Eva-Cornelia Hummel, *Krankenpflege im Umbruch (1876–1914). Ein Beitrag zum Problem der Berufsfindung "Krankenpflege"* (Freiburg, 1986), 35–38.

26. Hummel, *Krankenpflege im Umbruch,* 7–8, 33–37; Sachsse and Tennstedt, *Geschichte der Armenfürsorge,* 230–31; and Stacey Freeman, "Medicalizing the Nurse: Professional and Eugenic Discourse at the Kaiserin Auguste Victoria Haus in Berlin," *German Studies Review* 18, no. 3 (October 1995): 422–25. Freeman glosses over the contradiction noted by Hummel *(Krankenpflege im Umbruch,* 32) between those willing to serve in war yet unwilling to take on wage work in peacetime.

27. These changes in expectations were captured well in the feminist collection *Handbuch der Frauenbewegung,* ed. Helene Lange and Gertrud Bäumer, vol. 4, *Die deutsche Frau im Beruf* (Berlin, 1902), 28, in which the desire to study nursing was described not just as an economic necessity but as meeting an inner need. For demographic changes affecting women's lives, Quataert, "Demographic and Social Change." For the broader processes of change, among other works, Ute Frevert, *Women in German History: From Bourgeois Emancipation to Sexual Liberation,* trans. Stuart McKinnon-Evans (Oxford, 1989).

framed within a conservative, patriotic, and limited gender vision. The patriotic community struggled with a collision of values between the Christian world of charity and the modern capitalist economy.

So, too, did evangelical groups to its right. A parallel move to promote the volunteer services of laywomen to supplement the work of the deaconess nurses' stations and provide charitable relief at the parish level bore fruit in Protestant communities. In 1899, the empress gave her imprimatur to the founding of a Protestant Women's Relief Auxiliary (Evangelische Frauenhilfe), which coordinated the growing female philanthropic mission of the Protestant Church. The work of the auxiliary proved successful; the number of associations rose from 85 with 13,634 members in 1900 to 2,407 with a following of 249,000 members by 1912, an impressive growth by all accounts.[28] It proved to be a serious rival of the Patriotic Women's Associations, particularly in smaller cities and towns of old Prussia. The potential for jurisdictional conflicts was so acute that it forced the empress in 1906 to instruct the Ministries of Interior and Religious Affairs to work out, at least theoretically, the normative operational boundaries. These official statements of principles, sent to the district presidents for distribution to local bureaucrats, are indicative of official nationalist interests.

Ostensibly establishing a judicious division of labor, in effect they favored the Patriotic Women's Associations because of their indispensable role in war. In the eyes of officials, at stake was the women's valuable services to "army and people" *(Heer und Volk),* an invocation that highlighted the symbolic duo at the very center of actions in the name of the "caring" state. Government officials, thus, supported the expansion of patriotic women's chapters in more remote areas of Prussia; and "so the ministerial decree does not want to restrict the Patriotic Women's Association in this direction." Therefore, if a locality already hosted a Protestant group, officials were instructed nonetheless to encourage the founding of a patriotic women's chapter and work to see that evangelical women restrict their activities to all manner of Christian work with families.

In the local context envisioned by official nationalists, Red Cross women were given the sole responsibility for municipal welfare tasks.[29] In

---

28. Despite dynastic moral and financial encouragement, its parent organization, the *Hilfsverein,* had been floundering in the 1890s, graphic testimony to the fact that an infusion of dynastic support from above—ranging from money to personal involvement—could not guarantee success at the grassroots level; patriotic philanthropy never simply was a question of imposition on a passive population, but of its continuous reformulation through official interactions with civil society. See Baumann, *Protestantismus und Frauenemanzipation,* 139–49; Sachsse and Tennstedt, *Geschichte der Armenfürsorge,* 229–32.

29. *DRK,* 2:337–39, describes the rivalry and official nationalist efforts to work out a compromise; also Baumann, *Protestantismus und Frauenemanzipation,* 169–74, for details on the work of the *Frauenhilfe* in the locality.

practice, these decrees hardly could eliminate the conflicts between confessional and interconfessional philanthropy, although both groups shared fundamental commitments: dynastic loyalty, a Christian vision of service easily identified as patriotic, and a female voluntary imperative for the care of neighbor. Their day-to-day work established an institutional pattern of church, state, and associational involvement in social welfare on the local level.

Red Cross leaders, furthermore, could not remain insulated from the debates among Protestant and Catholic women who, by the early twentieth century, were grappling with aspects of the "woman question" from their own religious vantage point. Indeed, to the left of the state women's associations—forcing a slow accommodation to the forces of change in women's lives—were the moderate and right-wing feminist confessional groups like the German Protestant Women's League (Deutsch-Evangelische Frauenbund) founded in 1898 and the Catholic Women's League (Katholischer Frauenbund), which emerged in 1904. The Protestant leader Paula Mueller and the Catholic-convert Elisabeth Gnauck-Kühne were moderate voices in the feminist spectrum to be sure. But they were part of wider debates that were helping to organize the new professions of social work and nursing. The process of professionalization received an added impetus with the formation of an independent German Professional Organization of Nurses (Berufsorganisation der Krankenpflegerinnen Deutschlands), under the leadership of Agnes Karll in 1903. Together, professional and religious feminist organizations made the conditions of women's work and remuneration an explicit part of the national agenda. They also raised the demand for women's vote—for the trade and industrial courts and, in the case of Protestants, as of 1904, even for the local parish administrative councils.[30]

In addition, there were other moderate organizations in the bourgeois women's movement, for example, Lina Morgenstern's People's Kitchen in Berlin, the Lette Association promoting women's educational and occupational advancement, and Helene Lange's teachers' organization. The leaders of each of these avowedly feminist organizations had close personal ties with the *Landesmutter,* other royal female patrons, and Patriotic Women's Associations. Many were plugged into dynastic patronage and its rituals of celebration and reward, forging relationships that have gone largely unexamined by German feminist historians. For years, for example, there was an active correspondence between Empress Augusta and Lina Morgenstern. They exchanged publicized annual New Year's greet-

---

30. Baumann, *Protestantismus und Frauenemanzipation,* 88–98, for the religious feminist voices of Protestants and Catholics; for the professionalization of nurses, Hummel, *Krankenpflege im Umbruch,* 84–90, 101–18.

ings in the conservative press; the contact later was continued with Augusta's daughter Luise.[31] Part of the feminist message fit in well with the ideologies upholding the state. On one level, feminist egalitarianism and a dynastic social hierarchy undeniably are antithetical positions. In certain contexts, however, they became transmuted into shared commitments around the pursuit of waged employ and old age security, which were transforming the bases of women's lives. The impact of these interlocking forces can be explored in some detail through an examination of the organizations of Red Cross nurses and aides in Baden, recipients of special attention by the Baden royal house.

The Baden Association of Red Cross Sisters

For decades, literally, leaders of Baden's Section III grappled with what they defined as a serious shortcoming: their inability to recruit educated, well-off women for the nursing sisterhood. This elite element, or so the leaders intoned, would set a respectable example for the less privileged working sisters. But despite the most creative strategies and direct appeal to the "educated groups" in Baden society, the Association of Red Cross Sisters found its base among young women of rural and servant backgrounds and, as the long nineteenth century wore on, also from the popular classes *(Volksklasse)* in towns and small cities. Although the evidence is scarce, apparently there were proportionately more Catholics than Protestants among the recruits in the confessionally mixed state.[32] And the group wavered in its use of *Schwester* (sister), a traditional designation associated with the religious female nursing orders, and *Pflegerin* (nurse), a more modern term conjuring up the individual professional salaried employee.

The contradiction was inherent in the original accords between the *Land* Red Cross overseeing civilian war preparation and the Baden Women's Association implementing it. In the early 1870s, arrangements stressed the professional training of nurses and the need to provide, in the terminology of the day, the necessary scientific know-how *(wissen und*

31. Ute Gerhard, *Unerhört. Die Geschichte der deutschen Frauenbewegung* (Reinbeck bei Hamburg, 1990), 138–77; Frevert, *Women in German History.* For the exchange of greetings between the female court and Lina Morgenstern, *KZ,* no. 304, December 28, 1880, no. 5, January 7, 1881, and no. 6, January 7, 1888; and with Luise, GK, Abt. 69, no. 228, Aufenthalt der Grossherzogin in Berlin am 25 February–2 März 1906, letter, n.d.

32. GK, Abt. 69, no. 1130, Ausbildung von Wärterinnen aus gebildeter Ständen, 1888, and no. 1132, Einladung der Abt. III des Badischen Frauenvereins zur Beihilfe für die Krankenpflege. The language in these appeals is very carefully crafted. For the confessional divide, no. 890, Verzeichnis der Lehrschwestern, welche am 18. November 1910 das Dienstzeichen erhalten. Of the forty recipients, 55 percent were Catholics.

können), however rudimentary. The first plan of study in 1872 established courses running for two to three months in various clinics throughout the state along with "regular religious instruction" *(regelmässige Erbauungsstunden)* to awaken and strengthen the "requisite spirit."

Two Baden women leaders (table 3), Baroness von Berstett and the wife of District Judicial Officer Wielandt, together with Dr. Spemann, took their case for this indispensable instruction to the German Red Cross women's meeting in Frankfurt in 1874. On the agenda was the effort to establish uniform regulations for Red Cross nursing training in the new German nation. True to the federal character of the Red Cross, only the most general principles were agreed on, leaving each state association free to fill in the details. However, under the promptings of the Baden contingent—so its annual report proudly noted—the meeting successfully banished once and for all the claim that lay nursing was redundant, given the place of religious nursing orders. Rather, the Red Cross assembly affirmed the indispensability of trained lay nurses and used the Baden "[war] experiences, statutes and contracts" as its models.[33]

This turn to the science of medicine was hailed as a sign of a growing "understanding" of the new requirements that were affecting at once medical doctors and public opinion—let alone the world of dynastic service. By the 1870s, the professionalization of medicine was well under way in the states of Germany; and in the workplace, the newly trained nurse was put squarely under male doctors' authority—even if the members of Section III later on would take pride in Fräulein Lina Schiemann, the first female head physician in Germany appointed in 1908 to the municipal hospital in Pforzheim in Baden.[34]

Affirming the medical gender hierarchy, Red Cross practice nonetheless affected the ongoing formation of the profession of nursing. The association saw nursing as a viable employment option for women. As formulated at a meeting in 1874, just as "the man" so, too, "the girl" had to have an opportunity to secure her existence, eliding yet differentiating the two claimants. Nursing as an occupation had to command an "adequate wage" and extend a pension similar to that offered by the religious orders, which took care of their aged and disabled members through prebendary provisions.[35] But the Baden Red Cross shunned the logic of the capitalist wage system, distancing itself, indeed, from the position of the bourgeois

---

33. GK, Abt. 233, no. 2848, *Dreizehnter Jahresbericht* (1872), report on Section III; *Fünfzehnter Jahresbericht* (1874), containing a lecture by the army doctor von Corval. For curriculum matters, Abt. 69, no. 891, Lehrplan für den theoretischen Kurs der Schulerinnen des Bad. Frauenvereins, n.d. (around 1913).

34. GK, Abt. 69, no. 890, Die Abteilung III des Frauenvereins betr. 1908–10, Notiz.

35. GK, Abt. 233, no. 2848, speech by Dr. von Corval, 1874.

women's movement to its left, which stressed the individual benefits of wage employment for women. More in line with the religious orders, it centered nursing around the institution of the motherhouse. In Baden, this was the women's association clinic and, after its consecration in 1891, the Ludwig-Wilhelm Hospital in Karlsruhe.

The arrangement reflected the conservative logic that looked to the preservation of intermediary institutions to safeguarded collective values and serve as a buffer between the individual and the bureaucratic state. Reifying the principle of the motherhouse made all movements for reform difficult to implement, however, even though over the years numerous voices within the Red Cross community itself sought to improve the sisters' working and living conditions.

Two critics stand out in Baden around the turn of the century, the matron Hedwig von Schlichling and the Red Cross sister Elisabeth Storp; each offered trenchant criticism of the harsh conditions in the sisterhood and called for growing state role in training and placement. Storp later joined Karll in founding the professional union for "free" nurses.[36]

The Baden Women's Association leadership, however, continuously rallied around the motherhouse as the necessary structure to safeguard the sensitive training and holding of nurses in readiness for war. The "state" in its crass bureaucratic calculations could insure only the nurses' formal medical instruction but not their overall moral values nor their "politics." The leaders feared that a strengthened state supervisory role and a separate employment bureaucracy would loosen the bonds of dependency deemed necessary to uphold loyalty to the dynastic state to meet its medical requirements for war. Besides, the motherhouse imagery was useful for military-dynastic purposes, easily lending its social relationships on the micro level to the conception of a larger family community under the authority of the *Landesmutter.*

The duchess made ample use of such terminology when in 1912, as was the custom, she offered the concluding remarks at a Red Cross meeting. She praised the representatives of Section III and the matrons of the nurses' stations for their careful attention to details in securing the "firm foundation" of the nursing association. It was built on the "world of samaritan acts, the charitable love of neighbor" and on hard labor but was not slavish before the "world of egotism, superficiality, and material pleasures." This proper balance prompted her positive assessment, "for all of you are in a very special sense my children for whom I am permitted to feel quite motherly."[37] Activating the authoritative voice of the *Landesmutter*

---

36. These reform efforts are examined more fully by Hummel, *Krankenpflege im Umbruch,* 73–84.

37. GK, Abt. 69, no. 891, Oberinnen-Konferenz, March 25, 1912.

in this close work setting, she praised her children for their restraint and proper balance, offering motherly warmth that also affirmed her power to define the norms of behavior.

This "firm foundation," in the words of the duchess, helped perpetuate a set of normative values that were remarkably consistent over time, even as the field of nursing expanded in scope and task. The organizational goals and strategies described in 1872 and the revised statutes governing the "profession of sisters" *(Schwesternberuf)* presented to the duchess forty-two years later in 1914 deviate only in details. According to those in charge, the profession of nursing had to be saturated with "deep religious conviction of the spirit of Christian love and compassion as well as a loyal, unflagging devotion" to the cause of nursing. This was the sentiment in 1914; but the 1872 principles already stressed "a sense of duty and love for the sick." They also affirmed the values of "devotion . . . compatibility and, . . . as the highest goal of the spirit of Christian love, humility before God." These Christian moorings, however, embraced all denominations. Furthermore, both pronouncements reiterated the association's motto, unchanged over half a century: God is with us! *(Gott mit uns!)*. This same slogan was on the belt buckles of the enlisted men fighting in the two world wars.[38]

The persistence of the religious appeal is striking, a graphic testimony to the living force of the Christian message of patriotic service in the admittedly slowly "modernizing" conservative culture of imperial Germany. Meetings were infused with religious references played out in subtle psychological dramas; in another of her concluding remarks, Luise evoked a contemplative ideal, asking the audience to visualize a beautiful landscape and place itself at the top of a mountain looking down on the arduous routines of daily life. The quiet envisioning of this unsullied landscape was necessary to replenish the soul and restore strength, energy, and purpose, so the members could return again, reinvigorated, to the life of toil and trouble. Adding a dose of political memory to this vision, for the year was 1913, the duchess evoked the great patriotic centenary celebrations marking "German" victory over Napoleon. Her mountain vista, indeed, had revealed the many contributions of patriotic women who then, as now, demonstrated "serious willingness to sacrifice and fulfill their duties."[39]

---

38. GK, Abt. 233, no. 2848, *Dreizehnter Jahresbericht* (1871–1872) and Abt. 69, no. 892, Statut über Ausbildung und Verwendung der Krankenschwestern der Badischen Frauenvereins, March 18, 1914. I thank my colleague Professor George Stein for the information on the belt buckles. It demonstrates the profound interconnection between military and civilian war preparation forged first under dynastic-military authority.

39. GK, Abt. 69, no. 892, Oberinnen-Konferenz, March 14, 1913.

Within the milieu of wage labor, then, the Red Cross organization continuously reproduced the values of the wider dynastic philanthropic culture that also enclosed secular political identities and behavior in religious idioms. It proved a seductive message; in Baden, the Red Cross nursing assocation benefited from considerable public support. The minutes of its statewide meetings are filled with references to donors and benefactors, reproducing the politics of gift giving that we explored in chapter 3.[40] Section III operated in the black as well, thanks to a regular infusion of dynastic funds and public monies allocated by parliament for various projects around the Ludwig-Wilhelm Hospital.

On a more pragmatic level, the motherhouse served additional purposes. The Red Cross sisterhood was at once a hierarchical structure and a living community. In this way, too, it seemed to encapsulate the wider dynastic culture with its festivals and celebrations of rule that affirmed horizontal ties while simultaneously reinforcing social hierarchy. The intricate set of rules and regulations governing the assocation worked to maintain discipline and loyalty in a fashion similar to the military model, which was extended to the male stretcher-bearer units and cooperatives in the Red Cross organization.

In command at the top, so to speak, was the duchess, the nurses' patron, who had the final say over the assocation statutes. The nursing organization was placed under the authority of Section III and, thus, inserted right into the civilian plans for war. The symbolic service pin—a silver medal with the Red Cross against a white background—that the student nurses received upon graduation carried with it the requirement to be registered for medical war service. Annually, the names of the available personnel were placed on a list for the upcoming year (*Mobilmachungsjahr*); the names of at least half of the total Red Cross nurses had to appear on the list.

The statutes also stipulated the requirements for admittance into the sisterhood. The applicant had to be at least twenty years old, present various testimonies of good birth and character, and a statement of purpose, procedures designed to claim respectability in the eyes of a skeptical public, which in midcentury still identified "lay nursing"—both female and male—with social outcasts and ne'er-do-wells.

Applications were screened carefully for suitability. For example, in the case of Anna Heringer, from the town of Lahr, whose application came to the duchess's attention in 1900, the Section III business advisor, State Councillor and General Major Stiefbold, recommended rejection.

---

40. For example, GK, Abt. 69, no. 891, 1911–13, Verzeichniss der bis jetzt eingekommenen Gaben für den Bau im Ludwig-Wilhelm-Krankenheim, n.d.

Her father, an actuary, had been dismissed from state service for irregularities, and her brother, too, had been fired from his job for embezzlement. The family had been receiving regular poor relief support from 1887. Ostensibly, the grounds for rejection were her advanced age of thirty-five and reputed ill health; in fact Stiefbold expressed concern whether her upbringing in such a family context might taint her own ethical outlook. For her part, Anna Heringer's motives were solely financial. Financial need also accounted for a number of the young women (all unmarried) who attended nursing training courses offered by Professor Kneske in Freiburg in 1899. The fathers of three of the fourteen women attending his first class had died; in the second course, 42 percent of the young women (eight out of nineteen), similarly, were on their own, seemingly in need of a livelihood.[41]

Over and above the practicing nurses were the matrons *(Oberinnen)* in hospitals and nursing stations, women responsible for the deportment, training, and placement of the sisters—powerful figures in the negotiations over the nurses' tour of hospital duty who worked with the duchess and the women volunteers of Section III in the practical day-to-day running of the Nurses' Assocation. The statutes set them as "shining example[s] in the performance of duty, sacrificial love, and tolerance." If the Baden Red Cross failed to recruit young, educated, well-off women for the business of nursing, it drew on the elites for its supervisory personnel—matrons from aristocratic backgrounds like Fraulein von Schlichling, a smattering of baronesses, and women from other well-placed families. The majority were single and, thus, apparently more able to reconcile a salaried post with high social status.[42] The composition and hierarchical structure of the association introduced and reproduced social power differentials within the gender-specific community of nurses.

Power, of course, is not simply centered nor institutional, although to be sure external bureaucratic rules and regulations help maintain order and discipline. Association practices combined the authority of rules with the persuasive rituals of solidarity to affirm a sense of community—a horizontal sisterhood that linked the members together in pursuit of work

---

41. GK, Abt. 69, no. 889, Karlsruhe, January 1, 1900, and her petition to the duchess, December 10, 1899. For earlier prejudices against "nursing," see Hummel, *Krankenpflege im Umbruch*, 28. Loetz, *Vom Kranken zum Patienten*, makes the point that until midcentury nursing was hardly a female monopoly; in staffing the *Vormärz* charity hospitals, for example, the state encouraged both men and women to apply. For backgrounds of the students in Freiburg, GK, Abt. 69, no. 562, Besuch in Heiterheim und Freiburg, April 29, 1899.

42. GK, Abt. 69, no. 892, for the statutes. The background of the matrons is gleaned from the list of participants at the Red Cross meetings, from obituaries, and descriptions of their life and service in the nominations for state awards.

deemed both personally rewarding and collectively valuable. The woman's identity as Red Cross sister was conferred partly through her dress, a sumptuary policy explicitly designed "to increase consciousness of belonging together in the execution of the *Bund's* duties and to improve its economic position" in the wider society. Originally, the uniform arguably distinguished the Red Cross sister from others and helped raise her salary among a population still skeptical of the newfangled practice of "nursing." The dress code was established in December 1871. While it also mirrored the hierarchy of authority that existed within the association—matrons dressed differently than sisters and head nurses—over the years identity became tied up with the uniform and service medal.[43]

Group identity had added importance in the context of Red Cross service. It was linked to cultural practices that affirmed dynastic loyalty, as was true among many male medical volunteers and, independently, veterans' associations. The Red Cross sisters were deeply enmeshed in honors and festivities dispensed through the dynastic house: "in order to raise devotion to duty *(Pflichttreue)* and to honor faithful service," a "festive award ceremony" in the company of the duchess was established to celebrate ten, fifteen, and twenty years of continuous service. The event soon became a familiar sight in the annual patriotic calendar.[44] The ceremony worked to preserve state identity; it brought together people from all over the state who similarly were engaged in furthering the dynastic project. Paradoxically, these types of state ceremonies gave living meaning to official nationalism: its embodiment in dynastic state identity that had resonance beyond state borders—in this case in a wider German commitment to a common policy of civilian training for national defense. Furthermore, the recipient of the honors—in the midst of, for her, such exalted company—arguably became a more willing participant in the dynastic mission.

In-house festivities, too, punctuated the daily work routines of the Red Cross sisters. In this level of small group formation, the conservative dynastic leadership implemented a strategy of celebrations that it simultaneously was extending to the wider culture in its struggles for power and dominance. The statutes spelled out the intent unmistakably: "periodic festive gatherings . . . would be a way to affirm the nobility of the profession solemnly consecrated by moral-religious sentiments." Even the critic

---

43. GK, Abt. 233, no. 2848, *Dreizehnter Jahresbericht* (1871–72), report on Section III. The emotional identification with the uniform is reflected in Red Cross nurses' memoirs. For example, Henriette Riemann, *Schwester der Vierten Armee. Ein Kriegstagebuch* (Berlin, 1930), 14–15.

44. Considerable time and energy went into determining the guest list, drawn up by the president of the league in consultation with the dynastic court. GK, Abt. 69, no. 891, Anna Lauter, May 17, 1911, and May 11, 1912, letters.

Elisabeth Storp commented positively about the psychological benefits of the festivals for morale and cohesion. The celebrations provided a time of joy and diversion to assuage the daily encounter with suffering and pain. For the sisters without family, she went on to assert, the gatherings had particular value, creating kin ties that assured support and nurturance.[45] The power of these bonds, too, was revealed at the death of a sister or matron. The colleagues would travel great distances to attend the funeral, a coalescence that tangibly put the collective sisterhood on display. The intimacy they had gained in shared endeavors now bound the group together as they collectively offered their last farewell. The moment, too, was a statement about permanence and longevity: while the individual had died the group continued as a collectivity.[46]

From its inception, the Baden Assocation of Red Cross Sisters experienced steady although unspectacular growth. It counted 59 nurses and matrons in 1873; by 1889 their numbers had more than tripled, although the organization also struggled to contain an equally rapid turnover: recruits enjoyed the advantages of "free education," or so the leadership complained, but after a number of years left permanently for private practice or other work and were lost for the municipal philanthropic mission. In 1895 there were 267 sisters; a decade later their numbers had nearly doubled, rising to 522. By 1910, the state organization had 720 members, and the last years before the war saw continued gains: an increase to 768 in 1911 and to 900 in 1914.[47]

The work of the nursing sisters undeniably was hard, involving long hours and poor pay. Table 5 compares the salary scale of Red Cross nurses with "free" nurses and several other female professions. Nurses' pay was way below that of women teachers, for example. Furthermore, unlike the salaried employee or "free" nurse, the Red Cross nurse was under tight supervision—literally day and night—by the motherhouse and the

---

45. Details come from GK, Abt. 233, no. 2848, *Dreizehnter Jahresbericht* (1871–72); Hummel, *Krankenpflege im Umbruch,* 74–77, for Stolp's critique.

46. GK, Abt. 69, no. 889, August 6, 1905, letter from the executive committee on the funeral of Sophie Roys, who long had been the chief matron of the Karlsruhe Motherhouse.

47. Membership statistics are unclear for the early years because of confusion between the categories of league sisters and lay nurses. I have given the statistics for the former. GK, Abt. 233, no. 2848, Verzeichniss der Vereinswärterinnen nach dem Stand vom 1 January 1873. In 1873, in the jurisdiction of the Fourteenth Army Corps, there were 310 to 320 nurses and fifty-two to sixty-two Sisters of Charity available for war service. In 1889, a handwritten number of 174 was inserted into the report. See GK, Abt. 69, no. 1132, Einladung der Abt. III des Badischen Frauenvereins zur Beihilfe für die Krankenpflege. For the later period, the statistics of organized sisters come from no. 890, Karlsruhe, August 10, 1910; no. 891, Pflegekraft des Badischen Frauenvereins, 1911; and no. 892, Oberinnen-Konferenz, March 20, 1914.

TABLE 5.   Average Annual Salary of Baden Red Cross Nurses and Other Female Occupations in Select Years, 1874–1910 (in marks)

Date	Red Cross Nurses[a]	Free Nurses[b]	Sales Personnel in Berlin	Berlin Elementary School Teachers[c]	Specialized Teachers in Baden[c]
1874	140–300				
1901		500–900	1,068–1,116	1,432	1,450–2,350
1909	240–480				
1910	300–520				

Source: Eva Cornelia Hummel, *Krankenpflege im Umbruch* (Freiburg, 1986), 75–76; Helene Lange and Gertrud Bäumer, eds., *Handbuch der Frauenbewegung. Die Deutsche Frau im Beruf,* vol. 4 (Berlin, 1902), 143, 257; *DRK,* 3: 12–13; GK, Abt. 233, no. 2848, *Fünfzehnter Jahresbericht des Vorstandes des badischen Frauenvereins,* January–December 1874 and Abt. 69, no. 892, Die Abteilung III des Frauenvereins betr., executive committee report, March 18, 1914.
[a]By 1910, a clothing allowance, pension, and vacation time were paid in addition to the salaries.
[b]Caring for orphans in the Leipzig Poor Law Administration.
[c]Includes housing supplement.

women's association. Only in 1912, for example, did the duchess agree to reform the statutes and permit the sisters to attend the theater in the evenings; circuses continued to be off-limits, as did the new leisure space of the movie theater.[48]

Despite the drawbacks, for women of the popular classes this area of organized lay nursing opened undeniable opportunities for professional growth. Critics noted little active complaint among the permanent rank and file; perhaps the absence of visible discontent reflected the stifling social hierarchy in the association and the average sister's economic vulnerability; besides, many saw their work as a "calling," a noble Christian sacrifice that was impervious to change. The benefits of community life— personal advancement through education, an intimacy among the sisters, and the sharing of life's celebrations and sufferings—sustained a new female vocation that maintained its foot in older religious traditions and culture as well as the capitalist educational and wage systems. And the dynastic state benefited precisely from this particular combination of social and gender factors—which it had helped to constitute.

The Baden Nurses' Aides League

The work of the Baden Nurses' Aides League reflected an equally compelling mix of traditional and modern notions about gender roles. The league was formed in response to a number of contradictory pressures that began to coalesce around the turn of the century. One was clearly prag-

---

48. GK, Abt. 69, no. 891, Oberinnen-Konferenz, March 14, 1912.

matic: a growing recognition in Red Cross circles of the need to alleviate the workload of the overburdened nurses. The Congress of German State Women's Associations, in 1899, heard a proposal for a several-week course in rudimentary aspects of nursing, which would be open to women and daughters of the "educated classes" in German society.

The plan was cast in the language of patriotism, drawing on notions of a female "voluntary year of service" swirling about in nationalist circles. In one sense, it was but a new form of an old conservative effort to define and channel women's roles in the nation-state along nationalist lines—without conceding formal citizenship. Undeniably, it reflected also acknowledgment that changes were affecting the lives of young people; as the speaker at the conference put it candidly, "Today's young women yearn for meaningful activities in public life." One acceptable option was to study medicine and work as a volunteer in "the arena of organized philanthropy."[49] Two distinct goals had been artfully crafted together: the principle of voluntarism, which was at the heart of the call for female aides, meant that only well-off women would apply for the training; in turn, these privileged women could couch the venture—which easily shaded into wage work—in a veneer of patriotic undertakings.

That the schema returned to "voluntarism" was part of the point. Other speeches by the conservative-military leadership—for example, in 1909 by General Limberger, who headed the Baden State Red Cross Association—recognized the many "changes . . . in the life of the people, particularly in the area of social welfare." In the slow, seemingly inexorable shift from voluntary to state welfare initiatives, he was facing the erosion of the fundamental principle at the root of patriotic philanthropy: its reliance on organized volunteerism as an expression of conservative subjectivity. Grousing in the *Kreuz-Zeitung* in the years prior to World War I testifies to a similar preoccupation with welfare transformations among wider Conservative circles as well. Willy-nilly, top leaders in the Red Cross were determined to reinvent the female volunteer for the future, whose work, however, now required a higher level of medical training.[50]

Courses for privileged women turned this potential avenue into a reality. For example, in 1901, Section III organized a series of lectures on "nursing in war and peace" at the Ludwig-Wilhelm Hospital for "ladies of the educated classes," and the lecture became a standard fare in the clinics

---

49. GK, Abt. 69, no. 1133, according to a retrospective analysis at the third yearly meeting of the league, Karlsruhe, May 17, 1911.

50. For Limberger's speech, GK, Abt. 69, no. 1133, Festversammlung, December 3, 1909. Conservatives were becoming increasingly hostile to the growing cost of social reform and municipal services. See *KZ*, no. 542, November 18, 1913 "Ausblicke in die Zukunft"; and Eley, *Reshaping the German Right,* 316.

and hospitals throughout the state; a similar undertaking, advertised in the press, was occurring simultaneously in Prussia (and the other states of Germany) as well. Indeed, Baroness Spitzemberg's diary shows that in the late 1880s she, too, began to attend first-aid courses in Berlin with her women friends.[51] By 1904 in Baden, the so-called lecture had become a six-week course of twenty-five hours (extended a few years later to thirty-two hours) in theory, plus a month internship at a hospital, leading to certification as a voluntary nurses' aide *(freiwillige Hilfskrankenpflegerin)*, placed at the disposal of the state Red Cross association.[52] With this step, by its own testimony, the Red Cross accepted the education of women as a compelling "question of the day." Its apparent embrace of the woman question, however, was fraught with difficulty, as the social prejudices of the gender order again intruded into patriotic calculations in a different way.

According to official statutes of the Nurses' Aides League, the members worked for no remuneration, although, in the same sentence, the organization sanctioned a salary of one to two marks daily, plus board and travel money. A closer look at league minutes and reports reveals a wide range of employment that many aides, indeed, undertook. As the favored option, the opportunities in private practice—in effect as glorified nannies and helpmates—were of most concern to the leaders, who feared such work would interfere with the league's commitment to staff municipal hospital and poor relief agencies. In the case of private employment, a dose of social snobbery admittedly was appealing on both sides. According to a league pamphlet,

> It is a question of "ladies" who, unlike the Red Cross sisters, do not make nursing a career for life but rather take the work temporarily. Aides are used in cases in which an ill employer wants a nurse fully the equal in education, distinguishable only by her uniform.[53]

In addition, the aides learned skills necessary for hospital administration such as bookkeeping, stenography, and typewriting, which they also took into the marketplace. But the basic ambivalence about wage work among privileged women leaders and members meant the league philosophy itself reproduced prejudices that negatively affected the wider culture of

51. *Tagebuch der Baronin Spitzemberg,* 232.

52. GK, Abt. 69, no. 889, September 6, 1901, "Vorträge." For the curriculum of nurses' aides, no. 1117, Mitteilungen, "Lehrgang" and a copy of the certificate from December 2, 1904. Also in the same collection, no. 1, January 27, 1906, "Ausbildung von Helferinnen vom Roten Kreuz." For the standard curriculum approved by the Central Committee in 1908, *DRK,* 2:341–42.

53. GK, Abt. 69, no. 1133, Bund, Vermittlungsstelle, n.d. (around 1910).

women's work. The serious option of private employment was dismissed as work simply for "pin money" *(Taschengeld)*—a justification too often used by employers for the differential wage scales paid to men and women.[54]

Table 6 presents the social background and religious affiliation of nurses' aides who studied in Baden between 1906 and 1913. The sample is of 228 women, roughly half of the four hundred or so aides the state Red Cross counted in 1913 who could be put on the list for war mobilization.[55] Significant, of course, is the essential absence of Jews, who comprised, however, only a small part of the Baden population. Their names almost can be counted on one hand alone. Coming exclusively from the business community, these Jewish families, arguably, were highly assimilated, embracing an ethic transcending religious and class divides through patriotic service.[56] In a population in which roughly 60 percent were Catholic,

TABLE 6.   Religious Affiliation and Social Background of Nurses' Aides Studying in Baden, 1906–13

Religious Affiliation		Social Origin[a]		Population in Karlsruhe 1905	Population in Baden 1905
Protestants	91	Aristocracy	1		
		Business	13	50,630	701,964
		Mastercraftsman	10		
Catholics	38	Government Officials	31	42,188	1,124,057
		Military	6		
Old Catholics[b]	2	Medical	4		8,356
		Education	7		
Jews	8	Independently Wealthy	10	2,576	26,123
		Engineer	4		
		Architect	3		
Total available	139		89	95,394	1,859,500

Source: GK, Abt. 69, no. 1117, Mitteilungen, Ausbildung von Helferinnen vom Roten Kreuz, 1906–10; nos. 1133–34, Der Helferinnenbund beim Roten Kreuz, Wiederholungskurs, 1911, Liste des Ausbildungskurses von Helferinnen, March 8, 1912, Ausbildungskurses, January 21, 1913, *Neumanns Orte-und Verkehrs-Lexikon des Deutschen Reichs* (Leipzig, 1905), 42–43.

[a]According to father's occupation, when available.

[b]Those who refused to accept the doctrine of papal infallibility.

<hr>

54. GK, Abt. 69, no. 1133, Protokoll über die Versammlung im Helferinnen-Bund, October 7, 1908.

55. GK, Rep. 456, F 113, no. 13, Ärztliche Untersuchung und Wiederimpfung des Personals der freiw. Krankenpflge durch Sanitätsoffiziere, Karlsruhe, June 14, 1913.

56. Christoph Sachsse makes a similar argument in the case of Alice Salomon, who came from an assimilated Jewish family and used her vision of social reform and motherhood to transcend class divisions. See Seth Koven and Sonya Michel, eds., *Mothers of a New World: Maternalist Politics and the Origins of the Welfare States* (New York, 1993), 14.

the aides attracted proportionately greater numbers of Protestants. Yet this area of voluntary service was a space for Christian intermingling, as was true of the other patriotic philanthropic institutes in the state. Government officials made up the largest category of member households; those from professional occupations as well as business and artisanal groups split nearly evenly. By contrast there were few young women from aristocratic and military backgrounds studying as aides; the ambitious among them seemed to have preferred the more rigorous nursing training course with an eye to high administration later on. Whether or not they came from the "very best social groups," as a report from Freiburg asserted, these young trainees, undeniably, were "modern" women—relatively well off, leisured, and searching for a meaningful set of shared activities.

League membership reconciled seemingly contradictory motives. The financially privileged backgrounds of the aides as compared to the nurses elevated patriotism as a motive for study. The women who joined the Baden Nurses' Aides League entered a fiercely patriotic milieu of war preparation and its active celebration. The league president, Julia Limberger, and her husband, the state Red Cross head, were staunch patriots, whose primary identity lay with the dynastic court. Participation affirmed a sense of family in the embrace of the dynastic family, but it reflected as well more modern notions about women's capabilities and needs. In addition, it offered plenty of opportunity for excitement on the streets, enacting relief dramas to the awe of the crowds, or in writing, directing, and performing scripts in-house.

In the final analysis, it was the security of family and the ability to define as patriotic the ascribed female attributes at the heart of the vocation—self-sacrifice, duty, and care—that molded a new subjectivity. It worked to contain—however imperfectly—the modern pressures toward change in ways that, ultimately, were politically conservative and supportive of the gender hierarchy. At the same time, the presence of these trained "volunteers" in hospitals and clinics affirmed the scientific advances of the modern, technological nation-state. Their credentials inserted new medical knowledge into older forms of charity and largesse. The combination of modern medical practice rooted in a conservative culture of largesse must have been compelling indeed to these well-off young women.

For the members, the league functioned as a large, familiar, and supportive family.[57] Business meetings routinely were preceded by reports of important family events in the lives of the associates, as, for example,

---

57. GK, Abt. 69, no. 1133, Festversammlung der Helferinnen vom Rothen Kreuz, November 5, 1908, and December 3, 1909. My argument is drawn from these details of the league's festivities.

acknowledging the birth of a healthy daughter to "our loving league sister," Irmgard Stoelzel, and the gift sent to Fräulein Simon for her pending marriage; a card was passed around for all to sign. If the royal patron did not attend the meeting, an exchange of greetings took place by telegram, often composed in rhyme by a league would-be poet. Annually, the members laid a wreath at the grave of the deceased Baden duke Frederick. Commemorating the life cycle events of birth, death, marriage, and motherhood offered these self-styled patriots a link to the royal Baden house. The league's annual festival typically coincided with the birthday of Luise, although it also celebrated the birth of her daughter Hilda, the reigning duchess at the time of the league's founding.

The festive time was an opportunity to tie league members to the dynastic house through their common identity as women. Speeches regularly reminded the celebrants that the so-called natural female characteristics of sacrifice, care, love of neighbor, and a deep abiding loyalty linked the two "circles" together—the members saw themselves as a mirror image of the ideal royal figure, the beloved *Landesmutter*. Expressed another way, the dynast herself became a projection of these assumed female characteristics, which expressed the values of the privileged social milieu out of which they came. This powerful psychological mechanism underscores a basic characteristic of political symbols: their essential malleability and ambiguity. In this context, the esteemed *Landesmutter*, as a widely shared symbol, perfectly mirrored back the values of the group doing the imagining. And it hints at the mechanisms arousing deep emotions by something as abstract as national identity: the intimacies and ties of distinct local worlds were connected to the larger spatial frame through cultural and aesthetic forms.[58]

These forms were nurtured in the festive lives of league members. Their annual celebrations unleashed cultural energies that had been formed partly by these young women's early exposure to art, literature, and music appreciation; dabbling in "high culture" was part of what made a society woman in Germany.[59] But in the context of the league, these sensibilities were transformed into patriotic creations. The young women

---

58. Agnew, "Representing Space," 263–64, looks at how place, as an object of identity for an individual, can be projected onto a region or a nation.

59. For norms on manners and breeding that, arguably, influenced the lives of society daughters, Günter Häntzschel, ed., *Bildung und Kultur bürgerlicher Frauen, 1850–1918. Eine Quellendokumentation aus Anstandsbüchern und Lebenshilfen für Mädchen und Frauen als Beitrag zur weiblichen literarischen Sozialisation* (Tübingen, 1986), particularly the works of Henriette Davidis (1897), 51–52; Elise Polko (1871), 169–206; Ch. Oeser (1876), 461–67, for the place of poetry in the forms of advice. Also, Marie Martin, *Aus der Welt der deutschen Frauen* (Berlin 1906); and Albrecht Goerth, *Erziehung und Ausbildung der Mädchen. Ein Wegweiser für gebildete Eltern, für Lehrer and Erzieher*, 2 parts (Leipzig, 1894).

wrote in verse, gave recitals, sang songs, and created and produced plays; participation was personally satisfying and admired by the group. Simultaneously, in a process that linked their world to a much wider territorial community, they drew on cultural forms that reproduced a common national heritage.

Their annual festival on December 3, 1909, is a good case in point.[60] It was held in a decorated room in the museum in Karlsruhe, and the content alternated between expressions of German high culture, a specific Baden identity, and individual creations: members heard Beethoven's *Egmont* Overture and Schubert's military march and listened to several of their own group give piano recitals. These musical events were interspersed by a crafted prologue spoken by Gertrud Berg, cheers to the duchess Luise, and songs of tribute sung together. The evening culminated in the performance of a one-act play entitled "Scenes from the Professional Life of Nurses' Aides," composed in rhyme by Countess Hermine zu Leiningen, a member who came from Baden's old mediatized *(Standesherren)* families, by now loyally conservative. Earlier accounts indicate that she had been working for a time in Berlin-Pankow at a children's hospital. A copy of the script was sent to the duchess as a tribute and gift to solidify anew the bonds that tied the dynasty and the league together.

The play is a classic example of "art" imitating "life," a stylized enactment of the conflicts surrounding the new work world of nurses' aides as the members, arguably, experienced them. The plot can be stated simply. It is set in a hospital at a time of a typhus epidemic; the regular sisters are overworked, and the doctors are forced to rely on the aides, who overcome all doubt and suspicion by their hard work and professional competence.

The psychological mechanisms at work for actors and audience, however, make this drama important in sustaining the group; more was at work than entertainment, however much fun it was to write or act or sit in the audience. The performance allowed the members to confront in art the real-life prejudices that existed against these well-off and privileged women: as one character admits, although fondly, aides are "neither fish nor fowl" but "eccentric" *(wunderlich Gemisch),* between sisters and ladies. In this performance, the group acts out and experiences on "stage" its own anger and frustrations in working with doctors and sisters, who were superior to aides in the medical hierarchy; and it tests its own identity and commitments.

---

60. GK, Abt. 69, no. 1133, Festversammlung, December 3, 1909.

Not even the gender hierarchy is exempt from critique, as one aide says to her colleague who is planning to marry: "remember that as a bride you lose your rights." Ultimately, the aides reconfirm the gender expectations of the dynastic order: they experience solidarity in the memory of Luise (it was, after all, her birthday both in the play and on the day of the performance) and in common celebration of the importance of duty to the state. As sisters of the league, protected by the duchess, they prove willing to build a solid foundation "stone by stone" (in their own words) out of each individual contribution; and they link this effort to a wider national identity. Their own league will become known "throughout the whole of Germany, from the west to the east" for this important work of building national health and strength.

In its specific imagery and choice of words, this play drew on and reproduced a set of signs that were becoming part of the public domain of patriotic construction. The effect extended far beyond the Karlsruhe league. Figure 3 is a Red Cross poster from 1917 entitled "War Mosaic," in which the artist offers the exact duplication of the image of a slow, methodical, and solidly constructed stone-by-stone patriotic effort at home—in this case to care for soldiers' families under the deteriorating conditions of wartime. The artistic design draws the eye immediately to the white hands in the center, a mother's (identified by the wedding ring) and child's, in prayer and folded in thanks. But it is the stone-by-stone effort of the Red Cross that sustains hope, as do the accumulated contributions added to the edifice by the public. The poster is, after all, an appeal for money. Red Cross patriotic wartime images remained rooted in the older tropes and concepts that once had served the dynasty well.

Performance was not exclusively in-house nor a matter of dividing the members temporarily into actors and audience. As a branch of the Red Cross, league associates participated in the dramatic public enactments of projected civilian wartime services, which were crucial ingredients of Red Cross methods of popular persuasion. With the other men and women volunteers, they were drawn regularly into the streets to demonstrate the technological know-how of the medical volunteers ready at all times for national defense. They dramatized imaginary rescue missions in front of high-level dignitaries and generals from around the country who were invited guests; or they collaborated in demonstrating just how efficiently civilians could arrange food for an army contingent, which had appeared unexpectedly. On the fortieth anniversary of the founding of the Karlsruhe Men's Relief Association in May 1910, to cite another example, twelve of the nurses' aides participated in what was billed as a "large exercise and performance" *(Vorführung)* of the work of wartime medicine.

Fig. 3. Red Cross Section for Mother and Infant Care, calling on the public to join the stone-by-stone war effort, 1917. (Courtesy Hoover Institution Archives, Poster Collection, GE 201.)

Explicitly under doctors' orders, their dramatic assignment was to provide first aid to seventy infantrymen, who arrived on a hospital train, and also to "refresh" and "revive" their charges.[61] These performances must have been quite exciting for the women "actors" who, in their other lives as society wives or daughters, had difficulty even walking some streets!

This public appearance was not always playacting, of course. Along with Red Cross sisters, league aides were deployed in Müllheim to help out at the time of the disastrous train wreck in July 1911. Busy at the site of the collision itself, they also provided "aid and consolation" to the injured in the hospital.[62] The accident, which left thirteen dead and many more seriously hurt, was met by swift medical intervention and by the personal involvement of Duchess Luise. Her gifts of solicitude to the grieving families and the subsequent correspondence with these common people reaffirmed, as they expressed it, her "all too human compassion." In popular conceptions, the *Landesmutter* seemed once again to emerge as the "kindhearted helper of the unfortunate."[63] Aided by her female patriotic troops, she had stood at the helm of a concerted medical effort designed to reassure the general populace.

Medicine, Hygiene, and National Strength: Peoples' Sanatoria

In its original conception, the philanthropic infrastructure was poised for medical emergencies. Remember, epidemics, like floods, were defined as natural disasters in the original charters of the state Patriotic Women's Associations in the mid-1860s. A sudden outbreak of contagious disease would intertwine state and private relief measures for common purposes. In time, the Red Cross sisters, with their medical certification, were deployed to urban and rural areas as part of a growing state commitment to public health measures. The sisters met immediate needs as, for example, during a typhus epidemic that broke out in the village of Bauschlott, near Karlsruhe, in 1888; and they also staffed the permanent "nurses' sta-

---

61. GK, Abt. 69, no. 1117, Übung der freiwilligen Krankenpflege in Mannheim, 30 Juni 1907, and no. 1133, Der Helferinnenbund, *Jahresbericht* (1911). Also, reports in *KZ*, supplement to no. 199, June 15, 1888, exercise before a representative of the Ministry of War and the Central Committee of the Red Cross, and no. 53, February 2, 1892, report on the International Exhibition of the Red Cross in Leipzig, where a "mock" feeding of the army was arranged by the Ministry of Interior.

62. GK, Abt. 69, no. 1133, *Jahresbericht,* 1910–11. For the accident, no. 1134, Bericht der Monatsversammlung von 14 Februar 1912.

63. GK, Abt. 69, no. 579, Das Eisenbahnunglück bei Müllheim am 17 Juli 1911, letter Friedrich and Anna Bohnet (whose daughter died), April 14, 1911 and Amelie Stehlin from Neuenburg (Prussia), Konstanz, August 2, 1911.

tions" that proliferated throughout the states, helping spread new medical knowledge and hygienic standards among the common people.[64]

By the early twentieth century, new nationalist fears and concerns began to intrude into the medical training of nurses' aides in Baden. The curricula in 1906 included studying subjects necessary for war work: anatomy, circulation, breathing, nutrition, dressing wounds, and dealing with internal injuries. But their training also included detection and prevention of dangerous contagious diseases like tuberculosis, seen to undermine the strength and vitality of the nation. Expanding the scope of responsibilities into the arena of disease prevention and social hygiene was part of new assumptions driving welfare measures.[65]

The prescribed path of study for the Baden nurses' aides—a small auxiliary medical contingent in the larger Red Cross organizational hierarchy—nonetheless reveals a profound shift in the conception of war preparation: its growing intersection with the nationalist discourses around public health and hygiene. Starting in the mid-1890s, several independent lines of development had coalesced to redirect Red Cross praxis toward social engineering, in a new medical departure that blended hygienic and nutritional considerations. The treatment stressed "fresh air" and "square meals," with attention to personal hygiene in the controlled environment of a sanatorium.[66] In this context, state and society interacted to drive social change—this time along the lines of expanded medical management.

On the one hand, there was the army's continued interest in the fitness of its recruits and the growing preoccupation of state and imperial officials with public health—in part for the same reason. "From above," so to speak, these high government and military officials sponsored laboratory and scientific medical research and orchestrated national campaigns for

---

64. GK, Abt. 69, no. 1142, Die Einrichtung eine Pflegerinnen-Station in Badenweilen betr., 1888; no. 1144, Die Absendung von Pflegerinnen nach Bauschlott betr., 1888; no. 1131, Landkrankenpflege. According to a newspaper report in 1909, seventy-seven stations employed Red Cross nurses, and 188 women's association branches were overseeing the work of 374 nurses in the state of Baden. GK, Abt. 69, no. 951b, das 50-jährige Jubiläum des Badischen Frauenvereins am 16. und 17. Juni 1909, clipping of *Deutscher Reichsanzeiger,* Berlin, June 19, 1909.

65. GK, Abt. 69, no. 1117, "Ausbildung von Helferinnen vom Roten Kreuz," January 1906.

66. LK, Abt. 403, no. 8357, Volksheilstätten für Genesende und Kranke, 1897–98, which places Red Cross efforts in a wider context of the grassroots sanatoria movement. For example, Bl. 85–86, *Hygienische Rundschau,* November 1, 1897, survey of the origins of sanatoria; Bl. 487, clipping "Plannmässige Schwindsuchts-Bekämpfung in Deutschland." Also, Weindling, *Health, Race,* 177, notes that by 1910 Germany had more public sanatoria than any other country.

inoculation and disease prevention. On the other, in civil society itself, the advances in medical science were being picked up by a public drawn into the medical discourses around national health, strength, and well-being. Fueling the debates was a widespread grassroots movement of medical practitioners, independent pressure groups, and all manner of organizations, ad hoc committees, publications, and associations.

Even the older patriotic philanthropic organizations expanded their purview to embrace tasks now elevated to the national limelight. After 1905, for example, the Baden Women's Association added two new sections to its charge. The one, Section V, which later joined a statewide committee in 1911, coordinated the fight against tuberculosis; the other, Section VI, addressed the "national" implications of the demographics of infant mortality. In part, the new tasks represented a response to the empress, who was seeking to direct national attention to the decline in birth rates, channeling the state's continued interest in reproduction into new nationalist and power arguments. One historian of science, although not fully attuned to the intersection of dynastic power and philanthropic purpose, acknowledged nonetheless the "crucial" involvement of the empress "in giving the infant health movement social prestige and moral ardour."[67] Dynastic patronage flexibly matched changing notions about proper state welfare and medical provisions.

These shifts, too, were mirrored in the expansion of Red Cross fields of action to include the Sanatorium Association (Volksheilstätte-Verein), placed under the authority of the Central Committee (table 4). In the daily running of its thirteen sanatoria, the Red Cross relied on its nurses, aides, and the volunteers in the women's associations. But it also had support from the directors of the old age and disability insurance funds in urban centers, among them even socialists and progressives. This was true for the oldest Red Cross sanatorium, at the Grabowsee, near Berlin; the adult patients were mostly Berlin working men whose cure had been authorized by the insurance boards. Simultaneously, the Red Cross managed several institutes of special interest to the army.[68] For specific purposes, this cam-

67. Weindling, *Health, Race,* 194. For examples of a nationalist campaign to bring medical knowledge to the average person, LK, Abt. 403, no. 8366, Volksheilstätten für Lungenkranke, 1908–10, Bl. 91–92, describes a mobile tuberculosis museum sent around to the countryside. Attendance by the general public as well as schoolchildren was a way for the state to bring hygienic measures indirectly into the private domestic setting, particularly in rural areas, which were less impacted by state and private welfare interventions.

68. The army was interested in the work of the German Association for People's Hygiene. GK, Rep. 456, F 113, no. 17, Ministry of War, Berlin, January 21, 1907. For ties between socialists and Red Cross medical administrators, Weindling, *Health, Race,* 165, 175–80; an overview of the Red Cross sanatoria movement, with attention to the insurance funds, is in *DRK,* 2:305–6, 704–24.

paign of national health could transcend the divides of right and left in the volatile political life of the late *Kaiserreich.*

Those on the right had a ready-made argument for the health measures deemed to have such a grave "social and national necessity." Redeploying the metaphors of war, science, and humanitarianism, they placed the philanthropic imperative into a new nationalist formula. The initial Red Cross public appeal to support the sanatoria movement was cast in military idiom; tuberculosis was the "angel of death" insidiously destroying the vitality of the people. The patriotic response was stated boldly: to do battle with the "enemy" and "defend [German] territory."

In this campaign, the public was mobilized to combat an enemy, the silent killer of disease and, by implication if need be, the more flagrant threat of the enemy rifle. Support was couched in the language of humanitarianism made all the more compelling because it was said to promote the scientific advances that were deemed a German inheritance. Drawing on the older vocabulary of patriotic philanthropy, too, made the departure seem less radical. But it was. It opened up medical surveillance on a larger scale and imposed new hygienic standards in the domestic lives of the patients and their families. Furthermore, it added so-called medical criteria to the calculations of job referral agencies, which emerged as part of the social provisions available to "cured" patients. Agencies were told, for example, to screen the male applicants for apprenticeships or other jobs according to their state of health, dividing work in the economy into "light" and "heavy" categories. Similar calculations simultaneously were restricting women's job opportunities in the "heavy" work deemed inappropriate for future mothers.[69]

The new medical assumptions increasingly were insinuated into philanthropy as well. In the process, they were helping change the very basis of nation-state legitimacy in dynastic Germany that had been linked to notions—however contested—of the common good, Christian neighborliness, and community responsibilities. Now, these older understandings partly were being medicalized in a new scientific definition of health for the sake of national power. Thus, what I have called the "caring" state, rooted in the traditions of Christian and civic voluntarism, also was becoming the "curing" state, involving medical and hygienic interventions in a context of heightened nationalist concerns over power and strength. The pressures for change were constituted in mutual interaction between state, municipal institutions, and private associations.

---

69. *DRK,* 2:704. The Red Cross was concerned with the future employment of its patients but, here, medical calculations entered employment advice in a new pattern of social intervention.

A dramatic illustration of the shift that was redefining nation-state legitimacy is contained in a set of archival documents on a children's clinic in Heidelberg, the Luisenheilanstalt, which had been founded in 1860. The clinic was a typical private medical institution with links to the dynastic court. Over the years, its members had raised money to supplement the dues and donations by periodically sponsoring a bazaar. Its secretary, then, sought permission from municipal authorities to hold the fund-raising event, contacted Duchess Luise to serve as official patron, and publicized an appeal in the press. In obtaining official patronage, considerable correspondence moved back and forth between Heidelberg and the court at Karlsruhe. The old mechanism of raising money by hosting bazaars was perpetuated in the *Kaiserreich,* giving an appearance of structural continuity. Beneath the surface, however, the basis of the appeal—the very self-definition of the clinic's place in social and national life—was being transformed inexorably.

Compare, for example, the arguments that were publicized in 1897 and 1904 and, then, developed in a letter in 1908. The 1897 announcement of the pending bazaar—after a seven-year hiatus—still is cast in the traditional language of charity as a affirmation of Christian living. The secular institution itself is described as a "family" that substitutes for the mother and father who are too poor themselves to finance the necessary treatment. But the attention is on the private donors, its main financial backers, and the importance of their gifts. It likens their Christian deeds to the duchess, the "shining example of active charity for the poor" and symbol of the wider state involvement in the day-to-day needs of the unfortunate. The duchess's patronage, including her generous donations for the benefit sale, the gifts from other aristocratic and well-off patrons, and the support of the wider public comprise the basis of an extended community united in its obligations to help vulnerable and poor children.[70]

The close alliance between the clinic and dynastic state was maintained even as the original contract was being reformulated. The year 1904 offers an interesting transition moment partly for the language, which becomes more calculated and specifically medical. The appeal still is to the "well-off classes" *(die bemittelten Klassen)* for their charitable acts, which are acknowledged as a rich source of revenue; indeed, the institute is surviving because of the yearly donations, although, given rising demand, it can no longer meet expenses. In the clinic's advertisement, the public will support its venture because it recognizes that the "handling and nursing of

---

70. GK, Abt. 69, no. 1094, Die Luisenheilanstalt in Heidelberg betr., 1897–1914, November 17, 1897, Allerhöchste Besuch des Bazars zu Günsten der Luisenheilanstalt in Heidelberg. It contains the correspondence of Professor Dr. O. Vierordt and various mayors and also the flyer announcing the upcoming event.

sick children and the spread of sensible *(vernünftig)* principles for the care of the healthy are . . . [at the basis of] the well-being of all the social groups *(Stände)"* in society. Community well-being is defined by the level of public health that is subject to continued improvement through preventive measures and medical treatment. Although absent from direct reference, the duchess's ongoing patronage expressed state acknowledgment of the new understanding of the general good.

A 1908 letter from the director, Dr. Esser, to the duchess at the time of still another bazaar links the medical argument more explicitly to dynastic authority and national power. Speaking for the wider administration, he thanks her for her "gifts" and for the timely intervention with the Ministry of Culture, which has meant additional public monies for the clinic. Indeed, in return, the clinic hopes by "following the same spirit of its noble protector to be able to continue the great and beautiful work for the well-being of suffering children and for a healthy and strong nation in the future."[71] Together, the dynasty and the clinic were allies in the medical efforts to safeguard a strong German population. This alliance pointed to the intersection of health and nationalism. It expressed a grassroots understanding of the nationalist mission in medical terms that continued to be mediated by the personal involvement of the *Landesmutter*.

The volatile atmosphere of nationalist commitments, however, opened these institutes to the more dangerous discourses of racial hygiene and eugenics that also were part of the larger medical debates. In his detailed study of racial politics in Germany, the historian Paul Weindling notes that "racial and hereditarian ideas could easily be injected into the nationalist ideology of welfare organizations." Indeed, he argues that racial hygiene gained its first public exposure in the welfare organizations that were primed for the nationalist goals of preventing crippling diseases and infant mortality.[72]

The Red Cross infrastructure—with its ties to the military-dynastic leadership and its feet in the new movement of people's sanatoria and expanded public health provisions—both mirrored and reinforced these bonds between nationalism and medical science, so clearly expressed in Professor Esser's letter to the duchess. The ties linking war and science were equally close. In Red Cross experience, raising money to train nurses and medical orderlies for war work depended on convincing the public that the state had the most sophisticated medical, technological, and

---

71. GK, Abt. 69, no. 1094, *Dreiundvierzigster Jahresbericht über die Luisen-Heilanstalt für kranke Kinder in Heidelberg,* Heidelberg, 1904, and also letter of Dr. Vierordt, October 17, 1904; letter of Professor Esser, director, February 29, 1908.

72. Weindling, *Health, Race,* 168, 185.

hygienic advances at its disposal to wage a modern war. Increasingly, these calculations drove the commitments to "perform" and "display" the civilian war tasks out in the public limelight. And they encouraged new approaches to raise money for patriotic purposes: by the early twentieth century, Red Cross solicitation boxes, earmarking the proceeds for the work of the sanatoria, were placed at transport nodes and in hotels, cafes, and restaurants throughout the country.

The sanatoria movement led to direct Red Cross collaboration with the army as well. The buildings for the Red Cross Sanatorium at Grabowsee were constructed out of war barracks donated to the Central Committee, and, in 1906, on request of the chief medical officer of the army, the Red Cross established Section X, a Seaside Home for Wives and Children of Noncommissioned Officers located near Swinemünde. The home reflected the army's interest in the curative approach of social hygienic interventions, including diet; but since, apparently, the military had limited funds to promote the health of the families of low-level officers, this "private" philanthropic institute would do the important patriotic work.

As expressed in the correspondence between Red Cross officials and army medical doctors, the sanatorium would boost army morale and strengthen the "commitment to service" *(Dienstfreudigkeit)* as well as the work "performance" *(Leistungsfähigkeit)* of the noncommissioned personnel.[73] Information on the founding and purpose of the home spread through the battalion commanders and down the Red Cross publicity chain as well. The first annual report took the readers into a world of precise statistical measurements: symptoms, length, course, and outcome of treatment were demonstrated on charts and tables. The original group of thirty female patients were disembodied medical statistics. They became, in short, a database for the emerging debate over whether social or hereditary factors caused disease.[74]

Red Cross medical work was important in army calculations again in 1913. Passage of the military budget that year—in Gerhard Ritter's words, it was the "greatest army bill Germany had ever seen"—evoked concern in the Ministry of War that the increase in recruits was not matched by a concomitant rise in the numbers of civilian medical volunteers. In particular, the ministry wanted to expand the total number of medical corps and

---

73. *DRK,* 2:721; details and justification of the institute are in GK, Rep. 456, F 113, no. 17, correspondence between the Volksheilstättenverein Abt. X (Seeheim) and the Generalarzt, Berlin November 27, 1907, and with the military doctor of the Fourteenth Army Corps, including a copy of the original "Aufruf."

74. GK, Rep. 456, F 113, no. 17, *Seeheim für Unteroffizierfrauen und Kinder in Osternothafen bei Sweinemünde. Erster Bericht* (Berlin, 1906).

cooperatives and called on retired officers to support the training of these volunteers; and it also directed local Red Cross branch associations to target appropriate persons for war service. It singled out for particular attention the Seaside Home, which in peacetime, by the ministry's own admission, had "provided the military with so many benefits." The men and women on its medical staff now should be placed under direct mobilization orders.[75] In seeking to handle its short-term needs, the army extended its reach further into sectors that were medical and philanthropic. Once again, the health of the army blended with the health of the people and vice versa.

The gendered civilian war preparedness infrastructure was not alone in keeping the issues of war alive in the public limelight, although it was the largest civilian group to come under direct mobilization orders. In its daily operations, performances, and accounts of relief, it helped spread militaristic values deep in society and intertwined the worlds of empire and health in nationalist messages of battles, enemies, and victories. As the next chapter shows, patriotic women and the figure of the *Landesmutter* also forged important links to past wars through distinct cultural performances. They mobilized a social memory of individual and community sacrifice that was duplicated annually in commemorative festivities with the veterans of Germany's wars.

---

75. GK, Rep. 456, F 113, no. 13, circular from the Prussian war minister Erich von Falkenhayn, Berlin, April 27, 1914. On the army bill, Gerhard Ritter, *The Sword and the Scepter: The Problem of Militarism in Germany,* vol. 2, *The European Powers and the Wilhelmine Empire,* trans. Heinz Norden (Coral Gabels, Fla., 1969–72), 225; and Stig Förster, *Der doppelte Militarismus. Die deutsche Heeresrüstungspolitik zwischen Status-quo Sicherung und Aggression, 1890–1913* (Stuttgart, 1985), 247–95.

CHAPTER 6

Mobilizing Social Memory: Gendered Images of War and Sacrifice

A large international art and garden show opened in Düsseldorf in September 1904 to considerable fanfare. After all, the duchess of Baden, Luise, was the honored guest, a point of extensive attention in the newspaper and official accounts of the inaugural events.[1] The appearance of the royal figure prompted the magistrates to arrange the requisite ceremonies of homage that, in turn, worked to the credit of the same officials tied at that moment into the dynastic state system of honors and rewards. The crowds of common folk lined up to greet the duchess were large and enthusiastic, according to officials, but even more impressive were the young schoolgirls on display in front of the Palace of Art—by one account over three thousand in total. The duchess proceeded to wade through these layers of cheering participants, speaking to the one and then the other, a "triumphal march" *(Triumphzug)* as one local newspaper put it in an effort, perhaps, to place a mantle of consensus on the events in the streets.[2]

The welcoming speech was given by Professor Roeber, president of the exhibition's planning committee. Perhaps somewhat surprisingly, given the nature of the exhibit, it centered on a distinct memory of the wars of German unification. The trigger for such recall is easy to pinpoint: the

---

1. GK, Abt. 69, no. 227, Besuch der Grossherzogin in Koblenz und Düsseldorf vom 18–20 September 1904. The collection contains clippings of the *Düsseldorfer Zeitung,* September 20, 1904, and of the *Städtische Nachrichten;* the *Offizielle Ausstellungs-Zeitung für die Internationale Kunst-Ausstellung und grosse Gartenbau-Ausstellung,* Düsseldorf, 1904, and a clipping of the *Anstädter Tageblatt,* October 13, 1904.
2. Kaschuba, "Von der Rotte zum Block," 87–89, for a discussion of the procession *(Zug)* used by the Left to mobilize sympathy and pressure opponents. For a compelling recollection as a child of waiting for the arrival of the royalty, Bäumer, *Lebensweg durch eine Zeitwende,* 73.

genealogical connections of the Hohenzollern dynasty. The presence at the ceremony of the daughter of William I—the duchess Luise—prompted Roeber's memories about war. It was the present context—a speech before colleagues and friends with an eye to its publication—that emboldened his patriotic sensibility. His political inheritance seemed to prove the glory of past events. "Now that the light of the sun's rays of peace is shining, the second generation can burst forth with rich harvests, . . . the seeds of which were given by the life and work of the father."[3] Besides, Roeber could remind everyone in the audience of the close and special ties that Empress Augusta had established with the people of the Rhineland and West-phalia.

Professor Roeber's memory of war, however, went beyond the stan-dard litany of phrases in patriotic invocations of the founding of the *Reich,* although they were, of course, part of his presentation. He, too, drew on familiar, if rearranged, tropes, describing, for example, the unification era as a "phenomenal" *(gewaltig)* and "iron" *(eisern)* age. But his memory attached itself to the person of the *Landesmutter* Luise, whom he specifically praised as a "loyal and steadfast companion and advisor in times of difficulty." He conjured up the work she had performed in war, the ministerings by her own hands that had "bound the wounds and helped them heal and mend." These expressions of sacrifice were all the more necessary since war in his view was "inexorable" *(unerbittlich).* Indeed, the memory of past service had direct consequences for the future, in which the same pattern of care would be awakened again to meet war's inevitable sacrifices. These words seemed to lend authority to his charac-terizations of time, in which the past was a projection for the present of a particular vision of the future.[4]

These temporal connections were enacted in a stylized exchange that accompanied the opening speech. In carefully choreographed dialogue, a young daughter of the mayor recited a poem to the "noble princess of the Hohenzollern dynasty" whose very name awakened "sacred memory"; for her part, Luise stressed the significance of a deepening understanding of the events surrounding the founding of the *Reich,* as she saw it, preserved today as a "precious achievement" by her husband and William II; its future, too, was safeguarded by the strength of the dynastic line. Further-more, lest anyone question the relationship between gardens and war, the exhibit itself drew gardeners from all over Germany as proof of the "bless-ings and precious fruit" of the idea of nation *(Reichsgedanke),* which had

---

3. GK, Abt. 69, no. 227, *Düsseldorfer Zeitung,* September 20, 1904.

4. I found useful Diane Owen Hughes and Thomas R. Trautmann, eds., *Time: Histo-ries and Ethnologies* (Ann Arbor, Mich., 1995), for understanding multiple expressions of time in culture and the coexistence of distinct collective memories.

been realized in war. The duchess left unmentioned another possible correlation: the cultivation of flowers for the many ceremonies around military graveyards, which indisputably had become quite a business in the
Reich of her day.[5]

The subsequent letters of Professor Roeber reveal his reasoning for
setting the speech in the context of war. Claiming to speak for the general
populace, he wrote the duchess that "your visit has rekindled the memory
(*Andenken*) of the glorious days of German history"—the code expression
for the Wars of Unification.[6] Indisputably, it had for him and his own personal recollections found a receptive airing. It is unclear whether Roeber
had actually fought in the war or whether his memory reflected a "historical" consciousness.

Dynastic display, however, provided ample opportunities for a collective exchange of memories that were based on personal experiences.
Several years later, in 1910, the centenary of the death of Queen Luise of
Prussia was celebrated in the public reading room of the Educational Institute in Heidelberg, among many other sites in Germany. Although unin-
tended, two letters by the city librarian, Georg Zink, to the Baden duchess
Luise show how the *Landesmutter* image itself structured social memory in
the context of a group.[7]

Luise had loaned the exhibit a number of historic artifacts that had
been on display, and Zink was seeing to their return. He was proud of the
success of the exhibit, itself designed to strengthen a historical memory
and reinforce a common "German" identity in this Baden urban setting.
Indeed, its purpose reaffirmed the powerful connection between dynastic
rule and community largesse that was so much a part of political legitimacy: postcards of many of the items in the show were being sold and the
proceeds earmarked for the city's poor. (They sold out completely, neces-
sitating a rerun.)

The *Königin-Luise-Gedank* exhibition had been well attended, primarily by women and girls from all walks of life, according to Zink's
account. An exhibit on Pompeii running simultaneously drew twenty-two

---

5. GK, Abt. 69, no. 227, *Düsseldorfer Zeitung,* September 20, 1904. Nationalist struggles in the late nineteenth century began a process of commercializing commemorative memory. For example, *KZ,* no. 482, November 26, 1888, and no. 540, November 17, 1892, reports
on the flowers that were sold for the "commemoration of the dead," while red flowers were
available for the socialist festivals honoring the memory of the March victims of 1848. See
also *KZ,* no. 132, March 18, 1893. For a later period, Karin Hausen, "Mothers, Sons, and the
Sale of Symbols and Goods: The 'German Mother's Day,' 1923–1933," in Medick and
Sabean, *Interest and Emotion,* 371–413.

6. GK, Abt. 69, no. 227, Düsseldorf, October 2, 1904.

7. GK, Abt. 69, no. 175, Teilnahmebezeugungen zum 100-jährigen Todestag der Königin Luise von Preussen 1910, Heidelberg August 12, 1910, and August 18, 1910.

hundred visitors; Queen Luise had attracted twenty-four hundred! But it is his description of the interactions at a lecture—away from the glare of the public limelight—given to around 170 persons that is of particular interest.

The theme purported to turn on several episodes from the life of Queen Luise. There was a veteran in the audience who had had his leg blown off by a bullet fragment in the Franco-German war. (This is one of the few instances of specific mention of the mutilated veteran's body, typically hidden in the patriotic musings about war.) The veteran recounted that as he lay recovering in a hospital barrack in Mannheim, he was attended to by Duchess Luise herself, who subsequently sent him her portrait. Thus, in this forum, the veteran chose to speak not of his own pain and suffering but of the charitable undertakings of the duchess. His words prompted Frau Stratz, Zink's volunteer collaborator in the planning of local exhibits, to reminisce about her own work as a volunteer in those same military barracks in 1870–71, "and she told me lots about the exemplary . . . ministerings of [the duchess] in those great days *(in jener grossen Zeit)*," encoding the complexity and tragedy of war in the simple and sterile trope. Zink added that Frau Stratz was the first of many women who wanted to offer a new gloss on the exhibition of Queen Luise. Her shibboleth would memorialize "the great Luise of 1870" *(die grosse Luise von 1870)* in the person of the great Luise living in Mainau, her castle retreat on Lake Constance.[8]

The *Landesmutter* and Memory

These two examples, based partly on private correspondence, reveal a number of important elements in the complex workings of memory, at once essential to individual and collective identity. Without memory, the individual has no cohesive identity; but more to the point for this study, the creation of a wider (nation-)state identity was being shaped by sets of memories that increasingly were shared, differences not withstanding.[9] This apparently self-evident statement, however, masks another layer of complexity, for memory, like time, is "irregular" and varied; social mem-

8. GK, Abt. 69, no. 175, August 18, 1910. The reference was to Mainau in 1890, the meaning of which I have not fully understood, demonstrating the importance—and the difficulty at times—of placing group memory in its own traditions and specific references. For these difficulties, Hughes and Trautmann, *Time*, 9.

9. I am drawing here on Bernard S. Cohn, who works on India, a country in which there are multiple pasts, rendering the effort to construct a national identity on a common past counterproductive and divisive. He defines "modernity" partly by the extent to which there is one past that is accepted by a vast majority of society ("The Pasts of an Indian Village," in Hughes and Trautmann, *Time*, 29).

ory can coexist in different patterns in a society. It can be temporal, as is true of the illustrations above, which were drawn from literate, professional voices. In the examples, then, the memory was linear, linked to a specific "historic" event and activated by an object, a person, in this case the dynastic *Landesmutter.* Her person was the excuse for the specific individuals' recollections—those of Professor Roeber, Mrs. Stratz, and even the veteran, Sieber-Mitgenhaufen, recipient of the Iron Cross. But the same object can be a source of different memory structures among other groups in the population. Popular memory was shaped less often around events in time, appearing, rather, as the embodiment of attributes and qualities in space.[10] If in all cases, furthermore, it is the particular individual who remembers, memory is social; individuals remember as part of a group, stimulated by images, objects, and ideas that facilitate recall. At any moment in time, therefore, the taxonomy of memory in society is a complicated grid of different collective memories, overlapping, partly conflicting, and partly reinforcing each other simultaneously.

In mobilizing social memory, the *Landesmutter* image (in texts and monuments as well as in commemorative praxis and performances) had a particular cogency for the long nineteenth century. As a dynastic symbol of rule, it partook, of course, of older mechanisms of collective memory at work in a society that long had reinforced aristocratic identity. For one, time was preserved in generational memory, through a genealogical knowledge of the place and exploits of the noblewoman within the larger lineage. After all, it had been these generational ties that still informed Professor Roeber's speech in 1904. For another, identity was solidified, also in portraits, statues, or sculptures, visual media designed to impart the "natural" aura and authority of the nobility and safeguard its memory. As we have seen earlier, portraits regularly were given as keepsakes to preserve the moment of personal interaction between a commoner and the royalty. The calculation was not without effect, as witnessed, for example, by the veteran's account of the gift thirty-four years later. During the century, there also were a growing number of biographies of the royal figure and other forms of institutional memory—including the Baden court archive that provides such rich material for this study—necessary for dynastic state rule. Indeed, the image of the *Landesmutter* was neither inci-

---

10. In popular conceptions, the "heart" of Queen Luise was said to rest beneath her gravestone. See the discussion in 1904 in Berlin when the magistrates planned to move her gravesite to a different location in the Tiergarten (*KZ,* no. 94, February 25, 1903). For the classic statement on collective memory, Halbwachs, *On Collective Memory.* Maria Minicuci, "Time and Memory: Two Villages in Calabria," in Hughes and Trautmann, *Time,* 83, interrogates the notion that social memory reflects the social effects of history itself.

dental to social memory nor accidental—its display was an important and conscious instrument of dynastic state rule.[11]

From its origins in the early nineteenth century, furthermore, this dynastic female symbol was tied into and, in turn, reinforced the social memories of individual and collective sacrifice in war. In this sense, the *Landesmutter* image carried into the new world of state-building and, later, nation-state building older aristocratic identities, which had been located originally in warfare. But, after 1815, they were part of new gendered messages that expressed the memory of community participation in the war effort and not solely the military exploits and sacrifices of generals and soldiers. Indeed, it was the ministerings of the *Landesmutter,* activating an ethic of care for those wounded and maimed in the war of 1870, that had been remembered at the exhibitions in Düsseldorf and Heidelberg in the early twentieth century.

The dynastic narrative, and the patriotic institutions and practices that kept it alive, rewrote the rituals of sacrifice appropriate for conservative politics in the emerging century of modern democratic war. Commemorating sacrifice expressed more than an instrumental acknowledgment of a gift, however; it reenacted social organization and hierarchy through the active force of its gender dynamics.[12] Its ritual forms included celebration of the memories and stories of women's exploits and efforts in war. Indeed, a highly stylized embrace of female sacrifice was one logical product of the gendered nature of the dynastic patriotic public sphere.

These memories of sacrifice increasingly became attached to two other objects that intertwined with the older *Landesmutter* image as a framework for remembering the gendered obligations in war: the disabled veteran and the medical nurse. In the patriotic imagination after 1871, the "abstract" German state could be "seen" through the very people who had shed their blood for it and whose labor had bound the wounds. In addition to the honors given to dead soldiers and commemorations at gravesites, what could be a more graphic testimony of the "reality" of the national community itself than the living examples of those who had served it so nobly in war? The day-to-day care of disabled veterans and the commemorative practices, award ceremonies, and medals given to veterans and

---

11. For a valuable assessment of different types of memory and the relationship between memory and power, see Jacques Le Goff, *History and Memory* trans. Steven Rendall and Elizabeth Claman (New York, 1992), 4–58.

12. I was helped in this section on sacrifice by numerous talks with Richard Trexler. In working out the evidence, I found particularly useful Nancy Jay, *Throughout Your Generations Forever: Sacrifice, Religion, and Paternity* (Chicago, 1991); and René Girard, *Violence and the Sacred,* trans. Patrick Gregory (Baltimore, 1972). Jay's work is a stunning feminist analysis of the links between sacrifice, gender, and social organization, although I part company with her in my inclusion of women in the rituals of nationalist sacrifice.

nurses were testimonies to a new contract at the heart of national identity: a reciprocity of sacrifice and obligation that bound individuals to the state.

These same commemorative and philanthropic practices after 1871, however, capture a more complex identity than typically is assumed in nationalist narratives. The symbols of shared national sacrifice continued to be mediated by state and dynastic loyalties. In effect, the veteran and nurse singled out for public praise could be a link to the national imagination and simultaneously keep alive a collective memory of specific battles, which reinforced the constituent state's or region's pride and identity. Furthermore, these patriotic festivities commemorating the battles of war changed over time to meet new historic conditions. As Halbwachs reminds us, memory always is about the present.[13]

It was the complex interactions between the present and the past that sustained the potency of the *Landesmutter* symbol in the German states of central Europe. Thus, it never shared the fate of the French queen who, in the late eighteenth century, already was the object of public vilification and ridicule; for many of the oppositional male voices, the ills of the old order were condensed in the person of the queen—or the court lady or educated salon matron—whose pernicious public roles seemed to embody the decay of the whole political and social order. The attack in illustrated pamphlets and broadsheets culminated in 1793 in the actual trial and execution of the person of Marie Antoinette for "counterrevolutionary" conspiracy, a charge that also included the fear of "dissimulation," a transformation of men into women as a by-product of women's public prominence, as well as the crime of "incest," proof of the degeneracy of the aristocracy and its false genealogy. Lynn Hunt, the analyst of this deadly "family romance" played out in the French Revolution, states simply that queens in France "never seemed to qualify as mothers of the people."[14] At the end of the eighteenth century, the body politic in France was being redesigned to curb the public expression of feminine influence and power, although in the next century women continued to insert their voices into the debates over the political life of the state.[15]

Across the Rhine, the dynastic *Landesmutter* image had few vocal detractors. By the 1890s, the socialist subculture had emerged full-blown as a powerful alternative to monarchical rule and a public critic of its blend of nationalism and militarism. For August Bebel, one of the most

---

13. Halbwachs, *On Collective Memory,* 137–38, 183.

14. Lynn Hunt, *The Family Romance of the French Revolution* (Berkeley and Los Angeles, 1992), 89–123, 89 for the quote. Hunt recognizes that royal figures are subject to such attacks, but not all royal figures at all times (91).

15. Joan Wallach Scott, *Only Paradoxes to Offer: French Feminists and the Rights of Man* (Cambridge, Mass., 1996).

prominent leaders of the German Social Democratic Party, the *Landesmutter* symbol was a deception, a false promise of virtue and propriety. It masked the hypocrisy of "bourgeois" marriage that, in his analysis, was prostitution anyway, a "disgrace based on money" *(Geld und Schandesehe)*. In his highly influential feminist tract, *Women under Socialism* (1879), which went through numerous editions and translations, he attacks the aristocracy for its sexual promiscuity and scandalous, shameful lifestyle. His, however, is a class critique and not an individual vilification. In a backhanded way, it even recognizes the potential appeal of the *Landesmutter* image to the wider population, which repeatedly drew on the language of dynasty for its own purposes. But a discussion of the dynastic *Landesmutter* is peripheral to his purposes. In the same influential study, however, Bebel acknowledges the extensive practice of "patronage." In seeking aristocratic patrons, bourgeois women were emulating their male counterparts, who also "enjoy such protection in their enthusiasm for [philanthropic] efforts."[16] In many ways, Bebel was sympathetic to bourgeois women and the social constraints that limited their autonomy; however, in his analysis their ties to the aristocracy precluded any potential feminist alliance with the working class for meaningful reform, however much that strategy itself was contested in socialist circles.

A contemporary of Bebel's in the socialist movement, Lily Braun, offers an explicit commentary on the *Landesmutter* motif. To be sure, Braun was hardly a typical voice in the socialist community; she, herself, came from an aristocratic background. Her grandmother, Jenny von Gustedt, had been a childhood friend of Queen Augusta in Weimar; and the two women remained in contact throughout their lives. Braun's biography of her grandmother, *In the Shadow of Giants* (the reference is to Napoleon, Goethe, and Augusta), demonstrates a peculiar logic that led from the "imagined" concern and care of the *Landesmutter* for her children, which is described amply in the text, to Braun's own eclectic brand of feminism, which centered on the significance of motherhood as a right—irrespective of marriage—and supported by national insurance.[17] While idiosyncratic in her blend of socialism and feminism, Braun's usage

---

16. August Bebel, *Die Frau und der Sozialismus,* 27th ed. (Stuttgart, 1896), 111, 172. For the work's importance and its place in the political debates of the day, Ursula Herrmann and Volker Emmrich, *August Bebel: Ein Biographie* (Berlin, 1989), 218–37.

17. Lily Braun, *Gesammelte Werke,* vol. 1, *Im Schatten der Titanen. Erinnerungen an Baronin Jenny von Gustedt* (Berlin-Grunewald, n.d.), 80–81, 176–78, 242–50, and, on war, 320, 332–36. Braun reproduces Goethe's conversations with Eckermann on Marie Pawlowna and describes the "profession of the *Landesmutter*" in the work of Pawlowna, founder of the Patriotic Women's Institute in Weimar (chap. 1). Through her grandmother's letters, she takes the reader to her family's estate in West Prussia and the philanthropic work on behalf of the poor in the context of Junker power and authority. In Braun's account, the

of the *Landesmutter* tradition recreated its historic evolution in a way that drew a sympathetic reading for progressive purposes. However, in the biography, both Augusta and Jenny are shown to be deeply concerned with the impending war against Austria in 1866 (and again in 1870), lending the narrative an antimilitarist gloss that was a far cry from the operative values of the conservative dynastic political culture.

The *Landesmutter* symbol, in effect, was deeply embedded in the collective memories of war. Apparently, this partly shielded it from attack by the political Right, for whom war, after all, was the supreme guarantor of the integrity and autonomy of the state. The philanthropic setting for female volunteers "protected" by the dynasty, furthermore, rarely was subjected to frontal attack in the cultural "wars" of the *Kaiserreich* that, in the artistic imagination, found sustenance in overlapping and conflicting images of sacrifice: virginal, avenging, as in the figures of Judith or Salome, or devouring, the *vagina dentata*.[18] As aesthetic image, "charity" was on one end of the spectrum, fixed somehow, essential and tranquil, embodying women's bounty and self-sacrifice. The philanthropists themselves, however—powerful and privileged wives of aristocrats and high government and military officials and their "virginal" daughters (the patriotic *Jungfrauen*)—were persons of high public profile, who operated in liminal spaces outside the stifling domestic routines and in the company of other women. They seemingly eluded the modernist critique of the feminine public presence—the working-class woman, said to seduce "with the simple undulation of her rump," or the prostitute, caught up more directly in artistic male erotic fears of castration and fantasies of transcendence.[19]

"royal model" expressed a mobilization of "motherliness" inspired by a Christian commitment to the deed *(Religion ist Tat)*. For Braun's place in the socialist subculture, Jean H. Quataert, *Reluctant Feminists in German Social Democracy, 1885–1917* (Princeton, N.J., 1979); and Alfred G. Meyer, *The Feminism and Socialism of Lily Braun* (Bloomington, 1985).

18. Bram Dijkstra's *Idols of Perversity: Fantasies of Feminine Evil in Fin-de-Siècle Culture* (New York, 1986), 294, 373–401, is a fascinating study of the iconography of misogyny in modern art, although, at times he presents too transparent a reading of the texts and glosses over the agents. Also, Susan Rubin Suleiman, *Subversive Intent: Gender, Politics, and the Avant-Garde* (Cambridge, Mass., 1990).

19. I deliberately say "seemingly," because certain forms of imagination—the fantasies of soldier-males in the *Freikorps* in the 1920s, for example—reflected deep ambivalences about "white" (loyal) nurses and aristocratic mothers. On one level, even if the soldiers decried the affront to aristocratic authority and dignity, on another they welcomed it. While they separated out good women from whores, their psychic power was an identity with other males and a distance from all women. This marks the fascist "brotherhood" as a radicalized and different vision of the "family" than was proposed and deployed by dynastic institutions and patronage. For soldier-males, Klaus Theweleit, *Male Fantasies*, vol. 2, *Male Bodies: Psychoanalyzing the White Terror*, trans. Erica Carter and Chris Turner (Minneapolis, 1989). Also, Dijkstra, *Idols of Perversity*, 123–24 (for images of charity), 358–64 (and for the quote from Victor Barrucand in 1895, 358).

As revealing, the radical Right, too, differentiated among feminine spaces. When Adolf Stöcker sought women's support for his brand of popular nationalism in the early 1880s, he drew the boundaries of proper female participation in nationalist causes against the bourgeois women's movement. He singled out, however, several of its Jewish leaders for personal attack, among them Lina Morgenstern and Jenny Hirsch. On the one hand, he could draw a positive picture of the traditions and memories of the *Landesmütter,* praising their energy and activity for charitable undertakings: "so we can say that our patriotism runs not only through the king but also through the queen." On the other, he condemned the feminist understanding of women's social and welfare activities in the national community.[20] In his endeavors at grassroots mobilization, Stöcker used the public spaces opened by the *Landesmutter* but distinguished between patriotic and feminist activism. His anti-Semitic politics, however, meant a displacement of his more generalized hostility to feminism onto specific Jewish women.

Many male members of the Red Cross and of veterans' associations, however, unequivocally embraced the *Landesmutter* as their patron "saint" or historic "inspiration"; in October 1889, for example, the unit of Berlin stretcher-bearers hailed the dowager, Augusta, as the second queen Luise. The allusion was explicit. For many in the wider nationalist community, Queen Luise had become the "guardian angel of the fatherland," who at once embodied anti-French sentiments and Prussian honor; as one of her many biographers put it in 1876, her memory continuously worked to inspire "unity and unflinching resistance—as it must be in war, which is unavoidable."[21]

The Wars of Unification had revitalized the memory of Luise and added to the nationalist myths: Luise as patriotic guardian had returned to oversee the war of 1870 just as she so propitiously had inspired the young "volunteers" in the battles of 1813. A good illustration of this seemingly logical progression is a poem sent to the Baden duchess Luise by a Mrs. Zimmermann in 1910 at the time of the centenary celebration of the queen's death.[22] In honor of "July 19," numerous Baden subjects felt empowered to send their thoughts, poems, and memories about Queen

---

20. Reports of Stöcker's mobilization efforts are in *KZ,* first supplement to no. 135, June 12, 1881, and first supplement to no. 136, June 14, 1881.

21. For the Berlin *Sanitätskolonne,* see *KZ,* no. 458, October 1, 1889, which also simultaneously honored Auguste Victoria, the reigning empress, in a self-evident acceptance of dynastic family transition. For one of the multiple biographers of Luise, Eduard Engel, *Königin Luise* (Berlin, 1876), 4–5.

22. GK, Abt. 69, no. 175, Randern, July 18, 1910. The collection contains numerous other poems and letters.

Luise to her granddaughter. The selections capture in poetry what was being echoed elsewhere in historical and biographical forms. Theirs was a legitimizing yet popular myth, affecting a complex alliance of prince and people that had saved the nation.

"Disaster" *(Unheil)*, the poem begins, has visited the German people twice; once, a hundred years ago when "a loving heart" died, one filled with "sadness and worry for the fatherland." The people swore revenge (Luise was often described sacrificially as a "martyr" to Prussia's humiliation at Jena), and "it was her one son who saved Germany from such shame." Sixty years later, the poem continues, "disaster" struck again, with another Bonaparte on the throne. Her son, at the sarcophagus of his mother, then appealed to her for the "strength for war." As a "talisman she followed him step by step, steering the weapons in this difficult battle"—until victory. And should a thousand years go by, the poem predicts, Luise still will toil to insure that "our Germany never again is enslaved." The parallel with the legend of Barbarossa is unmistakable except that, in this case, it is cast in feminine form. These patriotic myths had a common currency among an increasingly politically aware public and, through the gender idiom, further drew into the nationalist orbit some of the very groups excluded from formal citizenship. Other poems and letters in the collection reproduce the same patriotic lessons about the histories of war, framed in the context of the intersection of past and present *Landesmütter*. The memory triggered by both the symbol and the person spoke of the inexorability of war in the political life of the state, even as it promised to honor its sacrifices and ease its pain.

Commemorating Veterans' Sacrifices

Women's philanthropic associations, too, stood at the same crossroads of memory work and the politics of care. Particularly those associations that supported disabled veterans typically combined a commitment to regular social and family relief with commemorative practices designed to keep alive the memory of distinct military battles. Well insinuated into local society, they usually were overseen by dynastic figures whose versions of war they worked to memorialize. The activities of the Prussian Women's and Young Ladies' Association in Berlin society offer a thick lens through which to see the subtle transformations in what nonetheless clearly remained dynastic and military loyalties and identities.

In chapter 2, for the period up to the 1860s, we followed the association's slow evolution in a converging "royalism from below," which was sustained in the *Kaiserreich*. The strength of its loyalty, nonetheless, permitted considerable change in the content of its messages. Furthermore, its understanding of war, as was true for large numbers of veterans after 1870, differed from the bourgeois nationalist groups, many of which tended to celebrate war as a nationalist moment of collective emancipation and liberation.[23] While nationalists of different creeds could agree that united Germany had been the product of war, to most veterans as well as patriotic women, unification had been the direct result of the propitious integration of dynastic military forces.

The flow of history, however, had a way of complicating the commemorative work. The Prussian association had resurfaced in late 1863 under the leadership of the wife of Lieutenant von Markatz; it was, undeniably, a Conservative and monarchical force in the Prussia of the "New Era," which openly pitted liberals against conservatives in the move to define the political nature of the state. Surprisingly, its own historical memory counted 1863 as "Year One" and, thus, the group celebrated its fiftieth anniversary in 1913. The archival documents indicate no such radical break, however. The president's appeal to the monarch in 1867 for continued financial "gifts" for its commemorative work reminded the court of the group's long ties to the Hohenzollern dynasty and the consistent backing it had received from Frederick William III, his successor, Frederick William IV, and the queen mother, Elisabeth.[24]

The 1867 appeal, however, contained a new element. The leadership now proposed to commemorate the battle of Königgrätz each July 3, joining in its festive celebration around a meal the old veterans still alive from the liberation battles of Gross-Beeren and Dennewitz with the new veterans from the recent war against Austria. The date was significant. This battle in the previous year had sealed Prussia's recent victory over Austria, deciding the 1866 war and, as was already clear, setting the stage for German unification under Prussian domination. After seven years of commemorative work, however, the victory celebration collided with the shifting political exigencies on the right.[25]

Indeed, in July 1871, the brewing problem already was anticipated by a *Kreuz-Zeitung* report, which encased the celebration in a carefully

23. Düding, "Kreigesvereine im wilhelminischen Reich"; Thomas Rohkrämer, "Heroes and Would-Be Heroes—Veterans and Reservists' Associations in Imperial Germany," in *Anticipating Total War: The German and American Experiences, 1871–1914*, ed. Manfred F. Boemeke, Roger Chickering, and Stig Förster (Cambridge, 1999), 189–215.

24. GSPK, no. 15607, Bl. 71, Berlin, June 13, 1867. In the leaders' own words "the radiance of the royal name elevated the association to an esteemed position," as found in Bl. 145–50, *Sechsundzwanzigster Jahresbericht des Preussischen Frauen-und Jungfrauenvereins* (for 1889).

25. For official requests to host the festival, GSPK, no. 15607, Bl. 74–87 (1868–73); and detailed descriptions of the celebrations, notably, *KZ*, no. 153, July 5, 1870, no. 153, July 5, 1871, supplement to no. 156, July 7, 1872, no. 139, June 18, 1873.

worded explanation: all efforts, the paper said, were made in the festivities "to conceal the memory of our triumph of 1866, which might have offended our former brave enemies"; after all, most of the states had collaborated in the subsequent struggle under "our heroic kaiser," while even "our main opponent—forgetting the old animosity—followed the . . . events in 1870–71 with a certain German sympathy."[26] While the same memory was celebrated in public again next year, and the speech by General Freiherr von Troschke included a pointed reference to the queen, "whose merciful attendance to duty during the hardships of the war brought in its train so much for the good," the commemorative date no longer found a sympathetic echo.

In 1873, the women's association appropriated June 16 as the date to honor the living veterans and continued to celebrate it for the next four decades. The celebration marked the entry of the "victorious troops into the splendidly decorated capital city of Berlin two years earlier," signaling the end of a war that was said to have "no parallel." Commemoration, indeed, always is political, designed to reinforce a sense of group cohesion by constructing a shared narrative of identity and purposefully excluding contentious elements. In conservative memory, the "German" civil war, after all, took place in 1848, not in 1866, and a festival marking the victory of one ally over the other in the emerging system of international alliances had no place in official nationalist politics. As Sherman notes persuasively, commemoration is as much about organizing forgetting as it is about "causing" to remember.[27]

The Prussian women's association, then, entered the *Kaiserreich* with a new social memory kept alive in the traditional annual public banquet for disabled veterans, which was held at a prominent locale in the urban landscape—at the Potsdamerbrücke or the Zoological Garden, for example. The organization was well positioned in Berlin high society, drawing on military and aristocratic elites for its organizational core. It had a higher proportion of military families among its active members than was true of the leadership of the Patriotic Women's Association.

A group of fifty active women members and several male advisors comprised its administrative center. The leadership consisted of an executive committee of between nine and eleven women; eleven so-called *Sammel-Damen*, typically the unmarried "young ladies" of the association, who were responsible for collecting the dues as well as the art, artifacts, and goods that were donated to its fund-raising events; and twenty-

---

26. *KZ,* no. 153, July 5, 1871.
27. Daniel J. Sherman, "Monuments, Mourning, and Masculinity in France after World War I," *Gender and History* 8, no. 1 (April 1996): 84.

two older investigators, the *Recherche-Damen,* whose important assignment was to "research" the lives of the disabled veterans and their families who were applying for temporary or permanent relief. In 1889, of the eleven executive committee members, five were titled military officer wives; in addition there was Baroness von Schwartzenberg and Countess Maximiliane von Oriola, born von Arnim, whose house was an active center of artistic and literary life, according to Baroness Spitzemberg. Mrs. von Krause, a member, served simultaneously on the Executive Committee of the Prussian Patriotic Women's Association.[28]

The association was well integrated into the extensive philanthropic nexus in Berlin. It maintained close ties to the municipal *Invalidenhaus,* the residency of many of the old veterans under its commemorative wing. The governor's wife, Frau General von Grolman, served on the executive committee in the late 1880s. Several of its leaders, including the duchess Oriola, were "honorary members" of the all-male Invalidendank, a local branch of the national philanthropic organization that had emerged to assist veterans or their widows and orphans find "suitable" employment. In addition, the Prussian group received subventions from the Patriotic Women's Association and maintained a close working relationship with the city Poor Commission as well as the Protestant philanthropic hierarchy: the City Mission, the *Frauenhilfe,* and the parish relief organizations throughout the metropolitan area. Clients were referred back and forth among these relief organizations and agencies. Financial backing came from a group of local contributors who paid dues on a regular basis; their numbers reached 524 in 1875 but dwindled to about half that number by the 1890s.[29] The association also was given free publicity by the mainstream daily press.

The Prussian association's high public profile came from a banquet, which it hosted annually for around 120 disabled veterans, whose numbers in the 1870s still included a few noncommissioned officers and rank and file from the wars against Napoleon. The festivities worked simultaneously to reinforce two distinct experiences of "nationalist" time. On the

---

28. The active members consistently came from the "highest" of Berlin society. In 1871, of nine women on the executive committee, three were titled, two were countesses, one was the wife of a state minister, another of a master builder, and the third a member of the high clergy. Membership statistics are in the archival collection: GSPK, no. 15607, Bl. 76, Berlin, June 3, 1869, Bl. 125–30, *21ster Jahresbericht des Preussischer-Frauen und Jungfrauen-Vereins* (for 1884), and Bl. 145–50, *Jahresbericht* (1889). Newspaper reports supplement the archival holdings: *KZ,* second supplement to no. 265, November 12, 1871, no. 63, March 15, 1874, no. 57, March 9, 1875. Also, *Tagebuch der Baronin Spitzemberg,* 137–38, 197, 220.

29. By 1889, the paying members has declined to 282, see GSPK, no. 15607, Bl. 145. For the "Invalidendank," *KZ,* supplement to no. 119, May 25, 1872.

one hand, the meal each June 16 was part of the patriotic calendar of events, a recurring cycle of celebration that offered a sense of regularity and security in the present. On the other, it kept alive an explicit historical memory, drawing a continuous line between the present and the past. In speeches and toasts, the banqueters celebrated the memory of past wars, reproducing a version of Prussian dynastic history that stressed the military victories from the battle of Fehrbellin (1675), which led to the expansion of Brandenburg at the expense of Sweden, to the recent wars establishing German unification. It helped define the future identity of the nation by constructing a grand historical narrative that came with a clear definition of enemies as well. In the words of Major von Ohlen-Adlerskron, whose speech in 1873 delineated a sequence of battles comprising his "history," hardly had the wounds of 1864–66 healed up then "our old arch enemy, who had no patience for the unity of Germany, . . . France forced us . . . into fiery, bloody war. Our heroic king led the loyal allied German army from victory to victory until the kaiser dictated the peace at Versailles."[30] The condensed tale was as much a dynastic triumph as a national one.

The patriotic festival worked to reinforce a sense of history—and create a living connection to the past. These ties were not only a way to safeguard the status quo, infusing it with what was claimed to be the sanctions of time and the very "successes" of history itself. The imagery of male generational continuity meant a transfer through time of the lessons that sustained the "heroic" war efforts. The same major, for example, singled out the "old veterans" from earlier wars as "the [living] examples of soldiers' virtues passed on to the child and the child's child." The earlier generations of war "heroes" had transferred their memories and values to the next and so on, comprising an unbreakable chain into the distant future that, in the conservative imagination, worked to perpetuate the beliefs and attitudes necessary to sustain war. The festivals themselves functioned as a way to insure continuity of the fighting force in face of the disruptions caused by time—by the inevitability of aging and death.

And, yet, the new context of unification disrupted "sacred" time even as it secured nationalist military traditions in new memory. The politics of memory transformed another festival in Berlin, which had paralleled the commemorative work of the Prussian Women's and Young Ladies' Association for over six decades. Dedicated to the volunteers of 1813–15, this celebration took place each February 3, the anniversary of the king's "call" for citizen-volunteers to enter the army in 1813. The year 1873 was

---

30. *KZ*, no. 139, June 18, 1873. For the festive entry in the eyes of the baroness, *Tagebuch der Baronin Spitzemberg*, June 16, 1871, 126–27.

the sixtieth anniversary of the proclamation, yet it was to be the last traditional celebration because the old "loyal" group was dying out (a loyalty that, pointedly, had been demonstrated in 1848, according to the account).

The closing festival, however, arranged a transition to pass its mantle of fidelity onto the heirs; the celebration constructed a ceremonial bridge between the old "volunteers," whose mission now was declared completed, and the recipients of the Iron Cross in 1870–71, who henceforth would gather together on the same day of remembrance. "Voluntarily, the volunteers lay down their honorary post" and through the solemn ceremony "pass on their whole inheritance, their way of thinking, their devotion, their loyalty to the Knights of the Iron Cross."[31] The Iron Cross medal had been rededicated in 1870. By design, the very values at the core of military life would be preserved, maintained, and proclaimed in a similarly recurring annual public ceremony by those living recipients of the Iron Cross. Indeed, a new nationalist memory celebrating the living maintained its ties to the old sacred date with its links to the dead, but it represented a break in historical consciousness even as it synchronized anew festive time to affirm social continuity. In addition, whatever emancipatory potential there might have been in the memory of the "patriotic volunteers"—those who, after all, had formed the first people's army—was submerged purposefully in this transition to commemorate, in the words of the speaker, the "splendid" organization of the royal army.[32]

The memory kept alive in the patriotic celebration of veterans was not that of the soldiers' sacrifices alone. It was not only about, to borrow again the compelling phrase of Nancy Jay, "intergenerational male continuity" secured through sacrifice.[33] At the banquets organized by the Prussian association, the speeches thanked the women whose organization originally had been formed to thank the soldiers for victories against Napoleon. Indeed, the ceremony linked soldiers and civilians in a chain of shared sacrifice and thanks. Thus, the annual festival was intended as much to keep alive the efforts of the "ladies," whose multiple undertakings, as one speaker reminded the audience, included the care of the wounded and injured soldiers of Prussia's past wars; their solicitous ministerings and gifts at each festive meal; and the philanthropic commitments

---

31. *KZ,* no. 28, February 2, 1873, "Die Freiwillige und ihre Erben." The festival had become a regular event by the 1830s and, in 1863, at the fiftieth anniversary of the mobilization of volunteers, the king attended to honor the participants.

32. For an overview of the rededication of the Iron Cross, *KZ,* no. 453, November 9, 1888. My thanks go to Kevin Slick and Matthew Lungerhausen, graduate students in German and Austrian history, for helping me ponder these changes in military festive life.

33. Jay, *Throughout Your Generations Forever,* 37–39.

to aid the needy disabled veterans and their families on a daily basis as well. The memory of these sacrifices in the past was kept alive and linked to the work in the ever-evolving present.

The reference to sacrifice is striking. It was a fundamental trope itself, found already in the 1844 survey of "patriotic" women's institutes in the Germanic Confederation. According to the author, the work of these private associations in their fundamental core embodied "sacrifices for the fatherland." The formulation duplicates the self-definition of the women's organization, which enclosed its own activities in a spirit of self-sacrifice *(opferbereite Thätigkeit)*.[34] On one level, the annual ceremony was a public enactment of the principle of community obligations to disabled veterans proposed in gendered script already in 1813–14, as a patriotic "duty" of mothers and sisters and encoded in the language of sacrifice. On another, the same ceremony reinforced the memory of the specific battle or entry and, thus, affirmed social continuity by its linkage to the past.

After 1871, furthermore, the "nation" was put on stage and made palpably visible through the preparation, presentation, and gift of the festive meal. As Major von Ohlen-Adlerskron affirmed in no uncertain terms in 1874, the festival was a "public demonstration of just how much the nation honors the army."[35] The ceremony was interpreted to express the reciprocities binding soldier and civilian; it worked partly to uphold the nation's honor and, thus, at once, to affirm its authority and power. In the politics of conservative commemoration, nationalist obligations and sacrifices mutually reinforced one another for state purposes. The ceremony, however, deployed its messages in multiple and complex ways, communicating specific messages about authority, hierarchy, and community and relying for its meanings on the subtle effects of the gender dynamics.

Celebration around a meal often was a useful medium to evoke family life and communion. Mary Douglas reminds us that meals are for family, good friends, and honored guests. While Douglas here is reflecting the English middle-class culture of her day, she equally could have analyzed the centrality of food rituals in constituting traditional religious or civic communities.[36] Indeed, rituals around food reflect both "communion" and "expiation," to borrow the expressive polarities at the heart of Jay's thinking on alimentary sacrifice. They work as two complementary sides

---

34. Gräfe, *Nachrichten von wohltätigen Frauenvereinen,* 17. Also, GSPK, no. 15607, Bl. 125–26, *Jahresbericht* (1884), offers a description of their own work.

35. *KZ,* supplement to no. 141, June 20, 1874.

36. Mary Douglas, "Deciphering a Meal," in *Implicit Meanings: Essay in Anthropology* (London, 1975), 256. For food in civic rituals in Republican Florence, Trexler, *Public Life,* 216, 237, 265–68, 324–26, and 433–35.

of one logical system that produces and reproduces social organization. Each functions separately to differentiate insiders from outsiders through integration and exclusion.[37] Seen through this lens, the annual patriotic banquet in effect intertwined older civic bourgeois as well as military-aristocratic gender patterns.

In the patriotic culture of imperial Berlin, the publicized meal each June 16 constituted the idealized national "family" bound in sacrifice. It simultaneously played out several distinct historic understandings of family, however. In Old Europe, public banquets had been integral to marriage rituals, serving family needs to present the young couple to the community and prevent clandestine marriages. In Italy, the engagement parties were for men only; but Renaissance art captures well the domestic gender relations among the great urban families newly allied in marriage. For example, Botticelli's *Story of Nastagio deglie Onesti* depicts a public banquet at the marriage of a knight: men sit together on a long table on the right facing women on the left. If such strict gender placement appeared less pronounced in northern Europe and among the plebian orders, public banquets nonetheless served to bring men and women together for festive occasions.[38]

Similarly, banquets became part of princely rule simultaneously accompanying and promoting court authority. At the meal, the prince could demonstrate his powers and wealth and cement social bonds and allegiances. In the politicizing of "domestic intimacy" that accompanied European state-building, however, men alone dined together with women in attendance. In some contexts, indeed, the "family of men" meant just that, a sacred male community created through sacrifice as the basis of political authority. This was the structure for classical Greece and Renaissance Florence in their heyday.[39] Furthermore, by the nineteenth century, military rites and feasts had appropriated the family trope for the brother-

---

37. Jay, *Throughout Your Generations Forever,* xiv.

38. Edward Muir, *Ritual in Early Modern Europe* (Cambridge, 1997), 33–38, including the plate of Pieter Brueghel the Elder, *The Peasant Wedding.* An excellent reproduction of the four secular paintings of Botticelli is in Ronald Lightbown, *Sandro Botticelli: Life and Work* (New York, 1989), 114–20.

39. The place of the banquet in the emergence of princely rule is stressed by Trexler, *Public Life,* 433–44. For the Greek linkage of family and male community, Jay, *Throughout Your Generations Forever,* 133. As she notes, this concept was distinct from the Nazi *Männerbund,* which shunned the term *family.* For transitional notions of male community, which foreshadowed fascist ideology, Jürgen Reulecke, "Männerbund versus the Family: Middle-Class Youth Movements and the Family in Germany in the Period of the First World War," in *The Upheaval of War: Family, Work, and Welfare in Europe, 1914–1918,* ed. Richard Wall and Jay Winter (Cambridge, 1988), 439–52.

hood of soldiers. The militarized sanitary corps of the Red Cross celebrated together as a male family.

In the festival of June 16, therefore, the twin forces of differentiation and integration intertwined in a way that both affirmed male bonding and reproduced the extended kin family of men and women. The festive meal enacted a family of brothers, united in memory of their patriotic sacrifice and pain, and the domestic family—compatible with the pervasive nationalist trope of "the German people" as a patriotic community of women and men, young and old, rich and poor, civilian and military, those crippled as well as whole. In the ceremony, this patriotic group stood apart from the rest by virtue of its participation in the banquet.

That women orchestrated the festival gave it an aura of "naturalness," helping to re-create a sense of a larger kin gathering, reinforced by the mingling of the ages at the meal. The meal was attended to by older and younger women—women who were someone's mother, wife, or daughter. In this interpretation, it helped fortify the parallel effort to define the state as a large family, insuring the well-being of its members through food and security and caring for their emotional needs as well.

But the choreography also worked to communicate strong feelings of intimacy and affection, rekindling the bonds of male comradeship that had been an essential part of military life. To the backdrop of a chorus of songs sung by *Verein* women, each veteran was escorted personally to his seat at a table decorated with flowers; in the words of one reporter, the women took the arms of the "younger disabled soldiers" and the "hoary old veterans," conjuring up a vision of intergenerational harmony among the soldiers ready and willing to defend their "family."

Glaring were the omissions, however: tensions over memory that came to divide the generations of veterans and ex-servicemen and tensions over money, reflecting the inequities of pensions and other material benefits.[40] Neither was there mention of the obvious: the injured veteran's body, the fact that he walked with difficulty, perhaps, or lacked an arm. The rhetorical garb surrounding the ceremony—in association protocols or newspaper reports—reproduced a sanitized version of war: the hero's death, a noble struggle, wounds that transcend pain. These myths contrasted with the life situation of the disabled and infirm veterans present at the meal; many were very old, and others were sick and maimed. The only concession was an acknowledgment that some of the women had been caring for the very same veterans in the hospitals. And, yet the ladies' spot-

---

40. For tensions among different generations of soldiers and conflict over levels of economic support, Rohrkrämer, "Heroes and Would-Be Heroes," and also his larger study, *Der Militarismus der "kleinen Leute." Die Kriegervereine im Deutschen Kaiserreich* (Munich, 1990).

light on the veterans must have been comforting: the meal was a fellowship feast that normalized the disabled soldiers and at the same time perpetuated a veneer that coated the horrors of war.

The meal opened with a religious prayer, intertwining God and country and imparting an explicit patriotic and Christian glow that grew more pronounced with the rise of grassroots radical nationalism. It concluded with the singing together of many patriotic songs, rekindling the bonds of brotherhood and camaraderie.[41] In between were the speeches and toasts, which stamped the event with an official rhetorical line. For those honored, however, the ceremony affirmed fellowship and intimacy through the sharing of food and song. And the German readers of the daily papers knew the patriotic songs and hymns and could imagine themselves singing along simultaneously.

The gender dynamics were more complex, however. Gender served to mask other forms of hierarchy and dominance. Indeed, as Jay demonstrates, its seemingly natural quality "makes gender unequalled as a cornerstone of domination."[42] Relations of power cut both horizontally (aristocratic and upper-middle-class women in Germany undoubtedly had a more restricted field of action than the men of their backgrounds) and vertically. These well-off, privileged women who, arguably, ate better food than what they served the veterans, reproduced the power hierarchy in German society, eliciting deference in the forms of address and indebtedness. Not only was the food a gift; but the less privileged soldiers received other gifts of cigars and champagne donated by local industrialists or other people who had more power and money.

At the festive meal in 1874, for example, a "friend of the *Verein*" donated the wine; a "patriotic neighbor" gave the champagne used for the toasts; and a woman member of the association passed out cigars—testimony, indeed, to a wider community of patriotic insiders. But at the very moment of paying back the "nation's" debt, new forms of indebtedness emerge. The circulation of gifts, as Mauss recognizes, draws "two moments in time" together; the act of transfer is both a payment now and

---

41. This was pointedly affirmed at the time of the Stöcker controversy, GSPK, no. 15607, Bl. 156–61, *Jahresbericht* (1890), and Bl. 182–89, *Jahresbericht* (1894): "Die ganze Feier war von echt vaterländischen, christlichen Geiste getragen."

42. Jay, *Throughout Your Generations Forever,* 37. Gender could not always mask class tensions, however. For example, in 1910, the "old, gray" veterans and widows in Elberfeld lodged a grievance against the local Patriotic Women's Association, seen as rich and propertied, over monies reputedly collected in the Franco-German war. In this case, the hope to create community cohesion through shared memory foundered over economic antagonisms in the present. For the conflict, LK, Abt. 403, no. 7366, Bl. 253–59, June 7, 1910, and June 20, 1910, Oberbürgermeister, report.

a new set of obligations enjoining the recipients or their heirs later.[43] Besides, the ceremony magnified the honor of those who organized it as much as those who, ostensibly, were honored. Food, after all, is a symbol of wealth, and the women who distributed it freely in public were demonstrating the power and authority of their high rank and status. On a more mundane level, the presence at the ceremony of a few key generals as well as the president of the police and prominent members of the Prussian government unmistakably reinforced the power hierarchy, should the more subtle workings of gender be missed.

The ceremony, therefore, affirmed community while it simultaneously underscored deference. It helped legitimize the conservative power hierarchy by enacting a complicated performance of sacrifice, drawing women into the ritual mechanisms that were designed to insure intergenerational continuity. The banquet, furthermore, reintegrated the disabled veteran into the patriotic family, silencing his pain while offering him solace.

In imperial Germany, the work of the women's association was placed squarely under the old Conservative slogan "With God for king and fatherland." Its annual celebration was a familiar sight on the local political scene. As one commentator put it in 1874, the banquet "is one of the peculiar features to observe that has given the face of Berlin its particular character."[44] And it remained a part of the city's commemorative life for the next four decades. Memory, in turn, works in subtle ways. According to his biographer, the prominent industrialist Hugo Stinnes was approached in March 1915 by a local Berlin businessman who envisioned a new ceremony to celebrate the triumphal "entry of the troops into Berlin" after the anticipated German victory in World War I. He wanted to rent out prime Berlin real estate in advance. To Stinnes, the move was "premature," but the effort to duplicate such "joyous welcome" in renewed ceremonial form, arguably, is a testimony to just how embedded the memory of June 16 had become in everyday consciousness.[45]

Patriotic Memory and Consumerism

If the ritual meal offered ample opportunity for patronage—and the association's annual reports meticulously recorded the nature and amount of

---

43. Mauss, *The Gift,* 35–36.

44. *KZ,* supplement to no. 141, June 20, 1874, "Erinnerungsfest."

45. Gerald D. Feldman, "War Aims, State Intervention, and Business Leadership in Germany: The Case of Hugo Stinnes," paper presented to a conference at Münchenwiler, October 9–12, 1996, 1. The reference to "joyous welcome" comes from the 1914 report on the festival, *KZ,* no. 269, June 12, 1914.

each gift given by the wealthy—so, too, did the other visible face of the Prussian women's organization: its annual fund-raising bazaar. Hosting a bazaar was a popular method of raising money in the patriotic culture of the *Kaiserreich:* all manner of gifts were solicited and, in turn, sold at the event for the benefit of targeted clients. The annual date of the Prussian women's bazaar settled on early December, coinciding with the Christmas season and linking this patriotic moment of giving—as was true for many of the local philanthropic institutions throughout Germany—to the joyous memory of gifts at the time of Jesus' birth. It further intertwined patriotic and Christian messages of sacrifice.

The yearly bazaar found ample backing for decades; many of the donations came from the very highest members of the Hohenzollern court, including art and artifacts they had acquired on trips abroad. For example, in 1881, the princess Frederick Charles, the association's patron, contributed an oil painting entitled *The Arab and His Steed,* the title alone seemingly objectifying the "essence" of the Orient. In turn, these same royal figures made generous purchases. Donations also came from far and wide, testifying to a circulating patriotic exchange network that, for the moment, effectively neutralized political distinctions; besides, the contributions were an opportunity for wealthy families to become associated with such exalted company. Thus, for example, in 1893 the Krupp family in Essen donated goods to the bazaar.[46] The association might have been a small urban organization, but it had wide currency reflecting its powerful backers.

The bazaar was very much a Prussian event, however. Over the years, space was provided by various state ministries—Public Works or Justice—and, in addition, the Prussian House of Deputies, off limits to women politically, nonetheless opened up its second floor to the event. The iconographic display was a forceful reminder of Prussian identity: busts of the Hohenzollern dynasty adorned the rooms; a table showed pictures of the association's patron and her family; the female organizers proudly paraded around with black-and-white ribbons on their left shoulders. In 1875, with the federal decision to shift from the old Prussian thaler to a new German mark, the *Kreuz-Zeitung* groused about the change that, it claimed, "reduced the value of philanthropy by threefold."[47] Prominently highlighted, too, was the red cross on white background.

But the impact of the Christmas bazaar moved beyond the so-called

46. GSPK, no. 15607, Bl. 172–78, *Jahresbericht* (1893); also, *KZ,* no. 282, December 1, 1881, and supplement to no. 286, December 6, 1874, "Der Weihnachts-Bazar des preussischen Frauen-und Jungfrauen-Vereins." For art, diplomacy, and influence, Jarchow, *Hofgeschenke.*

47. *KZ,* first supplement to no. 289, December 11, 1875.

sacrifices of patriotic gift-giving. It reflected a set of changes that also were duplicated in the many other benefit events and auctions that punctuated the patriotic year in German social life. An emerging consumer culture increasingly was drawing on patriotic messages for the sale of goods; the bazaar itself was a shoppers' paradise, however much its proceeds were earmarked, in our Prussia case, for the welfare of disabled soldiers. Booths sold children's dolls and toys, cosmetics, and Karlsbad porcelain, for example; there was a green room for wool items and a garden room for fresh and dried flowers. Many of the association members had met throughout the year at monthly meetings *(Nähversammlungen)* in the president's home to sew lingerie and underwear, aprons, jackets, skirts, and other "beautiful linens," which were sold at the bazaar. In their own description, this was the work behind the scenes *(still und unbemerkt)*, an obligatory platitude that was belied by the meticulous attention to publicity.[48] Most significantly, however, it became common practice for "established" Berlin firms to exhibit at the bazaar and also for "new businesses" to donate goods, hoping thereby to become known among potential customers. In 1894, the firm Louis Hirschberg organized a room for home furnishings and all manner of cooking implements and kitchen appliances, and in that same year a brewery in Munich donated beer for the buffet.[49] The business community, in short, was using these bazaars to promote its products.

As we saw in the case of the Heidelberg clinic, these bazaars were a routine part of patriotic fund-raising. But they also were opportunities to display "oriental" objects and artifacts and bring the exotic world of empire to the daily consciousness of the consumer. Over time, "oriental" booths and "exotic" rooms were added to the events and "oriental" portraits as well; other bazaars were set up to raise money specifically for medical work in the colonies; and exhibitions earmarking the profits for the German soldiers wounded in southwest Africa became more commonplace after 1904.[50]

The case of a bazaar sponsored in 1903 by the Berlin branch of the German Women's Association for Medical Services in the Colonies exemplifies, perhaps, the worst of the nasty business of appropriation. Held in the district building of Teltow, the bazaar let shoppers purchase Cameroon chocolates, New Guinea cigarettes, or drawings from Mesopotamia, among other items. On display, however, were the

48. GSPK, no. 15607, Bl. 145–50, *Jahresbericht* (1889).

49. GSPK, no. 15607, Bl. *Jahresbericht* (1894); also, *KZ*, supplement to no. 286, December 6, 1874, and, particularly, no. 288, December 8, 1880.

50. GK, Abt. 69, no. 573, Allerhöchster Besuch in Mannheim, November 7, 1904, Veranstaltung zur Gunsten der Verwundeten in Südwestafrika.

"natives" in the flesh: "the small Ferida," daughter of Emin Pascha; "Joli" brought from New Guinea by the Anthropological Society; the "Negro" of Dr. Ehler from Mauritius. Here, the foreign person was transformed literally into a show for the purposes of selling goods to benefit imperial colonial domination. According to the keen eye of Baroness Spitzemberg, these bazaars were popular, attracting a wide range of shoppers, including those from the lower orders *(untergeordnete Leute)*.[51]

Significantly, they did not operate in isolation. Research by other scholars confirms the effect of colonial ties on Germany's emerging consumer culture. Already in the early twentieth century, advertisement campaigns were using African and orientalist images to sell their mass products more widely. In the marketplace, German identity was being molded by its contrast to others of different colors and racial makeup.[52] Undeniably, the dynastic patriotic culture had become integrated into new consumption and leisure patterns, helping to make its messages part of the everyday exchange of goods. While it is not clear if the dynamics of capitalist development co-opted patriotism or vice versa, this world of patriotism, so politically intertwined with dynastic models, memory, and money, also was being anchored in the rituals of consumption that would long outlive dynastic interests.

Commemorating Nurses' Sacrifices

Official nationalism reproduced a story of the collective outpouring of support for the wars of 1813 and 1870 to sustain an identity that would reinforce loyalty and legitimacy in the present. As the Prussian banquets and bazaars reveal, these "myths" of war included memory of feminine— and not solely masculine—sacrifice.[53] Tellingly, an official commemora-

---

51. *KZ*, no. 574, December 7, 1903, bazaar of the Deutsche Frauen-Verein zur Krankenpflege in den Kolonien. Also, *Tagebuch der Baronin Spitzemberg*, February 7, 1889, 259 and, for her remarks on the Prussian Association's bazaar, 197.

52. May Opitz, Katharina Oguntoye, and Dagmar Schultz, eds., *Showing Our Colors: Afro-German Women Speak Out*, trans. Anne V. Adams (Amherst, 1992), 34–37. For new thinking on the relationship between commercialism and empire, Timothy Burke, "'Fork Up and Smile': Marketing, Colonial Knowledge, and the Female Subject in Zimbabwe," in the special issue "Gendered Colonialisms in African History," ed. Nancy Rose Hunt, Tessie R. Liu, and Jean Quataert, *Gender and History* 8, no. 3 (November 1996): 440–56.

53. Mosse, *Fallen Soldiers*, offers an analysis of the "Myth of the War Experience," although his is only a masculine discussion. For its gendered power in "causing" to forget, Joan Wallach Scott, "Rewriting History," in Margaret Higonnet et al., *Behind the Lines: Gender and the Two World Wars* (New Haven, 1987), 21–30. For the place of war myths in shaping historical events, Johannes Burkhardt, "Kriegsgrund Geschichte? 1870, 1813, 1756—historische Argumente und Orientierungen bei Ausbruch des Ersten Weltkrieges," in Johannes Burkhardt et al., *Lange und kurze Wege in den Ersten Weltkrieg* (Munich, 1996), 9–86. I want to thank Stig Förster for giving me a copy of this useful study.

tion of the civilian nurse in wartime was inserted into the construction of community—not individual—experience. As such, it served conservative ends. After 1870, in patriotic imagery, the lay Red Cross nurse—and to a lesser extent the trained aide or religious sister—was a shorthand symbol of an understanding of community mobilization at home for the war effort. Together with the patriotic volunteers, her place in the public arena activated a discourse of community obligations in war, which made the recurrence of war more imaginable.

No wonder, then, that the dynastic state singled out the wartime nurse for special commendation in ceremonies that were part of its rituals of rule in the *Kaiserreich*. Such expressions of "thankful remembrance" were orchestrated carefully to serve multiple purposes. In 1911, for example, Luise of Baden honored the surviving nurses who "during that glorious but bloody war [of 1870–71] had cared for the wounded and sick soldiers in the Baden homeland *(Heimat)*."[54] The date of the commemoration was chosen to coincide with the celebration of the fortieth anniversary of the founding of the *Reich* on January 18, thus simultaneously evoking the sacred moment of unification that, in her version of the past, formally concluded the "heroic" struggle.

What the volunteer nurse had accomplished was "great" *(gross)*, Luise declared in the public commendation; her work was "serious" *(ernst)* and "unselfish" *(selbstlos)*, the words alone consecrating a set of values through which to speak of women's wartime work. Although appropriated and deployed for dynastic state purposes, the "female" language of care never lost its connection to individual women, whose actions were said to symbolize the sign.[55] Thus, each nurse was sent a portrait of the duke, Frederick I, who had led the Baden troops to victory, and a special reception with the duchess was arranged for later that year. In the official pronouncement, Luise expressed the hope that the "gratitude I feel at the memory of our common experience of forty years ago continues to work to bind the past and the present in mutual trust." This dynast acknowledged readily that memories in common reinforce loyalty.

Indeed, the recipients momentarily were drawn into the dynastic orbit and helped perpetuate its memory through their own. Most professed

---

54. GK, Abt. 69, no. 1174, Erinnerungsgaben an Krankenpflegerinnen und Krankenschwestern die im Krieg 1870–71 die Verwundeten gepflegt haben, zum 18 January 1911. For other commendations, no. 1152, Die Verleihung einen Erinnerungsgabe an Schwester Noloska in Freiburg, 1888, betr., and no. 1155, Die Gewährung einen Auszeichnung an Schwester Xaveria, Oberin des Landesspitals zu Hüfingen, 1888.

55. This important observation contrasts with analyses that define, for example, the artistic "surreal" project as feminine but overlook the contributions of women artists to the movement. This point about "woman" as discursive entity that has little to do with women in the flesh is in Suleiman, *Subversive Intent*, 13–14.

themselves deeply touched by what they called such "noble attentiveness" or the expression of "female official graciousness" *(landesmütterliche Huld)* and, in return, offered their prayers for the dynasty, for Baden itself and its people and for the women's association, which in many cases had acted as intermediary in dispensing the gift. And they used the contact with the dynasty to profess their loyalty, often in graphic form. Take the particular formulation of Emilie Lahr from Illenau.

> It couldn't have been more unexpected and wonderful for me as a German who also has the fortune to be a Badener *(Badisches Landes-kind)* to receive the gracious keepsake. For those like me . . . whom God permitted to experience already in 1866 the blessed efforts of our deceased duke—God rest his soul—for the cause of unification, the happy memory of the German Reich always is tied up with the person of our beloved duke, Frederick I.[56]

As she described it, to receive the portrait was especially meaningful. "For all of us who forty years ago were able to help care for the wounded, it will keep alive and strengthen sentiments of gratitude and joyful enthusiasm."

Others took the opportunity to reassess the nurses' role "in those memorable times," as a Catholic superior in Freiburg expressed it. A number of the sisters in his congregation had been singled out for the honor. He equated their efforts in "nursing the poor, wounded soldiers in the hospitals" with the soldiers themselves. They, too, had taken their lives in their hands. In his schema, the old sisters now were the honored "veterans" *(Veteraninnen),* who had done their "duty." Another wrote about the "conviction" and "joy" at the heart of the women's "service to the fatherland and its wounded soldiers," offering a personal definition of the more abstract ideal of female patriotic sacrifice. One recipient of the honor, Mrs. Anna Sartori, widow of a court purveyor, wrote self-deprecatingly about her "limited strength," which she nonetheless had dedicated to the military hospital in Bruchsal, near Karlsruhe. She was being overly modest, to be sure, for other nurses' memoirs testify to the long hours of difficult hospital work and administration, which required considerable physical strength and inner fortitude. It had taken real conviction to rise above the many obstacles placed by male doctors and staff in the way of women's medical wartime roles.[57]

---

56. GK, Abt. 69, no. 1174, Illenau, January 31, 1911.

57. GK, Abt. 69, no. 1174, K. Meyer, Freiburg, January 21, 1911; Mother Superior Conrada Bilger, Hegner (?), January 28, 1911; Karlsruhe, January 28, 1911. Among the nurses' memoirs, Rosa Behrends-Wirth, *Frauenarbeit im Krieg;* and Mary Olnhausen, *Adventures of Army Nurse.*

Undeniably in 1911, the dispensing of dynastic honors had opened up a space for the expression of a range of emotions around the memories of women's wartime activities. It reconfigured institutional solidarity, linking the state Red Cross leadership, which had researched the names and locations of the surviving nurses, and the local women's associations, often the conduits for the gifts, with the sisters' religious superiors, various lay matrons, and other nurses and their circles. Besides, the visual nature of the gift and its display served as a reminder of women's work in war. Its depiction of the genealogical line anticipated similar configurations in the future.

Direct contact with the *Landesmutter,* too, had reinvigorated the commitment to the values that helped sustain dynastic legitimacy in the present. "With God's will," as one nursing sister from Alsace wrote Luise, "you will continue your charitable efforts for the welfare of the poor, sick, and needy and for the joy and consolation of your loyal [Baden] children." Emilie Lahr mirrored a view found in countless dynastic biographies: the personal devotion of the women of the royal houses "set an example in the present for all to emulate so that, through Christian love of neighbor, the social inequalities can be mitigated and more people will join together in joyful devotion to throne and altar."[58] The shared experience of women's ministerings reaffirmed the common bond of patriotic identity.

Women and War: European Comparisons

This commemorative moment in 1911 reawakened a memory of women's wartime services bound up with the birth of the German nation under dynastic leadership. It fit into a much wider discourse about women and war that, in Germany, had been strengthened and sustained by the full-scale embrace of the organized female nurses and volunteers in German Red Cross service from the 1860s on.

The German model was not adopted by the French, who, early on as we saw, had been skeptical of the principle of voluntarism. Nursing training for war, therefore, remained in private and religious hands and, at best, a bare minimum. But French participation in colonial wars (particularly the Boxer Rebellion in China, 1900–1903), brought home the problem of a shortage of nurses to an increasingly concerned nationalist public. Under government prodding, the Central Committee of the French Red Cross began to coordinate nursing training after 1907; the second Moroccan crisis in 1911 saw, in Hutchinson's words, a "patriotic revival" sweep

---

58. GK, Abt. 69, no. 1174, Sister M. Anysia, Oberbronn in Alsace, and Emilie Lahr, January 31, 1911.

over France.[59] There was a rush to train nurses with an eye to matching the levels of medical support of the Germans, Russians, and Japanese. To avid converts, in the event of war the Red Cross societies would mobilize to provide the necessary support for the nation's struggle. Addressing women in the audience in 1911, for example, Chief Physician Berthier employed a language that was remarkably similar to the German rhetoric.

> In a national war . . . you will respond en masse, you will form an army, an army of charity, in which all the women of France, coming to help and encourage the combatants, will be enrolled under the flag of the Red Cross. But, to best fulfill this role, you must begin now to prepare your mobilization.[60]

According to Margaret Darrow, the "discourse of the War Myth" in France centered on men, masculinity, and male sacrifice. It essentially "left French women immobilized, frozen out of the discussion of the envisioned war."[61] Her point is not that French public opinion was less consumed by the debates about war than was the German nor that French women were more pacifist. Rather, she argues that the political culture of the republican citizen-soldier appears to have placed obstacles to a societal engagement with the image of women and war. But clearly by 1911, the climate had changed dramatically with an emerging patriotic public.

Across the channel, the British drew on several German models of medical war preparation in the 1860s and, again, between 1907 and 1909.[62] In Britain, a process was under way for over half a century, reinforced also by continental and colonial wars—in the 1850s in the Crimea, in the wars of empire in India, Egypt, and the Sudan, by the "senseless deaths" during the Boer War (1899–1902), and by mounting fears of impending war and invasion in the early twentieth century. In the evolving world of people's war, debates in England opened a conspicuous role for women in the figure of the military nurse and, later, the volunteer aide,

---

59. Hutchinson, *Champions of Charity,* 259. The distinctions between patriotic publics in different political cultures require further careful monographic analysis.

60. Ibid., 260. Prior to the outbreak of war in 1914, Germany had trained ten times as many civilian wartime nurses as the French, according to a worried French source.

61. Margaret H. Darrow, "French Volunteer Nursing and the Myth of War Experience of World War I," *American Historical Review* 101, no. 1 (February 1996): 80–106. Darrow focuses on the wartime itself and its subsequent memories; no effort is made to place the volunteer prewar nurse in any wider political or nationalist context, and she slights the Red Cross.

62. Anne Summers, *Angels and Citizens: British Women as Military Nurses, 1854–1914* (London, 1988), 132–42, 247.

active in home defense; as in Germany, well-born women volunteers also took on a host of other types of war-related philanthropy that, indeed, contributed to making civilians "war-minded." In 1912, there were three hundred regular army nurses, three thousand women in nursing service, and over twenty-six thousand females in volunteer aid detachments, coordinated by British Red Cross local chapters, which had been revitalized after 1905.[63]

These new institutional patterns reflected the force of a patriotic public—from various nursing and reserve associations to philanthropic groups to high aristocrats and the female royalty—that pressured for women's inclusion in the work of war and empire. In Britain, however, it was civilians who had pushed their views on an often reluctant Army Medical Department and War Office. Women found "public status" and "political validation" in joining the cause of war. By the turn of the century, according to Anne Summers, "it was as if femininity itself . . . had been militarised, and provided with a new uniform: a nurse's dress, the Red Cross emblem, and war service medal."[64] Furthermore, the calculations of modern national war were encouraging similar institutional forms among the member states of the International Red Cross, including, as the French were well aware, imperial Russia, Austria-Hungary, and Meiji Japan.[65]

In their guise as Red Cross organizations, therefore, women's associations throughout Europe were helping shape the discourse, praxis, and memory of war. The German case was not exceptional. A brief return to the Baden Nurses' Aides League demonstrates the patriotic visions of this volunteer nursing association, emboldened by its memories of women's contributions in the war of 1870–71.

The Baden Nurses' Aides League was anchored squarely in the

---

63. Ibid., 162–66, 211–28, 253. Also, Janet S. K. Watson, "Khaki Girls, VADs, and Tommy's Sisters: Gender and Class in First World War Britain," *International History Review* 19, no. 1 (February 1997): 32–51; and Hutchinson, *Champions of Charity,* 241–53, for the tensions among British private and governmental groups leading to the establishment of the British Red Cross in the early twentieth century.

64. Summers, *Angels and Citizens,* 153, 204.

65. For reference to British reading of women's participation in the Russo-Japanese War, Summers, *Angels and Citizens,* 246–47; for Russia, Lindenmeyr, *Poverty Not a Vice,* 125–26, 203–17, for women, female royalty and the Russian Red Cross. Also, Olive Checkland, *Humanitarianism and the Emperor's Japan, 1877–1977* (New York, 1994). The primary sources reflect this flow of information. For example, GK, Abt. 69, no. 1133, *Jahresbericht des Helferinnenbundes vom Roten Kreuz, 1909–1910,* a retrospective presentation of women in the Japanese wars and in Red Cross work in Manchuria.

nationalist memory of 1870–71, a memory that it shared with others.[66] This historic moment became, so to speak, the Ptolemaic center of an activist female patriotic imagination around which the events of the past and the ever-changing present were made to revolve. The aides' diploma served vividly to remind each graduating class of the heroic past, as did the league's stationery: inside circular rose branches were the words "Memorial tablet of the Baden Women's Associations—under the Protection of Her Majesty the duchess Luise. Accomplishments: 1870–71. Care for 42,000 wounded in a total of 500,000 days in 60 hospitals by 1,000 Sisters and Aides."[67]

The league festivals and celebrations continuously re-created this particular historic "universe," which, in turn, was reinforced by the ongoing practical measures taken to satisfy the civilian medical war mobilization orders. In 1911, the passage of forty years since the end of the war also prompted league leaders to offer a historic reconstruction of volunteer nursing, just as it had encouraged the duchess to commend the living nurses from the earlier era. The speaker at the festive meeting, General Limberger, presented a linear argument that focused on 1870; it set 1866 as a prelude *(Vorspiel)* to the great achievements four years later, which, in his analysis, continued to inspire and justify the training of nurses and volunteer aides in the present.[68] It appears that a precise formulation of women's wartime services in the past remained essential to the construction of their future wartime roles. The appeal to a historical memory was a way to mute critics and counter deep ambivalences about women's public roles that undeniably were part of the wider culture. Besides, by redeploying the patriotic narrative, the women's organizations were able to reconnect to the power, prestige, and protection of their *Landesmutter.* The memory of shared activities once again reinforced the ties between them and the logic of the connection also projected the past directly onto the future.

This strategy also was women's own formulation. The league president, Julia Limberger, gave an address at a festival on December 3, 1912,

---

66. Imperial officials and military leaders devised military strategy with reference to 1870–71, but the lessons were complicated, and many different historical metaphors characterized their arguments. They embraced a blitzkrieg strategy (a victory through limited cabinet war) yet acknowledged the possibility of a longer struggle (a people's war), which could take years. Useful here is Stig Förster, "Dreams and Nightmares: German Military Leadership and the Images of Future Warfare, 1871–1914," in Boemeke, Chickering, and Förster, *Anticipating Total War,* 343–76.

67. GK, Abt. 69, no. 1117, Mitteilungen, "Ausbildung von Helferinnen vom Roten Kreuz," contains copies of the stationery and diploma.

68. GK, Abt. 69, no. 1133, Der Helferinnenbund, Jahresversammlung, May 17, 1911, and also no. 1134, Monatsversammlung, February 14, 1912.

the birthday of Duchess Luise. Hers, too, was a narrative of women's volunteer medical services in Baden during the war of 1870. As she wrote the duchess, the "choice of themes seems to me particularly appropriate, given the seriousness of the times *(ernste Zeit)* today and all the more so since the whole history of medical voluntarism works in such an exemplary *(vorbildlich)* fashion."[69] Much of her talk was spent describing the activities of Luise herself in 1870, "moving from city to city with loving care to oversee the hospitals, console the sick and the wounded." But some of the glory must have spilled over to the women's own war work going on simultaneously. And the speech stressed those popular celebrations with a "mass appeal," as, for example, the gathering when word spread of the victory at Wörth.

Julia Limberger had a didactic purpose in mind. "God preserve us from the horrors of war," she said, employing a sentiment that prefaced many statements by those convinced of war's inevitability. "If war comes, however, we will be sure that, as in the past, German women will be willing to join the sacrifice. As in the year 1870, women in our Baden homeland will follow the call of our noble protector."

This mobilization of memory served to contain a sense of unease, which arguably had influenced the choice of the rhetoric: the optimistic predictions about Baden women's future behavior in the face of war, in fact, masked deep uncertainty. At the time, patriotic groups were embroiled in a serious gender crisis over women's place in the conservative nationalist community, as the next chapter demonstrates. On the one hand, they confronted new political expectations among their female constituency. On the other, they feared their own rhetoric, which had dismissed the international pacifist movement as feminine and "dangerously" humanitarian, raising unsettling questions about women's proclivities for peace. Besides, there was competition from a small but vocal pacifist movement in Germany and a growing antimilitarism on the left, which spoke another language of gender, motherhood, and care.[70]

Despite the opposition, the myths and commemorations in the patriotic war culture were working to perpetuate war sentiments through their tales of individual heroism and glory. They reverberated through the culture in multiple, overlapping forms and styles, deepening the cognitive appeal by their emotional force and power. To the extent that they become part of the psychological processes of identity-formation, their effect is

---

69. GK, Abt. 69, no. 1134, "Aus der freiw. Hilfstätigkeit im Grossherzogtum Baden im Kriege 1870–71," and letter, December 5, 1912.

70. Roger Chickering, *Imperial Germany and a World without War: The Peace Movement and German Society, 1892–1914* (Princeton, N.J., 1975). For a discussion of how to assess the extent of antiwar sentiments among the population, Dülffer, "Einleitung," 9–19.

magnified. Indeed, they are an added ingredient in the creation of patriotic subjectivities, another layer affecting how people think about themselves as gendered beings. In the German national imagination, war myths were rooted in definitions fundamental to gender identity.

Historical writing to date has analyzed this process principally in terms of masculinity. There was, indeed, a powerful link between assumptions about manhood and war: the battles of war were the ultimate test of masculinity. In practice, the soldiers and veterans of Germany's wars never banished the horrors of war from their memories, although the wider patriotic culture, as we have seen, worked to sanitize war and turn it into a splendid collective memory. The gender expectations of the war myths, however, served to transcend its terror in the ultimate affirmation of the proof of manhood. As we have seen, Red Cross organizational strategy sought to tap these sentiments. These notions were so powerful that in the 1890s, according to Thomas Rohkrämer, Germany's veterans and the reservists—those who had served in the army but had not fought a war—divided over the memory of 1870.[71] Both could agree that the ultimate test of masculinity was war. But in the main, veterans continued to identify with the specific battles in which they had proven their "manhood" under fire, whereas the reservists turned to the future, anticipating "war" with a passion. Only then would they be able to demonstrate to themselves and others the solidity of their own masculinity.[72] Men could be passionate about war because they had accepted it as an act of manhood, an affirmation of the self that, in the daily life of the patriotic culture, was reinforced by the comradeship of festive meals and the militarized play at drills and games.

But these myths echoed in other gendered forms as well. As little as the soldiers did wartime nurses banish the horrors of war from their memories. They continued to be haunted by the countless numbers of "boys who go off [to the front] and die or return and are cripples for life." In their memories, the soldiers remained "shattered human being[s]," their wounds "atrocious," the deaths painful: "they die[d] slowly, alone . . . although now and then one [was] 'healed' and sent home." The wartime realities, indeed, had turned the war myth on its head and made a mockery of any "heroism mania," as Henriette Riemann, a Red Cross nurse on the west-

---

71. Rohkrämer, "Heroes and Would-Be Heroes," 211–14.

72. For gendered war notions manifest already in the Napoleonic era, Karen Hagemann, "Heldenmütter, Kriegerbraute und Amazonen. Entwurfe 'patriotischer' Weiblichkeit zur Zeit der Freiheitskriege," in *Militär und Gesellschaft im 19. und 20. Jahrhundert,* ed. Ute Frevert (Stuttgart, 1997), 174–200, and also her "Of Manly Valor." See as well Derek S. Linton, "Preparing German Youth for War," in Boemeke, Chickering, and Förster, *Anticipating Total War,* 167–87.

ern front, bitterly reflected.[73] Her premium was on female self-control and forbearance, however, and the reports of the Baden's Nurses' Aides League prior to the Great War may offer an added insight to the shaping of memory and speech in this terrain of civilian life.

Direct parallels exist between the sexualized construction of male and female patriotic identities. As I have shown, nurses' aides acquired one important identity in civilian war work, as did the women volunteers in philanthropic activities in a public arena that had been named "patriotic." Theirs, too, was an activist posture, reflecting abstract notions about patriotic duty mixed in with religious beliefs and self-understandings of femininity. At league meetings, the members were encouraged to talk about their work experiences in the hospitals, at charitable institutions, in the poorhouses, and in private clinics. While the evidence is sketchy, in these descriptions the German women learned to veil the obvious—pain, sickness, and sadness. In the words of one report, "from the applause" it is clear that the "necessary discretion had been maintained."[74] Part of belonging to the group—the constitution of female comradeship and solidarity as volunteer nurses—was learning in a public forum to mask the feelings and emotions aroused by the illnesses and needs of others. In this group socialization of the educated, elite women volunteers in Baden, the premium was on self-control so that in a context of patriotic ecstasy the woman also transcended for the moment the experiences of personal sadness and horror.

The mobilization of the memories of war was an important ingredient in the political culture of dynastic patriotism, activated in the presence of the *Landesmutter* as well as by public banquets and state awards and commendations. Through distinct cultural performances, it raised to public prominence men's and women's sacrifices for the nation, singling out veterans, nurses, and patriotic volunteers as palpable symbols of national solidarity, even if social memory could not always overcome the particular experience of gender, generational, or class differences. Such public acknowledgments kept alive the vision of past wars, themselves deemed "unforgettable," just as the peacetime rhetoric deemed women's war ser-

---

73. Riemann, *Schwester der Vierten Armee,* 79, 98, 257. To Riemann, "heroic" sentiments were possible only among the families of soldiers back home, reinforced by the work of the press and welfare/philanthropic institutions. These nurses' memoirs are a fascinating though largely untapped source: they combine self-effacement and doubt with feminist wit and an anger at the massive suffering and pain of war. See, in addition, Helene Mierisch, *Kamerad Schwester, 1914–1918* (Leipzig, 1934); and Anne-Marie Wenzel, *Deutsche Kraft in Fesseln: Fünf Jahre deutscher Schwesterndienst in Sibirien (1916–1921)* (Potsdam, 1931).

74. GK, Abt. 69, no. 1133, Jahresversammlung, May 17, 1911

vices "unforgettable," promising them a permanent place in the flow of collective memory. But the gender alliance at the base of patriotic praxis proved volatile. The next chapter explores a gender crisis in the patriotic community that surfaced at a moment of national commemoration in 1913. The crisis, indeed, spoke of deep fissures in the dynastic system itself. The eventual overthrow of the monarchy under the strains of war, mass deprivation, and enormous casualties provided a new setting for social memory, one that, however, destroyed the repeated promises to sanctify women's patriotic sacrifices.

CHAPTER 7

Testing Patriotic Alliances, 1913–1916

In the late *Kaiserreich,* veterans' and soldiers' gravesites offered ample opportunity for nationalist musings. The centrality of the dead soldier's sacrifice in the national imagination elevated cemeteries to sites of official patriotic celebration and mourning. Historians such as George Mosse interested in the distinctive "styles" of German nationalist thought see cemeteries as increasingly important spaces in shaping the "myths" about war in the long nineteenth century.[1] But cemeteries also were contested places in the *Kaiserreich,* a point overlooked in the totalizing myths of nationalism too often reproduced by its historians. Celebrations over soldiers' graves were not a monopoly of the nationalist Right. There were the graves of "heroes" singled out for other memory, those who fell in March 1848 defending "democracy," for example, and honored later by the socialists in the Wilhelmine era.

The war dead played into contemporary political struggle over definitions of the German nation that took on added urgency in the crisis years between 1912 and 1914, as war seemed to loom on the horizon. Neither the patriotic Right nor the socialist Left was immune from public taunting. On March 12, 1914, for example, the marble platform on the Kaiser Frederick memorial in Charlottenburg was painted red and inscribed with the words "red week," eliciting a frantic police search for the culprits. A few days later, against the backdrop of thousands of socialists honoring those buried in Friedrichhain who had died in March 1848, a veteran's association in a small cemetery laid two bouquets of flower decorated with black-and-white ribbons on the graves of soldiers of 1848, appropriating their sacrifice for Crown and fatherland.[2]

---

1. Mosse, *Fallen Soldiers,* 44–50.
2. *KZ,* no. 119, March 12, 1914, and no. 130, March 18, 1914.

Cemeteries and Nationalist Doubts

Patriotic reflections around military gravesites revealed deep uncertainties in the nationalist community itself, even as they worked to reproduce legitimate authority. These ambiguities also have been largely ignored in the literature on the cultural forms of national identity. In July 1913, for example, the *Kreuz-Zeitung* printed the ruminations of Karl Ruhkopf about an "old veteran's grave" (that of Karl von Reitenkamp, who had died in 1868) in his hometown.[3] In the narrative, Ruhkopf describes how as a boy he often walked through the cemetery and noticed a gravestone emblazoned with the patriotic inscription, "Whoever fights for the right cause will win" *(wer recht kämpfet der wird gekrönt)*. The boy fantasizes that the veteran, a fighter in the Wars of Liberation, came from old aristocratic lineage, as the name implies; his sacrifice, indeed, had been crowned in the "glorious years of 1870–71," which led to one, single, and free fatherland. In Ruhkopf's words, German unity promised "new and splendid rights for princes and people *(Fürsten und Völker)*, legal guarantees for all the social orders . . . [and] laws tearing down the restrictive custombarriers." The new state "also did not forget its poor and dejected and sought to protect them from misery and hunger when they became ill, ailing, or old." This description in many ways reproduced the official nationalist imagination that drew together elements of a conservative legitimacy, with its links between dynasty and folk, the rule of law, and care for the poor and the downtrodden.

But then, Ruhkopf says, "I went from my fantasy to daily life *(Alltag)*." An inquiry with his mother revealed that von Reitenkamp was not a nobleman but an ordinary man, indeed a petty *Dienstmann,* a "poor man of the people" *(ein armer kleiner Mann)*. This "old soldier" had lived a "hard, impoverished, and depressed life," which did not diminish the author's admiration, since heroes come in many forms. He had received few accolades in life, however, although he was honored in 1863 at the fiftieth-anniversary celebration of the battle of Leipzig. His comrades and friends provided the tombstone because his widow could not afford it. Somewhat bitterly, Ruhkopf notes that "when she was buried next to him . . . perhaps to save money the *von* was left off her name." But the point of the story was in the ending. On a recent trip back home, Ruhkopf found that the gravestone had disappeared; according to the church supervisor, it had been sold to make room for other burials and now, presumably, had found a spot in another edifice; it was serving alien functions.

Ruhkopf pointedly drew a contrast to other markers that had been

---

3. *KZ*, second supplement to no. 311, July 6, 1913, "Ein Altes Veteranengrab."

deemed more culturally and historically significant; they still were standing. The author expressed anger at this "forgetting." In the *Alltag,* the
existing order did not preserve the memory of those poor people who had
fought for it; by extension, its social claims for the "the poor, the ailing,
and the sick" were ringing hollow as well. Although he never directed his
critique to the political realm as such, Ruhkopf's message expressed deep
unease with the contemporary evolution of daily life. His metaphors were
religious, envisioning a retreat toward the eternal against the uncertain
progress of earthly life. "With God, each fighter has his memorial that no
church administration can remove and no movement of time can destroy."
The "paradoxes of time" had demonstrated to Ruhkopf the ruin of things;
in mundane terms, time threatened the national foundation. The edifice
was less solid than its appearance, for its underlying promises were not
always honored.[4]

Ruhkopf's morality tale was not an isolated case. Similar concerns
had surfaced earlier about a burial site of those who had died in the hospitals from their wounds in the battles of Gross-Beeren and Dennewitz. One
account was written by a former gymnast in 1904; it, too, expressed anger
that the graves of "these brave soldiers" now were threatened by a proposed expansion of a military cemetery; the author did not understand
why this "holy place" for 2,382 "soldiers on watch" could not be
redesigned and preserved.[5] As young gymnast, he, personally, had joined
the celebrations at the graves, which had been an annual gathering until
1863. The commemorations had kept alive the memory of the "sacrificial
work" of the doctors, many of them volunteers who later went into private
practice in the city, as well as of the women from "the most reputable"
Berlin families. Those crisis years had spurred on "rich and poor, old and
young" to provide the necessary "aid through deeds" *(werktätige Hülfe).*
The gymnast's recollections was remarkably similar to the official "histories" of gendered patriotic service for the nation in danger. But, now, it
appeared that one part of the nationalist community was encroaching on
the space of another. Even burial places could fall into ruin, and the
threatened change disrupted nationalist solidarity; it forced a disturbing
contrast between the internalized ideals of the national community and the
situation in daily life, where heroes were expendable and familiar land-

---

4. For the paradoxes of time as duration, Peter Hughes, "Ruins of Time: Estranging
History and Ethnology in the Enlightenment and After," in Hughes and Trautmann, *Time,*
276; also, Rudy J. Koshar, "Building Pasts: Historic Preservation and Identity in Twentieth-
Century Germany," in *Commemorations: The Politics of National Identity,* ed. John R. Gillis
(Princeton, N.J., 1994), 222–23.

5. *KZ,* no. 138, March 22, 1904, "Die Ruhestätte der in den Jahren 1813 und 1814 in
den hiesigen Lazaretten an ihren Wunden verstorbenen Soldaten."

scapes redesigned. This tension, perhaps, accounted for the deep anguish about the war sacrifices expressed by the aging gymnast: "If these war gravesites could speak, they would tell the most shocking tales of human misery." The gymnast had found solace in the memory of care but also intense resentment at the ease at which the nation seemed to be changing its priorities.

Commemoration and Division: 1913

The patriotic edifice, indeed, was exhibiting cracks from the inside. New and disturbing fault lines emerged in 1913, paradoxically during the months of official nationalist celebration of the one hundredth anniversary of the wars against Napoleon. From the perspective of the imperial center, the centenary seemed to open multiple vistas for patriotic remembrance, opportunities to reconnect the present age with past glories of military victories against the French through collective sacrifices. In different commemorative events throughout the year, official nationalists sought to proclaim a unity via a connection with a time when, it was maintained, the dynasty and its people were one in common "national" purpose.[6]

The focus on "Germany's" earlier wars, furthermore, reactivated contemporary reminiscences about peace, demonstrating the fundamental interconnection between images of war and images of peace in official nationalist thought. The celebratory rhetoric universally stressed the long reign of peace under the present kaiser, who, the argument went, had become "the protector *(Schirmherr)* of peace." But it simultaneously warned those who had benefited from the blessings of peace to be ready for the "storm." *Kreuz-Zeitung* reports pointedly drew the historic celebrations into the heart of contemporary political debates over national defense and military expenditures. In circular fashion, one author affirmed peace as a laudatory goal but made it contingent on "large sacrifices" in the form of increased funding for military purposes.[7]

The momentum of celebration was not lost on the Reichstag, which, during the spring months, was debating the largest increase in military

---

6. For an analysis of the commemoration that, however, misses the gender implications and replicates the major political divisions between the bourgeoisie and the working classes, Wolfram Siemann, "Krieg und Frieden in historischen Gedenkfeiern des Jahres 1913," in Düding, Friedemann, and Münch, *Öffentliche Festkultur,* 298–320. For an assessment of the historic memory of war in shaping dispositions to go to war, Burkhardt, "Kriegsgrund Geschichte?" His also is an exclusively male analysis.

7. For the peace/war continuum, *KZ,* no. 44, January 27, 1913, and no. 90, February 22, 1913.

expenditures in imperial German history. Officials timed the commemorative celebrations to influence the Reichstag deliberations: activities peaked between March and June to coincide with the debates on the military bill. The kaiser's message in February in Königsberg made the connection explicit. He stated in no uncertain terms that "if strengthening the foundation of universal conscription proves necessary, I have no doubt . . . that the German people will be ready and willing to take on further personal sacrifices, following the honorable example of our forefathers."[8] This paean to individual and collective sacrifice was the most repeated refrain in the official nationalist rhetoric of remembrance that year. Once again, the official strategy used commemoration to link a narrative of the past to a desired course of future action.

Hosting far-flung nationalist celebrations over numerous months could not guarantee a harmonious memory. At a minimum, the patriotic groups already predisposed became temporary coauthors in the official narrative, following its topographic and historic maps, which led back to the dynastic houses. In the volatile political climate of 1913, however, some of these same male "patriots" might have harbored considerable antagonism toward the imperial government and the person of the kaiser.[9] The power of ceremonies, as I show in this study, lies in their ability to produce sentiments of solidarity in the absence of consensus; but the danger resides as well in the spaces commemorations open for alternative memories and public pronouncements.

Official nationalists could not monopolize the lessons of the past; in 1913, other groups celebrated alongside, as did, for example, the reform feminists, who had their own memory and a different logic. In ceremonies on March 10 in Berlin, for example, the League of German Women's Associations (Bund deutscher Frauenvereine) centered its messages around "freedom." While fundamentally patriotic and nationalist, the moderate feminist festival had little to do with the dynastic narrative. It identified women with the emancipatory struggle of the Prussian bourgeoisie in 1813. Leaders such as Gertrud Bäumer linked the great historic "struggles for freedom" to a future that would bring women "freedom" as

---

8. In Siemann, "Krieg und Frieden," 313.

9. Eley, *Reshaping the German Right,* 316–21, analyzes the emergence of a national opposition against the government in 1913, as does Chickering, *We Men Who Feel,* 277–91. The division also is expressed in alternative memory. Instead of celebrating the one hundredth anniversary, some articles in the conservative *Kreuz-Zeitung* remembered events fifty years earlier and, thus, Bismarck's conflict with democratic groups in the Prussian constitutional crisis. For example, *KZ,* second supplement to no. 147, March 30, 1913, "Vor fünzig Jahren."

well, defined less in political terms than as the "free autonomous development of individual capacities."[10]

But opposition could threaten the fundamental basis of conservative
legitimacy as well. Many Social Democrats were active that year organizing street demonstrations against the authority behind the nationalist celebrations. They called on their ranks, for example, to participate in five
mass gatherings in Leipzig to protest the so-called patriotic "hubbub"
around the building of a new monument to the "battle of nations" (*Völkerschlacht*) in 1813. Workers marched with placards that warned,
"Against the Falsification of History!" and "Against Hurrah Patriotism."
These protests so angered the *Kreuz-Zeitung* that an article in October
called for a "new, true *Völkerschlacht* against the Social Democrats."[11]

Socialists intensified their antimilitarist agitation among the new
army recruits in September 1913, and they brought their different memories right into local politics. When several city officials in Schöneberg
(Berlin), for example, proposed to increase public funds for veterans in
honor of the anniversary date of the Prussian king's call "to my people"
(February 1813) the Social Democratic delegate Bernstein demanded the
amount be doubled. During the ensuring debate, he argued that whereas
socialists "oppose war" in principle, the soldiers who had fought for the
fatherland should receive adequate levels of support as a right. With this
claim, Bernstein challenged the conservative social state at its core, which
skirted a language of "rights." And he provided an alternative interpretation of the historic events of 1813. Circumstances had "forced" the king to
turn to the people, he asserted, claiming that "the facts" authenticated his
version of history. In his narrative, the political and military reformers
Yorck, Stein, and Scharnhorst were more appropriate figures for veneration. City officials decisively rejected Bernstein's view; such talk "belonged

---

10. Gertrud Bäumer, "Vom politischen Frauengeist des Jahres 1813," *Die Frau*, vol. 20,
no. 6, March 1913, 321–29; also, "Frauenbewegung und Nationalbewusstsein," *Die Frau*, no.
7, April 1913, 387–94, and in the same paper, "1813–1913," a poem, 385–86. For Bäumer, the
memory of the wars was proof of women's contributions to nationalist causes and power.
Also, *KZ*, no. 116, March 10, 1913, "Die Jahrhundertfeier der Frauen," an interesting report
in which the speech of the male speaker Dr. Harnack was reprinted but not Bäumer's.

11. For the socialist view from the conservative perspective, *KZ*, no. 485, October 16,
1913 (protests in Leipzig). Throughout the year, *Gleichheit*, the paper of the Social Democratic women's movement, followed events with a sardonic tone, drawing important lessons
for its reading public: the first linked the celebrations to a renewed militarism in the culture,
and the second offered a relentless critique of the official notion of patriotic "sacrifice." See
Gleichheit, vol. 23, no. 14, April 2, 1913, 219–20; no. 15, April 16, 1913, 226–28; no. 21, July
9, 1913, 331–33. Undeniably, the terms of the debate were set by the official nationalist celebration, itself placed against the backdrop of struggle over military expenditures in the
Reichstag.

more at a workers' rally than a city council meeting, which was monarchical by persuasion."[12] But Bernstein had made his point, one that even found its way into the conservative press. Indeed, the socialist opposition had turned the celebration on its head to force a radical redefinition of the caring state.

For students of the *Kaiserreich,* the particular physiognomy of the political divisions in 1913 comes as no surprise. Historians long have identified the last years before the war as a time of serious political crisis and stalemate. Carl Schorske's early study of German social democracy drew attention to generalized feelings of malaise after 1912, a *Reichsverdrossenheit,* which affected the political Left as it did the Right. Subsequent historians have looked at this malaise from the perspective of coalition-building and interest-group politics and tied it to broader structural tensions between socioeconomic modernization and continued authoritarian state power. For the ruling groups, coalition building became a complicated process of anti-socialist alliances to stave off democratic reform. Indeed, one influential line of analysis concludes that the ensuing domestic political stalemate propelled imperial German officials into war in 1914.[13]

Wolfram Siemann inserts the nationalist centenary celebration into this simplified view of polarized politics. In his analysis, the ceremonies pitted a homogeneous nationalist community against the progressive groups of Social Democrats, left liberals, and bourgeois feminists. The cultural conflict, however, exhibits more complicated divides. Outside the formal sphere of party politics, the gender antagonisms, which had been festering in the patriotic community itself, could no longer be contained. The debates laid bare the limits of the official nationalist rhetoric of sacrifice.

The Patriotic Crisis of Gender

The 1913 celebrations offered contemporaries a historic reconstruction of an earlier era of war and national regeneration. Significantly, they painted a "national" memory of "people's" involvement in war. The tales touched on the lives of the volunteer soldier and the low-level officer, of the old widow and the young seamstress, who gave their time and energy to the

---

12. *KZ,* no. 90, February 22, 1913, and first supplement to no. 455, September 28, 1913.

13. The literature is legion but among many possible sources, Carl E. Schorske, *German Social Democracy, 1905–1917: The Development of the Great Schism* (New York, 1955), 224. It was a central argument in Fritz Fischer's analysis of the crisis years leading to World War I, *Griff nach der Weltmacht* (Düsseldorf, 1961). For more recent analysis, Wehler, *Deutsche Gesellschaftsgeschichte,* 3:1152ff.; Nipperdey, *Deutsche Geschichte, 1866–1918,* 2:729–57.

war effort. In addition, there were the ladies who turned in their jewelry "for iron" and children who contributed their savings of pennies. The willingness of the whole population to sacrifice for the war and the royal figures who inspired the domestic mobilization (as Queen Luise and her contemporary, the Prussian Princess Marianne, or the living symbol Luise of Baden) were woven together in the dynastic narrative of nationalist cohesion. It told a story of collectivities of people under dynastic tutelage, contributing to the survival of the nation in wartime.

Though hardly new, the gendered narrative was performed, displayed, and exhibited in multiple forms throughout the year. For example, a memorial site opened in Berlin on the Jägerstrasse in January 1913. The old renovated house one hundred years earlier had been the central depot where Berliners came to donate their personal belongings for the cause of war. On display were the artifacts of civilian war sacrifices and the patriotic tropes that sought to define their meaning.[14]

This exhibition, and others going on simultaneously in Breslau and Königsberg, reinserted into popular consciousness many historic descriptions of the people's sacrifices during the Napoleonic wars. Reproduced, for example, was the slogan to "turn gold into iron" (*Gold gab ich für Eisen*) for the jewelry that had been donated for the war effort. By official accounts in Berlin alone, the populace turned in 160,000 gold rings and bracelets. There also was the image of the women who cut off their hair and gave it as a valuable natural resource for the war effort. In one case, the hair alone was said to be worth 196 thaler. But in the highly charged atmosphere of sexual tensions in 1913, these images were provocative and ambiguous. The cutting of hair, perhaps, symbolized voluntary sacrifice, but it spoke equally of submission to the state. It inverted the biblical story of Samson, yet simultaneously acknowledged the state's need for women's services in the calculations around "the people in arms." At the time, too, gold was telling multiple stories on artists' canvases and murals: of time-honored patriotic sacrifices but also of "modern" women's sexual hunger and false, unnatural pursuits (of autonomy and independence) uncontrolled by maternal, caring roles. Significantly, these same historic themes and images later became the central artistic designs in German Red Cross solicitation posters during the First World War, as figure 4 demonstrates.[15]

---

14. *KZ,* supplement to no. 17, January 11, 1913.

15. For the exhibits in Königsberg, *KZ,* no. 61, February 6, 1913, and supplement to no. 65, February 8, 1913; for tensions in Breslau, no. 103, March 2, 1913, which involved efforts by radical right-wing groups to close down a play of Gerhart Hauptmann produced by Max Reinhardt. For hair and body as symbol, Firth, *Symbols,* 262–98; and Douglas, *Implicit Meanings,* 83–89. For gold in the misogynist imagination of Gustav Klempt or Fritz Erler, see Dijkstra, *Idols of Perversity,* 366–71.

Fig. 4. Red Cross solicitation of women's hair. (Courtesy Hoover Institution Archives, Poster Collection, GE 190.)

Through a highly stylized yet erotic figurehead, the artist calls on women to place their prized yet replenishable resource at the service of the state, as they had done in earlier times. The hair was used for industrial purposes, for example to strengthen the driving belts on machinery, or for other thickening requirements.

Commemorating a narrative of community cohesion in war unleashed a full-blown gender crisis in conservative patriotic circles. In part, the rhetoric of many conservative nationalists returned to haunt them. The widely derogatory usages of *feminine* as a term for pacifists or as a synonym for the weaknesses and degeneracies of the age suddenly made the question of women's loyalties in war seem problematical. This explains the rush to memory, but, for some commentators, women's patriotic roles became partly unmoored from their dynastic anchor in civic activism. They were domesticated and enclosed in the language of private, behind-the-scenes *(stillen)* acts. This clash was long in the making, reflecting a subtle but significant change in authority from the aristocratic model of the *Landesmutter* to the private hearth and familial gender roles. While both positions reproduced essentialist notions of women's nature and character, the stage of entry into national life was strikingly different.

Compounding the debate were new political agendas among women whose public skills and reputations reflected their voluntary services for the state. Now, they sought partial entry into "formal" political life and, thus, were drawn into a confrontation with party politics and feminism. To be sure, the world of patriotic philanthropy continued to integrate its privileged women volunteers with no reference to "formal" politics and mask the power implications of the particular relief and welfare structure behind notions of disinterest and the common good. But after 1908, many prominent female volunteers and activists entered politics under the new laws of association that finally opened party life to women after over a half century of exclusion. In 1913, even the Conservative Party faced the formation of a Union of Conservative Women (Vereinigung konservativer Frauen).[16] This explicit step to party politics expanded the borders of the patriotic public, intensifying debates about the relationship between duties and rights at the basis of monarchical legitimacy.

The gender tensions unfolded in the public limelight, partly in the pages of the *Kreuz-Zeitung*. The paper was designated the political organ

---

16. For background on this move by Conservative women, Raffael Scheck, "German Conservatism and Female Political Activism in the early Weimar Republic," *German History* 15, no. 1 (1997): 34–55; and Baumann, *Protestantismus und Frauenemanzipation,* 216–26. For the Conservative constituents, James Retallack, "The Road to Philippi: The Conservative Party and Bethmann Hollweg's 'Politics of the Diagonal,' 1909–14," in Jones and Retallack, *Reform, Reaction, and Resistance,* 274–75.

of the Union of Conservative Women. It was as if the cacophony of patriotic commemoration added to the disquieting questions about the present. While there were almost as many solutions as distinct voices, most agreed with the characterization given by Countess Selma von der Gröben at the centenary celebration hosted by the German Protestant Women's League in Hanover in May 1913: "we live once again in grave times."[17] The parallel with the war clamor one hundred years earlier seemed compelling.

But even a retreat into gender stereotypes failed to square the circle. At stake for the women and men on the right, according to a lead article, "War and Women," in April, was the solidity of the "male war instinct" as a fundamental basis of national life. A secondary-school teacher in Kiel was even more direct; in his view, the prerequisite for the existence and flowering of the nation was an "army of manly warriors" who perfected a "masculine bravery that scorned the fear of death," a sentiment he called "primitive masculinity" and identified as necessary for all free peoples. Both authors, however, feared "atrophy" *(verkümmern)* in the "fanatical war" waged on masculine strength by the forces of women's emancipation and their corollary, cosmopolitan and international thinking. Other voices sought the explanation for men's collective identity and certainty of national purpose in the common bonds that had been forged during military service. In contrast, "we women stand apart from this path."[18]

Whatever the perspective, most of the contributors to the *Kreuz-Zeitung* debate thought in polarized terms that fed the crisis: a reified definition of manhood simply drove home insecurities about womanhood at a time of perceived national emergency. Indeed, those conservatives who entered the public debate dismissed as dangerous the "fantasies" of the women's movement and the peace movement, elided in the analysis; both represented "weakness," "self-indulgence," and "narrow-mindedness."[19] If men were warlike by nature, what was women's instinctive attitude toward war and patriotic duty?

The debate about women and patriotism in the Conservative press divided into several distinct, if interconnected, parts. It reflected considerable uncertainty about men's and women's "nature," the self-confident claim to natural male war-instincts not withstanding. And it demonstrated the limits of dynastic authorization, even for many who identified with the monarchical state.

---

17. *KZ,* supplement to no. 229, May 20, 1913, "Ein Mahnruf an die deutschen Frauen."

18. *KZ,* no. 167, April 11, 1913, "Der Krieg und die Frauen"; no. 244, May 28, 1913, "Frauenbewegung und Antimilitarismus"; no. 44, January 27, 1913, "Ein Wort an die deutschen Frauen."

19. *KZ,* May 28, 1913, also no. 293, June 26, 1913, "Zur Frauenfrage."

Most of the women contributors to the *Kreuz-Zeitung* advanced a didactic solution. Some, however, sketched a model of patriotic motherhood anchored in women's domestic roles as educators of their children. For them, patriotism, arguably, was a learned identity that was shaped in the "quiet routines of the home" and in the daily practices of motherly love. On the kaiser's birthday, for example, one author contrasted this "quiet" work in the home with the insufficiency of dynastic rituals: "To be sure, all the external pomp of a military parade dazzles the child, but just as quickly . . . it is forgotten" unless patriotic values are planted and nourished in his heart from earliest childhood. The monarchy was not absent from discussion, however; its narrative provided the educational content. Already in the child's room, "The mother sits and tells of Queen Luise and of the old kaiser . . . and, so, the love of the dynastic house" grows in the child's breast.[20]

The setting framed the argument purely in terms of domesticity, however; a proper gender division somehow would insure the warlike character of German men who, in the author's stretch of the imagination, in wartime would be supported by women's sacrifices at home. The structure of the argument demonstrates the pervasive appeal of normative "bourgeois" values that, in this line of development, supplanted the older patriotic "religion" of the deed. Equally significant was the absence of any claim to improve women's access to education, although, admittedly, the immediate debate was limited in scope to issues around war. Yet, in contrast to most of the women contributors to the conservative press, German reform feminists used the same arguments of women's didactic maternal roles to press for significant educational and social change favorable to women's lives.[21]

A number of articles, to be sure, acknowledged the time-honored place of women's patriotic philanthropy in wartime. Looking back at the Wars of Liberation, several authors claimed that the role of nurse and attendant was the most visible of women's wartime contributions early in the century, kept alive later by those who had joined the Red Cross in its valuable work of serving "humanity and the fatherland," simultaneously. For others, voluntary charity was placed simply alongside gainful employment or time devoted to associational life, sport, or travel. These were activities of the "modern" woman, but ones too often lived at the expense of her role of mother and wife—and, thus, ultimately of the patriotic

---

20. *KZ*, no. 44, January 27, 1913.

21. Helene Lange, *Die Frauenbewegung in ihren modernen Problemen* (Leipzig, 1924). For a historical assessment, James Albisetti, *Schooling German Girls and Women: Secondary and Higher Education in the Nineteenth Century* (Princeton, N.J., 1988); and Allen, *Feminism and Motherhood*, 95–131.

benefits and contributions of motherhood. In the debate, many roads, indeed, seemed to lead back to the domestic sphere, for it was here that women most profoundly influenced "public life." As the lead article in April put it, "the willingness to go to war" was a direct product of the sentiment of love of fatherland. This passion spread most naturally from mother to child: "Children must imbibe the love of the fatherland with their mothers' milk." Despite the rhetorical flourishes, however, the process of creating patriotic identities in family life was left vague, and the predicted outcome was only an affirmation, a testimony of faith. In the final analysis, the fatherland could count on the "conviction *(Gesinnung)* of its women and the deeds of its men."[22]

A group of articulate conservative voices had moved away from the philanthropic imperative that placed the formation of women's patriotic identity in a set of voluntary actions in civic life. In their reformulation, patriotism became instinctual, located essentially in the routines of family life and childrearing. This revision, indeed, dampened the agency of the patriotic public sphere.[23]

The conservative reliance on "faith" reflected a second line of argument that appeared in the debate. This line was historical, drawing the "lessons" of the past from the concrete examples of its "great men" or, to be more precise, the "great women" who had inspired patriotic deeds and devoted their lives to the fatherland in wartime. High on the list of "women worthies" were, of course, queens and princesses of the dynastic realms.[24] Once again, the specific dynastic imagery evoked normative patriotic sentiments.

But in the commemoration much also was made of the "brave *Jungfrauen,*" among them the woman-warrior Elenore Prochaskas, who cross-dressed, volunteered in 1813 for the Lützow brigade under the name August Renz, and died for the fatherland. Simultaneous with her invocation in print were patriotic gatherings at her gravesite in Potsdam, and

---

22. *KZ,* no. 167, April 11, 1913, article by R. v. H (Frau von Heydebrande, who served on the Executive Committee of the Conservative Union?) Similar sentiments were raised by an author in response to a work by the novelist Thea von Harbou in the third supplement to no. 503, October 26, 1913.

23. Davis, "Reconsidering Habermas." Davis offers a suggestive reading of the public as agent in the construction and transformation of gender identities. She points to the prominent place of urban women "of little means" in mounting the opposition in wartime. They constituted a powerful female plebian public that emerged to challenge the patriotic public.

24. For references to dynastic and other heroines, *KZ,* no. 115, March 9, 1913, re-creates the celebration of Queen Luise's birthday in Berlin in 1808, which had been turned into a protest against French occupation of Prussia; also, supplement to no. 281, June 19, 1913, "Eine fürstliche Vorkämpferin" (Princess William [Marianne] of Prussia); and supplement to no. 565, December 3, 1913, a long article on Luise of Baden.

similar ceremonies also were arranged at the monuments of the royal women figures throughout the year of 1913. October 6, for example, was the one hundredth anniversary of Prochaskas's death; a large parade ambled its way from the shooting field to the cemetery in Potsdam. The parade consisted of delegates of army officers and representatives of the military orphanage, members of veterans' and military associations displaying their flags, units of stretcher-bearers, and the women of the local nurses' aides association. Through speeches, the participants (and the reading public) learned about Prochaskas's life and sacrifice.[25]

Prochaskas, perhaps, seems an unlikely heroine for the Right, more of a threatening Amazon symbol of women's vigor and power. But she was an ideal figure for conservative co-optation; her actions seemed to demonstrate women's "natural" warlike proclivities and, thus, dispel the anxieties created by the rhetorical linkages between feminine and pacifist. Equally to the point, she died in battle and, therefore, did not return after military service to demand rights. Like the heroines of many popular bourgeois novels of the nineteenth century—plots in which the female authors could not reconcile women's gainful employment and marriage and, thus, had their heroines tragically die or disappear in the end—so, too, this war heroine died, obviating any need to accommodate woman's rights or claims as a result of her patriotic service.[26]

But the issue of rights haunted conservatives; the move by Conservative women to organize for political work in 1913 brought potential gender claims into the limelight. The leadership overlap with the bourgeois women's movement most disturbed Conservative Party members, many of whom otherwise cautiously accepted the new political reality, although they were determined to contain it. The more open-minded among them recognized that the Conservative Party had suffered a very serious electoral setback in 1912; while adhering to traditional Christian monarchical principles, they publicly tested ways to rethink and expand the basis of a "patriotic people's party" *(vaterländische Volkspartei)* and were willing to address the woman issue.

According to the Prussian deputy von Gossler-Schätz, who explained the unprecedented step of women's political organization to *Kreuz-*

---

25. *KZ,* no. 468, October 6, 1913.

26. On nineteenth-century novels, among others, Louisa May Alcott, *Work: A Story of Experience,* intro. Sarah Elbert (New York, 1977) (for the author, spinsterhood is the only way to reconcile work and family), and her *Moods* (New Brunswick, N.J., 1995). Also, Alcott's "Enigmas," *Frank Leslie's Popular Monthly,* April 1876, 467–80. See as well Elizabeth Young, "Confederate Counterfeit: The Case of the Cross-Dressed Civil War Soldier," in *Passings and the Fictions of Identity,* ed. Elaine Ginsberg (Durham, N.C., 1996), 181–217. I want to thank my colleague Sarah Elbert for helping me with this point.

Zeitung readers, "We no longer can do without the support of women." Indeed, he acknowledged that the whole "world of women *(Frauenwelt)* to our left" in the political arena, "from the Social Democrats to the National Liberals," was arrayed against Conservatives.[27] Women could, indeed, be valuable aides in the spread of "conservative Christian" values, but only within narrowly prescribed limits and out of "feelings of duty," not "passion for political struggle." In no uncertain terms, he cautioned the Union of Conservative Women not to join forces with the bourgeois women's movement. But tensions persisted, partly because Paula Mueller, on the new executive committee of the Union of Conservative Women, simultaneously affiliated with the reform feminists as president of the Protestant Women's League.[28]

Women's move toward formal political association, which had extended its reach to the recalcitrant Conservatives by 1913, seemed further to blur gender identity. It represented a breach in a sphere that had been masculine by definition. At a minimum, it forced a rethinking of the relationship between politics and philanthropy that in the late *Kaiserreich* still was posited, ideally, as opposite endeavors, neatly divided by gender, even if in reality men, too, volunteered their services for a variety of medical and philanthropic causes and some women were employed for wages in the Red Cross associations. For some on the right, however, the feared politicization of women's public roles called into question the dynastic norm of patriotic service, reinforcing a further retreat into the domestic.

The philanthropic arena of church and municipal life was the training ground for many Conservative women. The Union of Conservative Women's manifesto shows that the leaders approached politics through a charitable imperative, arguably shaped by monarchical and religious values. The goal of women's politics was not power for their own sex but for

27. *KZ,* supplement to no. 113, May 9, 1913, and second supplement to no. 467, October 5, 1913. The women's step to political union had been prompted partly by the formation in 1912 of the rabidly antifeminist German League against Women's Emancipation and its spin-off, the Christian National Group, which made the German Protestant Women's League its main target. For more details, James Retallack, *Notables of the Right: The Conservative Party and Political Mobilization in Germany, 1876–1918* (Boston, 1988), 182–90, 209–15; Baumann, *Protestentismus und Frauenemanzipation,* 202–16.

28. Retallack, *Notables of the Right,* 184–85. For the work of Protestant women from the perspective of moderate feminists, Gertrud Bäumer, *Gestalt und Wandel. Frauenbildnisse* (Berlin, 1939), 619–55, on Countess Selma von der Gröben. From the other side, see Paula Mueller, ed., *Handbuch zur Frauenfrage. Der Deutsch-Evangelische Frauenbund in seiner geschichtlichen Entwicklung, seinen Zeilen und seiner Arbeit* (Berlin, 1908). Mueller writes that she published her handbook because of the neglect of religious women's activities in the manual of the bourgeois feminist movement.

the well-being of the whole people—connecting public activism back to older patriotic visions of state service for the common good.[29]

But the motives of such leaders as Bertha von Kröcher and Elisabeth Stackmann were more complex. On the one hand, they openly expressed considerable frustration at their daily treatment by male municipal and church relief officials on the ground; too often, the leaders charged, women were overlooked in decision making, and there was no formal mechanism to communicate their views. These shortcomings did not translate into advocacy of women's vote, however. In this regard, Union of Conservative Women members toed the official party line, which opposed, in principle, women's right to vote in all areas of life, including Protestant Church administration. Rather, women's contributions to public life would be sealed "if the work committees of the church and the municipal administration were required to draw on women as expert witnesses in the fields that demanded women's input." These prominent women expected their party to work for such a formal arrangement in the future.

The same leaders, however, were disheartened that the party had failed adequately to address the "woman question" in its economic dimensions *(Notstände)*. It may be well and good to oppose women's gainful labor, they wrote, but not if "the opponents have no adequate measures to deal with economic hardships." The woman question as an expression of economic and social misery required attention; moreover, this commitment would broaden the base of the Conservative Party, seen as representing "agrarian" interests alone. In the leaders' analysis, the "woman question" was an urban question, a formulation, of course, that obviated any focus on the plight of poor rural women or Junker social power in the countryside. While muted and limited, Conservative women nonetheless recognized the need to address issues directly facing women. Offering a veiled threat, they claimed that without their input, many "honorably minded *(ehrlich denkende)* conservative women" would be lost to liberalism because of the intransigence of Conservative men.[30]

The step to political union, however, merely uncovered unbridgeable divides, which cut a number of ways. This was true not only for conservative men, many of whom clung stubbornly to a narrow view of women's spheres of life, but even for some women readers of the *Kreuz-Zeitung.*[31]

Entering the debate, one female author fell into a number of contradictions when she addressed the "masculine" sphere of politics. For her, the burning issue among women was the question of public rights and

---

29. *KZ,* supplement to no. 349, July 29, 1913.

30. *KZ,* supplement to no. 349, July 29, 1913.

31. *KZ,* second supplement to no. 467, October 5, 1913, and no. 293, June 26, 1913.

social duties. The feminist movement had made these themes compelling, and she also chastised conservative men for their "derision" and indifference. Breaking ranks with the Union of Conservative Women, however, this author saw the women's movement as a serious threat that her male colleagues neglected at their peril. Women in politics contradicted femininity and threatened all the "beauty, love, gentleness . . . and nobility at the basis of our life *(Volksleben)*." She contrasted the "organic" nature of family relations with the "mechanic" organization of statecraft: "Work in the family and work in the service of the state principally are distinct endeavors," even if family life promotes the religious and moral guidelines for statecraft. Her manifest concern with the corrupting nature of (male) politics seemed to undercut the old dynastic norm of women's civic activism in the name of the "caring" state. With the same breath, however, she acknowledged women's multiple and important "social and philanthropic activities" on behalf of the state. Striking at the heart of the matter, she admitted no consequent reforms or political claims. Women should "step back from demanding any public rights" *(jegliche öffentliche Rechte)* as a result of their civic, charitable, or religious work. And she criticized the German Protestant Women's League for demanding votes for women in church affairs, the lay assessor courts, and other legal institutions.[32] Despite the widespread hostility to the Protestant Women's League among Conservatives in prewar Germany, in 1917, when the reform feminist community publicized a manifesto that demanded women's political rights for their wartime services, the German Protestant women left the feminist league in protest.[33] They feared the step to women's formal citizenship as a breach in the authoritarian political order. In the alliance between conservative and moderate feminists to improve females' economic and legal status, there was no agreement over political rights.

Hardly coincidental, the principled disagreement among women mirrored a fundamental characteristic in Germany's social welfare project. The philanthropic milieu, which inspired and trained the many female volunteers in relief and social services, admitted no systematic discussion of rights. It remained embedded in conservative social and Christian notions of obligations—"gifts" of the privileged—that, in 1871, had been updated in a new nationalist contract based on the reciprocities between sacrifice

---

32. *KZ,* no. 293, June 26, 1913 and no. 331, July 18, 1914, a report on the International Women's Congress attended by Helene Lange and Paula Mueller. The Conservative Union defended Mueller's participation and reiterated her opposition to the feminist *Bund*'s position on women's suffrage.

33. The formal break came in March 1918. On the wartime tensions, Baumann, *Protestantismus und Frauenemanzipation,* 250–53 and Scheck, "German Conservatism," 36–37.

and obligation. Within its logic, there was no necessary next step to an assertion of women's rights as part of the relationship. Admittedly, dynastic philanthropy was only one element of a wider nexus of social services in the municipality, although, as we have seen, it was an essential component of imperial German planning for civilian medical war preparation. But the wider issue of rights continued to be the weak link in the official nationalist chain of policies, practices, and performances.

The 1913 gender crisis, which spilled over into the realm of rights and claims, thus, addressed a core issue of monarchical legitimacy in the *Kaiserreich:* this legitimacy rested on the reciprocal promise of state obligations to those with needs in exchange for sacrifices of every kind in times of national emergency. Yet the connection between sacrifice and needs was seriously out of balance: it would not adequately give weight to social and political rights, and, tragically in the end, it would demand too much sacrifice.

Civilian War Planning and the Transitions to Total War

The nationalist commemoration in 1913 that, in a heady brew, combined the memory with the anticipation of war was matched by renewed efforts at medical war planning. Despite the controversies swirling in the conservative press over women's patriotic roles for the nation, women's associations joined the festivities in 1913. Capitalizing on the heightened nationalist fervor, Red Cross leaders introduced a series of campaigns to solicit public monies and support. In May, for example, as a tribute to the twenty-fifth anniversary of William II's ascension to the throne, the Central Executive Committee of the Prussian Patriotic Women's Association put together a mobile exhibition of its history. Available to any chapter free of charge, it featured carefully arranged "pictures" and "charts" designed to explain Red Cross work to the general public *(die Öffentlichkeit)*. Among the eight themes was a detailed display on "war preparation and war work"; another concentrated on nursing training. To raise money, furthermore, a committee was organized in Brandenburg that August to sell postcards and pictures of the dynastic family as well as memorial teacups with an eye to reinforcing "valuable historical thinking." One cup was modeled on a hundred-year-old style, with 1813 encircled by a wreath of oak leaves and laurels; the saucer duplicated the campaign plan of the "battle of nations" at Leipzig. Another cup carried the portrait of the living empress.[34] These common items of domestic use worked on memories right in the home.

---

34. *KZ*, no. 246, May 29, 1913, and no. 369, August 9, 1913.

The next year, the Red Cross coordinated a nationwide solicitation campaign (Rote Kreuz-Sammlung 1914), which opened on May 10, the anniversary of the Peace of Frankfurt ending the Franco-German war. The poster, "appeal to the German people," which was plastered around Baden in April, gave up all pretense to political neutrality. The text fully identified with the need for a strengthened German fighting force and applauded the outcome of the Reichstag debates on military appropriations the previous year. It praised the German people for taking on the burdens of armaments to "protect its most valuable possessions" and called on them now to be equally generous in their national duty to donate goods and money for volunteer medical war preparation. "Our emperor and empress, the territorial princes and free cities of our fatherland, the male and female patrons of the state and women's associations of the Red Cross have accepted this task, as have the state governments," it proclaimed. In one breadth it identified the broad alliance of dynastic and state forces that was orchestrating much of official nationalist war planning, even if it omitted the army, as both the arbiter and beneficiary of the voluntary services. In Baden, the campaign was spelled out down to the attire of the women collectors (dressed in white or light colors and donning hats), with contingency plans for bad weather. The collection bins were decorated in the state colors, and the timing was specified as well: no solicitation during morning church services but otherwise house-to-house canvassing from 9:00 A.M. to 8:00 P.M. and, for those on the streets, from 7:00 A.M. to dusk. Evening solicitations were possible at railroad stations, restaurants, theaters, and resort areas (the women worked in pairs), and it was recommended as well to be at factory gates between noon and 2:00 P.M.[35]

Fund-raising campaigns were matched by accelerated efforts to expand medical war planning. Details from Baden demonstrate a sustained coordination after 1907, which coincided with British efforts to strengthen its own civil defense. General Limberger's "instructions" that year, for example, called for the work of medical war preparation to be set in motion with "renewed intensity."[36] The numerical plans for war would be matched, he argued, by equal statistical certainty among the civilian medical corps. Thus, Limberger demanded a careful counting of local associations and corporations; of the hospitals and the numbers of beds available; of the male and female medical staff, clerks, and supervisory personnel; as well as of the linkages to the religious orders.

The assignments of civilian medical personnel during the transition

---

35. For details, GK, Abt. 69, no. 1118, Mitteilungen, *Sonderblatt,* March 28, 1914.
36. GK, Abt. 69, no. 1117, Mitteilungen, "Kriegstätigkeits vorbereitung," Karlsruhe, January 9, 1907.

days to full war mobilization were communicated more effectively down the chain of command. The military mobilization calendar (MMK) contained specific orders for the designated Red Cross organizations according to day 1, day 2, day 3, et cetera, of mobilization. In Baden, Plan Number 6 spelled out the sequence by task for the women's associations according to each day of the initial mobilization. On the first day, for example, the women would be assigned to the different hospitals, which had to be operational within ten days. Only on day 3, however, would women's workshops be set up, responsible for producing clothing and undergarments for hospital use.[37]

As "rumors of impending war" *(Kriegsgerüchte)* developed momentum in 1913, furthermore, the numbers of applicants for nurses aides' training increased steadily, exceeding space in local Karlsruhe hospitals, according to Julia Limberger. Expectations, however, still were guided by the lessons of the Franco-German war, and Limberger proposed no expansion of course offerings. Rather, she predicted that inadequate supplies of medical personnel could be surmounted during the actual days of mobilization through special courses arranged for nurses. "That is the experience of 1870–71," she concluded confidently. The length, intensity, and unprecedented human costs of the war confounded these expectations. In the months before the war, however, the agenda of the Baden matrons' conferences included a new topic, "the business of mobilization" *(Mobilmachungsangelegenheiten)*.[38]

In the literature on German history as well as research on peace studies, the apparent popular enthusiasm for war in August 1914 in Germany has elicited considerable attention.[39] It seems to stand out as a particularly striking moment of war ecstasy, culminating in the Reichstag votes for war credits on August 4 in which even the Social Democratic antimilitarist principles all but evaporated. Of course, government propaganda in the weeks before mobilization carefully portrayed the impending war as "defensive" and thus "just," combining older Christian notions with the modern imperatives of righteous national defense. Nonetheless, the masses milling about the streets and the near flawless implementation of mobilization seemed to express a new sense of community united in com-

---

37. GK, Abt. 69, no. 1117, "Muster-Pläne für den Übergang zur Kriegstätigkeit," no. 1, January 27, 1909.

38. GK, Abt. 69, no. 1134, Julia Limberger, "Ausbildung für Helferinnen vom Roten Kreuz 1913," and no. 891, Oberinnen-Konferenz, March 20, 1914.

39. A particularly useful collection is Marcel Van der Linden and Gottfried Mergner, eds., *Kriegsbegeisterung und mentale Kriegsvorbereitung. Inderdisziplinäre Studien* (Berlin, 1991). Also, see the reflections by Jean Bethke Elshtain, *Women and War* (New York, 1987).

mon purpose. The politically charged memory of such unified nationalist outpouring is organized under the rubric "August days."[40]

Recent research offers a more nuanced picture. It reveals, for example, considerable tension between the majority of Social Democratic leaders in parliament, seduced by the war fervor, and their rank-and-file members, many of whom maintained a fundamental opposition to war. Letters of workers and reports by clergy of the popular mood in many localities in those early August days spoke of despondency, despair, and fear. A detailed study of the ties between South Bavarian soldiers and their kinfolk at home during the First World War uncovers an anxious mood in 1914; soldiers entered the war with "tears," concludes the historian Benjamin Ziemann.[41] My own reading of the *Kreuz-Zeitung* from June 28 (the assassination date of the Austrian heir to the throne, Archduke Francis Ferdinand, in Sarajevo) until August 2 (day 1 of the imperial German war calendar) finds considerable uncertainty among high government leaders about the popular mood. In Berlin, for example, officials were so concerned about mass expressions of any sort that they banned all demonstrations in the heart of the city, including those by acknowledged patriots! Furthermore, official propaganda in those tense weeks reenacted some of the historic themes staged during the previous year—to conjure up once again the memory of men and women's selfless sacrifices under dynastic blessings in 1813.[42]

These observations, of course, beg the question of the role of official nationalist policies and performances in the creation of war sentiments in Germany. The answers, ultimately, may be unsatisfactory. Can one measure with precision the political implications of a military parade set against the backdrop of a dynastic visit to a philanthropic institution; a street theater that used scientifically advanced medical interventions promising to ease the pain of battle; or a choreographed national cam-

---

40. For its continued importance in the explorations of the ties between German nationalism and fascism, Peter Fritzsche, *Germans into Nazis* (Cambridge, Mass., 1998), 13–82.

41. Wolfgang Kruse, "Die Kreigsbegeisterung im Deutschen Reich zum Beginn des Ersten Weltkrieges: Entstehungszusammenhänge, Grenzen und ideologische Strukturen," in Van der Linden and Mergner, *Kriegsbegeisterung und mentale Kriegsvorbereitung*, 78–79; in the same volume, Jürgen Rojahn, "Arbeiterbewegung und Kriegsbegeisterung: Die deutsche Sozialdemokratie, 1870–1914," 58–70. For the southern Bavarian example, Benjamin Ziemann, *Front und Heimat. Ländliche Kriegserfahrungen im südlichen Bayern, 1914–1923* (Leipzig, 1997), 33, 463. I want to thank Deborah Cohen for telling me about this helpful study.

42. A good example is *KZ,* supplement to no. 358, August 2, 1914, commemorating the centenary of the Order of Luise. For the effort to control Berlin streets and patriotic response see the following issues in 1914: no. 346, July 27; no. 349, July 28, which contains the police decree; no. 350, July 29; and no. 352, July 30.

paign of assistance during a frightful natural disaster? Similar uncertainty confounds all analysts who enter the realm of identity-formation through ritual performances—irrespective if the media are advanced by ruling groups or their opposition.[43] I can propose, however, several arguments that help broaden the discussion of war planning and national identity through a focus on the gendered workings of the Red Cross.

First, official nationalism, which relied on dynastic rulers, rituals, and symbols, established a political legitimacy based on "care" and justified by war. Through its philanthropic praxis, expressed in the principle of "organized voluntarism," a gendered war culture of patriotic duties extended deep into civil society. However wide the spectrum of views in August 1914—admittedly ranging the gamut from enthusiasm to dread—the war signaled the onset of a preestablished promise of care, and one that had been on stage in the streets, hospitals, and exhibitions and during floods and epidemics in the years of peace. Such expectations, arguably, were part of popular sentiments, glimpsed in the letters of thanks for dynastic solicitude. Indeed, more detailed studies of sentiments at the onset of the war show the breadth of monarchical sentiments—among soldiers in the Bavarian army, for example, even if it was a loyalty to the Bavarian king and not necessarily to the German kaiser.[44] National defense went through the state; national loyalty was understood at the start through dynastic and religious idioms. In time, both soldiers and civilians alike had to make sense of the sacrifices asked of them. Then, the patriotic vocabulary of the August days, which had defined the sacrifices in the name of God, king, and fatherland, quickly faltered.

Second, the organizations of the Red Cross were mobilized smoothly and successfully in August 1914 as specified by the war calendar. The evidence appears incontrovertible. This official mobilization was matched by an outpouring of all manner of civic activism—from the formation of a National Women's Service in early August to the proliferation of makeshift soup kitchens or day care centers throughout the country—that expressed the powerful hold of notions of patriotic deeds in the national imagination. It affirmed the seeming ease with which earlier commitments to philanthropic and municipal relief efforts became war work for the national defense. Such linkages were perfectly clear to Wilhelm Kuhleweis of the Institute for the Blind in Ilvesheim, Baden. Rejected by the army because of a "weak constitution" and unable to volunteer with the Red Cross because of the "throngs" of applicants, he turned to the duchess in

---

43. For ways to assess working-class ritual forms, Lüdtke, "Trauerritual und politische Manifestation," 120.

44. Ziemann, *Front und Heimat,* 265, detailing the importance of the Wittelsbach cult in those early months of the war.

early August in total desperation. He wanted her to get him work in a medical transport unit because "in the years of peace . . . [I worked] in the arenas of social welfare *(auf sozialen Gebiete)."*[45] Furthermore, whatever gender tensions had surfaced earlier revealing fissures over understanding of women's contributions in wartime, they seemed to close when war broke out. The *Burgfrieden* (a political peace at the root of the "ideas of 1914") was matched by a temporary gender peace as well.[46]

The German Red Cross took on functions essential to the war economy, tasks that were increasingly difficult to meet as industrial mobilization at home became more and more essential for military successes on the battlefield. Its volunteers, for example, were called on to stock municipal hospitals with food and supplies. But an internal memo of the Baden State Relief Association already on August 4 acknowledged that "our preparations are inadequate, and we need considerably greater planning and production," particularly to "replenish the needed supplies."[47] Thus, from the start, Red Cross organizations were embroiled in the improvisations of social and political "crisis management" that characterized imperial and state responses to the prolongation of war and the privations added on by naval blockade.[48] Managing the public was a critical task, and the Red Cross, long dependent on the public's goodwill, was deeply implicated in the work of patriotic indoctrination. Furthermore, its reliance on organized voluntarism in the figures of the knowledgeable woman, trained nurse, or aide, sustained the prewar dynastic model of philanthropic-state alliances for relief. During the period that the historian Frie labels "muddling through," from the outbreak of war until mid-1915, this alliance remained operative on the local level, overseeing services for the war wounded, the permanently disabled, and survivor families—whole categories of clients that were expanding at rapid rates as the war continued to take its relentless toll on limbs and life.[49] This work, furthermore, remained linked to political legitimacy, through such organizational umbrellas as Thanks of the Fatherland (Dank des Vaterlandes).

---

45. GK, Abt. 69, no. 620, Den Feldzug, August 1914.

46. For reports on this early political peace, Ernst Johann, *Innenansicht eines Krieges: Bilder, Briefe, Dokumente 1914–1918* (Frankfurt am Main, 1968), 16–18, 22–23; and Roger Chickering, *Imperial Germany and the Great War, 1914, 1918* (Cambridge, 1998), 13–17, for an assessment of the "spirit of 1914."

47. GK, Abt. 69, no. 619, Die Mobilmachung 1914, August 4, 1914. For the transition to the war footing in Baden, Hugo Ott, "Die wirtschaftliche und soziale Entwicklung von der Mittel des 19. Jahrhunderts bis zum ende des Ersten Weltkriegs," in Josef Becker et al., *Badische Geschichte. Vom Grossherzogtum bis zur Gegenwart* (Stuttgart, 1979), 129–34.

48. The term is in Frie, *Wohlfahrtsstaat und Provinz,* 19, 81.

49. Ibid., 100.

The year 1916, however, proved a decisive turning point in the evolution of German social welfare ideologies, institutions, and provisions.[50] The army's voracious need for human and industrial resources was pushing Germany toward "total war," symbolized at home by the Hindenburg Program of late 1916 designed to subordinate civilian industry and labor to military requirements. Social resources were channeled toward armaments production; food rationing policies favored munitions workers; and the crucial task of job referrals became centralized. If military policy exempted women from this civilian draft, it nonetheless set up a national commission to persuade working-class women (through wage, day care, and other incentives) to take on work in armaments industries. Similarly, Red Cross lists of female volunteers were sent directly to local military commanders.[51]

Increasing coordination and centralization of resources by military, state, and local officials inexorably transformed the philanthropic milieu. Old organizations such as the Prussian Women's and Young Ladies' Association could no longer compete in the scramble for public support; pointedly, its archival documents cease in 1916. Needs clearly outstripped resources. The clients themselves—the four million war cripples, who were a visible testimony to the costs of battle on the streets of Germany, soldiers' wives and widows—and growing numbers of officials managing resources put forth new claims to social services as a matter of rights. The principle of social rights competed with the tradition of charity. Significantly, too, centralization tilted the balance toward administrative and "expert" personnel in social welfare agencies at the expense of the knowledgeable volunteer; it favored bureaucrats and professionals, reducing the scope of private initiatives for the general good. By 1916, indeed, the patriotic public, long integrated into dynastic rule, no longer provided a cohesive image of the nationalist contract, which had spoken of an equitable relationship among sacrifice, care, and reward.

The remaining chapter looks at Red Cross participation in the war economy in Baden. It concentrates on the state level, which oversaw the civilian medical war services, and on the Karlsruhe Nurses Aides' League, which did much of the voluntary labor on the ground. In the vocabulary of the day, aides formed a veritable "female auxiliary troop" (*Frauenhilfs-*

---

50. This is a common argument in the literature. Among others, Frie, *Wohlfahrtsstaat und Provinz,* 183. It also is measured by the erosion of state legitimacy (Ziemann, *Front und Heimat,* 52, 121–24, 252–60).

51. GK, Abt. 69, no. 648, Den Feldzug, 1916, 131st Sitzung (state Red Cross meeting), December 11, 1916; no. 649, Monatsitzung, November 11, 1916; no. 1134, 10th Jahresversammlung, April 3, 1918.

trupp) for all manner of social services on the home front.[52] The necessarily restricted inquiry nonetheless permits a focused examination of the wartime crises affecting the medical philanthropic associations of the royal house and their place in a service culture sustained by active correspondence as well as artistic images duplicated all over Germany. It helps answer a question often glossed over in the literature on war: what are the mechanisms that sustain a group's patriotic identity as the legitimacy of the state erodes around it? A more systematic investigation of the war years would require a much longer and, arguably, a different book.

Baden Patriotic Communities in Wartime

During the heady days of war mobilization in August 1914, Baden Red Cross officials turned directly to the public for support—soliciting cash as well as foodstuffs, matériel, and volunteer labor. From the start, they counted on "public solicitations" *(öffentliche Sammlungen)* to make up the shortages of money and supplies that, by their own admission, were fairly serious. These shortcomings were felt all the more sharply in Baden because of its proximity to early battles on the western front; by August 10, six ships had arrived from Strasbourg bringing the wounded from the campaigns around Mülhausen—"well over one thousand men"—to the hospitals in Karlsruhe; on August 16, the medical transport units and nurses' aides were helping unload wounded soldiers from the first hospital train to arrive at the local station.[53]

Five months into the war, the Baden State Red Cross had nothing but praise for these early efforts; the work had been "successful" and "smoothly handled," it wrote in retrospect. In no uncertain terms, officials agreed that "with enthusiasm as its driving force, the mobilization had laid to rest any earlier concerns about the reliability of calling up medical volunteers." The "public" *(die Öffentlichkeit)* deserved high marks as well, for it had emerged as an important "ally" *(Bundesgenosse)* in the "work of charity" *(Liebeswerke)*.[54]

The report devoted a whole section to public opinion, a crucial area of domestic pacification that needed continuous time and attention despite the imposition of martial law and press censorship at the start of the war. Along with other quasi-official patriotic groups, the Red Cross did its part to present the war as "just and holy," sentiments that in these early months

---

52. GSPK, no. 15613, Bl. 17–19, Berlin, August 21, 1916, national executive committee retrospective. Also, GK, Abt. 69, no. 619, eighth meeting (state Red Cross), August 8, 1914.

53. GK, Abt. 69, no. 619, ninth meeting (state Red Cross), August 10, 1914, and thirteenth meeting, August 16, 1914. Also, Ott, "Wirtschaftliche und soziale Entwicklung," 132.

54. GK, Abt. 69, no. 1118, Mitteilungen, Karlsruhe, December 3, 1914.

it attributed to the public. In Red Cross imagery, the public became an active agent in the war effort as well—a persona whose willingness to donate money and goods to the hospitals provided "bountiful harvests." In December, officials expressed the hope that these voluntary contributions would prove lasting, prophetically noting that "the war in no way has reached its climax." One artist captures the ambiguities of these sentiments in a poster for 1917 (fig. 5). Here, the public still is a bountiful female figure giving gifts for soldiers at Christmastime. The image also is of birth, of a broad-hipped peasant women bearing children for the fatherland. The use of light draws attention to the apron, covering yet suggesting the womb. The handshake in the background speaks of reconciliation, even between, perhaps, rural and urban areas of Germany. But by 1917, the harsh wartime requisitions had deeply embittered the countryside and widened the gulf between village and city.

At the start of the war, however, the Red Cross solicitation campaigns fell on receptive ears. They pulled out all the old familiar tropes that long had been part of the patriotic landscape. The images, artistic designs, and written appeals were those of the old dynastic narrative of collective sacrifices in war. Assurances were made of the personal concern of the *Landesmutter* for all her children in these difficult days, and the imagery was deeply religious as well. It drew on and reinforced the religious symbolism through which many people in the population were trying to comprehend the dangers of war. A grassroots piety *(Kriegsfrömmigkeit)* had emerged at the beginning of war among soldiers and civilians alike. Figure 6 graphically connects these two worlds. It is an evocative image of a wounded soldier set against the red cross (which is bright red in the original colored poster). His sacrifice is likened to Christ's, and the public is asked to make its own sacrifices to support the voluntary medical war services. The power of this edifice of religious meaning began to crack only in 1916, under the onslaught of mass death, hunger, and lack of fuel.[55]

Figure 7 re-creates another familiar theme: the patriotic deed. In this gendered setting, a young woman is reading to a wounded soldier, and the poster is appealing for donations of books for use in hospitals and reconvalescent homes. It suggests that Red Cross artists participated in the work of glorifying German "culture," which many educated voices in World War I saw engaged in a battle to the death against enemy values. The connection is made through explicit identification with "our thinkers and poets" and communicated more subtly in the classic fatherly figure on

---

55. Ziemann, *Front und Heimat,* 51–52; and Chickering, *Imperial Germany and Great War,* 127–29, on the "war theology."

Fig. 5.   "The thanks of the kaiser and people to the army and navy, Christmas, 1917." (Courtesy Hoover Institution Archives, Poster Collection, GE 1863.)

Fig. 6.   Red Cross collection to benefit volunteer nurses, 1914, Munich. (Courtesy Hoover Institution Archives, Poster Collection, GE 200.)

the bench with its Doric columns. In time, this "cultural" battle, too, met mounting hostility among the lower classes, for whom German "culture" easily translated into war profiting, low pay, and the inequalities of sacrifice. Importantly, the poster also has an erotic aspect, suggested in the woman's exposed neck and the curls around her face; it spoke of both modesty and desire. Indeed, the images of the wounded soldier (fig. 6) and the woman donating her hair (fig. 4) are similarly sexualized. Despite his downcast face, the soldier's eyes have the look of power to them; the woman's red lips simply jump off the poster. Beneath the conservative gender stereotypes were subtle erotic messages, embedding patriotic giving in a modern consumer mode, which intrinsically relies on the evocation of desire.

Figure 8 returns to past practices; it is an appeal to the female public to donate jams and preserves on the birthday of the empress in 1915. Again, German women were invited to participate in the dynastic celebrations of life, of birth in the face of death and collective family festivity in light of individual family tragedies. This early poster campaign drew on historic memory in its efforts to sustain all manner of patriotic acts.

Equally to the point, these artistic forms were matched by real-life actions of dynastic rulers, duly noted in the controlled press. On August 4, for example, Empress Auguste Victoria attended the meeting of the German Red Cross and turned over the royal castles in Strasbourg, Wiesbaden, Königsberg, and Koblenz to the organization for the use of wounded soldiers, an act of official benevolence duplicated in Braunschweig, where the duchess, too, transformed the resident castle into a hospital of 150 beds. In the early phases of mobilization, the empress was visible at the Neukölln railroad station in Berlin greeting the departing troops and at other symbolic points in the city.[56] Her appeal on August 6 to German women to join the war effort became a propaganda poster of its own.[57]

The duchess of Baden also made regular trips to the work stations in Karlsruhe in rites that reaffirmed personal concern and official support. Through much of the war, she actively participated in state Red Cross executive committee meetings. The dynastic courts, furthermore, continued to give sizable amounts of cash to the Red Cross, a practice matched by well-heeled individuals, but in the growing climate of shortages and mistrust, such "largesse" easily was turned upside down by the vocal critics. "If a businessman gives a thousand marks to the Red Cross, then he bilks the people a hundredfold," or so the accusation went in Berlin in

---

56. *KZ,* no. 361, August 4, 1914, and for her visits, no. 368, August 7, and no. 374, August 11.
57. "An die Deutschen Frauen!" GE 3, HIA.

Fig. 7.   "Commune with our thinkers and poets! The book offers joy and comfort."
(Courtesy Hoover Institution Archives, Poster Collection, GE 196.)

Kaiferin-Geburtstagsgabe

Deutfche Frauen

gebt uns am **Freitag, den 22. Oktober d. J.**

für unfere Truppen im Felde und in den Lazaretten

eingefochtes Obft, Kompotts, Marmeladen, Gelees, Mus, Honig, Beeren- und Fruchtfäfte.
Keine deutfche Frau bleibe zurück. Auch die kleinfte Gabe ift willkommen.

Der Vaterländifche Frauen-Verein
Provinzialverein Berlin

Gaben-Sammelftellen
(geöffnet von 9 Uhr morgens bis 8 Uhr abends)

Fig. 8.   Commemorative gift celebrating the empress's birthday, October 22, 1915, calling on women to donate jams and preserves to support the troops at the front and in the hospitals. (Courtesy Hoover Institution Archives, Poster Collection, GE 246.)

1915. As the war progressed, publicity remained central to the work of patriotic communication; at a Red Cross meeting in late 1916, indeed, city officials in Mannheim wanted their specific contributions clearly identified in the published record of the fund-raising effort. And minutes of Red Cross business meetings show that pieces of jewelry—as in 1813—became donations of specific amounts of cash.[58] Significantly, the old symbolics of gift giving transported patriotic volunteer and donor alike into an earlier world of war, which had seen victory.

On closer analysis, the Red Cross leadership in Baden already in August 1914 had trod especially cautiously in its dealings with its so-called ally, the public. Tensions had flared for a time between Red Cross and Karlsruhe officials over the display of posters; the fear was that the public might become confused by too many solicitations or, worse, "resent[ful]." More serious, perhaps, were the rumors circulating as early as August 8 about a firm that reputedly had failed to supply bakers with grain to make bread for the hospitals. A representative of the firm and some of the bakers appeared at a meeting of the Red Cross to dispel the rumor, but officials had their first glimpse at the volatility of the public mood. And they had to deal with several cases of price gouging: unauthorized persons had been selling lemonade at exorbitant prices to the troops at the train stations.[59]

The solicitation campaign, however, laid claim to shared practices designed to express national cohesion. At the level of the state, however, fund-raising heightened regional identification while exacerbating geographical tensions among patriotic groups in the nation. The Baden Day of Sacrifice planned for September 19, 1915, was geared to the specifics of Baden historical memory. The populace was called on to "renounce a pleasure" or "a treat" and turn the unspent money over to Red Cross solicitors, who would be out on the streets that day throughout the state. The event was timed to fold into a Day of Thanks on September 20, the wedding anniversary celebration of the Baden dynastic house: both Frederick and Luise (1856) and the reigning couple, Frederick II and Hilda (1885), had been married on that date. The official voice of the imagined community was cast in the first-person plural: through the donation "we

---

58. The Baden examples are in GK, Abt. 69, no. 619, seventh meeting, August 8, 1914, and ninth meeting, August 10, 1914, which reported the continued flow of gifts, including twenty thousand marks from Prince and Princess zu Loewenstein, scions of an old mediatized aristocratic family, and two thousand marks from a Frau Eugenie Bumüller. Also, the fifteenth meeting, August 18, 1914, details the sale of jewelry, which netted 3,058 marks. For the concerns over publicity, no. 649, monthly meeting, November 11, 1916; and Davis, "Home Fires Burning," 164, for the socialist charge that profits were incompatible with "patriotism."

59. GK, Abt. 69, no. 619, seventh to eleventh meetings, August 8–13, 1914.

would render our thanks to the troops at the front in the same manner as the dynastic pairs." The campaign linked dynasty and people in common cause by appealing to a distinctive Baden history and identity.

As resources became more scarce, campaigns by those outside the state met with increased hostility in patriotic circles. There had been, to be sure, a "kaiser's solicitation of German women" in August 1915, which yielded 345,000 Marks in Baden alone. Red Cross meetings, however, reveal growing antagonism toward groups outside Baden, such as the Prussian branch of the Navy League or the peasant *Hansabund*. Leaders groused that these organizations came into the state, solicited money to buy war goods, and then favored exclusively Berlin merchants and distributors to the detriment of Baden businessmen and artisans. A growing perception of the inequalities of sacrifice fed interregional and state tensions, a logical outcome of the way German national identity had been mediated and shaped by distinctive and evocative state allegiances. So serious was the charge of favoritism that in March 1917 the Baden state sent a representative to Berlin to safeguard Baden interests in the procurement of wartime contracts. In turn, many poor Berliners believed that they were being disadvantaged in government food distribution schemes as against Bavarians or Rhinelanders, not to mention the "rich," who were seen to have unlimited access to better-quality goods.[60] German politics was fracturing badly: divisions appeared along class, gender, regional, state, and ideological lines.

Furthermore, by July 1916, the Baden Red Cross leadership acknowledged a deep crisis of conscience. Two years after the outbreak of hostilities, the report by General Limberger was grim; as he called it, each person in the audience "alone had to come to grips" with the "colossal events" around them, as did the whole German people. "Mars rules the world," he said and admitted, in effect, that all assumptions are "null and void." It was "useless" to ask about the future, the length of the war, or the outcome. His profoundly pessimistic voice, however, drew no unsettling conclusions. Rather, he expressed pride that there were no complaints about an unwillingness to "tough it out" *(Ausdauern)* in his association. He recommended that attention be given to winning over a "new generation" *(Nachwuchs)*—calling, in effect, for new blood for the struggle. And he retreated back into a self-congratulatory view of the German character: "After all, we Germans are capable of acting purely altruistically." Ulti-

---

60. GK, Abt. 69, nos. 632–33, eighty-third to eighty-fifth meetings, August 11–16, 1915; Ott, "Wirtschaftliche und soziale Entwicklung," 138–39; Davis, "Home Fires Burning," 316. Also, Belinda Davis, "Food Scarcity and the Empowerment of the Female Consumer in World War I Berlin," in *The Sex of Things: Gender and Consumption in Historical Perspective,* ed. Victoria de Grazia (Berkeley and Los Angeles, 1996), 287–310.

mately, he turned to the seemingly neutral and humanitarian stance that had underwritten war—all war, irrespective of its costs, goals, or aims.[61] Thus, the Red Cross maintained its image as merely caregiving, denying that it had any active role or responsibility in the perpetuation of the horror.

In light of the mounting strains of war and the acknowledgment of grave doubts, official nationalist efforts to sustain patriotic loyalty by encouraging domestic sacrifice rang hollow. Red Cross solicitation appeals, however, remained static, at odds with the changes tearing at social and family life. Posters continued to affirm the bonds between kaiser and *Volk*. Old themes were dressed up in modern, art deco images, and slogans were turned upside down so that "gold" was seen to destroy "iron"—the iron chains that had kept Germany encircled—but the links to the past were immutable (fig. 9). The posters continued to duplicate a vision of earlier wars and an imagined unified dynastic polity.

Red Cross leaders quickly learned differently. Even the Day of Sacrifice in Baden had proved disappointing; the women's association in Sandhofen, for example, simply refused to pass out postcards; the Oppenau women's group had voiced "reservations," and others opposed the use of posters. All in all, the results were "poor." By November 1916, the state association had to face the fact that, in the words of a delegate from Freiburg, the "charitable donations gradually have dried up." Not surprising, in September 1918, when the Patriotic Women's Association leaders toyed with the idea of raising funds for a new school for German nurses and set the date for the campaign on January 27, 1919 (the kaiser's sixtieth birthday), it tried to plan around the "hostilities to open-handedness" (*Anfeindungen der Gebefreudigkeit*), as it dismissively mislabeled the sentiments in the wider population.[62]

Despite disagreements over means and strategy voiced now and then by some local women's associations and growing disciplinary action against individual nurses and aides who, in the face of hunger and deprivation, reputedly stole hospital goods and supplies, the medical corps stayed intact and muddled through; its trained personnel remained wedded to the dynastic house.[63] Given the disruptions in communication and internal travel, the familiar ceremonial bonds that had tied dynasty, volunteers, and nurses were kept alive as far as possible. For example, the

---

61. GK, Abt. 69, no. 644, 123d meeting, July 31, 1916.

62. GK, Abt. 69, no. 632, eighty-seventh meeting, August 30, 1915; no. 633, ninetieth meeting, September 20, 1915; no. 649, monthly meeting, November 11, 1916. For the national proposal in 1918, GSPK, no. 15613, Bl. 78, September 13, 1918.

63. GK, Abt. 69, no. 892, Die Abteilung III des Frauenvereins, betr., April 19, 1918, for concerns over theft.

Fig. 9. "Gold smashes Iron." (Courtesy Hoover Institution Archives, Poster Collection, GE 1776.)

annual "festival" at the Ludwig-Wilhelm Hospital was suspended during the war, but the duchess substituted a personal letter of thanks and used the opportunity of the written word to reinvigorate the linkages between female sacrifice and patriotic identity. In March 1916, furthermore, she attended a meeting between Section III and the matrons, the first since the outbreak of war.[64]

The duchess used the opportunity to comment on the present. Although preaching to the converted, she spoke of duty, loyalty, and service to the fatherland only. She called on the participants to remember "the old times of the past" and "our quiet, peaceful evolution" and think of the great events of the day "that forge us into a steadfast unity, insuring our ability to stand together and carry on." Ultimately, her recourse was to trust in God, who, at the right moment, would transform the "miseries of war" into the "blessings" of peacetime.[65] The premium simply was on stubborn stoicism, with only the vaguest vision of peace to come. In the context of the crisis of monarchical legitimacy, dynastic voices in Baden—as elsewhere—were unable to embrace a discourse of rights that was integrative. Resources were being strained beyond the breaking point, and the growing exhaustion showed just how intertwined the issues of morale and resources had become at home and on the front. Bringing the battlefield home, the meeting remembered by name the nursing sisters who had died in the line of duty.

Throughout the war, nurses' aides were a familiar sight in Baden, helping arrange exhibits and benefit concerts as well as collecting money on street corners and at factory gates. With their special uniforms—a high-necked dress with a loose skirt, white cap with polka-dot gauze, a red cross on a white apron, and the league's official brooch—the aides seemed to personify the prewar alliance of science and humanitarianism that had promised to ease the pains of war. Their continued presence on the streets, however, was contradictory, reassuring to some that the older mechanisms of care still were operating, yet equally alienating to groups who increasingly blamed the state for the hardships and miseries of wartime.[66]

In the hospitals in Karlsruhe, the aides provided medical assistance but also cooked, prepared and served food, and wrote letters for, as well as read to, sick and wounded soldiers. Under the Office of War Relief, and together with the volunteers of the National Women's Service, they organized infant day care centers in factories for soldiers' families. In Baden,

---

64. GK, Abt. 69, no. 892, October 21, 1916, "Meine Liebe Schwestern" from Luise (n.d.).

65. GK, Abt. 69, no. 892, Oberinnen-Konferenz, March 24, 1916.

66. GK, Abt. 69, no. 1134, Helferinnenversammlungen, February 18 and April 23, 1917, and June 3, 1918.

the National Service was a coalition of more "progressive" women's groups, including teachers, suffragists, socialists, and female clerks, which had been founded on August 6, 1914, responding to a call from Berlin. While nominally separate from the older Women's Association, by its own admission, the National Service's work was underwritten partly by Red Cross financing. Both organizations formed a joint information bureau to help track down wounded soldiers or those missing in action and, together with the Karlsruhe Catholic Women's League, the three groups took over the tasks of "reeducating" the populace on nutritional matters. They arranged courses and lectures for poorer urban women on food preparation and nourishment and set aside space in city hall for consultations, making available cookbooks as well.[67]

Under government encouragement, women in the patriotic, feminist, and religious associations responded to the emerging food crisis with goals of more rational household management, an approach that—however much it drew on earlier models and programs of domestic interventions—proved woefully inadequate. While in the short run the national emergency seemed to bring diverse women's organizations together for shared goals, it masked serious long-term differences in the conclusions each would draw for the official payback; and a growing independent understanding of claims by the "women of lesser means" added another volatile element into the fractured politics of wartime Germany.

But for the service groups like the Baden Nurses' Aides League, continuities of the visual culture worked to maintain the illusion of the older familiar world that had taken Germany into the war with such confidence. As a living part of daily work and festive life, these images reinforced group solidarity and identity. The number of nurses' aides rose steadily, increasing fourfold to 1,613 by 1917. Training courses multiplied, and, repeating the bureaucratization process affecting social agencies throughout Germany, a new administrative hierarchy was introduced to coordinate the war work of the aides in 1916.[68]

Although the performative side of patriotic work was muted greatly, the aides were assigned to accompany the Karlsruhe public on tours of a model trench, which men of the *Landsturm* (militia) had set up at the Exerzierplatz to raise money for Red Cross purposes. Within several

---

67. GK, Abt. 69, no. 632, August, report of the Baden Women's Service, August 11, 1915. Also, *KZ*, no. 362, August 4, 1914, which announced the formation of the Women's Service on the national level. For an overview of women's war work, Ute Daniel, "Fiktionen, Friktionen und Fakten—Frauenlohnarbeit im Ersten Weltkrieg," in *Arbeiterschaft in Deutschland 1914–1918: Studien zu Arbeitskampf und Arbeitsmarkt im Ersten Weltkrieg,* ed. Günther Mai (Düsseldorf, 1985), 277–323.

68. GK, Abt. 69, no. 892, Sitzung, Abteilung III, September 26, 1916.

weeks of its opening, the net profit reached 2,608 marks. Seemingly macabre, the replica reflects a process that George Mosse calls "trivialization," a psychological need to keep the horror of war at bay by making it part of the everyday, in this case a mundane family excursion to a fully sanitized space to imagine war.[69] League members also unquestionably supported the wider patriotic efforts to draw the young into their causes. In the dark days of war, in February 1917, they eagerly formed a youth group, made up of their own biological sisters "as well as other young girls with secondary education."[70] The patriotic family was working to reproduce itself, a normative value reaffirmed in the poster campaign through its idealization of mothers and children as Germany's future (fig. 10). The nurses aides continued to hold their annual celebrations in December on the birthday of Duchess Luise.

The events of the annual festival in 1916 capture vividly the world that sustained the home front service.[71] Despite the war, the celebration maintained its familiar structure. It opened by reporting the gratitude of the duchess for her gift. As was the custom, this year league aides had stuffed a wicker easy chair with toys for children and activities for soldiers and sent it, in her name, to the Home for Cripples in Heidelberg. The business side of the meeting followed next. Members were reminded of the important work they had been doing: their help during the "day of sacrifice" for the navy (and a special letter of thanks was read from the president of the German Navy League) and their house-to-house and street collections for the Red Cross, among others. The president noted that a new list of openings (in paid and volunteer work) for Patriotic Auxiliary Service had been posted in the office and urged members to take on additional tasks. Four new members were introduced and made to feel welcome.

Business then was followed by entertainment, a suspension of the "normal" work time that allowed for a release of emotions in the supportive environment of familiar relations.[72] There were speeches, the singing of a "lovely duo," and the playing of a violin solo. One league "artist" had written a poem, which was added to a collection league members were compiling on their own wartime experiences. Someone else recited a poem written by Hans von Pezold, a military doctor at the front who had been a familiar figure in nursing circles before the war; another member read a

---

69. Mosse, *Fallen Soldiers,* 126–27.

70. GK, Abt. 69, no. 632, eighty-third meeting, August 2, 1915, and eighty-fifth meeting, August 16, 1916; no. 1134, Helferinnenversammlung, February 18, 1917.

71. GK, Abt. 69, no. 648, Protokoll der Festversammlung des Helferinnenbundes, December 10, 1916.

72. On ritual time, Turner, *From Ritual to Theatre.*

In unseren Kindern liegt Deutschlands Zukunft

Tragt alle bei

zu

Deutschlands Spende
für Säuglings- und Kleinkinderschutz

Fig. 10.   "In our children lies Germany's future." (Courtesy Hoover Institution
Archives, Poster Collection, GE 1774.)

firsthand report from the eastern front, and someone quoted "in a fresh way" two patriotic poems. League identity was sustained in part by a continuous exchange of views between the home front and the battlefield. Over the course of the war, an astonishing 30 billion pieces of mail passed between these two realms of "experience" and worked to integrate them.[73] Disillusionment, sadness, anger, and sorrow originated from both sides, ultimately bolstering republican sentiments among the larger population as the surest way to end the war. In the case of the league, however, such exchanges provided substantial support for the medical war work of doctors and nurses still in the name of the monarchy.

The festive celebration was overwhelmed by the war around it but became a way to maintain acceptable illusions about war itself—and foresee peace and German victory in its very symbols. Together, members acknowledged individual and collective sacrifices of all kinds. On an individual level, participation was diversionary and, quite possibly, served to hold in check the day-to-day trauma of ministering to the wounded, ill, and needy. Affirming the patriotic messages certainly helped justify the pain and loss around them.

The evening culminated in a choral performance "for three voices," composed and choreographed by league members themselves. Actors and audience merged in this private theatrical performance. The scene opened with two characters, a guardian angel and a genie beneath the busts of the young duchess and duke of Baden, which had been set on a laurel branch. The plot was a powerful recitation of a set of values—charity, love, work, harmony, and happiness—replicating the old cornucopia of patriotic sensibilities, which the two characters offered to the royal couple as tribute.

The performance was both entertaining and instructive and ended with the appearance of an angel of peace, "whose thoughtful words allowed the circle to see a better world for themselves in the future." However mechanical or hackneyed the scene may seem, through the performance the amateur actors and audience were transported directly into the wider patriotic culture, which posted identical symbols and images in public spaces. It was the ongoing ties to the larger patriotic public that reinforced small-group cohesion: the shared images and symbols kept alive and meaningful the old patriotic emotions and feelings that had been experienced in the past and worked to sustain an ongoing identification with the dynastic state and its defense. The wider world of medical service, too, found sustenance in the traditions, symbols, and practices of care of the

---

73. Chickering, *Imperial Germany and Great War,* 101; and Ziemann, *Front und Heimat,* 21, 30, who points to three mechanisms that inextricably bound home and front together: the soldiers on leave, the flow of private correspondence, and the ongoing mobilization of soldiers.

Baden royal house, which spoke of a familiar order promising predictabil-
ity and continuity. But the world of dynastic Germany, able to oversee the
passage from peace to war in 1914, had lost its aura to take the process to
peace again.

The transition to republican life after 1918 was traumatic for the
women and men who had fashioned their identity in dynastic service. The
Baden Women's Association as well as the Association of Red Cross Sisters and Nurses' Aides League continued their work immediately after the
war with the same leadership and many of the same members, but in a
political climate they resented deeply. As one woman put it, the postwar
era seemed to be "a time of sheer madness by the people." In the words of
Anna Lauter, the turmoil in the streets and the ongoing changes had tested
her "courage" and "confidence." Other letters to the duchess, who continued to reside in Baden until her death in 1923, pined for a return to the old
days and the political security that had come from the mutual interaction
between association and royal patron.[74]

Although deprived of formal authority by the abdication of Frederick
II on November 22, 1918, the duchess, nonetheless, worked tirelessly
behind the scenes to effect social relations in her image. For example, the
old pattern of dynastic gift-giving from endowments of birthday funds and
other monies was sustained at least until her death, preserving a foothold
back into the older world for the recipients. Despite the political changes,
the practice reconfirmed the tradition of the royal family as benefactor; it
enacted the old social hierarchy with those on top responsible for those
deserving poor below, mediated by the women's association. And, as in
the old days, people wrote to thank the duchess for her beneficence in these
"hard times" of spiraling inflation.

The duchess also was involved in a series of negotiations between the
women's association and the new municipal government in Karlsruhe
about the fate of the Ludwig-Wilhelm Hospital, owned by the association.
The hospital came out of the war debt-ridden. At first, the municipality
was hesitant to offer any public support. Its sale or lease, however, would
have been a blow to the association. In short order, municipal officials
became persuaded of its public utility and agreed to help underwrite hospital operations, drawing on a prewar precedent set in 1911; at the time the
city government had been willing to help fund an extensive renovation

---

74. GK, Abt. 69, no. 953, Dankschreiben von Frauenvereinen für Gaben aus der
Geburtstagsspende, 1922, letter of Frl. Elisabeth Brauer, December 31, 1922; no. 894, letter
of Anna Lauter, Karlsruhe, June 28, 1922. Also, for the last years of her life, Friedrich Hin-
denlang, *Grossherzogin Luise von Baden. Der Lebenstag einer fürstlichen Menschenfreundin*
(Karlsruhe, 1925), 116–27.

project for a number of years. The decision preserved the organizational core of the Baden Women's Association.[75]

Duchess Luise, however, adamantly opposed other aspects of the new political order, at least in associations that still offered her a voice. She kept in constant touch with the nursing matrons, and, although she no longer attended their conferences, she interceded in the debates directly by letter. In June 1919 in no uncertain terms she fought the move to unionize the nursing sisters, calling it a "very important issue." Acknowledging a new political reality, however, she cautioned that "the sisters cannot be directly forbidden [to join] . . . nor threatened with dismissal [from the organization]." But self-evidently, unionization was incompatible with the "old spirit," which had to be safeguarded at all costs. And she called on the matrons to keep a "watchful eye" on their charges. A year later, she still was seeking to influence the spirit of the conference, offering "the appropriate interpretation." Her letter spoke of the past in the language of "homesickness," a yearning for the "unforgettable hours of meeting" and working together. "I know that you will keep the old spirit alive and strong that had proved so successful over sixty years in the execution of the noble goals," she wrote the matrons in July 1920.[76] The vision of humanitarian actions prevented examination of the causes and consequences of war.

In microcosm, these tensions captured the unbridgeable gaps between the old female dynastic patrons and their network of supporting intermediary institutions on the one hand and the new authority of democratic officials on the other. Part of the new constellation—unions, workers' rights, and the expansion of state welfare guarantees—remained unacceptable to the old privileged service elites, even if they successfully adjusted to the new realities of women's suffrage. Behind the "old spirit" lay its power hierarchy, rooted in the reciprocities of social obligation and political loyalty. If the transition to the Weimar Republic formally ended the politics of dynastic-sponsored philanthropy, the conservative Christian principles behind community service and social responsibility at its base evolved into more permanent features of modern German identity.

---

75. GK, Abt. 69, no. 684, Der Verein Badischer Heimatdanks, 1920–21, includes eleven letters thanking the duchess for her financial gifts. On the negotiations surrounding the hospital, no. 893, Sitzung, Abteilung III, March 22, 1919, and report, Den Fortbestand des Ludwig-Wilhelm-Krankenheims, betr. Karlsruhe, June 24, 1920.

76. GK, Abt. 69, no. 893, Sitzung, Abteilung III, June 20, 1919, and Oberinnen-Konferenz, July 7, 1920.

Conclusion: A Gendered Reading of Patriotism and Power

The German figure of the patriot *(Vaterlandsfreund)* entered the public realm in the eighteenth century. Throughout German lands, authors penned pamphlets, titled newspapers, and wrote travel accounts and memoirs from the new perspective of the patriotic. Reform associations in urban settings adopted the name, and political philosophers rearranged the bonds of legitimacy between ruler and subject around allegedly shared patriotic commitments. Whatever its specific context or shade of meaning, at its core was a new subjectivity, which helped to create personal identities partly through civic activism in the name of a vision of individual and community well-being. Patriotism was a self-conscious identity acquired by service out in public. Indeed, these enlightenment practices reworked the linkages between charity, relief, and political legitimation, which were essential components of the struggles for power and authority in early modern dynastic and city states, even if their role is not fully credited in the historical literature.

In contrast, a wide range of scholarship has recognized the connections between patriotic structures and state-building in the "long" nineteenth century. The work is rich and suggestive, although largely unintegrated. Drawing on a tradition of thought in the West, political theorists, for example, point to new civic identities that transformed patriotism into the foundation of republican virtue: an armed civic commitment that was at the basis of definitions of male citizenship, realized first in North America and France. The ideal of a militarized male citizenry, in time, proved compatible with the royal professional armies of Prussia/Germany and imperial Russia as well as the system of territorial defense organized in early-twentieth-century Britain. A gendered formation from the start, the model citizen-soldier posited an equally formulaic female "other" and derived its full meaning from the juxtaposition of gendered polarities: war and peace, soldier and helpmate, militarism and pacifism, aggression and passivity. While inserting "woman" directly into the discourse of war and politics, much of this literature remains at the level of symbolic structures and political ideals.[1]

A second line of analysis is more common among German historians for whom patriotism and nationalism, understandably, are deeply complicated questions. It connects patriotism and nationalism to social organization, institution building, and political struggle in the emerging nation-states of Europe. With few exceptions, however, German scholars have failed to analyze women's place in shaping national identity and civil defense. Their focus, rather, remains fixed on the bourgeois nationalist movement and, after 1879, the increasingly radical male-dominated nationalist *Verbände*. This analysis leads to a tautology: "national identities" are a function of so-called nationalist debates over armaments, imperialism, or missionary work in the formal spheres of politics—in parliament, the press, and the pressure groups themselves. Even the feminist "politics" of reform are disconnected from the themes that are held to constitute nationalist discourse. Through this prism, nationalism, indeed, becomes a debate among German men.

My study has sought to overcome the limitations of both scholarly approaches. By offering a gendered analysis of patriotism and power, it works to integrate the distinct insights into a new and promising interpretative grid. This approach highlights social groups and behavioral forms that essentially remain peripheral in the dominant narratives of nationalism: the German dynastic courts, aristocratic women, and wives of medical professionals as well as their work of staging philanthropy for conservative political state ends.

Furthermore, an examination of the philanthropic milieu of patriotic women adds a new mix into debates over modernity, a concept that has been legitimized by the writing of history itself. The blend of traditional and modern elements in dynastic-sanctioned charity—for example, the alliance of humanitarianism and science, the face-to-face ties in bureaucratic organizations, or the political rituals of benevolence in contrast to rights—reveals the shortcomings of any model that posits a straight developmental line toward "modern" rational state-forms with a single unitary national identity. Indeed, scholars outside the West have offered trenchant critiques of the linear foundations of such arguments. For example, Dipesh Chakrabarty speaks of "deferral" and Mark Elvin of a "complex

---

1. I am drawing on here Elshtain, *Women and War;* and Elshtain and Tobias, *Women, Militarism, and War.* For England, Summers, *Angels and Citizens,* 237–90; and, for Russia, Joshua Sandborn, "Empire, Nation, and the Man: Conscription and Political Community in Russia, 1905–1925," Ph.D. diss., University of Chicago, 1998.

of power" divorced, however, from any end point, such as liberal democracy.[2] My gendered perspective on dynastic patriotism, too, defies an emancipatory teleology. The philanthropic prism seems rather to refract the multiple paradoxes that are a part of the slow and asymmetrical unfolding of modernity. Dynastic-sponsored philanthropic associations, institutions, and ritual worlds reshaped the arenas of public and private, blurring the lines between charity and politics as well as religious and secular identities. Over the century, its patriotic public, which was shaped by the interdependence of court and civil society, promoted the memory of war, helping to set the preconditions for the supportive home front; in peacetime, the practices of care forged growing identification with a wider state and, later, national community. In 1916, however, this public succumbed under wartime strains set in motion partly by the very paradoxes of its formation.

The key to the workings of the patriotic public in the German case is the intersection of gender, power, and privilege. Feminist scholarship shows unmistakably that women are not passive objects in history nor mere victims of its unsavory aspects, but active agents, even if, as Marx would have it, under conditions they do not fully control. If one line of feminist analysis nonetheless draws persuasive links between nationalism, war, and masculine aggression, in the context of social hierarchy and class privilege, patriotic identities, nationalism, and war were (and still are) embraced enthusiastically by some women.[3] Analyzing the historical gender patterns offers a more inclusive picture of the complexities of national identity-formation and struggle than does a focus on men's experiences alone.

As this study shows, patriotism was not a self-evident system of beliefs, a primordial identification with land and flora serving as the precondition for national identity. It was constructed, in part, by acts officially named "patriotic": in the "religious" ethic of civic voluntarism itself; through a charitable bequest; by purchases at a patriotic Christmas bazaar; or by the benefit proceeds earmarked for the needy from a piano recital. It inhered, too, in the hosting of a public banquet for disabled veterans and the confessional intermingling at dynastic festivals. It also was part of the memory of a "joyous" collective celebration of rule. Indeed, the continuous flow of personal correspondence between individuals, members of associations, and the dynastic courts testifies to the power and

---

2. Chakrabarty, "Difference—Deferral." Also, the scholar of China Mark Elvin, "Viewpoint: A Working Definition of 'Modernity'?" *Past and Present,* no. 113 (November 1986): 209–13.

3. Joane Nagel, "Masculinity and Nationalism: Gender and Sexuality in the Making of Nations," *Ethnic and Racial Studies* 21, no. 2 (March 1998): 242–69.

place of this self-conscious identity, which extended far into civil society. It sustained a deep, personal connection with the ruling houses and, particularly, with their female members, whose highly publicized private lives synchronized so well with associational festive time. Acquired through self-conscious action under dynastic patronage, it expanded individual horizons well beyond the locality. In circular fashion, its works, too, helped construct images of the state as "caring" and, in time, as "curing" as well. Similarly, the reaffirmations of loyalty in word and deed worked to produce allegiances; patriotic acts and rituals, therefore, did not simply reflect but helped to constitute identities. In this setting, too, patriotism was more than simply rampant "hatred," in the oft-quoted assessment that the prominent banker Ludwig Bamberger uttered in 1889, although distrust, social exclusion, and a mentality of "us" against "them" undoubtedly were part of the message.[4]

If patriotic acts dramatized notions of collective concern and cohesion, their forms simultaneously worked to reinforce hierarchy and domination. The staging of dynastic philanthropy combined the seemingly contradictory elements of horizontal community and social hierarchy; behind its language of solidarity stood social inequality. On this stage, the gender dynamics worked to reproduce and naturalize the inequalities of wealth and power. Deeply enmeshed in the dynastic state apparatus and its military force, the women's and men's patriotic associations helped define conservative "politics" in the century, a consistent loyalty to the dynastic houses and their military arm and a vision of rule that was realized in the demanding benevolence of intermediary institutions. As a surrogate for the state, at times they circumvented the bureaucratic formulas of authority as well. Conservative legitimacy, however, was not static, and its evolving forms represented an ongoing series of negotiations and compromises between dynastic, military, and government leaders, on the one hand, and their dynamic and, at times, volatile social base, on the other. Conservatism was "modernized" slowly by the continuous interpenetration of these mutually dependent contradictory elements.

In an ongoing process of social transformation, changes that had been set in motion by dynastic patronage long outlived the dynasty. The extension of dynastic family time into the routines of associational life helped sustain an interconfessional Christian service elite. Its formation was gradual, to be sure, mediated, paradoxically, by a language of *Untertan* that, through its horizontal embrace and voice of concern, worked to desacralize the dynasty and the titled aristocracy. Its evolution captures a complicated sociological process, which linked aristocrats and bourgeoisie

---

4. In Wehler, *Deutsche Gesellschaftgeschichte,* 3:954.

in voluntary service and underwrote a powerful conservative Christian national identity.

Aristocratic women took the lead in this politics of dynastic philanthropy. By assuming the legal protection of the liberal *Verein,* they made their labor increasingly essential to the state. The high leadership represented a balance of aristocratic families—estate owner and titled nobles, many of whom had cosmopolitan ties and diversified wealth. In Prussia, Junker voices consistently faced other perspectives from Silesia, Alsace, the province of Saxony, or the Rhineland as well as those from outside the state. And loyal Catholics also were included. The local case of Silesia demonstrates the importance of the inherited estate (the Lähnhaus or Matzdorf, for example) in conferring leadership; in Baden, aristocratic wives and daughters were doing the day-to-day work on local committees. Paradoxically, *Verein* life reflected the traditional authorities of birth, family connections, and marriage alliances, as well as the auras of court society and military honor, but in modern organizational form that was based on abstract criteria—political principles and ideology. Shared patriotic commitments and practices, therefore, drew aristocratic women together with women of high government service and the medical professions in loyalty alliances that transcended birth. If, collectively, the patriotic associations opposed women's political rights, they nonetheless expressed growing identification with the state, which they portrayed in their own image. The work, therefore, upheld traditional reciprocities of social privileges and obligations. This was the framework that brought men into the association halls in a gender formation of social power, however unequal, tense and, ultimately, detrimental to women's formal political rights. The dynastic state, in turn, reinforced this conservative compact with its medals and festivals honoring together women's and men's services.

These same patriotic volunteers oversaw, trained, and nurtured their own medical personnel, including, after midcentury, a cadre of nursing lay sisters from rural and working-class communities (as in Baden). And, later in the century, they also supported their "modern" urban wealthy daughters who, in studying to become nurses' aides, found a way to express their own vision of patriotism. In the patriotic mantle, these young women could camouflage wage work and find excitement in the streets by donning roles in choreographed relief dramas. The conservative organizations opened up wage work for some women, but in forms that sustained ongoing identification with the dynastic court. Their labor kept at bay the individualizing effects of the capitalist wage economy. And in patterns not previously fully recognized, the same groups of privileged women established mutually beneficial, if not always harmonious, relationships with veterans and with the zealous young male medical personnel under the

Red Cross. It was these specific social conjunctures—tested in the matrix of ideas, institutions, ritual performances, and philanthropic actions—that defined the conservative content of the performances.

Although outside formal politics, dynastic philanthropy nonetheless was enmeshed in central issues of statecraft and, thus, in political struggle with other formations of public opinion such as socialist, feminist, or radical nationalist. In constant battle in public, women's patriotic services successfully impacted the processes of state-building in three prime areas: in the overall authoritarian character of welfare provisions, in the expansion of medical war preparation, and in the communal architecture of hospitals, clinics, old-age homes, nurses' stations, and association headquarters, through which the patriotic culture of care itself, seemingly, was memorialized.

Private charitable associations proliferated at the very moment Germany made its transition to public welfare interventions; there was no linear shift to municipal and state authority at the expense of private charity. Until the crisis years of World War I, the German welfare state mixed official and private initiatives, offering a favorable climate for charitable endeavors underwritten by a host of diverse and effective public fund-raising campaigns. As part of a wider trend of municipal relief, state women's associations and institutions expanded in numbers and members over the decades. They came to embrace the largest numbers of organized women in imperial Germany prior to World War I, linking their participants horizontally over a widening expanse of territory and tying them vertically into the rituals and rewards of dynastic rule. After 1880, Patriotic Women's Associations helped develop, diversify, and expand social relief services in a growing number of municipalities across the country. But the patterns of care and the use of their sites for ceremonies and festivals were part of a strategy of rule that drew charity into the work of legitimation. Patriotic voluntarism, therefore, helped forge long-lasting social relationships between the "abstract" state and the people. Indeed, this work taught the wider public to see philanthropy as gifts mediated by the face-to-face relations of patriotic volunteers, in turn expressing the personal "concern" and "involvement" of the *Landesmütter*. This public role kept alive personalistic values in the heart of the bureaucratic state. Importantly, its presentation was designed to contain the pressures of democracy and keep at bay the entire question of rights.

Not surprisingly, similar calculations had affected the development of the Prussian/German professional army in an era of the people's war; patriotic philanthropy was a vital complement to the army. No other large civilian institutional structure was as deeply involved in medical war preparation as the state women's associations under the Red Cross. And, while people go to war for many different reasons, to be sure, the promise of "care" and the medical advances in "cure" seemed to change the face of war by expressing a solicitous concern for its victims. This caring imperative was reinforced by commemorative practices that wrote the narrative of war as individual heroism and community sacrifice and performed it before the public in annual celebrations and in choreographed street dramas. Finally, through its multiple building projects, patriotic philanthropy was changing the visual landscape in Germany; its many buildings took on a "public" character expressing communal values of care at the basis of the national imagination.

Ultimately, the work of patriotic philanthropy helped to construct national identity. After 1871, it entered the nationalist debates, but these struggles took place in arenas that hitherto have escaped investigation in the literature on German nationalism. Ever attuned to its own representation, the dynastic infrastructure organized disaster relief with an eye to constructing a conservative "national" community response. Inaugural rituals associated dynastic authority with community decisions to invest in public health and worked to tie medical science to notions of national strength and power. Its obsession with commemorative practices, indeed, bound memory to its purposes: the present status quo was presented as the logical outcome of history, which held the key to the future. The physical sites claimed by the patriotic groups, however, became points of contestation—at cemeteries honoring the war dead, or in the women's clinics over medical practices and reading material. These same sites also evoked serious reflection and self-doubt in the patriotic community itself.

As importantly, the spaces opened up by the patriotic organizations—the annual bazaars and auctions, benefit concerts, lotteries, museum exhibitions, and mobile displays—reabsorbed other nationalist debates over empire, German settlements abroad, the colonial troops, armaments, and hygiene, all of which simultaneously were swirling around the Reichstag and in the press. In the "oriental" booths of the Prussian Women's and Young Ladies' Association, through the sale of colonial goods and in monies earmarked for colonial troops, issues of empire and world power became part of daily routines, insinuated in the rituals of consumption and gift giving. Even Red Cross artists used messages of desire to market patriotic deeds and acts. Through these efforts, official national symbols, rituals, and practices had a lasting impact on German identity, even if they did not survive public anger over the inequalities of sacrifice and massive loss of life in World War I.

The technology of industrial war, ironically, turned the home front into a critical battlefield in military strategy. As the war settled into the trenches, efficient mobilization of civilian resources, labor, and morale became increasingly central to the running of war. As Roger Chickering writes persuasively, "the war was to be won elsewhere than on the field of battle."[5] Dynastic philanthropy long had prepared for war in peacetime, commemorating its history, honoring its veterans, and turning patriotic acts and donations into civic duties for the nation. But the unanticipated length, intensity, and strains of modern war overwhelmed its model of "organized voluntarism" and destroyed its public, permanently undercutting the visible prewar roles for the privileged patriotic women.

Dynastic philanthropy relied on the female volunteer as the visible embodiment of the caring state. In the early months of the war, organized voluntarism, indeed, remained the successful model for civilian mobilization. In fact, throughout the war years, the welfare policies at home that defined social needs as problems for "experts" continued to target experienced *(bewährte)* women and men. Thus, for example, the Westfalian agency for the war disabled in 1915 purposefully included women from the local Patriotic Women's Association and Red Cross personnel in the coalition.[6] Even in this case, however, decision-making authority increasingly was taken over by provincial bureaucrats and professionals.

But the contradictions of the gender dynamics contributed to the undermining of official nationalism. In the climate of professionalization and bureaucratization, the woman volunteer was losing her place, challenged by a potent equation of professionalization with male authority. Even Marie Lüders, who headed the National Commission for Wartime Female Labor in the War Office in 1917, came under increasing attack by male welfare administrators for not being a medical doctor.[7] The military-dynastic state in wartime could not contain the logic of women's public participation, which it sanctioned. It had faced a similar dilemma in the aftermath of 1848. Then, it reached a compromise with privileged aristocratic and state servitor families, in effect underwriting mutually beneficial conservative "politics" through a mode of female voluntarism that reinforced social hierarchies. In World War I, military-dynastic groups once again were dependent on women—now as crucial resources for running the war. While the patriotic ranks stoically carried on in the name of the dynastic fatherland, reform feminists in national and local service put forth renewed claims for democratic rights and political citizenship as paybacks for their wartime mobilization. Testifying to the ongoing fracturing of loyalties after 1916, furthermore, urban women "of lesser means" demanded equitable access to food as their first priority and not the vote.[8]

5. Chickering, *Imperial Germany and Great War*, 31.

6. Frie, *Wohlfahrtsstaat und Provinz*, 139–40.

7. Hong, "World War I," 364.

8. Belinda Davis, *Home Fires Burning: Food, Politics, and Everyday Life in World War I Berlin* (Chapel Hill, N.C., 2000).

But loyalty also divided by region and state, a function, too, of the way German national identity had been structured through official nationalist rituals and practices. Growing shortages of food and fuel and government rationing policies and forced requisitions provoked antagonisms along state lines. Social and class hostilities were expressed partly in geographic idiom. Badeners feared the economic advantages of Prussians, while rural Bavarians turned their anxieties about the war's prolongation into a "hatred" *(Preussenhass)*; in turn, Berliners felt disadvantaged by Rhinelanders and others. Significantly, these understandings eroded dynastic loyalty among the increasingly war-weary populace. But the persons of the monarchy also came under attack by the patriotic Right for making too many concessions to political parties and labor. In the short run, geographic antagonisms further eroded a sense of common struggle and shared sacrifice; and the German state and imperial dynastic houses ultimately succumbed to the anger unleashed by their own militarism. In the long run, these geographic divisions were reabsorbed into a German nation in republican form. With seeming ease, even those on the Right—significantly, veterans' associations and the conservative press, for example—substituted loyalty to the German fatherland for their earlier identification with the state dynasty in the imperial nation.[9] The Right entered Weimar with a nationalist identity encased in a vocabulary of Germanness, despite the early hopes of the service elite for a rejuvenation of the old order.

The new political context of republican Germany broke with the past in two interrelated arenas that had worked untiringly for dynastic legitimacy: the patriotic public and its social markers of historical memory. Certainly, the old patriotic public, tied so closely to the dynastic courts, lost its identity in the Weimar social state. But the new state's broad commitment to extensive welfare rights and entitlements created a decisively different milieu for the interaction between official welfare policies and private charitable initiatives. Weimar legislation transformed the confessional and lay philanthropic organizations of the *Kaiserreich,* which had been forced to centralize and pool resources in order to survive the war, into state-sanctioned national welfare bodies. Thus, for example, the Red Cross and its Patriotic Women's Associations (severed fully from the military by the Treaty of Versailles) jostled for influence in local agencies with representatives of different political and religious persuasions. These multiple coalitions, in effect, transformed the welfare service sector; it lost its semblance of "neutrality" and "disinterest" and no longer was able to provide social consensus. No favored institutional formation of ideology and praxis emerged to bolster state identity.

9. Fritzsche, *Germans into Nazis,* 111, for the press; and Ziemann, *Front und Heimat,* 422–23, for the veterans' associations.

Furthermore, for many clients and the public still called on to make donations, the relationship between state and private obligations seemed contradictory and mutually disadvantageous in the new context of social legislation in Weimar. The case of disabled veterans is a telling and tragic example of the mounting frustrations, according to an innovative recent study by Deborah Cohen.[10] Labor Ministry officials at the *Reich* and *Land* levels sought to anchor their new legitimacy partly in the full reintegration of veterans into economic life. They, too, wanted to reap the rewards of the "Thanks of the Fatherland." These generous provisions, however, came at the expense of private initiatives, which were curtailed by the government as unwelcomed competition. Therefore, veterans complained bitterly that "the public" had deserted them despite their multiple sacrifices for the fatherland. Tragically, with the massive dislocations caused by rampant inflation and subsequent depression that kept state monies at stagnant levels, veterans' anger turned against the presumed indifference of the public and the failed promises of the state. Disabled veterans became formidable supporters of the Nazi movement. Similarly, local officials in rural Bavaria complained that money for monuments honoring the war dead came at the expense of contributions for relief services for the living. The memory of "fallen soldiers" took precedence over the current needs of the poor and the disabled.[11]

Equally significant, sacrifice increasingly became defined as male in a postwar politics that glorified masculinity. In Weimar, German national identity continued to be shaped by its ties to war in the struggles over commemorating its memory. Festivals, monuments, and public ceremonies, however, offered little opportunity to dramatize women's contributions to the national struggle. The myth of the "stab in the back" blamed civilians and the home front for the loss of the war; this powerful sentiment, apparently, left many Conservative women deeply shaken. Furthermore, they no longer had recourse to the *Landesmutter* symbol, which had been a forceful trigger for collective remembrances of women's ministering to the war wounded and their care for veterans. In addition, to their right, the psychological mechanisms of fascist violence expressed profound ambivalences about social privilege. In the brutal attacks on the supposed "red" menace, the men of the *Freikorps* fantasized also about annihilating aristocratic women as well as "white" nurses, whom they feared as threats to their fragile egos.[12] Women's sacrifices and the imperatives of Christian

10. Deborah Cohen, *The War Come Home: Disabled Veterans in Britain and Germany, 1914–1939* (Berkeley, Los Angeles, London, 2001).

11. Ziemann, *Front und Heimat,* 446; and also Mosse, *Fallen Soldiers.*

12. Theweleit, *Male Bodies.*

neighborliness—once integral to official nationalist messages—were alien to the politics of the new fascist Right. In this heightened atmosphere of nationalist crisis, which increasingly turned against the state, republican groups seemingly were powerless to advance their own narrative of the past, and therefore they lost the ability to shape the future.

There is no need to place dynastic philanthropy in a teleology that leads to National Socialism to appreciate its significance in modern German history. Its work had opened up spaces outside formal politics for confessional intermingling. After the Nazi horror and the devastations of World War II, a shared Christian identity became the fundamental basis of West Germanness. This definition served the new state well partly because "patriotism" and "nationalism" had been discredited so thoroughly; it also seemed to contrast sharply with both the Nazi and Communist ideologies.[13] If Christian by default, the choice was not without its logic. A civic activism tied to German identity had been forged in part in the interconfessional philanthropic spaces of the *Kaiserreich,* in particular in the confessionally mixed areas of the Rhineland, Westfalia, and Baden. This interconfessional alliance was resolidified between 1944 and 1948; postwar biographical accounts of a number of leading lay Christian Democrats active in the movement place their formative development in the philanthropic milieu of the late *Kaiserreich.*[14]

Although lost to the historical record in the tumultuous years after 1918, dynastic rule and the patriotic groups, associations, and institutions under its authority had a decisive impact on the German national imagination. In the "long" nineteenth century, they worked to shape a national identity that greeted war as an inevitable part of modern life, while their gendered politics promised to ease its pain and agony. From the longer

---

13. Michael Minkenberg, "Civil Religion and German Unification," *German Studies Review* 20, no. 1 (February 1997): 63–81; and Hans-Jürgen Puhle, "Conservatism in Modern German History," *Journal of Contemporary History* 13, no. 4 (October 1978): 712.

14. The hypothesis needs further documentation, and it does not deny other places where interconfessionalism was tested and contested in the late *Kaiserreich:* in the Prussian House of Deputies or in debates over a Christian—interconfessional—or "integral" trade unionism. For biographical sketches see *Zeitgeschichte in Lebensbildern: Aus dem deutschen Katholizismus des 20. Jahrhunderts,* vols. 1–2, ed. Rudolf Morsey, vol. 3, ed. Jürgen Aretz, Rudolf Morsey, and Anton Rauscher (Mainz, 1973–79). I am referring, in particular, to the formative influences on Michael Kardinal von Faulhaber (2:101–13), active in the Catholic women's movement and teachers' associations; Christine Teusch (2:202–13), with her roots in social welfare during World War I; Maria Schmitz (3:204–22), a prominent Catholic teacher with close ties to the royalty; Helene Weber (3:223–34), parliamentarian in Weimar and the Federal Republic, whose career began in social work through the German Catholic Women's League; Hedwig Dransfeld (1:129–36), active in the prewar German *Caritasverband.*

perspective, the interaction of court and association imbued the secular national community with a broad interconfessional Christian identity inexorably linked through deeds to the German state. To this discussion of patriotism and war, I have sought to bring my feminist commitment to women's agency, voice, and place in history. It is my hope that such a gendered reading, paradoxically, may promote the cause of peace.

Bibliographical Essay

Primary research for this book centers on the archival collections of the Civil Cabinets of the German states, the "secret" offices that connected members of the court to state ministries in their interactions over the economy, civil society, and politics. It draws primarily on rich archival holdings in the states of Baden and Prussia. In Baden, the Genderallandesarchiv, Karlsruhe (GK) houses the collections Abt. 69 (Geheimes Kabinett der Grossherzogin Luise), Abt. 233 (Staatsministerium), and Rep. 456 (the Fourteenth Army Corps) and its Sanitary Bureau, F 113 (Sanitätsamt), 1871–1920. In light of the destruction of so many archival holdings on the German military in World War II, materials on the Baden Fourteenth Army Corps offer unique insights into the army-civilian relationship in war preparation and public hygiene.

For Prussia, I worked in the Geheimes Staatsarchiv Preussischer Kulturbesitz (GSPK), Königliches Geheimes Civil-Cabinet, I, HA, Rep. 89, nos. 15607–8, Preussischer Frauen-und Jungfrauen-Verein, 1818–1916 (Wohltätigkeits-Sachen, Generalia). Its archival location under the rubric "charity" maintained the useful fiction of the separation of philanthropy and politics. I also looked at nos. 15609–13, Vaterländischer Frauen-Verein und seine Zweig-Vereine, 1867–1919. This collection contains the extraordinarily detailed and personal letters from the local branch association in Lähn, Silesia, as well as other testimonies of the intimate connections between court and association at times of dynastic celebrations; it documents efforts to honor servitors with medals and awards. I also worked in the Landeshauptarchiv, Koblenz (LK) for the interconfessional Rhineland. It houses the archives of the St. Barbara Association, 1791–1922 (Best. 661, 23) as well as the regional women's association, 403 (Kommunalsachen, Vereine), Oberpräsidium der Rheinprovinz, nos. 7363–66, Frauenvereine im Oberpräsidialbezirk, 1835–1912.

The secret cabinet of Duchess Luise facilitated her multiple roles as state *Landesmutter* over her long reign (1856–1907) and life (d. 1923). It contains a wide range of documents, many previously untapped, reflecting the powerful interactions between court and civil society as well as the place of the royal figure in the evolution of municipal life (at times of natural disasters and at ceremonial moments consecrating hospitals and establishing nursing stations) as well as in the institutions and associations under her patronage. It holds the extensive correspondence from individuals from many walks of life as well as members of associations with the dynastic court. Typical here are no. 169, Glückwünsche verschiedener Frauenvereine zu verschiedenen Gedenktagen der fürstlichen Familie, 1882; no. 953, Dankschreiben von Frauenvereine für Gaben aus der Geburtstagsspende, 1922; and no. 175, Teilnamebezeugnungen zum 100-jährigen Todestag der Königin Luise von Preussen, 1910.

The Baden collection has extensive materials on the Frauen-Verein and its various sections. Because of my interest in the connections between nationalism and war, I concentrated primarily on Section III, Red Cross Nursing reports (Berichte der Abt. III des Frauenvereins und Antworteten, Baden [III] Rotes Kreuz-Krankenpflege, nos. 887–94, 1890–1922) and the documents on the state Red Cross, nos. 1117–18, Mitteilungen, 1906–1916. For a broad overview I also looked at Abt. 233, no. 2848, Armensachen (Der badische Frauenverein), which covers the period 1866–1919. I followed the work of these organizations into the First World War in more detail through no. 619, Die Mobilmachung, 1914, and nos. 620–49, Den Feldzug, 1914–17. I also consulted the holdings of specific nursing groups and activities, among them nos. 1133–34, Der Helferinnenbund beim Roten Kreuz, 1908–18; no. 1120, Die Oberinnen-Konferenz, 1889, 1891; and no. 1131, Landkrankenpflege, 1888, 1909–10. I consulted materials for local associations around the state, including nos. 942–44, Versammlungen der Frauenvereine des Seekreises auf Schloss Mainau, 1897–1913 and no. 932, Der Frauenvereine in Baden-Baden, 1888–92. No. 940, Der Frauenverein St. Barbara in Koblenz, 1910, contains additional materials on the connection between Koblenz and Karlsruhe. I also followed the duchess of Baden on her many tours to Säckingen, Buchen, and Sinsheim, 1892 (no. 586), Koblenz, 1897 (no. 225), Lörrach, 1900 (no. 571), Düsseldorf and Koblenz, 1904 (no. 227), Mannheim, 1856–1907 (nos. 572–73, 575b), Bühlertal, 1903 (no. 1147), Kork, 1904 (no. 1161), Sandhofen, 1904 (no. 1166) among others. I looked at the evolution of charitable life in Baden localities through nos. 1177–78, Verzeichnis der Pfründner-Kranken-Waisen-und Rettungshäuser und anderer Wohltätigkeitsanstalten in Baden, 1890, 1898, no. 1179, Zusammenstellung der Vereinsanstalten in Karlsruhe, 1891, and no. 1129, Namenverzeichnis der Krankenwärterinnen getrennt nach Kliniken in badischen Städten, 1888.

In addition to materials on St. Barbara and the women's associations, the Landeshauptarchiv, Koblenz, has detailed collections on charitable undertakings comparable to Baden and a wide range of materials on poverty and public institutions (Öffentliche Institute und Armenwesen) in *Vormärz,* which reveal the percolation of ideas of legitimacy. Among others, no. 744, Die Bevölkerung der Arbeitsanstalt zu Brauweiler, 1823; no. 796, Die bestehenden resp. eingerichteten Armenspeiseanstalten, 1831–33; no. 10200, Abgaben bei öffentlichen Lustbarkeiten zu Armenzwecken; no. 4399, Die Forderung des Stock'schen Armenfonds zu Braunfels an die Fürstin Luise zu Solms-Braunfels, 1832–36; no. 4447, Die von der Frau Fürstin von Liegnitz Durchlaucht und anderen Gliedern des Königlichen Hauses bewilligten Unterstützengen, 1843–47 (Unterstützungssachen). Furthermore, the collections no. 8357, Volksheilstätten für Genesende und Kranke, 1897–98, and no. 8366, Volksheilstätte für Lungenkranke, 1908–10, set a wider context for the growing Red Cross and military interest in public health issues in later years, which I pursued primarily through the eyes of the Fourteenth Army Corps. The Red Cross World War I posters duplicating the dynastic narrative are in the Hoover Institution Archives, Stanford, California. A fuller accounting of the archival sources is found in the footnotes.

A range of published primary sources augment the archival research. Only a partial account is noted here. The public nature of the philanthropic rituals was observed for the *Kaiserreich* through close reading of national newspapers, particularly the Conservative *Neue Preussische Kreuz-Zeitung* (Berlin, 1870–1914), supplemented, in 1888 and 1889, by the more Liberal *Vossiche Zeitung* and the *Berliner Tageblatt* and, for 1911, the Socialist *Vorwärts* and, in 1913, *Die Gleichheit, Zeitschrift für die Interessen der Arbeiterinnen.* Clippings of reports of local newspapers also are in the archival collections.

For the period of the Germanic Confederation, I drew heavily on the study commissioned by Crown Princess Augusta by Heinrich Gräfe, *Nachrichten von wohltätigen Frauenvereinen in Deutschland. Ein Beitrag zur Sittengeschichte des Neunzehnten Jahrhunderts* (Cassel, 1844). It centers on a detailed analysis of the Patriotic Women's Institute in the Duchy of Weimar. The sociological profile of the leadership of the state women's associations draws on "the Gotha," the official genealogical record of German aristocrats (from the court [*Hof*] to the *freiherrlichen, adligen* and *briefadligen Häuser*): *Gothaisches Genealogischer Hofkalender nebst Diplomatisch-statistischem Jahrbuch 1872,* vol. 109 (Gotha, 1872); *Gothaisches Genealogisches Taschenbuch der freiherrlichen Häuser,* vol. 22 (Gotha, 1872); *Gothaisches Genealogisches Taschenbuch der Adligen Häuser,* vol. 1 (1900); *Gothaisches Genealogisches Taschenbuch der Briefadligen Häuser,*

1909 (Gotha, 1909), for example. These records were matched with other compendia of aristocratic genealogies, including the useful collection of Ernst Heinrich Kneschke, ed., *Neues allgemeines Deutsches Adels-Lexicon* (Leipzig, 1860–70; rpt. Hildesheim, 1973). And I consulted as well numerous handbooks identified more fully in the footnotes. Among other sources, *Handbuch der Deutschen Frauenvereine unter dem Rothen Kreuz* (Berlin, 1881); Gertrud Bäumer and Helene Lange, eds., *Handbuch der Frauenbewegung,* 4 vols. (Berlin, 1901–2); *Handbuch des Vaterländischen Frauen-Vereins* (Berlin, 1910); *Handbuch über den Königlich Preussischen Hof und Staat für das Jahr 1909* (Berlin, 1908) (and other dates). I relied also on the three volumes of *Das Deutsche Rote Kreuz* (Berlin, 1910).

My decision to limit the bibliography to a representative sample of archival and published primary sources is dictated by space and financial considerations. My footnotes are explanatory in nature and underpin the theoretical arguments that frame the rich empirical evidence on which this book is based.

Index

Social History, Popular Culture, and Politics in Germany
Geoff Eley, Series Editor

(continued from pg. ii)